The
Gentlemen
Negotiators

The Gentlemen Negotiators

*A Diplomatic History
of the First World War*

Z. A. B. Zeman

The Macmillan Company

NEW YORK, NEW YORK

D
610
.Z44
1971

The Macmillan Company
866 Third Avenue, New York, N.Y. 10022

First published in 1971 as *A Diplomatic History of The First World War*
by Weidenfeld & Nicolson, London.

Library of Congress Catalog Card Number: 70-108149

First American Edition 1971

Printed in the United States of America

4-21-71

Contents

Maps

Preface

A diplomatic history of the First World War: there may seem to be a contradiction in terms in the subject. When diplomats fail soldiers are supposed to take over. On the outbreak of war diplomats disappear from the stage, perhaps into military uniforms. Their ways of conducting business, their particular skills, are not required for the moment. In every walk of national life, soldiers are paramount. They have in their hands the prize of victory.

Historical writing reflects that view. Most of the major printed collections of diplomatic papers stop short of the war. There is a big accumulation of work dealing with the origins of the war and the question of war guilt. On the whole, in August 1914 diplomatic history stops; military history takes over.

There are exceptions. Two American historians, Professors G.F.Kennan and R.H.Ullman, have written detailed and authoritative studies of the relations between America and Russia and between Britain and Russia after the revolution in 1917. They have set a new high standard for the writing of diplomatic history. The late Dr W.W.Gottlieb has described how and why Italy and Turkey went into the war; he has given us a considerable part of the diplomatic story behind the first two years of warfare. Apart from some more specialized monographs and articles, most of which the reader will come across in the notes, no more has been done on the diplomacy of the First World War.

In this connection another important category of writing should be noted. Since Dr A.J.P.Taylor's bright, panoramic survey of *The War Aims of the Allies in the First World War* in Essays Presented to Sir Lewis Namier (edited by R.Pares and

A. J. P. Taylor, London, 1956) there has grown up, mainly in Germany, a considerable body of 'war aims' literature. It is dominated by Professor Fritz Fischer's solid and imposing *Germany's Aims in the First World War*, published in London in 1967, six years after its original appearance in Germany.

It is an extension of the older 'war guilt' line of inquiry into the origins of the war, and aims to pinpoint the shifting patterns of ambition and hope, of greed and fear, at the time when victory was denied to those who were contesting it. Professor Fischer sees Germany's wartime policy almost exclusively in terms of war aims, of acquisition of territory rather than as a strategy and diplomacy forced upon the German leaders by the exigencies of the war.

The aims in the war of the Great Powers were likely to be as much what the states on one side wanted from each other as what they wanted from the enemy. The unexpected thing about peace without annexations was that it was first mentioned in an exchange between the Austrian and German Chiefs of Staff, a long time before the Russian revolution. After the Bolshevik victory in November 1917 Trotsky miscalculated the potential impact on the European public by his publication of secret diplomatic papers which revealed the rapacity of the European Powers. Milyukov, the first Russian revolutionary Foreign Minister was equally wrong in thinking that the promise of Constantinople would keep the peasants in uniform in the trenches. Lloyd George's gift to the English of Jerusalem for Christmas in 1917 was meant, not to stake out a claim, but to keep spirits up in a very bleak winter.

The study pursued in the following pages touches on those problems without placing them at its centre. It sets out rather to trace the broad movements of strategy and diplomacy and to show how the two means of winning the war – the military and the political – fitted together at the decisive points of those four years. Had the soldiers lived up to their early promise and finished the war in one decisive campaign, there would have been no need for a diplomatic history of the First World War.

In the process of constructing the study the author has drawn on the work and advice of many historians. He is greatly indebted to them, as well as to the librarians and archivists who have assisted him in his search. Mr Herbert Rees has taken much trouble in preparing the manuscript for the printer; finally, the author would like to acknowledge the understanding shown to him and his work by the Court of the University of St Andrews, and by the Carnegie Trust for the Universities of Scotland.

London, 1969

1   Rome

On Sunday 28 June 1914, the Italian Premier Salandra was taking advantage of the long, quiet summer afternoon to catch up on some work at his office. He was disturbed by the ringing of the telephone on his desk. San Giuliano, the Foreign Minister, was on the line: 'Have you heard? We are rid of that tiresome business of the Villa d'Este.'

'How is that?' said Salandra.

'The Archduke Franz Ferdinand was assassinated at Sarajevo this morning.'

For Salandra, this was good news. That business of the Villa d'Este had given him a lot of trouble. A house of great architectural merit and historical interest, it was originally built for Cardinal d'Este, son of Duke Alfonso of Ferrara by his second wife, Lucrezia Borgia, in the middle of the sixteenth century. Its park had terraces with good views and beautiful fountains; it had been empty for some time. Archduke Franz Ferdinand inherited the property in 1875 and, having no use for it, decided to sell it. When Salandra took over office in March 1914, he was told by his predecessor that the government had agreed to buy the Villa for the state for 2m. lire (about £80,000 at 1914 value). Salandra thought the price too high, especially as it was to be paid to a member of the House of Habsburg. In addition, the Austrian Ambassador to Rome, whom the Premier greatly disliked, kept urging him to bring the matter of the purchase at last before the chamber of deputies.[1]

The whole affair was distasteful to Salandra. He would have had to put the popularity of his government in the chamber to the test on a measure in which he had no interest, and which would have been expensive to the Treasury. And he may well have asked himself why the Italian government should pay a Habsburg for property on Italian soil. When Salandra put the receiver down that Sunday afternoon, he knew that the papers concerning the Villa d'Este could remain in the pending tray, perhaps indefinitely.

Sir Rennell Rodd, the British Ambassador to Rome, sensed a similar feeling of relief after the Sarajevo murders when he wrote to the Foreign Secretary:[2]

It has been curious to study here the effect of the abominable assassination at Sarajevo. While ostensibly the authorities and the press have been loud in their denunciations of the crime and full of sympathy with the Emperor, it is obvious that people have generally regarded the elimination of the late Archduke as almost providential. I heard from two bankers here that at Trieste after the news was received the Hungarian stock rose from 72 to 80. He was almost as much disliked it seems in Hungary as in Italy.

In the Habsburg capital, on the other hand, the event almost failed to make any impression whatever. On Sunday and Monday, the crowds in Vienna listened to music and drank wine at Grinzig and in the Prater as if nothing had happened. The Russian Ambassador to Vienna reported:[3]

The tragic end of Archduke Franz Ferdinand found little response in the financial circles here and on the stock exchange—this index of mood in business circles. The value of government stocks did not change, which is explained here by confidence in the continuation of peace.

Indeed, in all the capitals of Europe, the reaction to the assassination of the heir to the Habsburg throne was calm to the point of indifference. The people took little note; the stock exchanges registered hardly a tremor; the politicians continued taking their holidays. The diplomats in London, Paris, St Petersburg on the whole believed that some peaceful settlement of the differences between Vienna and Belgrade was possible.

The feeling of high summer euphoria lingered on. More than three weeks after Sarajevo, Sir Francis Bertie, the Ambassador to Paris, having planned to leave town for a cure at Montigny in August, wrote to London asking for permission to make an earlier start. He observed that the chimney flues of the Embassy building were in serious need of attention, and that the dirty work could be done in his absence. Sir Edward Grey remarked that the Ambassador's leave 'must depend upon the European situation; if

2

there is no acute and dangerous crisis Sir F. Bertie must of course avoid the soot.'[4] The Ambassador remained at his post.

There had been a few signs that the summer calm was deceptive. From Budapest, American Vice-Consul Frank Mallet wrote on 13 July 1914 that war between Austria-Hungary and Serbia was unavoidable as soon as the crops were harvested. On the following day, 14 July, San Giuliano requested the legal department of the Foreign Ministry to work out a note on Italy's international position in the case of a conflict.[5] The document, drafted by Guido Fusinato, an eminent jurist and a member of the Hague Tribunal, stated that on the basis of the fifth treaty of the Triple Alliance, concluded in 1912, a *casus foederis* would not obtain for Italy and that, in the event of occupation of Serbian territory by Austria-Hungary, Italy should claim compensation under Article VII of the alliance.* Two months after he had stated the case for Italy's neutrality, Guido Fusinato killed himself. He was affected by the war and by the divided mind of Italy. He became convinced of the overwhelming strength of Germany, and believed that his countrymen had made a grievous error in not supporting their former allies.

Indeed, the critical situation in Europe toward the end of July necessitated a drastic revision, by the Italian statesmen, of their customary diplomatic conceptions. For over thirty years – since 1882 – they had adhered to the Triple Alliance with Germany and Austria. They had used it with skill and to good purpose. Their recently united country had consolidated its position in Europe and in the Mediterranean; the treaty served as a check on Austria's

* Since much of the subsequent dispute between Rome and Vienna hinged on the interpretation of Article VII of the 1912 treaty of Triple Alliance, this was its full text:[6] 'Austria-Hungary and Italy, having in mind only the maintenance, so far as possible, of the territorial *status quo* in the Orient, engage to use their influence to forestall any territorial modification which might be injurious to one or the other of the Powers signatory to the present Treaty. To this end, they shall communicate to one another all information of a nature to enlighten each other mutually concerning their own dispositions, as well as those of other Powers. However, if, in the course of events, the maintenance of the *status quo* in the regions of the Balkans or of the Ottoman coasts and islands in the Adriatic and in the Aegean Sea should become impossible, and if, whether in consequence of the action of a third Power or otherwise, Austria-Hungary or Italy should find themselves under the necessity of modifying it by a temporary or permanent occupation on their part, this occupation shall take place only after a previous agreement between the two Powers, based upon the principle of a reciprocal compensation for every advantage, territorial or other, which each of them might obtain beyond the present *status quo*, and giving satisfaction to the interests and well founded claims of the two Parties.'

expansion in the Adriatic and in the Balkans; it even removed the
threat of co-operation between those Catholics in Italy who
opposed the House of Savoy, and Vienna. The French power in
the Mediterranean no longer looked so formidable, viewed from
behind the protective shield of the alliance, and it saved the
Italians from making an all-out effort to secure the support of
Britain. Nevertheless, Italian statesmen took good care not to put
themselves in a position where they might have to face Britain as
an enemy. Two days after the secret conclusion of the Triple
Alliance on 22 May 1882, the three signatory Powers issued an
equally secret declaration that 'the provisions of the Alliance could
not be regarded as directed against England'.[7] Though in 1912 the
provision concerning Britain was not added to the new text of the
Triple Alliance treaty, the considerations of English naval strength
had by no means disappeared from the Italians' calculations. The
country's open coastline, 4,160 miles long, was highly vulnerable
to assault from the sea, and Rome assumed that Britain would
completely paralyse any military action it might undertake. In the
summer of 1914, therefore, the policy of Britain was of decisive
importance for the Italian cabinet.

Austria-Hungary, on the other hand, might in the new circumstances have to revert to her old role of Italy's 'traditional enemy'.
The mass of the Italian people could be tempted into claiming
that not all of them had yet been gathered under one flag, and
many of their politicians were not averse to making the attempt.
At a conservative estimate made in the Austrian census of 1910,
when mother tongue was taken as the criterion of nationality,
768,422 Italians lived in Austria: in the Trentino, in south Tirol,
and in isolated ethnical islands spaced out along the Adriatic coast
south of the Istrian peninsula. The last group especially could
make an Italian patriot's heart beat faster. There was the spectacle
of his own people across the Adriatic Sea, under alien rule. They
were the relics of once flourishing communities, of the former
Italian dominions in the Adriatic: should they now be encouraged
to recover their former glory, or should they be allowed to
disappear altogether? From the hills around Trieste, the largest
maritime port of Austria-Hungary, the Slav barbarians were about
to descend and destroy an Italian town: if it could be shown that
they were encouraged to do so by the Austrian authorities,
another telling point against Vienna would be made. In Prince

Konrad Hohenlohe, the Governor of Trieste, the Italian chau-
vinists found a suitable villain of the piece. They bitterly resented
his decrees of August 1913 which required Italian officials in the
town to be Austrian subjects; they alleged that he protected the
Slovenes against the Italians whenever they fought in the streets;
that, in short, he had been conducting a sinister campaign against
the Italians and for the Slavs in the province he administered. In
Trieste, Vienna was blamed for supporting the Slavs; in the
Trentino and the south Tirol, the Austrian authorities seemed to
the Italians to prefer the Germans. Salandra was eloquent on this
subject:[8]

I had not forgotten a summer spent at Bormio, in the upper Val-
tellina. From the Stelvio pass came German tourists in serried ranks;
on they marched, with nailed boots and alpenstocks, in rhythmic step,
helping along the more obese of their party; and it reminded me of the
barbaric hordes that once descended upon *i nostri dolci campi*.

From Salandra's point of view, the Italians on the other side of
the frontier could be put to practical uses. The territories they
inhabited would compensate Italy for the disturbance of the *status
quo* in the Balkans, an enterprise on which Austria-Hungary was
now about to embark. The principle of compensations was one
of the corner-stones of the treaty of the Triple Alliance, as it was
one of the cardinal principles of the European balance of power.
Although in August 1914 all the Great Powers abandoned that
principle in favour of a rough game for higher stakes, the Italian
government remained cautious. The Habsburgs had decided to
make a move in the Balkans, a move which they had prepared in
a secretive way, in consultation with Berlin alone. (The Viennese
diplomats were convinced they had good reason for maintaining
complete silence in regard to Rome. They had received proofs,
during the Balkan wars, that their confidential dispatches to the
Italian Foreign Ministry were passed on to St Petersburg.) For
Italy, then, there would be compensations.

However devious the subsequent negotiations conducted by
the Consulta, the Italian Foreign Ministry, with both the belligerent camps may have been, Italy differed from the rest of the
European Powers in that it had formulated specific war aims long
before entering the war. The fact that they were based on the
concept of compensations was a hang-over from the past; that the

claim was made in terms of nationality, and to marginal territories only partly inhabited by Italians, pointed to a wartime diplomacy that was yet to come.

The reasoning of Jagow, the Secretary of State in the Wilhelmstrasse, moved on the same lines as that of his Italian colleague. On 14 July, San Giuliano had asked his legal department for a statement on Italy's international position in the event of war; the question of compensations was raised in it. On the following day, Jagow requested the German Ambassador to Vienna to draw the attention of the Austrian government to the necessity of discussions with Rome: 'In strict confidence, the only compensation regarded as adequate in Italy would be the acquisition of the Trentino.'⁹ When Tschirschky, the German Ambassador, called on Count Berchtold, the Austrian Foreign Minister, on 20 July, he tactfully omitted to mention the Trentino: Berchtold, for his part, denied Italy's right to any compensations, and proceeded to instruct his Ambassadors to Berlin and Rome in that sense. He stubbornly maintained that Austria did not intend to acquire any Serbian territory – which was at the time true – and that a temporary occupation of enemy territory was not a sufficient reason for compensations – which was foolish. A similar mistake was made in Rome where von Mérey, the Austrian Ambassador, failed to give San Giuliano, at the audience of 21 July, a specific assurance that Austria had no interest in the acquisition of Serbian territory.¹⁰ The pattern of the future relations among the partners of the Triple Alliance had emerged in the days before the definite rupture between Austria-Hungary and Serbia. The arguments from Rome as to why Italy should obtain compensations, and from Vienna as to why Rome should get nothing were developed; the Wilhelmstrasse showed more interest than the Ballhausplatz in keeping Italy on the right side of the dividing line, and prepared to exert pressure, if necessary, to make the cavalier Viennese take the problem more seriously.

By raising the matter of compensation San Giuliano raised the matter of war, and the chances that a general war might be avoided were growing smaller every hour. On 30 July, the day after Austria's declaration of war on Serbia, San Giuliano explained to Flotow: 'I do not say that Italy *will* not take part in the end; I merely register the fact that she is not *bound* to do so.'¹¹

On the following day, the Italian cabinet decided to remain

neutral on the grounds that Austria-Hungary was engaged in an offensive action against Serbia. In the circumstances, it was the only decision Salandra and his colleagues could take. They did not expect the conflict between Vienna and Belgrade to remain localized, and they had a great respect for the German army and for the British navy. The instability of the government, the lack of solid parliamentary support for it, the recent anarchist unrest in the Romagna and the railway strikes, Italy's economic and military situation, everything seemed to point in the direction of neutrality. Nevertheless, San Giuliano's statement to Flotow of the day before still remained true. Italy was not naturally neutral in the same way as, say, Sweden or Switzerland: from the outbreak of the war until May 1915, when Rome declared war on the Central Powers, Italian neutrality was nothing but a policy of expediency. By declaring the country's neutrality, Salandra and San Giuliano made a bid to preserve their freedom of action, and to place their country in a position of diplomatic strength. But they knew that if neutrality became a matter of habit, they would be opting out of the Great Powers' club.

Antonio Salandra was not a man to regard such a possibility with equanimity. Born in 1853 at Troia in southern Italy, he was old enough to have been deeply affected by the inspiration of the *Risorgimento*; by the time he completed his education at the university of Naples, the Kingdom of the Two Sicilies had ceased to exist. He became Professor of Constitutional Law at Naples, and went into politics when he was thirty-five, the earliest age under Italian law. Five years later he received a junior government appointment in the Ministry of Finance, later becoming State Secretary, and then Minister, in the Treasury during Sidney Sonnino's two brief terms in office. Salandra's political prominence derived partly from his interest in financial matters, mainly from his parliamentary skill. He treated the chamber of deputies in the same way as he treated the excitable, emotional public outside: there was, for Salandra, little difference between them. His southern eloquence aided his rise to the leadership of the liberal-conservative government party, and his career culminated in March 1914, when he was asked to form the cabinet.

He was then an impressive old man with a noble face, a drooping moustache, and dark, staring eyes; they could be cold and severe, or they could, unfocusing, quickly acquire a distant look.

He kept up the main enthusiasm of his youth. The *Risorgimento* was not yet complete, and now, in the summer of 1914, the time and the man in command were right. There was a promise of glory in the air, the final chapter in the history of Italian unification could at last be written. Salandra himself described his feelings at the time:[12]

> ... it was impossible to extinguish the sympathy in every Italian heart for the exiles of the unredeemed provinces, and for those who fought in defence of the Italian ideal against Germanism in the North and Slavism in the East. There are politicians who deny the importance of the warm impulses of the heart. They are wrong, for popular feeling is a reality that must be reckoned with. There are moments when it becomes a resistless force, . . .

Salandra, the son of the people who always kept a finger on their pulse, was complemented by his aristocratic Foreign Minister, San Giuliano. A man of 'vast and brilliant culture', who could keep up with his chief in the speed and facility of his speaking and writing, he drew upon a much larger fund of scepticism. This did not prevent him, however, from being 'like other sceptics of his generation, a fervid patriot'[13] or from keeping a steady eye on the advancement of his political career. Throughout the critical period of July and August, the Foreign Minister spent most of his time nursing his gout at Fiuggi, the spa south of Rome, where Flotow, the German Ambassador, who was also feeling below par, often kept him company. Although San Giuliano was regarded in diplomatic circles as a firm adherent of the Triple Alliance, he gave Flotow no information worth having during their sojourns at the watering place. In any case, the Foreign Minister's steadfastness in the cause of the Triple Alliance was rightly suspect: the British Ambassador was convinced that 'in the end we should have had San Giuliano on our side'.[14]

San Giuliano stayed in office until the day of his death on 16 October; Salandra then assumed temporary charge of the Foreign Ministry as well, and it was when he addressed his staff there that he made the '*sacro egoismo*' remark that reverberated throughout Europe. He said that the good Italian's mind must be liberated from 'every prejudice, from every sentiment save that of exclusive and limitless devotion to our fatherland and of a holy egoism for Italy'.[15] Until that point in the war, none of the European politicians had stated the obvious in such a forceful manner; there were, however, good Italians who did not much care for their Premier, and he had to defend his platitudinous indiscretion. In doing so, Salandra went even further. He rejected the idea that the war was fought for the sake of humanity, or the defence of justice, or democracy; he expressed his doubts whether anyone could be persuaded to die for such high ideals. Returning to the origins of the controversy, which foreshadowed the future discussions of war aims, Salandra explained that the meaning of the phrase '*sacro egoismo*' was more sacred than egoistic, that it was an attitude of mind of mystical rather than of cynical men. Despite a number of polemical lapses, there was nevertheless sound political sense in Salandra's calculations. For the time being, his policy was a stark necessity for Italy.

In retrospect, Salandra was critical of his predecessor for having done nothing to prepare Italy 'morally and materially' for the conflict: an autobiographer's exaggeration.[16] For twenty years, Giovanni Giolitti had governed Italy in his own way. When he ran into difficulties, or when he got tired of the cares of office, there always was one of his opponents inside the government party – Luzzatti, or Sonnino, or Salandra – who was only too glad to assume, for however short a time, the responsibility Giolitti himself was no longer prepared to carry. His zest renewed after a few months, Giolitti would overthrow that government and return to power once again. When Salandra became Premier in March 1914 Giolitti retained majority support in the parliament; the established pattern of Italian politics was finally disrupted by the consequences of the explosion in August 1914, rather than by Salandra's superior political skill.

As long as Giolitti remained in office he exerted himself to make Italy fit to take its place in the ranks of the Great Powers of Europe. He could do so only at a high price. In 1907, 117m. lire (about £4,600,000 at pre-war value) were spent on public works, 85m. on education, in contrast to 167m. spent on the navy and 376m. on the army.[17] For the financial year ending 30 June 1914, the estimates included 202,225,416 lire for public works, 145,746,297 for instruction, 256,736,511 for the navy and 424,330,058 for the army.[18] The burden of heavy military expenditure was imposed on a weak economy in which industry and agriculture, the rich families of the industrial princes and the destitute mass of the peasants lived uncomfortably side by side.

The centres of industry were few, their control concentrated in a few hands, and the overall level of industrialization low. The absence of a strong home market and the lack of raw materials forced the Italian industrialists to export a large part of their produce, but their prices were often too high, and they ran into stiff competition.[19] A large foreign debt haunted the Italian cabinets, and the question of foreign loans therefore ranked high on the agenda of the diplomatic negotiations after the outbreak of the war.

Italy's colonial adventures were also expensive: the politicians in Rome interpreted the facts of modern imperialism in their own way. A strong economy and a powerful industry in the mother country were the driving force of imperial expansion: in the case of Italy these were absent. The Italians therefore approached the problem differently, hoping that colonies would cure the economic ills in their own country; their hopes were usually disappointed. Libya, that 'vast sandpit', became a children's playground for an expensive Great Power game. One of the last tasks of Giolitti's Ministry had been to produce 47m. lire for the Libyan expedition: the tax was to be levied on 'buildings in construction, prices of admission to cinema shows, public carriages, furniture removers and mineral waters'.[20] The financial problem Salandra inherited from Giolitti upset the smooth working of the parliament. Toward the end of June 1914, the socialists obstructed every financial proposal made by the government. On one occasion a socialist deputy overturned the voting urn, a misdemeanour for which he was assaulted by other members of the Chamber.

The ill-mannered socialist deputy was one of the new men elected to the Chamber for the first time after the passage of the electoral reform bill of June 1912, which provided for universal male franchise: the bill resulted in a considerable increase in the vote for the Radical, Republican, Socialist and Catholic parties. And outside the parliament there were the anarchists of the Romagna who were by no means quiescent in the summer of 1914; the separatists in Sicily; the railwaymen ready to strike at the slightest provocation.

In August 1914 Salandra was not in a position to proclaim a civil truce as the German government proclaimed the *Burgfrieden*, or the French the *union sacré*. Such political and social cohesion did not exist in Italy. This was why Salandra wrote that his country had not been 'morally' prepared for the war. At the core of the Premier's political difficulties was the quest for a programme which would have inspired the diverse forces of Italy to a common effort. It was typical of him to find such a programme in the ideas of the *Risorgimento*. Almost half a century after the completion of the unification of the main body of the Italian states, the formula still worked.

From the outbreak of the war, Salandra and San Giuliano embarked on a course of rigorous advancement of their country's interests. The simultaneous conversations with the two belligerent camps, the *vagabondaggio* from Vienna to St Petersburg, from Berlin to London, was the mode of negotiations that suited the Consulta best.

It was one of the minor ironies of the war that, on the Allied side, St Petersburg was the most anxious to secure Italy's co-operation. From the very first day of the war, Sazonov, the Russian Foreign Minister, was torn between his desire to use Italy for drawing Austro-Hungarian forces away from the eastern front, and his unwillingness to encourage the Italians to take up positions in the Adriatic and on the west coast of the Balkan peninsula, for which he and the Serbian government had other plans. Nevertheless, the Russians got quickly off the mark in the competition for the favours of Rome. Shortly before Britain declared war on Germany, and on the day that Italy announced to the world her neutrality, Sazonov consulted Marchese Carlotti, the Ambassador to St Petersburg, as to what the Italian demands were likely to be. Carlotti replied that his country would be content with 'a preponderant position' in the Adriatic and that for this purpose Valona, the Albanian port, would have to be annexed and, he added, the possession of the Trentino would also be of interest. The Italian government, the Ambassador said, would not object if Serbia and Greece were to make certain territorial acquisitions on the Adriatic coast and that on the whole it would be more agreeable to Rome if Russia, and not France, conducted the negotiations.[21]

For some time after Britain came into the war the situation remained unchanged and Sazonov carried on the negotiations with Italy. By 7 August the Russian Foreign Minister had received an agreement from Paris and London on the terms of the offer to be made to Italy: preponderance in the Adriatic based on Trieste –

the largest Austrian port, a new addition to the original bait – and on Valona, with the Trentino thrown in. Austria-Hungary was therefore to carry the main burden of the Allied offer to Italy, which could of course be honoured only in case of Austria's defeat. The offer implied a severe denting of the periphery of the multi-national Empire: its total dismemberment was not yet contemplated by any European government.

Sazonov's impatience showed as soon as the proposal to Italy was made. He asked his British and French colleagues for an agreement that the offer to Italy should be made conditional. Italy was to get the spoils after the war, and her armed forces were to attack the Austrians at once. But neither London nor Paris would commit themselves to an official statement on those lines, and Sazonov received the first rebuke from his allies. The Italian public, they argued, could not be expected to accommodate itself to such a sudden switch in their government's foreign policy; the Allies would achieve nothing apart from delivering into the hands of their enemies a proof of their having exerted an unreasonable amount of pressure on the government in Rome; the Italian King would be placed in an awkward position. The offer had been made, and Paris and London would not, for the time being, go any further. In any case, Italy's temporary indecision was not without its uses, as it tied down at least a part of the Austro-Hungarian forces; Italy must, so ran the argument of the western allies, be given time to decide where its best advantage lay.

This was precisely the situation Sazonov had wanted to avoid. The tactics he had adopted for the Italian negotiations were quite different. He wanted to make a tempting offer to the Italians and indicate that it would not stand for ever; in this way, he intended to hustle them into accepting the first offer. Speedy military aid was what he was after; he knew that the more time the Italians were given, the higher their demands would become: so high, in fact, that Russia would have to abandon altogether the pretence of defending Serbia's interests on the Adriatic. His fears were justified. The Italians had a good hand and no wish to lay their cards on the table. They negotiated with both the belligerent sides, and since the negotiations remained necessarily secret, they alone knew what the state of bidding was at any given moment. The uncertainty of one of the parties as to the latest offer made by the other naturally made the bidding brisker.

After two weeks of intensive diplomatic activity, during which the winning over of Italy was Sazonov's chief interest, the Russian Foreign Minister gave way to pressure from London and Paris. He instructed his Ambassador to Rome to tread very cautiously, to confine himself to expressing satisfaction over Italy's decision to remain neutral and assuring San Giuliano that the Allies would do their utmost to satisfy Italian national aspirations.[22] The original draft treaty with Italy, offering a reward for immediate military action, remained unsigned in the archives of the Foreign Ministry in St Petersburg. By the middle of August 1914, the first phase of the Allied bid to secure the co-operation of Italy was over. From San Giuliano's point of view, Sazonov was too mean and too pressing; the Russian offers were too hurried as well as somewhat ragged. The Russian Foreign Minister was not a suitable negotiator, nor was St Petersburg the right place. On 15 August San Giuliano told Krupenski, the Russian Ambassador, that further negotiations on Italy's participation in the war should proceed 'in the most absolute secrecy and must take place in London, exclusively in London'.[23] Being removed from the main Continental diplomatic circuit, London had a reputation for discretion: more important for the Italians, Britain perhaps had more to offer, and certainly at a more leisurely pace.

In the subsequent months, after Sazonov had withdrawn from playing the leading role in the negotiations with Italy, the differences between Russia and its western allies emerged sharply. Sir Edward Grey thought Italy's co-operation in the war of supreme importance, while, as Italy's price continued to rise, Sazonov became more and more doubtful of its value. He may have suspected the British of wanting, by using the Italians, to limit any extension of Russia's influence in the Adriatic. Russia's role as the champion of Slav interests in the Balkans once more returned to a prominent place in Sazonov's thinking; in any case, there were the Serbs and other South Slavs to remind him of it.

It was inevitable that at some point on the 600-mile-long Adriatic coastline between Trieste and Valona, the interests of Italy and Serbia would clash. Both countries were pursuing policies that may be best described as a poor man's imperialism: they hoped that acquisition of new territories would solve their internal economic and political problems. In this regard, Serbia had recently done much better than Italy. On the conclusion of the Balkan wars in July 1913, it received, by the peace treaty of Bucharest, 15,241 square miles of Macedonian territory and over one-and-a-half million inhabitants, bringing its total population to over four-and-a-half million. The acquisition in fact brought Serbia no internal peace; it set off a fierce controversy between the politicians and the soldiers in Belgrade, a controversy which made its own contribution to the murder of the successor to the Habsburg throne.[24] The Macedonian territory did not satiate Belgrade. There were still more than two million Serbs living under Habsburg rule–according to the census of 1910, 1,106,471 Serbs lived in the Hungarian part of the Habsburg dominions, 783,334 Serbs and Croats in the Austrian part; the 1912 estimate for the provinces of Bosnia and Herzegovina was 856,158 Serbs–and then there were the Croats and the Slovenes, Catholic but racially related to the Serbs. They were at first not taken into account by Belgrade: the movement for South Slav unity and Great Serbian plans for expansion were then two quite distinct things. The Belgrade politicians on the whole preferred to work with the Serbs of the Habsburg monarchy, and especially with the Serbs in Bosnia and Herzegovina. The two provinces had been occupied by Austria-Hungary in 1878, and annexed in 1908; the Ministry of Finance in Vienna was responsible for their administration and in 1910 they acquired their own Diet. Bosnia and Herzegovina lay between Serbia and the sea: the aggressive majority of the Belgrade politicians believed that without access to the sea Serbia would never become economically and politically independent. For several years before the outbreak of the First World War, the Serbian population of the Habsburg monarchy had been regarded in Belgrade as the best means of exerting pressure in the direction of the Adriatic seaboard. For this policy the support of Russia was essential: diplomacy, religious and racial affinities, terrorist activities, were all used to weaken the influence of Austria in the Balkans and to push Serbia's western frontier toward the Adriatic coastline. This policy, pursued by Belgrade in close consultation with St Petersburg, had brought the two Slav partners no tangible rewards before August 1914. In the end it succeeded in irritating Vienna into an ill-considered military action; the opportunity that Pašić, the devious Prime Minister of Serbia, had missed in 1909, when his request for

Russian military support against Austria was turned down, came up again in July 1914.

But the outbreak of the war drastically changed diplomatic perspectives on the Balkans, when Russia's coming to Serbia's rescue in 1914 set off a chain reaction which brought all the European Great Powers into the war. As a member state of the Triple Entente, Russia lost much of its former freedom of diplomatic action. Apart from military necessity which often showed the value of old alliances in a new light, Russia was now constrained to bear in mind the interests and opinions of its allies. It was bound to them very closely. By the Declaration of London of 29 September 1914, Britain, France and Russia pledged themselves never to conclude a separate peace. It looked now as if the position of Serbia might become highly vulnerable; as if the hopes for which it had entered the war in the first place would dissolve like smoke above the battlefields. In a conflict of all the European Great Powers, Serbia was the odd man out: a small country, actually engaged in fighting. Though the claims of Italy to the status of a Great Power may have been tenuous, the possibility of its participation in the war appeared – to the politicians and soldiers in London, Paris and often enough in St Petersburg – more valuable than Serbia's actual war effort.

Pašić knew nothing about the course the negotiations with Italy were taking, nor was he aware of Sazonov's loss of diplomatic initiative. On 21 September, he at last officially informed St Petersburg of Serbian territorial claims. He did not ask outright for all the lands of the Habsburg monarchy inhabited by the South Slavs: on the contrary, he avoided the subject as far as he could. He conceded that the Istrian peninsula 'could be divided with Italy should it immediately join against Austria-Hungary'. A week later, he added that 'Dalmatia desires to be united with Serbia' and that 'Italy will be satisfied if it obtains Trieste, Trent, Pola, and Istria with Pulj'.[25] Especially in his second communication to St Petersburg, Pašić tried to accommodate Italy in the demands he thought it was making: he referred, on the other hand, to the 'desire' of Dalmatia to be united with Serbia. There was a simple explanation for this. The exiles from Austrian Dalmatia began supplying him with information about the Italian demands.

Bosnia and Herzegovina had before the war been supplying

EUROPE IN NOVEMBER 1914

	The Entente Powers and associates in November 1914.
	The Central Powers in November 1914.
	Neutral states in November 1914.
	The Western and Eastern fronts in November 1914.

FINLAND

Helsingfors

Gulf of Finland

ST. PETERSBURG

Reval

STOCKHOLM

Riga

Moscow

Libau

Memel

Kovno

Vilna

Smolensk

Königsberg

zig

Minsk

R   U   S   S   I   A

Grodno

en

Brest Litovsk

Warsaw

Kiev

POLAND

Dnieper

Lemberg (Lwow)

Dniester

Bratislava (Pressburg)

Tisza

Prut

Odessa

Budapest

TRIA - HUNGARY

Drava

RUMANIA

Sava

BUCHAREST

B   L   A   C   K   S   E   A

BELGRADE

Danube

BULGARIA

MONTE-NEGRO

SERBIA

SOFIA

Constantinople

ANGORA

ALBANIA

Salonika

OTTOMAN EMPIRE (TURKEY)

Brindisi

GREECE

AEGEAN SEA

Smyrna

IONIAN SEA

ATHENS

essina

RHODES

CYPRUS

SEA

CRETE

the terrorists who committed acts of violence against the Austro-Hungarian administration for the sake of a greater Serbia; Dalmatia, on the other hand, supplied most of the forceful advocates of the movement for South Slav unity. Dr Ante Trumbić, a former member of the Austrian Reichsrat and of the Dalmatian Diet, Frano Supilo, a former member of the Hungarian parliament, and Ivan Mestrović, the sculptor, had left the Habsburg realm for political exile a few days before the outbreak of war. They chose Italy as their base of operations, and it was a natural choice for them to make. Italian was the second language of the Dalmatians: they had before their eyes the example of the Italian unification, and they looked toward Serbia as the Piedmont of the South Slavs, as the focal point of their unity. It was ironical that in Italy the exiles met the greatest disappointment of their lives. They did not only find a complete lack of understanding of their political plans. They followed with anxiety the irredentist demands made daily in the Italian press; they were especially alarmed by the rumour of an expedition of Italian volunteers – shades of Garibaldi – which was soon to land on the Dalmatian coast. Had they known about the concessions to Italy Pašić had proposed to Sazonov on 28 September, they would have been appalled. It needed no subtle political instinct on the part of Supilo and his friends to sense that Italy would attempt to drive a hard bargain. They were afraid that they could not quite rely on Serbia and Russia to protect their interests and therefore decided instead on direct action.

On 28 September, the day of Pašić's second communication to St Petersburg, the three men called on the British, the French and the Russian Ambassadors to Rome. Their polite and non-committal reception left them depressed but not inactive. They had nothing if not persistence on their side. Supilo left immediately for Bordeaux, then the temporary seat of the French government; he met there Delcassé and Izvolsky, the Russian Ambassador. He gave the latter a memorandum on the unification of the South Slavs, in which he paid, for a Catholic, considerable deference to Holy Mother Russia. From Bordeaux, Supilo made two trips to London. Here he frightened Asquith, who described him as a 'boiling Stromboli' and who witnessed the eruption when he asked the deputy from Dalmatia, pencil in hand and map spread on the luncheon table, whether those Italian demands (Asquith's hand moving fast down the Dalmatian coastline) would be acceptable to the South Slavs.

Indeed, the first months of the war brought the advocates of South Slav unity nothing but disappointments. There were too many obstacles in the way of their cause. The Allies wanted to make certain of Italy and they were promising in return, as they saw it, enemy territory. They were naturally impatient with the South Slav exiles who claimed that the territory was inhabited not by enemies but by friends. The claim was hardly justified. South Slav unity was not a popular cause in the Habsburg dominions early in the war; in Vienna, the threat of Italy's intervention on the Allied side, and rumours of Italian territorial claims, were expected to strengthen the loyalty of the South Slavs to the monarchy: the Croats, the Slovenes, as well as many Serbs, in fact gave ample proof of this on the battlefield, after Italy's declaration of war. Finally, the plans of the exiles more than hinted at the possibility of the dissolution of the Habsburg territories, a very advanced idea at that stage of the war, especially for Paris and London.

But even St Petersburg proved unreceptive to it, as Supilo was soon to find out. True, he arrived there in February 1915, when the Russian army was being hard pressed. Sazonov was not allowed by Russia's western Allies to forget that at least a million fresh Italian troops were at stake. There were, however, other considerations in the mind of the Russian Foreign Minister. Supporting Serbia was one thing; supervising, as a diplomatic midwife, the birth of a united South Slav state quite another. The Russians knew from experience that they were able to influence the policy of Pašić's Serbia, and they saw no reason for disturbing that state of affairs, by supporting a federation of the Serbs with the Croats and the Slovenes. Early in 1915, Sazonov put it in this way:[26]

I can say nothing about the Croats and the Slovenes. They are fighting against us and I tell you now that if the Russian people had to fight for only half a day for the liberation of the Slovenes, I would not agree to it!

It was clearly going to be difficult to win the Russians over to the idea of a united South Slav state. But Supilo's journey to St Petersburg was not entirely wasted. When he arrived there early in February 1915, he had with him a letter of introduction to Sazonov from the Serbian Prime Minister. Sazonov was too busy, and Supilo was received instead by Baron Schilling, who was working on the Near East desk in the Russian Foreign Ministry. At one point in their conversation, Schilling startled his visitor. He asked Supilo what he thought would be the best way of safeguarding the national rights of the Poles, should Austrian Poland pass under the rule of Russia after the war. Supilo, who was a suspicious and imaginative man, did not like the question at all. It revealed to him an aspect of the official mind which he did not care for: if the Russian diplomats thought about the Poles in that way, there was no reason to suppose that they would think differently in regard to the South Slavs. The old dynastic arrangements would prevail; it was like living, Supilo may have felt, a century before, with Metternich making all the important decisions.

The fuss Supilo consequently made earned him an audience with Sazonov. He accused the Minister at once of having conceded Italy everything. Sazonov thought the exile knew more than in fact he did – after his lunch with Asquith, Supilo was able to refer to a few points that had actually come up during the negotiations with Italy – and spoke to him quite openly about the conditions Italy was making. He offered as an explanation the worsening of Russia's military position.

All that Supilo took back with him from St Petersburg was advance information on the concessions to Italy; their common plight brought the Serbian government and the South Slav exiles closer together. They alerted their friends in London and Paris – mostly journalists and university professors, none of them in high official position – to the danger of Italian greed. Their protests made no impression on the policy of the Allies. The negotiations with Italy had advanced too far.

Looking back at these negotiations, Salandra wrote:[27]

For the satisfaction of my conscience and for the glory of that political party of which my Ministry was the last uncontaminated representation, it is sufficient that we planned, desired, prepared and initiated the victorious War.

The preparations for that victorious war took eight months, and they occupied not only the Premier's time. We have seen that soon after the outbreak of the war, Britain took over from Russia the conduct of the negotiations: in due course, the conflict over Italy became a diplomatic contest between London and Berlin, with St Petersburg and Vienna playing rather unreliable and temperamental second strings. From the Allied point of view, the diplomatic situation in Italy was precisely the reverse of that in Turkey. In Constantinople the Germans were on the offensive and the Allies on the defensive: Berlin tried to get Turkey into the war, whereas London, Paris and St Petersburg wanted to keep Turkey neutral. In Rome, on the other hand, the Allies were bidding for the higher stakes while the Central Powers hoped, at best, to keep Italy out of the war.

In this regard Austria-Hungary was a heavy liability. Popular enmity against Habsburg rule was easy to kindle; the pre-war diplomatic marriage had been one of crude convenience. And during the crucial period in the relations between Austria-Hungary and Italy the two Ambassadors to Rome – von Mérey and, from December 1914, Baron Macchio – did little to ease the situation. The Italians thought them both too slow-moving, too slow-witted and overbearing; von Mérey had been even less popular than Macchio, and San Giuliano had taken great pains to avoid him. Prince von Bülow, a former Chancellor of the German Reich, who arrived in Rome soon after Macchio, disliked his Austrian colleague nearly as much as the Italians did. He thought Macchio 'indolent, without initiative, without personal opinions'. It was the Ambassador's misfortune to represent, in Rome, an unpopular state.

The man then responsible for Austrian foreign policy was Count Berchtold, Foreign Minister at the Ballhausplatz in Vienna since February 1912. He had taken over from Aehrenthal, but he preferred to think of himself as one of a line of more illustrious names, such as Metternich and Schwarzenberg. It is possible that Berchtold was wrong in his view. In 1912 he had behind him a record of mediocre, though by no means discreditable, service to the Habsburg state. Soon after his marriage to Ferdinandine, Countess Károlyi, in January 1893 he was transferred from home to foreign civil service. His first posting abroad took him to Paris, and he went on to serve his apprenticeship as a diplomat in London, where he witnessed the funeral of Queen Victoria and the coronation of Edward VII; he looked after Archduke Franz

Ferdinand when the latter came to London for the funeral, and
noted that the heir to the Habsburg throne had the 'eyes of a
hunter'.[28] In March 1903 he moved on to St Peterburg as a
Counsellor. He disliked the climate: his second son was constantly
ill, and his own weak constitution also suffered. After three years
in St Petersburg, he very much wanted to go home and devote
himself to the management of his estates. But when he returned
to Vienna in the autumn of 1906 he committed the error of going
to the Ballhausplatz to congratulate Aehrenthal on his appointment as Foreign Minister. The post of Ambassador to St Petersburg was mentioned in the course of the conversation, but
Berchtold seemed completely uninterested; he finally accepted it
in December, after unrelenting pressure by the Foreign Minister.
He left Vienna early in January 1907 with mixed feelings; 'an
ounce of happiness, two ounces of concern, and a hundredweight
of infernal anxiety'.[29]

With regard to the future relations between Austria and Russia
Berchtold was guilty of a fatal blunder. He had never liked his
post in St Petersburg, and was acutely aware of the dangers that
Russia's foreign policies, both official and unofficial – the activities of the various Panslav societies, political subversion through
the Orthodox religion, the collections in Russia for famine relief
on Austrian territory – presented to the internal order of the
Habsburg state. The threat was aimed especially at the marginal
territories of Austria-Hungary: Russian support for Serbia and
Serbian encouragement of the anti-Habsburg Serbs in Bosnia and
Herzegovina were the most dangerous of the Russian-sponsored
activities. But those problems were not new, and Aehrenthal had
always made a point of settling them with Russia direct. Berchtold,
when he took over the Foreign Ministry, abandoned the former
practice. During the Serbian crises in the summer of 1914,
Berchtold was out of touch with St Petersburg. He believed that
the incident could be localized and that, as he put it later himself,
'our action against Serbia was not intended to provoke Russia'.[30]

Berchtold came from a conventional Austrian aristocratic home:
his father loved horses and his mother took an interest in the arts;
their son Poldi was to do both, with the horses having an edge
over the arts. He felt most at home on his father's estate at
Buchlau in Moravia, and skipped the usual grand tour popular
with young men of quality. The broad acres and the deep woods

of Buchlau were young Berchtold's world, and in later life he returned to them as often as he could. The large estate was situated in the German–Czech border area; there were Czech, German, Slovak and Hungarian employees there, and Berchtold learnt to speak the languages of all of them. It was said that he was a true Austrian in that he had no national prejudices: his limitations lay elsewhere. His youth centred on a country house which represented a particular way of life, and that of a particular class. Berchtold never showed the slightest desire to break out of his enchanted circle. Like many Austrian aristocrats he looked down on the 'common people' and on one occasion he told Archduke Leopold Salvator that 'the people are in the last resort a flock of sheep blindly following their leaders'.[31]

The adult Berchtold was an easy-going, occasionally frivolous man with a strong sense of duty to the reigning dynasty and the established order. As Foreign Minister, he came to enjoy his audiences with Franz Josef, and three-quarters of an hour of the Emperor's time were always set aside for the purpose, whatever the importance of the matter in hand. Berchtold was impressionable and could be easily influenced. It seemed to some of his contemporaries that there was a certain lifelessness about him: what he said and did, did not sound unreasonable; it sounded as if it did not really concern him. He was incapable of making quick decisions; vacillation and procrastination were his favourite vices. He was, however, patient, adaptable, discreet and supremely polite. But even a man of Berchtold's patience found it hard to endure the negotiations with Rome. On 5 January 1915 he wrote in his diary that because of the 'Italian complications'[32] he wished to beg the Emperor to appoint Count Burián in his place. The request was granted and in July 1915 Colonel Berchtold left with his regiment for the Isonzo front. He preferred to fight the Italians rather than negotiate with them.

Berchtold never believed that there was any way of influencing the Italians in favour of the Central Powers. From the very beginning of the war his attitude was that the politicians in Rome were faithless, that the war would in any case be a short one, and the only sensible policy was to play for time. The basic Austro-Hungarian attitudes toward the Italian problem were expressed at a cabinet meeting as early as 8 August 1914. Berchtold still foolishly persisted in his view that Austria's conflict with Serbia did not come under Article VII of the treaty of the Triple Alliance, disregarding the fact that if Vienna had any aim in the war at all, it was the elimination of Serbia as a political factor in the Balkans. But he was ready to recognize the Italian claim in this case because 'Italy's existence is not at stake, as ours is'. Stefan Tisza, the Hungarian Prime Minister, said that Germany had no right to press Vienna to make concessions to the Italians; it was the German action against Belgium that had brought the British and the French fleets into the Mediterranean, before the eyes of the Italians, and made them think twice about joining their former allies in the war. Tisza went on to point out the bad impression that would be created both abroad and at home by territorial concessions to Italy; 'a state which . . . gives away pieces of territory from its own body degrades itself before the whole world'. He went on to say that 'our main endeavour should now be to play for time until [military] decision is reached in France and in Russia, and Italy loses her desire to take enemy action against us'. He believed therefore that the conversations with the Italian government should be spun out in some non-committal manner, while an energetic effort should be made to win over Turkey and Bulgaria. At this point the speculations of the politicians were interrupted by Field-Marshal Conrad, who flatly stated that successful resistance to Italian attacks on Istria, Trieste and the South Tirol would be impossible; in order to make the task of the soldiers at all possible, Turkey, Bulgaria and Rumania would have to be won over for military participation in the war, and Italy would have to be kept neutral. Conrad considered the neutrality of Italy of such importance that he could think of no price high enough to pay for it. Stürgkh, the Austrian Premier, thought that every subterfuge should be used against the 'Italian brigands'. The cabinet in the end resolved that

the negotiations with Italy should be continued in a non-committal manner so that the Italian government should stay neutral as long as no decision is reached in France and in Russia. . . .[33]

Berchtold was able to keep up his policy of spinning out the negotiations with Rome and of looking surprised when faced with Italian demands, for a long time. No military decision on the western and eastern fronts was made, and Berchtold's policy soon started taking its toll.

In the first five months of the war, diplomatic nerves had been under too great a strain. Both the Austrian and the German Ambassadors were replaced, and in January 1915 Berchtold himself resigned because of the Italian entanglement. The ailing, intransigent Mérey had been recalled already in October: his place was taken by Macchio, a lively and courteous gentleman of Dalmatian origin. Flotow, the German Ambassador, had also been unwell for some time; together with his Russian wife, who spoke German badly and kept a little statue of Ivan the Terrible in her drawing room, he left Rome to make place for Prince von Bülow. The new Ambassador came to Rome on 17 December; there would have been nothing unusual about his arrival in peacetime. Since his retirement as Chancellor, Bülow had spent every winter in Rome at his splendid Villa Malta; he was married to a daughter of Laura Minghetti, a member of an eminent Italian family and a descendant of Sir John Acton, who had been the Prime Minister of the Kingdom of the Two Sicilies. As a member of the exclusive order of the Collar of the Annunziata, Prince von Bülow could style himself a 'cousin' of King Victor. He was a highly cultured man with a sharp tongue and an even sharper pen; he was the most eminent emissary the Wilhelmstrasse had at its disposal. The Italian Premier himself wrote: 'Without doubt, Prince von Bülow was of all German diplomatists the one best qualified to exercise a political influence over Italy.'[34] During his mission to Rome the Viennese daily, *Neue Freie Presse*, commented that 'the hub of European politics today is in the Villa Malta'. After Bülow's arrival in Rome, Sir Rennell and Lady Rodd had to start entertaining at the British Embassy much more often than they had done before.

Bülow's commission was clear-cut and difficult. He was to keep Italy neutral, largely at the expense of Vienna. 'We have packed the Trentino in Prince von Bülow's trunk', Jagow, the Foreign Secretary, told the German Empress: a remark which was not, strictly speaking, true. The title deeds to the province were not held in Berlin. But Bülow had to behave as if they were, and to conduct negotiations in Rome on behalf of Berlin as well as of Vienna. He assumed that the Austrians were not in a position to make difficulties. After their initial setbacks on the eastern front and after their failure to hold on to Belgrade, they badly needed German military aid: their argument that the Germans had tended to neglect the eastern front on the outbreak of the war was as true as it was irrelevant. The military plight of Germany's ally was not expected to make Bülow's mission more difficult.

The Consulta, the seat of the Italian Foreign Ministry, where he was now to be a frequent visitor, was well known to him. It was an austerely beautiful palace, opposite the Quirinal, with an imposing double staircase and a view, from the Foreign Minister's windows, of the colossal statue of Castor and Pollux reining in their horses. There was a copy of the statue in Berlin; it was nicknamed 'Progress checked, retrogression encouraged'. On his first visit to the Consulta, Bülow may have reflected that this was precisely what had happened in Rome. Perhaps too many mistakes had been made in the past: 'that singular mixture of perfidy and stupidity' was his description of Germany's past policy in regard to Italy; Berchtold had been allowed to obstruct for too long. When Bülow later remembered his Italian mission, he gave a detailed account of the difficulties that faced him at its outset: had he foreseen them in December 1914, he would not have gone to Rome at all.

Like most of his colleagues in the Wilhelmstrasse, Bülow thought that the Italians were open to persuasion: a hope that nobody in Vienna entertained seriously. Military evidence on the whole told in Berchtold's favour. Soon after the outbreak of war, the Italians launched an ambitious armaments programme. The allocation for extraordinary military expenditure in that financial year, the previous one having conveniently ended on 30 June 1914, was in excess of 1,000m. lire, of which 750m. was to be spent on the army. The Italians were unable to afford this expenditure: the following year, the British loan of 1,250m. lire, which went with the signing of the Pact of London, only just covered it. The sum, and the allocation of a substantial part of it to the army, hinted at the Italian government's intentions. Though the German Military Attaché pointed out these facts to the Chancellor,[35] Berlin preserved its optimism intact.

Some aspects of the Italian situation favoured this optimism: the new Ambassador to Rome had more behind him than prestige and connections. Since the diplomatic breach between France and Italy in 1881, German private investment in the Kingdom had been steadily rising, and by the end of 1913 it had amounted to 40m. lire (£1,660,000), excluding investment through Swiss channels.

Although the total sum was dwarfed by the amount – at least 440m. lire – of Belgian, French and British capital, the German economic penetration of the Kingdom was more far-reaching than was indicated by a comparison between the figures of the Allied and the German investments. The shipping lines, the Hamburg-Amerika, the Norddeutscher Lloyd and Kosmos, were among the leading German companies in Italy, and commerce in several Italian ports was controlled by German firms; many companies, even those financed by Belgian or French capital, were under German management; the Italian concessions of many of the big British firms were entrusted to Germans. The influence of Berlin was especially strong in banking. The Credito Italiano was largely a German foundation; the important Banca Commerciale Italiana had been established with the backing of German capital and run in 1914 by Herr Joel, a German banker from Danzig and one of the most influential men in Italy.[36] A number of Italian politicians had risen to prominence through their connections with German industry and commerce; many more felt that the Reich was on the way to becoming the leading industrial and military power in Europe. When Bülow arrived in Rome on 17 December, Joel was in the group of men who were waiting for the Ambassador at the railway station; the funds that were to help Bülow's mission had been forwarded earlier to the Banca Commerciale.

At the Consulta Bülow found an old acquaintance. Sidney Sonnino had joined Salandra's reconstructed cabinet in November: an important step toward the consolidation of Salandra's position. Sonnino had been Prime Minister twice, for a few months in 1906 and then again in 1910. He was regarded as a partisan of the Triple Alliance and, as late as 10 November 1914, the Austrian Ambassador thought that there were no indications that Sonnino had changed his mind.[37] There was really no way of telling. Sonnino was in many respects an unusual politician in the Italian context. His father was an Italian Jew, his mother Scottish; Sonnino himself was of the Protestant faith. His father had made a fortune as a banker in Egypt; young Sonnino was a studious and rich man who was able to devote himself entirely to politics. He was taciturn and tenacious; he completely lacked Salandra's fluency as an orator, he disliked making speeches, and when he had to make one he read it laboriously from his notes: an uncommon sight in the Italian parliament. He had, on the other hand, a characteristic rare in Italian politicians: he was entirely impervious to criticism and was therefore independent of the forces by which most of his colleagues were influenced. He was too detached for Lloyd George's taste; the Welshman called the taciturn Italian Protestant a 'terrible man'. Nor was Sonnino always popular with his subordinates. One of his Ambassadors who could no longer bear the strain during the negotiations on the allegiance of Italy to one side or the other, said of the Foreign Minister that he was 'nothing but a little Jew out to make a big deal'.[38]

Prince von Bülow was unable to break Sonnino's silence. He later complained:[39]

> I could never manage to learn the exact extent of Italian commitments, made before my arrival, to the Allies; nor, above all, could I be certain that she had not definitely and finally pledged herself.

He assumed that the Italians had given the Allies no definite undertaking. At his first meeting with Sonnino, he immediately agreed that the Trentino should be discussed; Sonnino, on his part, made a brief reference to Trieste. Bülow would not go that far; the reference made him crosser than he cared to admit. At this point, he may well have reflected that patriotic greed had started overleaping the bounds of reason. The acquisition of Trieste would only have lengthened the coastline of Italy; Trieste would have become one of its supernumerary ports, and would have been deprived of its commercial hinterland, while Austria would have lost its only important outlet in the Adriatic; Germany also had an interest in keeping it open for central European trade. It is unlikely that Bülow thought Sonnino unintelligent enough not to see this; there must have been another reason for the mention of Trieste. It was that Sonnino had agreed with Salandra on the policy of intervention on the side of the Allies, and his asking Bülow for Trieste was his way of saying that there was little point in further negotiations. Moreover, it would have been uncharacteristic of him, had he wanted to achieve more than that. If there was no point in further negotiations, then Bülow's presence in Rome was unnecessary. Neither Salandra nor his Foreign Minister wanted him around in an official capacity while they were preparing their country for war.

In the light of subsequent developments it seems likely that Bülow had understood Sonnino's hint and that, early in his stay in Rome, the Ambassador had decided that Salandra's government would not play the role he had chosen for it. Yet Bülow had to behave as if nothing at all had happened and continue to treat the government as a partner in the conversations on Italy's future. Secretly, however, he set to work on a plan of subversion. A valuable prize was at stake: in wartime, interference with the affairs of a foreign country was not uncommon. If nothing could be expected from Salandra's government because it was moving toward intervention, then there existed an obvious alternative to that government. Giolitti could once more return to power.

On 3 January 1915, the British Ambassador to Rome was convinced that this was precisely the aim that Bülow had in mind: he added that the Prince, who had decided to use Giolitti and the Banca Commerciale to keep Italy neutral, had 'shown discernment' and that he might well 'accomplish something'.[40] Originally, Salandra and his government had been nothing for Giolitti but a stop-gap, a pilot to ride out the storm. But then the unexpected happened. During the war Salandra showed himself to be a more astute politician than Giolitti had taken him for; the Premier's reconstruction of the cabinet early in November 1914 strengthened its interventionist forces, while eliminating, in the words of the British Ambassador, the 'neutrality at any price' element. By the end of 1914 Giolitti knew that the Premier would be difficult to dislodge from office, especially with Sonnino lined up on his side. He nevertheless made the attempt. He was a skilful political manipulator who controlled the majority – some 300 out of 500 – of the deputies in the Chamber. Described by his enemies as the 'Minister of the underworld', Giolitti's influence, through a judicious application of favours and patronage, extended throughout Italian public life. Large numbers of senators and journalists, civil servants and mayors, were in one way or another indebted to him. He approached politics with a clear, open, opportunist mind: on one occasion he fought the socialists and suppressed strikers, on another he authorized an extensive programme of public works. In 1912, he saw the bill on universal manhood suffrage through the parliament, while at the same time taking care to neutralize its effects – an increase in the representation of the Left – by introducing Catholic deputies into the Chamber.

By the time Bülow had found his bearings in Rome, the respective positions of the interventionists and the neutralists in Italy had become better defined. It was now clear to influential groups in Italian public life that a war on the Central Powers would be harmful to their interests. Those members of the *haute bourgeoisie* with German business connections had no intention of giving hem up; the Catholics who let religion influence their politics disliked the attacks on the Habsburg dynasty; the Conservatives feared the chaos which they suspected the Freemasons, the Radicals and the Republicans of desiring and working for; Socialist pacifism had found a response among the masses of the people. All these diverse forces came together in the attempt to keep Italy neutral.

Giolitti knew that neutrality alone would satisfy no one; there would have to be some inducement. On 24 January 1915, he wrote to a friend:[41]

> ... certainly I do not, like the nationalists, look on war as a piece of good fortune; I consider it a disaster to be faced only when the honour and the interests of the country are at stake. It might be, and it does not appear improbable, that in the present state of Europe much [*parecchio*] might be obtained without war, but this no one outside the Government is fully qualified to decide.

Early in February, the letter was published in the Roman press, and the '*parecchio*' phrase reverberated throughout Italy. Giolitti was offering 'much' without involving the country in the war. The assumption of the interventionists – that Italy would be opting out of the Great Powers' club if it did not actively take part in their quarrel – could be countered by the argument that, at the end of the war, a strong Italy would confront an exhausted Europe. And Giolitti believed that the war would be long and exhausting.

In the letter that contained the '*parecchio*' formula, Giolitti also defended himself against the charge of his 'alleged relations'[42] with Prince von Bülow. In his autobiography, the Italian politician maintained that he had seen Bülow, since he came to Rome as Ambassador, on one occasion only: their second meeting never materialized; Giolitti was out when the Prince called on him, and on his return, he found the Ambassador's card.[43] Bülow, on his part, was even more reticent: he said nothing in his memoirs about his relations with Giolitti, apart from the remark that he was 'our best and surest Italian friend'.[44] The two men had a great many interests in common. Most important, Bülow wanted to keep Italy neutral and so did Giolitti. To achieve this, they had to use the same means: they had to create a suitable climate of political and public opinion, a climate that could be achieved mainly through their political connections and through the press. They could work for the same aim independently of each other; there was no need for constant consultation. But neither of them worked in isolation. Giolitti had been connected with the Banca Commerciale before the war, and Bülow's political funds deposited there were used to finance Giolitti's activities. The Ambassador also had to keep his Italian ally informed of the state of the Central Powers' offers: otherwise Giolitti would not have known what the definition of '*parecchio*' was, and how much exactly his country had to gain. According to one witness, the policy of Giolitti's paper *La Stampa* was due to the influence of the German Ambassador, who had no scruples in exercising it.[45] Nevertheless, Giolitti was not offering Italy some artificial, synthetic policy, the product of political graft and foreign influence. Under Italian conditions it was a genuine alternative to Salandra's plans, as the fierceness of the attacks on Giolitti was to prove.

For Bülow, in the meanwhile, it was sometimes difficult to decide whether Rome or Vienna presented him with the greater problem. It did not take the Austro-Hungarian government long to realize that in Bülow it had found a formidable opponent who was resolved to put an end to the policy of procrastination. Matters came to a head in Vienna on 10 January 1915. On the morning of that day Stürgkh, Tisza and three high Hungarian officials in the Foreign Ministry met Berchtold, who started the conversation by surveying the negotiations with Italy since its declaration of neutrality, adding a brief description of the worsening in Austria's military situation. It was a defence of his Italian policy, of which he knew that most of the men assembled in his room were highly critical. He wanted to prove to them that he had not softened in the past few weeks; once again, he said that Italy 'needs negotiations in order to pacify the war-mongers. Therefore negotiations must be spun out!' Once again, the Foreign Minister indicated that a demand by the Italians for the Trentino should be received on the part of the diplomats with frank amazement. Berchtold's speech failed to impress the Hungarian Premier. Tisza was not at all pessimistic about the military situation, and he accused Berchtold of trying too hard to please the Italians. He thought that Vienna should combat by every means Bülow's activities in Rome; one day perhaps Austria-Hungary might have to give up the Trentino in order to avert military disaster. But he was convinced that the moment had not yet come. Berchtold, concluding his own record of the meeting, wrote that 'all present . . . were of the opinion that in the first place we must firmly refuse to negotiate about the Trentino'.[46] Later in the morning, the two Prime Ministers, Tisza and Stürgkh, Burián, Tisza's admirer and close friend, and Tschirschky, the German Ambassador to Vienna, lunched with Berchtold. The conversation took on a quick pace and a sharp tone. Tisza attacked Bülow, and went on to accuse Berlin of having raised the Italians' hopes, thereby making negotiations with them more difficult. Tschirschky defended his government and stressed the common interest of Berlin and Vienna in preventing the dispersal of their armed forces. He was certain that such a dispersal would follow the declaration of war by Italy and Rumania. Tisza insisted that the situation of the Central Powers was far from critical, and renewed his attacks on Bülow. In his view, the German Ambassador to Rome was conducting a completely independent policy, and one calculated to do great harm to the interests of the Habsburg monarchy. The German Ambassador protested against the accusation.

The luncheon party was not going at all well. Tisza suddenly got up and asked Berchtold to come with him into the next room. There, leaning against a chest between two large windows, his eyes filled with tears (the eyes and the tears magnified by his spectacles), Tisza told Berchtold that he held him in high regard, and it was therefore going to be difficult for him to say what lay on his heart. He nevertheless said it. He told Berchtold that his conduct of foreign policy lacked the necessary energy, and that this caused him great concern at the present time, when the existence of the monarchy was at stake. He therefore saw it as his duty to tell the Emperor, at the audience later that day, of his view. If Franz Josef did not agree, then Tisza promised Berchtold his continued support. Berchtold was rather taken aback by this emotional scene in the middle of his luncheon party. He was, however, not a fighter like Tisza. He said that in the first place he had accepted the office against his better judgement, and Tisza's proposal that he should resign suited him very well indeed. He would have liked to add that Burián would be the best man to succeed him, but thought better of it. The Hungarian Premier might have wanted the Foreign Ministry for himself.[47] Tisza had, in fact, no intention of spending too much time away from Budapest, the source of his political power; he had a friend who would do just as well for the post.

Burián became Foreign Minister on 13 January: now Tisza was able to influence foreign policy without bearing responsibility for it. The Foreign Ministry in Vienna became a preserve of the Hungarians: apart from the Minister, two heads of the political departments, Forgach and Nemes, Wickenburg at the head of the trade department, and two other high officials, Szápary and Szécen, were all Hungarian. Tisza's victory was due to the dissatisfaction felt in Vienna at the conduct of the Italian negotiations. Tisza, Stürgkh and Burián were all agreed that no concessions should be made to Italy. Berchtold was forced to resign not because he basically disagreed with them, but because he was thought to be too impressionable, and because he had been seen to vacillate.

Burián, the new Foreign Minister, had a high opinion of himself. He was a more serious person than Berchtold, and had none of his frivolity. His logical reasoning sometimes lost touch with reality. He rarely asked anyone's advice, but behind every action and every policy of his there stood the formidable figure of Stefan Tisza. Their foreign policy was as tough and uncompromising as was Tisza's attitude to, say, the Slovaks or the Rumanians in Hungary; it reached its culmination on 11 February, when Burián sent a memorandum to Salandra's cabinet, claiming compensations for Italy's gains in the Balkan wars and, more recently, in the Adriatic. Burián boasted that he had made the Italians despair, and Bülow furious.[48]

The Austrian policy hardened at the very time when Berlin was making an all-out effort to negotiate in Rome. Early in February, Matthias Erzberger had arrived in Rome on his first mission. He was a valuable ally for Bülow: the Prince himself had asked that Erzberger should come to Italy. He was inconspicuous, uninhibited by diplomatic conventions; there were many things the Ambassador could not do and Erzberger could. He was a shrewd politician, a leading member of the Catholic Centre Party. A tailor's son from a small Swabian town, he had a deceptively open face, and there was something comic and over-eager about him; his appearance was described as that of an 'ornamental beer-cork'. He had never met Bülow before, but he had attacked the Prince, fiercely and on several occasions, in the Reichstag. In Rome, the two men left their former enmity behind.

In all, Erzberger came to Rome three times – early in February, in April and in May 1915 – each time eager to help, provided with unlimited financial means by the Berlin government, each time appalled afresh by the stupidity of Vienna and the duplicity of Rome. His great strength lay in his shrewdness, his tenacity, and the number of contacts he had in the upper reaches of the Catholic hierarchy. Reporting on his first mission, Erzberger wrote that the Pope, the Vatican Secretary of State Cardinal Gasparri, the Under Secretary Pacelli, the Jesuit General Count Ledóchowski, the Provincial of the German Jesuits Father Ehrle, and Father Foncke, the head of the Biblical Institute, were among the ecclesiastics with whom he had established contacts. Like Bülow, Erzberger was something of an optimist in regard to Italy: after his first visit to Rome he wrote in urgent underlined sentences:[49]

she will inevitably enter the war unless a settlement is quickly reached with Austria. The unconditional neutrality of Italy cannot be attained without Austrian concessions. But it can be said with equal certainty that the benevolent neutrality of Italy can be achieved for the entire duration of the war at the price of relatively small Austrian offers.

At this time Erzberger was still convinced that the Trentino, together with the promise of better treatment for the Italians under Habsburg rule, would secure the benevolent neutrality of Rome. In the course of his audience with Benedict xv on 23 February, Erzberger asked the Pope to use his influence in Vienna; he knew that the Pope abhorred the possibility of a conflict between Austria and Italy: in the midst of a belligerent country, the position of the Vatican would have become untenable and the running of church affairs difficult; moreover, the Pope wished Austria to remain a great Catholic Power. Benedict xv agreed with Erzberger on the reasons that made it difficult for Austria to negotiate. There existed the danger that Italy would use the first concession as blackmail to extort others, and that the agreement would not remain secret. There was no telling what would be the effect of such news spreading among the peoples of the Habsburg state; it might well be seen as the first step toward a voluntary liquidation of the Austro-Hungarian state. Firm guarantees would therefore be needed for Vienna.

When Erzberger returned to Berlin, the Chancellor was so impressed by his arguments that he arranged an interview for him with the Kaiser. Its purpose was to move Wilhelm II to exert the strongest possible pressure on Franz Josef. Though the Kaiser described the Habsburg ruler as 'his sole surviving friend in the world',[50] he promised to do his best. The forces mobilized by Erzberger to put pressure on the Austrians were formidable indeed. They included Ledóchowski, the Jesuit General; Cardinal Piffl, the Archbishop of Vienna; Frau Katharina Schratt, the actress friend of the Emperor. Count Monts, the influential retired diplomat, was dispatched to the Habsburg capital; the Ambassador was instructed to tackle the stubborn Burián; Erzberger himself contacted the leaders of the Austrian Christian Socialists. The concerted pressure soon produced results. At a meeting of the Crown Council on 8 March 1915 it was finally decided to give up the Trentino; the Emperor made the concession most unwillingly, saying that if Italy asked for more, Austria would rather fight it out.[51]

The decision of the Crown Council was an important achievement for Erzberger, and he received his due share of credit for it. There were, however, two ways of looking at the concession. In an optimistic mood, the Germans would talk of 'starting the heavy stone rolling' or 'breaking the ice'; in retrospect, in a mood of recrimination, it was merely another link in the chain of Vienna's diplomatic blunders: the Austrians gave away 'too little, too late'.

Nevertheless, Erzberger was back in Rome early in April, reporting to Sonnino the pressure that Berlin had put on Vienna, as well as the German intention of guaranteeing Vienna's compliance with the agreement. Erzberger's meeting with the Foreign Minister had been arranged by Bülow, and its main purpose was not so much to influence Sonnino as to find out whether he had entered into an agreement with the enemy. Erzberger gained the impression, rightly, that Italy had not yet fully committed itself to the Allies. There was no need, on the other hand, for him to cast around for information on Sonnino's attitude to the Central Powers. The Foreign Minister told him in a few words and quite plainly that the latest Austrian offer was far from satisfactory and that it must be improved on. He added – and this was for Vienna the crux of the matter – that he was unable to bind himself to the maintenance of the secrecy of any possible agreement. Both parliament and people must have proof of the successful outcome of the negotiations.[52]

It was now clear that Erzberger's easy optimism at the time of his first visit to Italy had not been warranted. On the return journey from the second mission he stopped in Vienna in order to work there for further concessions. Once again, the Catholic machinery was put into motion; the Archduchess Zita, who was to become the last Habsburg Empress, and some other members of her family, the House of Parma, were also won over for the policy of making further concessions; in Berlin, Jagow began to read Bülow's dispatches to the Austrian Ambassador whenever opportunity arose. But this time, the only outcome of Erzberger's activity in Vienna was to stir up the underlying hostility to Bülow. The Austrians never forgave what they regarded as that 'betrayal' in Rome: owing to their opposition, Bülow had little chance of succeeding Bethmann Hollweg as Chancellor in 1917.

In Rome, Bülow pressed Macchio as hard as he could for further concessions; in Berlin, Bethmann Hollweg saw Burián personally on 25 April. The Chancellor quoted the German Chief of Staff as saying that the entry of Italy into the war would result in the defeat of the Central Powers, and he referred, for good measure, to Germany's inability to come to the aid of Austria-Hungary on any Italian front that might come about as a result of Vienna's intransigence.

But on 26 April 1915, the day after Burián's meeting with Bethmann Hollweg, the secret pact that bound Italy to declare war on the Central Powers within a month was signed in London. When Erzberger arrived on his last mission to Rome a few days later, he found a changed atmosphere. His contacts were more cautious; more of his meetings with the Italians took place in the crypts of churches, or in deserted monasteries, than in the Villa Malta. And shortly after his arrival, Cardinal Gasparri told him of his suspicion that the Italian government had already committed itself to the Allies.

When Erzberger met Salandra for the first time on 4 May 1915, the Premier, with the Pact of London in his pocket, had to take extra care to give nothing away. He was very conciliatory and reasonable: he told Erzberger that the Trentino, and perhaps a free city status for Trieste, would satisfy Italy. Nevertheless, Erzberger and Bülow were not deceived: they were convinced that Salandra's government had by now committed itself to the side of the enemy. They had no proof, but in official quarters in Rome there was a subdued air of purpose that had not been there before.

At that point, early in May 1915, the two German emissaries began to move fast. Time was running out and they knew it. They carried on with their former activities, only more intensively – Erzberger recruited a Sicilian priest who started collecting signatures to a broadly based clerical peace petition – but they knew that merely to try to influence public opinion was not enough. If Italy were to remain neutral, Salandra's cabinet would have to go. It was not as united a body as Salandra later made out.[53] The Minister of Education, Signor Grippo, was the leading neutralist, and he could call on the support of the Ministers of Agriculture and of the Post; in the opposite camp Salandra, Sonnino and the Ministers of War and of Colonies were in favour of intervention, while between the two groups there were seven members of the cabinet not yet definitely committed. Grippo, who had been introduced to Erzberger by a mutual clerical friend, promised to encourage dissension within Salandra's government. He received, from the Germans, an adequate reward for his efforts.

The next item on Erzberger's agenda was to bully Macchio into making far-reaching concessions. There did not seem to be enough time for the Ambassador either to resign or to consult Vienna, so fast did events move, and so hard did Erzberger push. It was essential that the neutralists' hand should be strengthened by a really generous offer at Austria's expense. Erzberger met Macchio on the morning of 10 May and presented him with a ready-made offer: the Trentino; the Isonzo territory including Gradisca; municipal autonomy, a free port and an Italian university for Trieste; protection of cultural rights for the Italian minority in the Habsburg Empire; further negotiations about Gorizia and the islands in the Adriatic; Valona and a completely free hand for Italy in Albania – all this to be guaranteed by Germany.[54] Though Macchio refused to sign the document before consulting Vienna, Erzberger had a copy of it passed on to Giolitti, who asked for

Bülow's and Macchio's signatures. Macchio was then hastily summoned to the Villa Malta, where his two German friends made him sign the document. This by no means ended the tragicomedy. Giolitti, with a fine sense of propriety and of tactics, then reminded Erzberger that there existed a legal government in Rome, and that it should also receive the document. Erzberger, needing additional copies rather badly, was seen, late in the evening, pursuing Macchio at Roman restaurants and night-clubs – places where he himself was by no means a frequent visitor.

The document remained technically invalid for two days, until 12 May, when Burián endorsed it. On the same day, Erzberger provided it with further guarantees: one to be given by the Kaiser, the other by Franz Josef; an Austro-Italian commission was to be set up at once to supervise the transfer of the former Habsburg territory; soldiers in the Austro-Hungarian army who came from there were to be demobilized. Only the Austrian frontier fortifications were to be retained by the Austrians for the duration of hostilities: Erzberger, however, said nothing as to how he envisaged this part of the agreement working out in practice; the frontier fortifications were situated deep in the territory to be ceded to Italy.

The two documents, both of them of questionable validity, did not fail to produce the desired effect in Rome. Austria was to make important concessions, publicly and at once; there was perhaps no need for Italy to enter the war after all. Giolitti returned to the capital from his country house in Piedmont to command his followers in parliament. The confrontation of the two camps was about to take place.

By the time the Germans, together with their reluctant ally, had made the final offer, Salandra's cabinet was irrevocably committed to entering the war. The partisans of intervention had received steady encouragement from London and Paris. Sir Rennell Rodd, the British Ambassador to Rome, had never found it difficult to impress on his government the importance of Italy's entry into the war on the Allied side. He was popular in the Foreign Office, where he had the reputation of a minor poet; in Rome, he preferred the company of writers and artists to that of politicians. One of his best friends there was Axel Munthe, the fashionable doctor and writer, whom Rodd later defended against charges of spying for Germany.

The Ambassador got on well with Sonnino, because the Foreign Minister was so unlike an Italian politician; the first long conversation between them had taken place on 7 November 1914, Sonnino's second day at the Consulta. Rodd talked first to the Minister about the Balkans: a week before their meeting Turkey had openly joined the side of Germany and Austria-Hungary. There now existed a considerable body of opinion in Rome that this action offered the necessary pretext for Italy to come into the war on the Allied side. Sonnino indicated to Rodd that in this area the interests of their countries were the same, and the Ambassador was now able to get down to the discussion of the grounds of Italy's possible co-operation.[55] He returned to the point where negotiations with San Giuliano had stopped. In September 1914, Grey had not wanted to rush prematurely into definite obligations to the Italians; on 18 September he had instructed Rodd as follows:[56]

I should like you to take an early opportunity of telling the Prime Minister quite privately and informally that I am ready to discuss most sympathetically, as he already knows, with the Italian Ambassador here all the points that will require consideration, with a view to meeting the wishes of the Italian Government should the latter decide to join us. But, as I have repeatedly told the Italian Ambassador here, until such a decision is come to, I do not think any useful purpose would be served by discussing contingencies.

Now, at their first interview on 7 November, Sonnino told Rodd that he did not quite like Grey's insistence on not negotiating the details of the agreement until Italy had definitely committed herself; Rodd explained that his Minister

had not considered it opportune to enter into a long and elaborate discussion of points of detail constituting a state document, which would involve elaborate negotiations, until there was some definite indication of Italy's real intentions.

Despite the diplomatic quibble, Sonnino and Rodd knew that they were talking about the same thing, and that they could go a step further. Sonnino told his visitor that his country was not yet ready for action: in any case there was no particular hurry as the war was going to be a long one. But he thought it quite possible that circumstances might precipitate matters in this connection and he referred to an action by Turkey. Since some surprise might force the hand of Italy, compelling it to take a decisive step at a few days' or even hours' notice, Sonnino argued that it would be well to have ready some concrete scheme which could be signed by the two parties without delay. 'He did not see', Rodd wrote,

why some such draft scheme could not be very confidentially prepared between us. He would prefer that it should be known to the fewest possible people. . . . He thought it would be better not to deal with France and Russia directly at present. They were not always too discreet in treating such questions.

Nor did he expect them to be, Sonnino might have added, as generous as Britain.

As on the previous occasion, Rodd now again supported the Italian proposal. But this time, he thought, the situation was different. San Giuliano had been a 'scheming, contriving, subtle personality', but now the Ambassador was dealing with a 'man of direct and straightforward character'. In a more important regard, however, the situation remained the same. Rodd was positive, as he had been three months before, that Italy would not join the enemy because 'the opinion of the country would not allow that, and certain parties would provoke a revolution if they suspected it'. He nevertheless felt that 'there would be value in having got something tangible between us of this kind for holding Italy fast'.

There were too many obstacles in the way of a draft treaty. The Italians were not yet ready for a military engagement, and they wanted a concrete and detailed undertaking; Britain's allies would have to be consulted, and St Petersburg was certain to make difficulties. The negotiations were postponed until the Italians themselves made an approach.

Since the Foreign Secretary did not want to discuss the detailed conditions in advance, the Consulta was left to do all the work. On 16 February 1915, Sonnino informed Imperiali, the Ambassador to London, of the terms on which his government would be prepared to join the Allies in the war. But the Ambassador was to await instructions before contacting the Foreign Office.[57] Imperiali did not have to wait long. The events in the Turkish theatre of war quickened the Italians' interest in coming into the war. On 19 February British and French battleships commenced the bombardment of the forts guarding the entrance to the Dardanelles; a week later, a number of the outer forts had been blasted out of existence, and the Straits swept clear for four miles. At the same time, the interest of the Russians in Italy's co-operation reached the lowest point yet; Sonnino may have known about this, and he certainly kept a close watch on the events in the Dardanelles. On 4 March, Imperiali presented Sir Edward Grey with a document which started with a coy introduction ('nothing forces [Italy] to . . . encounter the immense risks and responsibilities of a war except the desire to free her brothers from a foreign yoke . . .'[58]) and ended with extortionate demands.[59]

The British Foreign Secretary carried the main burden of the subsequent negotiations, and Britain's allies caused him as much difficulty as the Italians. After the first glance through the terms when he had received them from London on 10 March, Poincaré knew that the Italians were demanding, as he put it, 'the lot'. Delcassé told the foreign editor of *The Times* that 'Italy put a pistol to our heads'.[60] But Delcassé attributed great importance to the alliance. There were those million Italian bayonets to be taken into consideration and the possibility that some more Rumanian ones might well be added later. Only in regard to Africa and to Italy's status as a naval power did Sonnino find it impossible to break through the united front of London and Paris. The goodwill of France and Britain in the Adriatic and on the Balkans was much more important for Sonnino and he knew that that goodwill would be forthcoming, at the expense of Serbia and Russia. Here, Grey was patient as well as accommodating. There was only one way for him to cut the Italian–Russian knot. On the same day, 11 March 1915, Sir George Buchanan, the British Ambassador to St Petersburg, passed on to Sazonov two documents: one of them informed him of Sonnino's terms; the other made the promise to Russia of Constantinople and the Straits. Then Sazonov was left in peace to consider and compare them.

It must have been immediately obvious to Sazonov that the offer in Turkey was an inducement to accept Sonnino's demands in the Adriatic. Although the Russian Foreign Minister later remembered that it had cost him 'a great effort to sacrifice to the advantages of the Italian alliance the interest of the Serbian people',[61] he nevertheless made the effort, less for the sake of the alliance with Italy than for the extension of Russia's influence in the Straits. When Sazonov replied to London on 15 March he was prepared to negotiate – an improvement on the situation a few weeks before. Although he agreed to the annexation by Italy of Trieste, Istria and the Quarnero Islands, he insisted that Serbia should obtain the Dalmatian littoral from the mouth of the river Krka down to a point north of Dubrovnik, as well as the offshore islands.[62] The Croats – Sazonov did not state whether Croatia was to remain a part of the Habsburg Empire – were to retain the coast north of the Krka to the Italian frontier near Volosca (Volosko, suburb of Opatija) including the offshore islands. Sazonov also objected to the Italian demand for the neutralization of the best part of the eastern Adriatic coast; he wrote that he agreed with 'the neutralization of the coast of the future independent Albania' as well as of the Greek coast between Chimara (now Himarë) and Cape Stilo, but he resolutely opposed the neutralization of the Bay of Cattaro in Bosnia.

Sonnino replied on 24 March to Grey's summary of the Russian objections. He felt at the time that there would be no point in exchanging Italy's 'present intolerable position of inferiority' in the Adriatic compared with Austria for the same condition that would arise as the result of the establishment of a 'league of young and ambitious Yugoslav states'. He argued that the different geographical conditions of the two shores – the open Italian coastline on the one hand, and the protected eastern Adriatic littoral, with its numerous offshore islands, on the other – a contrast aggravated by the development of modern naval warfare, made extreme caution on the part of Italy essential. He then enumerated all those parts of the littoral that would remain in Slav hands; though he knew that the establishment of a 'Yugoslav league' was far from a foregone conclusion, he nevertheless referred to its possibility in order to strengthen his case.[63] In the following weeks, the British Foreign Secretary had to insist that both St Petersburg and Rome should make concessions, impressing it on the Russians that the entry of Italy would mean the turning-point of the war, and attempting to show the Italians a united front on the part of the three Allies. In London, the supporters of the South Slavs were constantly reminding the Foreign Office of the sacrifice Serbia was making for the Allied cause, and of its natural rights; in Rome, Rodd had fallen under Sonnino's spell.

The argument between Rome and St Petersburg on the division of Dalmatia and the neutralization of the Adriatic coast, conducted through the good offices of Sir Edward Grey, went on until Easter 1915, when the Foreign Secretary could stand it no longer. He left London for Fallodon, his country house in the north of England, to recuperate from failing eyesight and insomnia; Sazonov may have seen other motives for his English colleague's illness. When Rodd wrote to London on 2 April, he addressed the letter to Asquith.[64] He put it to the Premier that if Italy did not obtain what it wanted in the Adriatic, Britain would lose its co-operation as well, probably, as that of Rumania and the other Balkan states. The Ambassador then assured Asquith:

> At the present moment she is ours – on the terms you know. These once accepted, she cannot go back. Once she escapes us, one cannot tell what may happen. It has taken months of careful nursing, and the avoidance of irritants, and the prompting of various influential persons to bring things to this point. The decision depends in the main on three people: the King, the Prime Minister, and the Minister of Foreign Affairs. We have them all favourable now – if the decision can be warranted by Italy obtaining the guarantee of that absolute security in the Adriatic which is the real inducement.

On the other side, there was Bülow hovering around with the offer of the Trentino and of something more on the Isonzo, and

> in a nation not very sure of itself and scared to death by the fear of Germany, there are an immense number of people who would prefer their security with a tolerable prospect of some compensation for neutrality to the enormous risk of war.

Although Rodd wrote that he himself had sympathy for the Dalmatians he thought that 'perhaps one attaches too much importance to the views put forward and appeals made by the small number of cultivated men, who are the protagonists of the Dalmatian unity movement'. The Cursolan islands – Cursola (Korčula), Lesina (Hvar) and the Sabbioncello peninsula (Pelješac) – were the hard core of the controversy between the Russians and the Italians: in Sonnino's view, the islands gave their owner the mastery of the Adriatic, and he would not move unless Italy were promised them. Rodd argued that no real British or French interest was involved, and 'only a sentimental one for Russia, unless she is farsighted enough to look at the future potentiality of these islands as a base'. Rodd asked Asquith to disregard the views of the Dalmatians and of Russia for the sake of British interests:

> I look on it, if not as a matter of life and death, at any rate as a matter of capital importance to secure the co-operation of Italy. . . . If we close the ring round Germany and Austria, the end is in sight.

The Cursolan islands impasse was finally resolved by Delcassé's formula – Sabbioncello to Serbia, the islands to the Italians – which was accepted by both Rome and St Petersburg. But the rich fund of difficulties was not yet exhausted. Still to be settled were the problems of the neutralization of the coast, as well as the extent of the Albanian hinterland. And when the tangle of the Adriatic coastline was at last sorted out, Sonnino produced his time-fuse. Italy was not to enter the war until the lapse of one month after the signature of the treaty. Salandra and his Foreign Minister found it difficult, as so often before, to commit themselves fully: there always existed the possibility that they might have made a mistake in their calculations, a mistake that would suddenly and glaringly become apparent. There were so many factors to be taken into consideration. On the western front, the second battle of Ypres began on 22 April, and it was now running its course in the midst of confusion, mud and poisonous gases; in the east the Russians had tried, for many weeks in vain, to storm the Carpathian ramparts. But a glance toward the south-east gave the Italians a much better lead. An Anglo-French campaign was then in progress in the region of the Dardanelles; on 25 April, British and French troops landed on both shores of the Straits. On the following day, the treaty with Italy was signed in London. Italy was to receive the Trentino, south Tirol, Trieste with Venezia Giulia, a third of Dalmatia and a number of Dalmatian islands (specific reference was made to several rocks in the Adriatic), a virtual mandate over Albania as well as outright possession of Valona and the Bay of Saseno, the Dodecanese islands, the promise of a substantial area in Asia Minor, the whole of Libya and some compensation in East Africa. The signatory Powers agreed not to conclude a separate peace and Italy was granted a loan of £50m.[65]

The Italian Ambassador to London signed the treaty in a hurry because his government feared that after a successful campaign in the Dardanelles the value of his country as an ally would diminish; the British and French governments signed it because they were convinced of the military importance of Italy's co-operation; the reluctance of the Russians was overcome by the promise of Constantinople. Sazonov accepted defeat on all the major Adriatic issues because of the hope that the eastern question would be solved in his country's favour, and for that hope he was willing to abandon the support of Serbia's ambitions for which Russia had entered the war in the first place, and to hand over some 600,000 Slavs to Italian rule. In addition, the secret Pact of London provided for 230,000 Germans, as well as many Albanians, Turks and Africans, to be ruled by Rome.[66] It seemed a small price to pay for Italy's entry into the war, for no one had yet realized how much of a liability an ally could be.

Berlin, on the other hand, could not give the Italians what they desired most of all: the domination of the Adriatic. Under an agreement with the Central Powers the Italians would at best have been able to carry out the final details of their national unification. Neither Bülow nor Erzberger, of course, knew how much the Italians had been promised; they believed that their offer of 12 May 1915 could still tip the balance in their favour. And the Germans, and perhaps Giolitti as well, underestimated Salandra. As soon as he heard of the German and Austrian bait, he made a dramatic gesture. On 13 May, he offered the King the resignation of his cabinet. Rome came to the verge of a civil war. The two parties, the interventionists and the neutralists, were proposing reasonable alternative policies: the conflict between them, however, had to be settled in a violent way. The Pact of London was secret and it could not be discussed in parliament; the neutralists dominated the chamber of deputies, whereas the interventionists were stronger in the government. Salandra and Sonnino therefore had to prove that the parliament was not really representative of the public mood: the issue was settled in the streets.

In those days, the parliament was invaded by angry mobs and the neutralist deputies were assaulted. The most vicious attacks were reserved for Giolitti: Saturday, 15 May, witnessed the most violent scenes outside his house in Rome. Neither the police nor the troops took any action against the demonstrators; the lives and property of the prominent neutralists went unprotected. Behind the violence of the mob – some of it was engineered, on a rent-a-mob basis, by Italian and foreign interventionist interests – there was much public speaking, charged with emotion.

Gabriele D'Annunzio, in Salandra's view 'the greatest living poet and writer that Italy could boast',[67] gave the interventionist cause valuable help.

After his return from France on 13 May, D'Annunzio declared at once that he had detected in Rome 'a certain smell of treason'. It came of course from Giolitti. In a number of dramatic speeches, the poet castigated Giolitti for having conducted an ignoble onslaught on the government, an onslaught that had been inspired by the foreigner. In the course of his campaign, D'Annunzio set a new standard in patriotic oratory:[68]

No, we are not, and we will not be, a museum, an inn, a village summer resort, a sky painted with Prussian blue for international honeymoon couples, a delightful market for buying and selling, fraud and barter.

D'Annunzio knew what he was talking about. He had had to flee from Italy in order to avoid his creditors, and he was now financially dependent on the editor of the pro-Allied and anti-German *Corriere della Sera*, and on Luigi Albertini, the wealthy politician engaged on the interventionist side who, many years later, compensated for his involvement in the events of 1915 by writing a most valuable, and detached, study of the origins of the First World War.

Like D'Annunzio, Benito Mussolini was also serving his apprenticeship as rabble-rouser; it was the first time their paths crossed. Though Mussolini was a fine patriotic speaker, and though he had made his mark as a journalist on the side of intervention, the fascist assertion that he brought Italy into the war single-handed was exaggerated. The years 1914 and 1915 were more important for Mussolini's personal development than for the impact he made on the history of his country. When the war broke out in August 1914, Mussolini was editing the socialist daily, the *Avanti*, and, like all his comrades, was a strict supporter of Italy's neutrality. The first number of his *Popolo d'Italia*, a daily committed to intervention, appeared on 15 November 1914. Mussolini quickly changed sides. He knew that Germany had failed to establish a decisive military preponderance on the western front: at the same time, he resented the limitations imposed on him by Socialist doctrine and discipline. He believed that the central weakness of pre-war European Socialism was that it contained too much class and too little national appeal. He wanted to have an independent newspaper in which to express his new views, and the fact that it was subsidized from Paris bothered him not at all.* In addition, Mussolini, together with Filippo Corridoni's Syndicalists, formed the Fasci di Azione Rivoluzionaria, an organization which specialized in demonstrations for war.

The popular enthusiasm for war was not as 'spontaneous' as Sir Rennell Rodd, for one, thought it to be: it was in fact the result of a blending of government action, press policy and foreign influence. After the disastrous harvest of the previous year and industrial dislocation on a large scale, the economic crisis was aggravated by natural catastrophes; the Tiber floods in the middle of February 1915, followed soon after the Abruzzi earthquake. By the end of the winter there existed in Italy a reservoir of popular discontent which could be tapped for political purposes. Early in March, the government's attitude to interventionist demonstrations became visibly more permissive than it had been in the previous year; the first clashes in the streets took place. They indicated that the neutralists still had the upper hand, and Salandra's government placed a temporary ban on the right of assembly. At the same time the voices of the large interventionist newspapers – the *Corriere della Sera*, *Secolo* and *Idea Nazionale* – began to grow shrill, with Mussolini's *Popolo d'Italia* usually outdoing them all. And shortly before Salandra prorogued the parliament for an unusually long Easter recess, it had voted for a bill for the 'military and economic defence of the State' and, with it, for a considerable limitation of its own powers.

The neutralists gradually lost ground among the mass of the Italian public. Although they used similar methods, they lacked on their side the force of government action. The Russian Ambassador to Rome was astonished by the ways in which Salandra played havoc with Italian politics and the Constitution.[69] Nor did their cause have the emotional appeal of war, of the *Risorgimento*, of Great Power aspirations. The neutralists had only one powerful ally on their side: the Catholic Church. On 12 May 1915, Sir Rennell Rodd complained:[70]

* The evidence of his dependence on French financial support for the *Popolo d'Italia* is discussed in Sir Ivone Kirkpatrick's *Mussolini: Study of a Demagogue*, London 1964, pp. 64 f.

...I cannot fight with priests. It is getting on one's nerves, this unassailable enemy. With the press we can manage, as all the decent papers almost are with us....

Among the newspapers, the *Corriere della Sera* gave the war party the greatest help. In a government-inspired article on 14 May it hinted at the existence of the Pact of London and it charged the Germans and the Austrians with interfering, by making their offer to the opposition and not to the government, with the internal affairs of the country. On the morning of that day, before he read the article, Erzberger was certain of victory; he may have had some doubts after seeing the newspaper. Against the background of rioting in the streets, a vicious press war and Salandra's resignation, Giolitti had to move with great caution. He knew that a completely new government with a programme that centred on an agreement with Austria could not become a popular proposition. He may therefore have wished first to join Salandra's cabinet, and to have Sonnino and Martini, the two men most committed to intervention, dismissed, before getting what he could from Austria and then becoming Premier himself. Salandra would at first provide continuity of government, and the appearance of a sharp break in policy would be avoided. He had, however, no desire to accept any part of such a deal, even if it gave him the support of the majority in parliament. In any case, the decision was not in the hands of the deputies. Faced with intimidation by the mob, with press attacks that branded him as a traitor, Giolitti took no action beyond advising against war. He was, after all, a politician of much the same kind as Salandra; in Salandra's place he would have behaved in the same way. No question of principle was involved for Giolitti, and he was acutely aware of the weakness of his position.

The King, whose sympathy lay with the war party and who feared the prospect of a republican revolution, refused, on 16 May, to accept Salandra's resignation. On 17 May, the Premier and Sonnino were back in office. On the same day, Giolitti left Rome for his house in Piedmont, and Erzberger was asked to leave the country. Before he got on the train that took him to safety, Erzberger signed a promissory note for 50m. marks, payable if Italian neutrality was maintained until the end of the war.[71]

2 Constantinople

On 15 August 1914, the Foreign Office transmitted a message to Constantinople from the First Lord of the Admiralty. The message from Churchill was for Enver Pasha, and it read:[1]

I hope you are not going to make a mistake which will undo all the services you have rendered Turkey and cast away the success of the second Balkan war. By a strict and honest neutrality these can be kept secure. But siding with Germany openly or secretly now must mean the greatest disaster to you, your comrades and your country. The overwhelming superiority at sea possessed by the navies of England, France, Russia and Japan over those of Austria and Germany renders it easy for the four allies to transport troops in almost unlimited numbers from any quarter of the globe and if they were forced into a quarrel by Turkey their blow could be delivered at the heart. On the other hand I know that Sir Edward Grey, who has already been approached as to possible terms of peace if Germany and Austria are beaten, has stated that if Turkey remains loyal to her neutrality, a solemn agreement to respect the integrity of the Turkish Empire must be a condition of any terms of peace that affect the near East. The personal regard I have for you, Talaat, and Djavid and the admiration with which I have followed your career from our first meeting at Würzburg alone leads me to speak these words of friendship before it is too late.

It did not much matter that the message was not friendly enough: it was dispatched too late, and to the wrong person. The Germans had concluded a secret treaty with Turkey on 2 August 1914, and on the Turkish side, Enver had been its prime mover.

Over the years the prestige of the Ottoman Empire had sunk so low that no Great Power, although their representatives went on competing for influence in Constantinople, would commit itself to an alliance with the Turkish government. Churchill himself had had occasion to turn the Turks down. In October 1911 Javid Bey, a financier and a leading member of the Committee of Union and Progress, wrote to Churchill asking for an alliance with Britain;

after consulting Sir Edward Grey, Churchill replied that he could do nothing to help in bringing about an alliance.[2] This was two years after Churchill's brief visit to Constantinople, in the summer of 1909, where he had met Javid and other members of the Committee, and a year after Churchill's first meeting with Enver at the German army manœuvres near Würzburg.

But there was a more recent incident which concerned Churchill and the Turks, and had done nothing to endear the First Lord to his friends in Constantinople. At the time of the summer crisis in 1914 the construction of two capital ships was nearing completion at the Armstrong Whitworth yard on the Tyne. The order was worth £7,500,000, and the Turks had collected the money by a popular subscription to which Constantinople stevedores, Anatolian peasants, women who had sold their hair, had all contributed. In Newcastle some 500 Turkish sailors were waiting to go on board the two new battleships when, on 28 July, Churchill gave an order to detain the ships. The Admiralty order set off the well-known and dramatic chain reaction: the chase of the German ships *Goeben* and *Breslau* by the British in the Mediterranean; their escape and arrival in Constantinople late in the afternoon on 10 August; their nominal sale to the Turkish government as a replacement for the ships the British had confiscated, and the effect of these events on the mood of the Turks.

The position of the ships in Constantinople was ambiguous. Although Turkish-owned, they remained under German command, and there was the farce of the Germans dressing up in parts of Turkish naval uniforms. It resulted one day in the comic incident when the German band on one of the ships, anchored near the Russian Embassy building, treated the Russians to a concert; when they had finished they replaced their own caps with Turkish fezes, and the ship steamed off.

The arrival of the *Goeben* and the *Breslau* greatly strengthened the Germans' position in Constantinople; Rear-Admiral Limpus, the head of the British naval mission, was stopped when he attempted to go on board the *Goeben*. Limpus was somewhat out of place in the Turkish capital after the arrival of the German men-of-war; once again, the First Lord vigorously set out to correct the situation. Shortly after he had written to Enver, Churchill ordered Limpus, early in September, to leave Constantinople and take over the command of the squadron watching the

Dardanelles. Sir Louis Mallet, the British Ambassador to Constantinople, sharply opposed the transfer; on 11 September he telegraphed the Foreign Office that he regarded it

as a grave mistake from a political point of view. It will be looked upon by all Turks as a piece of sharp practice on our part to transfer an officer from the nominal command of the Turkish Fleet for whose training, direction, and preparation for war he has been responsible, to the command of our own fleet, which is universally believed to be seeking an excuse for forcing the Straits. The appointment will re-arouse the bitter indignation caused by H.M. Government's detention of the ships, which is just beginning to die down. . . . [3]

The Ambassador's arguments caused the government to override Churchill's decision on the new appointment for Limpus; there could, however, be no doubt that the opening moves in the contest for Turkey had gone against the Allies, and against Britain in particular. By taking a sea-power's view of the situation, the British government did what it had been accustomed to doing: it argued from the position of naval strength. In the summer of 1914, however, the argument fell flat in Turkey. From the Turks' point of view, Britain failed, in two important regards, to support her claim to naval supremacy. Would the delivery, the Turks may well have asked, of two capital ships according to the contract really have made that much difference to Britain's position as the leading sea-power? And then there was the failure of the British and the French Mediterranean fleets to stop the *Goeben* and the *Breslau*: the concrete proofs of that failure loomed high over the other ships in the Constantinople docks.

Until his departure from Constantinople in November 1914, Sir Louis Mallet's dispatches grew more and more disconsolate; yet he held on, doing all he could to stop the Turks from lunging into the war. He knew that the international situation – all the Great Powers busy, at each other's throats – held out a great promise for the Turks; he knew that they had not come into the war only because of their agonizing uncertainty as to its future winner. Like his colleagues, Sir Louis resented the way in which the Turkish cabinet issued a notification to all Great Powers that it would abrogate the capitulations on 1 October 1914. The capitulations treaties, most of them signed in the seventeenth century, gave extraterritorial rights to foreign subjects: they paid no local taxes, they were not subject to Turkish law, they could be arrested or deported only on the order of their own Ambassador. These and other privileges had originally been granted by powerful rulers to small communities of foreign merchants; then, two centuries later, they were resented by weak governments, who were irritated by the capitulations and saw them as infringements of their power. The chance for the Turks to get rid of the capitulations came after the outbreak of the war: in the autumn of 1914 the Great Powers gave way on the capitulations, mildly protesting at the same time. Sir Louis Mallet later wrote that the Great Powers could have done nothing to prevent the abolition of the capitulations:[4]

From the moment that the Powers were at war, it was the opportunity of the Young Turk's life and he means to make the most of it. Djavid, Talaat and others say that the internal reforms are the safety valve to prevent war, and that they can point to this as the reason for and the wonderful achievement of mobilisation.

Indeed, on a number of occasions Talaat had told the British Ambassador that he hoped the European war would go on for at least twenty years, during which time the Turks would show Europe what their country could do if left to herself. It looked as if the Turks might stay out of the war altogether.

The important thing for Mallet was that the Germans and their friends in Constantinople had not, by the middle of October, achieved their main object: the entry of Turkey into the war. He had worked with his French and Russian colleagues for this end, and he regarded their achievement with satisfaction. Indeed, the Ambassador was convinced that many, quite possibly most, Turkish politicians viewed the prospect of a war on Britain and Russia with apprehension. The same men resented the growing dependence of their country on Germany, and Sir Louis Mallet was available on the spot, to explain to them how their position could become more uncomfortable. Sir Louis had, as he himself put it, 'incredible conversations' with the Grand Vizier, that 'absolute oriental and true grandson of Mahomed Ali, fanatical, intriguing and barbarous at heart'. The Ambassador made much of Turkey's position of servitude to Germany, called the Grand Vizier 'the slave of the German Ambassador' and generally annoyed him, in order to make him, in his fury, more communicative and more honest. He once screamed at Sir Louis that all soldiers, and Turkish soldiers in particular, were brutes, and that he was quite worn out fighting them.

Bearing in mind the economic and military situation of Turkey, and the vacillating attitudes of the politicians, the British Ambassador did not lose hope till the last moment. On 16 October 1914, he wrote to London that, given patience and some military success to show, 'it is not I but Wangenheim [the German Ambassador] who will have to leave first'.[5] Sir Louis Mallet knew nothing about the *coup* the Germans had pulled off in Constantinople as early as 2 August 1914. On that day, the Turks signed a secret treaty with Germany: a lot of preparatory work for it had been done by Baron Wangenheim.

A big German from a numerous noble family in Thuringia, Konrad Freiherr von Wangenheim had a very good command of English and French, a pleasant, easy-going nature behind an imposing appearance, and an unexceptional diplomatic career behind him, with perhaps more Balkan and Near East postings in it than usual. He has often been described as a 'typical *Junker*' or a sinister and compulsive plotter: he was not a *Junker*, and he plotted no more and no less than his colleagues in Constantinople. He was only more successful. There were many elements in the Turkish situation that played into his hands. Germany was the only Great Power in Europe that had never claimed or received any part of the Ottoman Empire: the animosity, on the other hand, between Russia and Turkey was a long-established fact of the international scene. In an argument the Turks were likely to take the opposite side to Russia. They disliked the Russians in the same way that the Italians resented the Austrians: a sentiment that affected the broad masses of the population and was backed up by long historical memories. The Russians had taken the Crimea and a part of the Caucasus from the Turks; the British had Egypt and Cyprus; the French, Algeria and Tunisia. On the other side, the Austrians had annexed Bosnia-Herzegovina: the Germans alone had never taken advantage of the weakness of the Ottoman Empire. In Constantinople, as compared with Rome, the roles of the contenders for Turkey's favours were reversed. In Italy it was the Allies who were trying to get the Italians to join the war, while the Central Powers wanted to keep them neutral; in Constantinople, on the other hand, Germany and Austria were playing for the higher stakes.

The recent internal developments in Turkey also worked in Germany's favour. In the revolution of 1908, the Young Turks – the Committee of Union and Progress – became the dominant force in Turkish politics. They wanted to take their country into the modern age; their endeavour to carry out reforms, however, was frequently jeopardized by the events that accompanied the decline of the Ottoman Empire: the peripheral wars, the contraction of Turkish territory, the impoverishment of the state. Among the revolutionaries of 1908, a young man called Enver Pasha was prominent. A soldier by profession – he had passed out of the staff college in Constantinople in 1905 – Enver left for Berlin as the Military Attaché shortly after the Young Turks came to power. He became an admirer of Prussian military efficiency; he believed that, of all the great European Powers, Germany would give Turkey the most disinterested help.

While in Berlin, Enver took time off on a variety of military assignments. In 1911, he fought the Italians in Libya: in 1912, he skirmished with the Bulgarians outside Constantinople. When, toward the end of the first Balkan War in the spring of 1913, the Turkish armies were defeated and the government was negotiating an armistice, Enver returned to Constantinople to take part in another *coup*. In its course the Minister of War was murdered; a new and more courageous cabinet emerged, in which Enver succeeded the murdered man. And then luck turned in the Turks' favour. Bulgaria's allies in the first Balkan War rounded on it, seeking to divide between themselves the territories the Bulgarians had won from the Turks; the Turks, for their own part, made a swift recovery and, under Enver's leadership, recaptured Adrianople.

Enver was then thirty-five years old and much admired in Constantinople. He was now Minister of War as well as Chief of Staff. Talaat Bey, the gargantuan former telegraph operator, who supervised the Young Turk party machinery, was the Minister of the Interior. Jemal Bey, an ambitious character, devoid of all charm, whose rather unpleasant appearance concealed an even more unpleasant disposition, became Military Governor and then Minister of Marine. Of the triumvirate, only Jemal could not stand the Germans, and he occasionally embarrassed his colleagues by swearing at German visitors in their presence, though only in Turkish. He was sent away soon after the outbreak of war, to pursue his ambition in the deserts of Syria and Sinai, leading the

Turkish expedition against Egypt. Talaat was, like the Grand Vizier, more stolid and neutral; a man of the people, who remained unaffected by his success.

In this triumvirate the influence of Enver was dominant. He had military experience, as well as a knowledge of the foreign scene. It did not seem to matter that his travels had been rather limited. He knew Berlin and the German army well: he was right in believing that of all the Europeans, the Prussians could run the best army. After his return to Constantinople and his appointment to the Ministry of War, Enver established close relations with Wangenheim, the German Ambassador, with whom he arranged the dispatch of a German military mission to Turkey. It arrived in Constantinople in December 1913, led by General Liman von Sanders. Such missions had visited the country before; Rear-Admiral Limpus was in Constantinople at the time, doing his best to get the Turkish navy ship-shape.

It soon became apparent that General Liman's was no ordinary mission. Liman was to command the First Turkish Army, which was stationed in, and in control of, the capital; his colleague General Bronsart was to become Chief-of-Staff. A protest by the British, French and Russian Ambassadors followed the announcement, and the Turks made Liman an Inspector General of the armed forces instead.

He was a quiet, efficient and non-political soldier who would have been content to act as a glorified drill-sergeant for the Turks. But Liman was meant to serve two masters, a position in which he felt uncomfortable and which caused some diplomatic complications. On one occasion, at the American Ambassador's dinner in February 1914, Liman sat glumly next to the Ambassador's daughter, at the lower end of the table. The Ambassador, Henry Morgenthau, was as new as Liman to his post and he had therefore asked the doyen of the diplomatic corps, Count Pallavicini, the Austrian Ambassador, to mark the list of guests according to precedence. Pallavicini put Liman at No. 13, below those holding the rank of Ambassador. At the end of the dinner, an agitated German diplomat told the Ambassador that he had made a horrible mistake, by putting the Kaiser's representative so far down the table.[6] The purpose of Liman's mission was two-fold: he was to reorganize the Turkish army and get it, as far as possible, under German control.

In the summer crisis of 1914 Enver, the man of action, sporting a Kaiser moustache and not hiding his German sympathies, was in a strong position to pursue his plans for Turkey. But trying to achieve a degree of influence over Turkey, and tying the country to Germany by an alliance, were two quite different things. The more acute the crisis grew, the more cautious did Wangenheim become. In the course of July, he raised various objections to binding Turkey to the Triple Alliance, and then, on 23 July, the Ambassador reported that

the Grand Vizier repeated the desire expressed to me by Enver Pasha yesterday that formal entry into the Triplice might be made possible for Turkey. Margrave Pallavicini, who had in the meantime discussed the question with me, replied that an alliance with Turkey would at the moment impose too great a burden on the Triplice. The Triplice could not defend Turkey against everybody.

When Wangenheim had raised his own objections to the alliance the day before, the Kaiser had disapproved. He had written on the margin of the dispatch:

Now it is a question of getting hold of every musket in the Balkans that is prepared to go off *for* Austria against the Slavs, thus a Turko–Bulgarian alliance leaning on Austria is most certainly to be agreed to!

But now, when Wangenheim reported on the attitude of his Austrian colleague, Wilhelm II was furious: 'Rubbish! Wangenheim must definitely reply welcoming Turkey's accession to the Triplice.'[7]

Jagow, the State Secretary in the Foreign Ministry, at once instructed Wangenheim to act according to the Emperor's wishes. The negotiations in Constantinople were opened on 27 July: at 9.30 p.m. on the following day, nine and a half hours after the Austrian declaration of war on Serbia, Wangenheim was informed, by Berlin, of the terms on which the German government was prepared to conclude the alliance. In the first place, Turkey and Germany would maintain strict neutrality in the hostilities, only just opened, between Vienna and Belgrade; if Russia, however, intervened in the war, thus occasioning intervention by Germany, Turkey would have to follow suit: the German military mission would exercise supreme command over the Turkish armed forces. The treaty, it was suggested, was to be valid for the

period of the conflict that might have arisen out of the war between Austria and Serbia.[8] The treaty was signed on those lines,
in Constantinople, on 2 August. On the following day, Turkey
mobilized, and declared itself neutral.

The Allies knew nothing about the treaty, and the Germans
were disappointed, though not really surprised, by its aftermath.
The changing fortunes of war gave the Turks no clue: they
wanted to know whether they had made the right decision,
whether they were on the winning side. There were times when
everything seemed to be going against the Central Powers: in
addition, the Turkish mobilization was a slow process, and it
occurred to them that they could now try to get concessions
without committing their armed forces. But further inducements
for the Turks were on the way. While the *Goeben* and the *Breslau*
were approaching the Greek coast on their journey to Constantinople, the Foreign Ministry in Vienna received, on 7 August, an
urgent telephone message from Berlin. A military train, it said,
was approaching the Austrian frontier, carrying four gentlemen
in charge of 1½m. marks' worth of gold, destined for Constantinople. They had a pass from the Austro-Hungarian Embassy to
Berlin, on which, however, 'the word gold does not appear'; they
were to send it on from Vienna to the Turkish capital, by the
safest and fastest route.[9] It took them from Budapest across the
Rumanian frontier to Bucharest, and then through the two frontier
towns south of the capital, Giurgiu on the Rumanian side and
Ruse (Ruschuk) in Bulgaria, and on to Constantinople. It was the
first of many similar transports of gold, as well as weapons: by
the beginning of October, the Turks had received 15m. marks'
worth (the exchange rate at the time was 20 marks to the £)
of arms and ammunition as well as a loan of 100m. francs in
gold.[10]

Pressure on Turkey to enter the war was intermittent. Early in
September, Wangenheim wrote to Enver that his government
thought the moment suitable for Turkey to fulfil its duties as an
ally.[11] But there were still some outstanding matters to be settled.
German naval officers in Constantinople were convinced that,
sooner or later, the Allies would attempt to force the Dardanelles.
Their security remained to be taken care of: the mines and other
equipment had been delayed on their way to Constantinople. In
addition, Berlin and Vienna had not yet settled what exactly they

expected of Turkey in the war. There existed several attractive possibilities: Turkey's strategic position was of crucial importance. An action against Odessa – either a pure naval operation, with shelling of the harbour installations, or a combined operation with military landings – was being considered; or a campaign against England in Egypt, with the Suez Canal as its objective; an action in the Caucasus or in the Balkans also came up for discussion.

On the whole, the two German Admirals in Constantinople, Souchon and Usedom, were pessimistic about the Odessa action. They argued that it could not be launched before the Straits were secure from forcing, that is at the end of September at the earliest. Until the Turkish navy established its supremacy in the Black Sea, a combined sea–land operation was out of the question. Apart from that, the harbour was mined, and although their Odessa army corps was currently employed in Galicia, the Russians had enough troops at their disposal to resist successfully an attempt at landing. The Germans seemed to favour the Egyptian campaign most of all, and then the expedition to the Caucasus which, they believed, would receive some support from the local population. Turkish action in Europe, in the Balkans – Vienna inclined more and more to favour that operation, especially as the Austrian campaign against Serbia ran into stiff resistance – was difficult to plan so long as the position of Bulgaria and Rumania in the war was not clarified.

As on so many other occasions, differences between Berlin and Vienna soon arose on the military uses that were to be made of the Turkish alliance. On 14 September 1914, the German Ambassador to Vienna told Berchtold that the planned action against Egypt by the Turkish Eighth Army Corps had been scrapped because of Austria's protest.[12] When Wangenheim reported on it to Berlin, his government was quick to put the blame on the Austrians. It did not consider the possibility that the Turks themselves wanted an excuse for their own inaction. At the same time, Pallavicini disapproved of the plan for a campaign in Egypt because he feared that it would provoke the Italians. The German Foreign Ministry thought differently: it believed that such an action would tie the Italians down in Libya, and put them off considering military enterprises in Europe. Anyway, Pallavicini was sharply instructed to mind his own business and to let the

Turks know that an action in Egypt, and especially the blocking of the Suez Canal, were highly desirable undertakings.

By the end of September, the concerted pressure on the Turks by the German and the Austrian Ambassadors had brought no results. The question of the capitulations had not yet been settled, as the Turks wanted to secure the agreement by Russia, France and Britain to their abolition; the Straits had not yet been secured against forcing; no decisive event had taken place on the battle-fields. The Germans therefore fell back on direct action: their two ships and two Turkish torpedo boats under German command steamed out into the Black Sea, on a Sunday expedition. They encountered no Russian men-of-war, but Admiral Usedom thought that he might be luckier next time, and that the exercise should therefore be repeated as often as necessary, drawing in more and more Turkish ships, with courtesy calls being paid at Rumanian and Bulgarian ports. It mattered little that the Turks opposed such expeditions.

Explorations in the Black Sea were not, however, without their dangers. The situation in Constantinople was far from settled, and the position of the government far from secure; Wangenheim could not press the Turkish government as hard as he may have wanted to. He threatened at one point to put the *Goeben* and *Breslau* to sea under the German flag; Pallavicini, however, reported:[13]

The fiction still prevails that the two ships had been bought by Turkey, and they made a very good impression on public opinion here. If it became now apparent that it was only an ostensible sale the people would feel cheated by the government. . . .

The Turkish government had to proceed carefully: public demonstrations, a cabinet crisis, were the last things Enver and Talaat, as well as the Germans and the Austrians, needed at that point. Wangenheim and Pallavicini knew, just as well as their adversaries did, how volatile the political scene in Constantinople could be. There were other reasons for restraint on the part of the German Ambassador. He was aware that Enver and his friends, provided they remained in power, had an interest in German victory and in the maximum weakening of Russia; that they served the cause of the Central Powers by holding the smaller Balkan states in check, at any rate for the time being.

As late as 22 October 1914, the Grand Vizier, the Austrian Ambassador reported, was against an immediate Turkish action.[14] Earlier in the month, the Turks had been making frequent references to a loan of £5m. which, they gave the Germans to understand, would speed up their decision: they were given the loan, and again nothing happened. It was, however, in the first days of October that the Turks began to realize, just as much as their future allies, that the maintenance of armed neutrality was a very expensive undertaking. The deliveries of German arms had in fact proved, from the Turkish point of view, an expensive gift. They had to be maintained, and supplemented, and manned: the Turks found that they could not afford to receive any more expensive presents. The Germans, for their own part, were in a position to make future benefactions conditional on Turkey's entry into the war: the same ruling would apply to official loans as well as to bribes for Turkish politicians.

The Turks were unable to resist for long the combined pressures upon them. On 27 October 1914 the Foreign Ministry in Vienna informed Count Tarnowski in Bulgaria that, despite the existence of the 'hard' and the 'soft' parties in Constantinople, the Central Powers would soon succeed in making the Turkish government act, and that, in any case, the fleet will now put to sea and attack any Russian ships it may encounter.[15]

In fact, early in the morning on that day, 27 October, the *Goeben*, the *Breslau* and five Turkish ships had entered the Black Sea, under the command of Admiral Souchon. The fleet divided as soon as it left the Bosporus, and individual ships were ordered to attack towns on the Russian coast: Odessa and Novorossisk were the main targets. The official communiqués issued in Constantinople about the Black Sea action were calculated to mislead: they made considerable play with a Russian minelayer, allegedly encountered and sunk near the Bosporus. It was in fact destroyed off Sevastopol. The text of the communiqué – that an unexpected encounter provoked by Russian ships had taken place – was in sharp contrast to the facts. The action had been plotted by Enver and Souchon – the Grand Vizier was furious when he got to know about it – and based on a detailed plan worked out in advance by the Germans. The order for the action was signed by Enver and Jemal, and Wangenheim carefully put away his copy of the document; he also handed over the sum of £300,000 for bribes, ostensibly to be distributed among Turkish naval officers.[16] Taking that and other expenditure into consideration, the Central Powers gained an ally at a bargain price.

This was not immediately apparent, even to the German and Austrian Ambassadors to Constantinople. They knew that the action of the fleet in the Black Sea, if it were to be regarded as a success and to make an impression in Bucharest and Sofia, would have to result in the destruction of the Russian fleet; that the landing in Odessa, or indeed anywhere on the Russian coast, would be impossible without the co-operation of Rumania. The Austrians favoured the idea of a combined Turkish-Bulgarian action against Serbia, but the politicians in Sofia were apparently content with their position as spectators. It was impossible to develop the campaign in the Caucasus before the onset of winter; there existed the danger that the Turks would run into superior enemy forces and that the Russians, in their turn, would invade Armenia. An action in Egypt was also threatened. Some 45,000 British troops were reported to be stationed there, and they would receive backing from warships in the Suez Canal; the Turks had the Damascus corps, an inferior force, at their disposal for an action in Egypt. Finally, there was, at any rate for the Austrians, a more generally unpleasant feature of Turkey's participation in the war. It had been known, before Turkey's entry into the war, that Enver and his friends wanted to strengthen their country's fighting potential by the proclamation of a Holy War. It was addressed to all Moslems, apart from the subjects of the German and the Austro-Hungarian Empires: when the proclamation was made in the middle of November 1914, the believer who fought in the war was promised salvation from the horrors of the Day of Judgement, provided that he carried

in one hand a sword, in the other a gun, in his pocket balls of fire and death-dealing missiles, and in his heart the light of the faith, and that we should lift up our voices, saying – India for the Indian Moslems, Java for the Javanese Moslems, Algeria for the Algerian Moslems, Morocco for the Moroccan Moslems, Tunis for the Tunisian Moslems, Egypt for the Egyptian Moslems, Iran for the Iranian Moslems, Turan for the Turanian Moslems, Bokhara for the Bokharan Moslems, Caucasus for the Caucasian Moslems, and the Ottoman Empire for the Ottoman Turks and Arabs.[17]

The Austrian Ambassador to Constantinople disapproved of the idea of the Holy War and tried hard to make the Turks abandon it or at least postpone its declaration. He thought that it would have an adverse effect in Rome because it would spill over into the Italian colonies. But Pallavicini was more disturbed when Tochev, the Bulgarian Minister, told him in the middle of November 1914 that in his country the proclamation had made the worst possible impression and enabled Russia to make a bid for a united front against Turkey. Though the announcement of the Holy War was greeted with a show of enthusiasm in the capital itself, its effects on Moslems outside Turkey were negligible. If the fortunes of war were to go against Turkey, the Austrian Ambassador thought, the Christians in the Ottoman Empire would be in a very dangerous situation: in any case, the blame for the incitement of religious fanaticism in the Islam world would fall ultimately on Germany, as well as Austria.[18]

Such considerations cancelled out, for Pallavicini, some of the value of Turkey's participation in the war. He was convinced that the Germans had been wrong to have put the Turks under so much pressure and that it would have been preferable to have them on the side of the Central Powers in a position of benevolent neutrality, holding the Balkan states in check. For Pallavicini, the German leaders moved too fast.

In peacetime the relations between the German and Austrian Ambassadors to Constantinople had been exemplary. At the time of Turkey's entry into the war Pallavicini felt irritated by his colleague. One of the main reasons why Germany had entered into negotiations with the Turks in July 1914 was their desire to secure the position of Austria in the Balkans. In the subsequent weeks, that motive was gradually pushed into the background. The various German military, naval and Middle Eastern experts had a number of ambitious plans for the Turks. Not one of them had any bearing on the position of Austria in the Balkans.

Nor did the Turks, once they committed themselves to participation in the war, remain content. All they had was a short-term, defensive treaty with Germany against Russia. They wanted something more, and they asked their allies for it immediately. A member of the cabinet, Halil Bey, left for a tour of Vienna and Berlin toward the end of October; in Constantinople, Talaat, Enver and Jemal put the same request to the two Ambassadors. The Turks wanted an alliance wider in scope, and for a longer time. The Central Powers were to guarantee their aid if (apart from Russia) England, France or a Balkan coalition attacked Turkey, and the guarantee was to run for ten years.[19] On this occasion, the Austrian Ambassador to Constantinople was taking a more active interest in the negotiations than he had before the conclusion of the treaty on 2 August 1914, and he was inclined to give the Turks what they were asking for. He argued that, since the end of the war would find Turkey in the Austro-German sphere of influence, it was in the interest of the Central Empires to protect and strengthen their ally. Wangenheim agreed, and there seemed to be no objections, in the respective Ministries, to the new and extended alliance with Turkey. Bethmann Hollweg, the German Chancellor, was alone in resisting the extension: his long-term thinking on diplomacy was then dominated by the desire to see Germany, after the war, free 'from the nightmare of coalitions', and he added, reasonably, that the victory of the Central Powers in the war would take care of Turkey's security; in any case he saw no reason why special conditions should be made for Turkey now, when it was taking part in the war.

The German Ambassador put his views to the Chancellor with force. He argued that the position of the war party in the Turkish capital would be strengthened by the new agreement (that point had originally been made by the Turks themselves, who maintained that the resignation of the pro-French Minister of Finance, Javid Bey, early in November, created a rallying point for the opposition forces), that no Turk thought a diplomatic agreement with a European Power absolutely binding, and that the whole thing would be a mere formality, costing Germany nothing.[20] After concerted pressure from his own as well as from the Austrian Foreign Ministry, Bethmann Hollweg gave way: the alliance with Turkey was to be extended until the year 1920, with an option running until 1926; he would not commit himself beyond the year when the alliance between Berlin and Vienna would lapse.

Despite the change in the German Chancellor's attitude, the treaty did not have a smooth passage. Early in the negotiations, Berchtold expressed his opinion that Italy should be informed of them; the Italians knew nothing of the first German-Turkish treaty, and the Germans could think of no reason why they should be told of the negotiations for the second. The more serious difficulty arose when the Turks presented the Germans and the Austrians with their own draft treaty. They asked for the broadest defensive alliance: Article I concerned Turkey's territorial integrity, and its defence against an attack by a Great Power or by a coalition of Balkan states. It was the second part of the clause, concerning the Balkan states, that had a specially disturbing effect on the Austrian Foreign Ministry. The Habsburg monarchy, holding sway as it did over territories bordering on three Balkan states, was more directly involved in the affairs of the peninsula than Germany; the Balkan wars had proved, if indeed proof was needed, the dangers of getting diplomatically involved in that part of Europe. Berchtold asked for the clause on attack by a Balkan coalition to be dropped; in Constantinople, relations between Pallavicini and Wangenheim cooled off again; even though the Germans demonstrated with impeccable diplomatic logic that the Austrian fears were unfounded (no *casus foederis* could arise between Turkey and Rumania as long as the latter remained bound to the Central Powers; a military convention would be drawn up, which would in fact eliminate Vienna's concern with *casus foederis*, should Bulgaria be involved in the coalition, so that Austria would have to come in only in the event of an attack on Turkey by Serbia and Montenegro). Nevertheless, the Austrians remained cautious, unwilling to make any specific commitments.

Early in January, the Germans could no longer wait for their ally: on 9 January 1915 Wangenheim was authorized to sign the alliance; Vienna delayed the declaration of its formal concurrence until 31 March. The two countries agreed to mutual aid in case one of them were attacked by either 'Russia, France, or England or a coalition composed of at least two Balkan states'; there was, in Article II, a special provision concerning England:

the engagement assumed by Germany will come into effect only in the event that Turkey finds itself engaged in a simultaneous conflict with England and a second European state.

A special military convention was to be agreed on immediately after the conclusion of peace: the treaty was to remain secret, and it was valid until 8 July 1920, the same date in fact as the Dual Alliance.[21] In spite of Vienna's temporary abstention, the treaty meant a diplomatic victory for the Turks. It was a broadly conceived alliance, and its details remained to be filled in: it bound Turkey firmly to the Dual Alliance, and put an end to that country's diplomatic isolation.

In the first months of the war both the belligerent sides scored a diplomatic victory in southern Europe. The Allies secured the adhesion of Italy, the Central Powers that of Turkey. Italy appeared, especially from London, the more desirable prize and the Allied diplomatic effort was concentrated on Rome. The situation in Constantinople was, however, more open than the politicians in London or Paris assumed. Churchill, the First Lord of the Admiralty, was especially interested in 'scandalous, crumbling, decrepit, penniless' Turkey. For the British government the Turkish question was one that could be dealt with largely in terms of sea-power. Its significance for the Balkans, for the conduct of the war in Russia, indeed, for the whole continental strategy of the Central Powers, emerged only later in the war.

The forcing of the Straits was an idea familiar to the British navy, and it cropped up again in government circles in London soon after Turkey's entry into the war. It finally took the form of a naval action which was launched on 19 February 1915, and which was not intended to be more than a limited commitment. On that day five British and three French men-of-war, most of them obsolete, opened up bombardment of the forts at the entrance of the Dardanelles. For a few days the action was hampered by bad weather; by 2 March, the outer forts had been reduced and the Straits had been cleared of mines for four miles. On the following days the inner forts were pounded, and the Straits apparently cleared up to the Narrows, at the entrance to the Sea of Marmara, at which point the action started running into severe difficulties. H.M.S. *Irresistible* and H.M.S. *Ocean* as well as the French *Bouvet* were sunk by mines. On 23 March the commanding Admiral informed London that he would suspend the operation, after which the original conception of the Dardanelles campaign as a purely naval strike was abandoned. It became an uneasy combined operation which was to break, in London, friendships, reputations and a government. When the weather at last cleared on 25 April, General Sir Ian Hamilton's forces stormed the tip and the waist of the Gallipoli peninsula; after many vicissitudes, none of which the men who had taken part in the expedition remembered with pleasure, the final evacuation of the peninsula was confirmed by the British government on 27 December 1915.

Throughout the year 1915 the cabinet in London was in a divided mind as to what exactly its expectations should be, what exactly was the strategic value of the Dardanelles expedition. That in itself was bound to contribute to the uncertain touch in the execution of the campaign: its failure had wider repercussions. Although the doctrine of the primacy of the western front was accepted in Paris as well as in London, the Dardanelles expedition was not as unimportant, for the western allies, as the mode of its execution suggested.

Early in January 1915, Grand Duke Nikolai Nikolaevich, the Commander-in-Chief of the Russian armies, had requested, through Lord Kitchener, a naval action against Turkey to relieve pressure in the Caucasus. On 19 January, Churchill replied to the Grand Duke that the Admiralty 'have decided that general interests of the Allied Cause require serious effort to be made to break down Turkish opposition'.[22] He then went on to describe the size of the force that Britain was going to use, and expressed the hope that the Russian government 'will co-operate powerfully in this operation at the proper moment by naval action at the mouth of the Bosphorus, and by having troops ready to seize any advantage that may be gained'. But this was not what the Grand Duke had meant. In his reply he stated that the appeal to the Allies had been made because he was determined not to weaken the forces operating against the Germans and the Austrians; the appeal was not accompanied by any suggestion as to the method of execution simply because Russia had no means of directly assisting an action against Turkey.[23] Russian dreadnoughts, Nikolai Nikolaevich let Churchill know, were not yet ready – the *Imperatritsa Maria* would be completed only in May; they had no modern submarines in the Black Sea, and only an insufficient number of destroyers. If all its ships were together, the Russian fleet could just about match the Turkish. Nor could Russia, the Grand Duke went on, assist its allies with troops. Two army corps at least would be necessary, but they could not be spared in the principal theatre of war.

The inter-Allied requests for military and naval assistance usually followed the same pattern – help was requested at point A when pressure became too strong at point B – and the inquiry by the Commander-in-Chief of the Russian armies was no exception. It was, however, unusual for one of the Allied Powers to ask its associates for military help in an area of its special interest (Sazonov greatly disapproved of the Grand Duke's request): Russia, Constantinople and the Straits was such an area. It was, first of all, by far the most important of Russia's trade routes; in the decade between 1903 and 1912, 37 per cent of its total exports passed through the Dardanelles. It was a cheap way, a factor especially important in view of the fact that Russia's exports largely consisted of corn and raw materials, items that cannot carry high freight charges. The commercial importance of the Straits was brought home to the Russians in 1912 and 1913, during their temporary closure, when Russian exporters incurred a loss of 30m. roubles a month. (The 1914 value of the rouble was 9·4 roubles to the £ sterling, i.e. the loss amounted to nearly £3m.) The fastest-growing industries in Russia, in the area between the Donbas coalmines and the Baku oilfields, were concentrated just to the north and north-east of the Black Sea, a development that gave freedom of passage into the Sea of Marmara and the Mediterranean a special significance in the last decade before the outbreak of the war. Russia's life-line was under foreign control, which, even in peacetime, had been sometimes unfriendly and always temperamental.

The strategic significance of the Straits was similar to their economic importance: the free passage of the Russian Imperial Navy could be obstructed just as much as the passage of the merchantmen; in addition, the government controlling the Narrows could imperil Russia's southern coast, as well as Russian supremacy in the Black Sea, by admitting enemy ships. The activities of the *Goeben* and the *Breslau* had recently confirmed precisely that point. The Russians knew that even if they controlled the Straits, including the group of islands in the Aegean facing the entrance to the Dardanelles, they still would not be quite certain of free access to the Mediterranean.[24] The Power with naval supremacy in the Mediterranean could easily stop them from entering that sea. Once the Russians controlled the Straits, their Black Sea fleet was in a position to combat such hegemony: new possibilities then opened up before them. Instead of maintaining four separate fleets each with its own organization, a very expensive and clumsy undertaking, they would have only one 'Grand

Fleet of the Open Seas', based on the Black Sea. Their country would become one of the leading naval Powers: a prospect that was especially attractive to the Russians in November 1914, with their second largest fleet corked up in the Black Sea, and their biggest all-year-round ports serving the needs of local offshore shipping.

Indeed, when the Russians thought in terms of world power, they always started by thinking about the Straits. Their politicians had all been agreed, in the years before the war, that the possession of the Straits was a virtual necessity for the welfare of their state. For liberals like Professor Milyukov, the leader of the Kadet party, the control of the Straits was to be the sole objective – the first, the boldest, and the last move they wanted to make. For the expansionists, on the other hand, it was to be only the beginning. Many of them were to be found in the Admiralty in St Petersburg: the Russians knew, from the British example, that theirs was an age when world power went hand in hand with naval power.

It was not easy for London and Paris to accommodate the Russians. Quite apart from their own more or less established interests in the Near East and the Mediterranean, the English and the French politicians became irritated and wary of the Russians because the latter appeared over-demanding, with their ambitions too vague and unbounded. There was not only the Straits question with all its immediated ramifications to be resolved. It appeared that Russia had, shortly after the outbreak of the war, put itself, once again, into the role of the protector of Slav interests everywhere, especially in the Habsburg dominions. There was of course the alliance between Russia and Serbia, that had proved itself in the July 1914 crisis and had played its part in plunging Europe into the war. It was an alliance which could be regarded in two ways: either as an expression of Russia's desire to gain a foothold in the Balkans, a firm base for further inroads into the Ottoman domains as far as Constantinople; or as part and parcel of a Panslav policy, an instrument of Russia's westward expansion, directed mainly against the Habsburgs. After the outbreak of the war, it appeared as the latter, a possibility rarely considered outside the Ballhausplatz. And if it were taken in conjunction with Russia's plans for Constantinople and the Straits, then London and Paris had an ally more ambitious than they had bargained for. On 14 August, Grand Duke Nikolai Nikolaevich published his proclamation to the Slavs of Austria-Hungary. It was a crude attempt at political warfare, the first one made in a war that was to see so many. It was noticed in London and in Paris. Poincaré thought it was 'an announcement of disguised annexations' which the Russians had kept secret from their allies: a few weeks later, the British Ambassador to Sofia flatly stated that the expansion of Russia to the west must be blocked by every means, especially by the preservation of the Habsburg Empire.[25] Although the western Allies placed great value on Russia's participation in the war, they were unwilling to stand by and watch St Petersburg prepare the ground for a far-reaching extension of its influence.

Apart from putting their disapproval on record, there was little the western Allies could do, for the time being, about Russia's plans for expansion to the west. But there was a way of blocking its advance in the eastern Mediterranean, by supporting Italy's claims. Rome would in that way be tempted to come into the war, and some counter-balance to Russia would be created. St Petersburg, on the other hand, would have to be satisfied by concessions in Constantinople and the Straits. Such was the diplomatic strategy behind the events of 2 March 1915. That morning the British Ambassador passed two documents on to Sazonov. One of them informed him of the Italian terms and the other promised Russia Constantinople and the Straits.[26]

Sir Edward Grey knew that his action meant a break with the traditional foreign policy of Britain. The Crimean War, the policy of Beaconsfield and his successors, had aimed at keeping Russia out of the Straits. Now the Ottoman Empire was no longer to be protected and the possibility of its break-up was hinted at. Though the promise to the Russians depended on the outcome of the war and though Sazonov saw it, in his more pessimistic moments, as a bait held out before him by the British, his doubts never lasted long.

The problem had been brought to a head by the prospect of British and French naval action in the Straits. It roused the Russian Foreign Minister to feverish diplomatic activity, which culminated in a memorandum for the British and French Ambassadors on 4 March 1915, in which Sazonov stated:[27]

The course of recent events leads His Majesty the Emperor Nicholas to conclude that the question of Constantinople and the Straits must be solved finally and in the sense of Russia's efforts for the past hundred years. Any solution will remain unsatisfactory and insecure so long as the city of Constantinople, the western shore of the Bosphorus, the Sea of Marmara and the Dardanelles, as well as southern Thrace as far as the Enos-Midia line are not included in the domain of the Russian Empire.

It was clear that Sazonov was ready to be difficult, and that he had no scruples about jeopardizing the success of the Allied action in the Straits. Indirectly aided by the French, he successfully quashed the prospect of military co-operation by Greece on the Gallipoli peninsula: there were so many ways in which the Russians could damage the Allied cause, starting with Greece and ending by their concluding a separate peace with Germany, that they had to be pacified. There was no longer any point in trying to win them over for the plan of putting the Straits under international control, on the lines of the Suez Canal arrangement. The Russians simply replied that Britain was the real master there: they hinted, at the same time, that they were aware of British and French interests in the Middle East. Something more was required; perhaps even the reversal of traditional British policy. It took place at the meeting of Asquith's cabinet on 10 March. Within the next forty-eight hours, Sazonov was informed that, provided that the war was brought to a victorious conclusion and that Great Britain and France also got what they expected from the war, London was ready to make concessions to Russia on the basis of his memorandum of 4 March. The Quai d'Orsay moved more slowly. The French had the reputation in London of being violently pro-Russian: in the Foreign Office, Delcassé was known as Delcassoff. In the case of Constantinople, however, French policy remained unaffected by such sympathies. After luncheon on 3 March, the Tsar had told the French Ambassador that Russia must have Constantinople; Paléologue, the Ambassador, reminded the Tsar of French interests in the Ottoman Empire. They were considerable, amounting at the time, it was calculated, to some 3000m. francs,[28] in addition to the manifold Catholic missionary and educational activities that had been developed under the auspices of the French Embassy. The Tsar was in an expansive mood: he, on his part, could be understanding about the desires of Paris; when Paléologue mentioned his country's direct concerns, Nicholas II said that he wanted

France to emerge from this war as great and strong as possible. I agree beforehand to everything your Government wishes. Take the left bank of the Rhine; take Koblenz; go even further if you think it wise.[29]

There were signs that Delcassé might follow the British example; too many influential men in Paris, however, continued to exert pressure on the government. Throughout March, various schemes for the internationalizing of the Straits were put forward and dropped; on 9 March, Poincaré, the President of the Republic, was unable to restrain himself from interference in foreign affairs any longer. He wrote to Paléologue in St Petersburg that

the possession of Constantinople and environs would not only give Russia a kind of privilege in the succession to the Ottoman Empire. It would bring her, by way of the Mediterranean, into the concert of the Western nations and enable her, through the freedom of the seas, to become a great naval Power. Thus the European balance would be entirely changed. Such an aggrandizement and such an increase of power would not be acceptable to us, unless we ourselves came out of the War with equivalent advantages.[30]

The Russians were indignant. After a diplomatic struggle lasting a month, in which the Foreign Office reluctantly took a part, Sazonov was informed that Paris was prepared to follow the London line.

The Russians received a conditional promise, but it was a promise none the less. It was meant to keep them in the war: at this stage, the question was not considered whether the peasants in the Russian army would be sufficiently impressed by the vision of Constantinople, their Tsargrad, to stay in the trenches. A decisive victory for the three principal Allies could cut through the Dardanelles knot; for the time being, in March 1915, the situation held out some promise. It was a situation created largely by British naval and diplomatic initiative, and complicated by the way in which the two activities did not quite keep in step. The diplomats removed the danger, not yet acute but already present, of Russia's defection, while making an important advance toward securing Italy's active participation. There existed, however, no agreement in London on what to expect of a successful naval action in the Straits. Its long-term effects on the course of the war were difficult to forecast. On a short-term basis, a successful operation would almost certainly have removed the Young Turk government from power and knocked Turkey out of the war: Kitchener and Churchill were agreed on this. The mood in Constantinople, in late February and early March 1915, bore witness to the immense prestige of the Royal Navy. In the Turkish capital, the action was generally expected to succeed. Wangenheim and his colleagues were ready to leave in a hurry; special trains were standing, their steam up, on the sidings; a German naval officer was reported to have said that he was going to change into his shroud, and keep it on; preparations were being made for firing the city and blowing up St Sophia. Of the members of the Young Turk cabinet, only Enver, recently back from the disastrous expedition to the Caucasus, remained calm and collected: he regarded the struggle in the Straits as his own personal confrontation with Churchill. The unexpected happened. By the end of March the naval action had clearly run into difficulties. Enver's most cherished desire, to demonstrate the vulnerability of the Royal Navy, was fulfilled. The panic in Constantinople subsided as fast as it rose: the Kaiser and the Sultan exchanged decorations, Wilhelm II receiving 10,000 cigarettes in addition to his medal; the Turks triumphantly published an abbreviated casualty list, including the loss of 'a mule of Hungarian origin'.

The failure of the Allied action in the Straits now left Russia isolated for the duration of the war, as well as weakening the position of the diplomats in regard to the smaller Balkan states. Since the beginning of the war, Bulgaria and Rumania had received from the Great Powers attentions quite out of proportion to their military importance. Bulgaria's strategic position was the more crucial: if it joined the Central Powers, then Serbia, exposed to a Bulgarian attack from the rear, would be doomed, and Turkey reinforced.[31]

Before the war Bulgaria had been technically uncommitted. The foundations of its independence had been laid under Russian protection, with the creation, in 1870, of a separate Bulgarian Orthodox Church. By 1914, Russia's special relationship with Sofia was very much a thing of the past. The aged Exarch Josef had nothing more to contribute to the controversy following the disaster of the second Balkan War than the injunction to his compatriots that their national misfortunes were the result of a deep-seated moral delinquency. The country's more recent fortunes, on the other hand, could largely be attributed to its connections with Berlin and Vienna. King Ferdinand, the youngest son of Prince August of Saxe-Coburg-Gotha, had been elected Prince of Bulgaria by the Grand Sobranie, the parliament in Sofia, in 1887, when he was twenty-six years old. He was an ambitious, clever person whom the Sobranie excused from professing the Orthodox faith; he had to make an undertaking, however, to reside in the principality. Ferdinand had no desire to become an absentee landlord: he regarded his personal fortunes and those of his family as being closely linked with those of Bulgaria. On 5 October 1908, the day of the annexation of Bosnia and Herzegovina, and in close consultation with Austrian diplomacy, Bulgaria was proclaimed an independent kingdom. Ferdinand assumed the title of Tsar, while he kept, locked away in a chest, for a special day in the distant future, the full regalia of a Byzantine Emperor: in Balkan politics everything was possible.

Vasil Radoslavov, the Premier, who was also Minister of the Interior and of Foreign Affairs, served his Tsar well. Before he assumed office in July 1913 he had argued that Bulgaria would have to disregard the cant about Slav solidarity, turn its back on Russia, make peace with Rumania, and take revenge on Greece and Serbia. For the time being, however, there was no interested Great Power to whom Bulgaria could turn. Austria-Hungary was reserved, and the Kaiser could not stand Ferdinand; toward the end of 1913 Wilhelm II thought it far more important for Austria-Hungary to win Serbia than Bulgaria, 'whose King was untrustworthy and always inclined toward intrigue'.[32] The Russians were even cooler. Their long-term plan for the Balkans was to reconcile Bulgaria with Serbia, and they were quite prepared to wait for Radoslavov's fall, or to help him on his way to it, before they made a move in that direction. For the time being, their new Minister to Sofia – he arrived there early in 1914 – A.A.Savinski, kept on annoying Ferdinand and putting him, as well as Bulgaria, in his place. At his first audience with the King, Savinski informed him that Bulgaria 'must prove by its actions that it deserves Russian support'[33] and then, shortly before the outbreak of the war, the Minister reminded Ferdinand that 'Russia has her own political tasks which exceed all others in importance; that is what the Bulgarians have so often overlooked'.[34] While Ferdinand was getting more and more irritated by Savinski and by Russian policy toward Bulgaria, Radoslavov remained in office despite attempts by Russia and France to unseat him. Some four weeks before the

Sarajevo murders, the French government offered Ferdinand a loan of 600m. francs (25·225 francs to £1 sterling at 1914 value) in instalments, provided that he got rid of Radoslavov. In the course of the summer crisis, however, the offer petered out: the Germans, on the other hand, acted faster and with more resolution. A consortium of bankers headed by the *Disconto Gesellschaft* showed themselves prepared to advance 100m. francs forthwith, and then two lots of 250m. were to follow. Bulgaria was able to convert its small liabilities into one big burden, at 5 per cent interest rates, set aside the sum of 50m. for the construction of a railroad to the Aegean Sea by German and Austro-Hungarian companies, and of 100 m. for purchases in Germany and Austria-Hungary. The loan was to be ratified by Bulgaria before 30 July 1914, and it could be withdrawn in case of the outbreak of war; the debate on its ratification occasioned one of those legendary scenes in a Balkan parliament, when all the opposition parties stormily refused the offer (there was Savinski's influence behind the refusal) and the government accepted it, without a division taking place.

In the course of the July crisis and then immediately after the outbreak of the war, the interest of the Great Powers in Bulgaria greatly increased. The interest was not, however, reciprocated on the Bulgarian side. Like many other Balkan politicians, Ferdinand and Radoslavov were unsure of themselves in the new, divided Europe. They hesitated to trust their political instinct, because, they felt, they could not afford to make mistakes. The situation suggested that Bulgaria should remain neutral until the issue among the Great Powers was settled, and that in the meantime there was no harm in trying to remain on good terms with the two sides. Ferdinand and Radoslavov were not yet ready to commit their country in a quarrel between the Great Powers. They were, however, prepared to act in the narrower Balkan context.

Four days after the conclusion of the treaty between Turkey and Germany the Bulgarians concluded, on 6 August 1914, their own treaty with Turkey. It was an alliance that affected nothing beyond the actions of the two states in the Balkans: it contained a promise of mutual help in the event of an attack by one or more Balkan states; it provided for consultation before either of the contracting parties embarked on any military action in the Balkans; a military convention was to be worked out. In addition, the Bulgarians reinsured themselves by having it stated in the treaty that they would not have to undertake any offensive military action in agreement with Turkey until they obtained an adequate guarantee from Rumania.[35]

The treaty remained an unusually well-kept secret until the middle of December 1914, when a member of the Turkish cabinet told Wangenheim about it. It made the Bulgarians feel more secure, but it did not move the King and his Premier to active participation in the war. And in order to maintain their precarious seat on the fence as long as they did, the Bulgarians had to exercise hard their skills. After a Russian inquiry, for instance, about a proposed landing of troops at Varna and the use of Burgas by the navy in September 1914, Radoslavov told Savinski that his country would not resist a *fait accompli* while, at the same time, he informed Vienna that such action, on the part of Russia, would certainly mean war.[36]

For over a year after the outbreak of the war, King Ferdinand and Radoslavov kept their country neutral. In practice, their interpretation of neutrality favoured the Central Powers: vehicles carrying arms, ammunition and gold to Turkey found a smooth passage through Bulgarian territory. But until the spring of 1915, military events provided the Bulgarians with no decisive bearings; with the initial failure of the naval action in the Straits, the situation began to change, and the unsuccessful Gallipoli expedition, combined with the victories of the Austro-German forces on the Russian front, put the minds of the King and his Premier at rest.

The Allied diplomats fought hard in Bulgaria. But they had little to offer the Bulgarians after their commitments to Italy, and these made it more difficult for the Serbs, in their turn, to give up territory in order to tempt the Bulgarians into the war. In addition, the relations between Serbia and Bulgaria had deteriorated since the beginning of the war because of the activities in Macedonia of the *komitadji*, the Bulgarian paramilitary terrorist organization, which were receiving secret support from Vienna. Among the Allied politicians, Delcassé alone placed greater value on the co-operation of Bulgaria than on that of Greece (another point of difference with Grey), and he was also prepared to risk the fury of the Serbs. It was feared in London that at a crucial point in the Bulgarian negotiations the French Foreign Minister would tell the Serbs and the Greeks to go to the devil, and then do his best for the Bulgarians.[37] It is doubtful if even that extreme measure would have changed Bulgaria's position.

In contrast to the latest offer of the Central Powers made in February 1915, the simplicity of which made a powerful appeal to the Bulgarians – they were offered everything they could take from their enemies by force of arms[38] – the Allies wooed Sofia in an intricate and confusing manner. Their note of 29 May offered to guarantee Bulgaria the possession, after the war, of that portion of Macedonia, then in Serbian hands, known as the 'uncontested zone'. (In the Foreign Office communications on that subject, a number of incredulous British diplomats changed its name to the more appropriate 'contested zone'.) The guarantee was conditional on Serbia's obtaining compensation in Bosnia-Herzegovina and on the Adriatic. The four Allied Powers also offered to use their best endeavours and induce Greece to surrender Kavalla, as well as facilitating negotiations between Bulgaria and Rumania with regard to the Dobruja. Sofia then replied on 15 June, making a number of inquiries, especially about 'equitable compensations' to Serbia.[39] At this point of the negotiations, Sir Henry Bax-Ironside, the British Minister to Sofia, left his post. He objected to the Allied treatment of Serbia as much as to the assumption that military assistance from Bulgaria could still be obtained. He was replaced, in the middle of July, by Hugh O'Beirne, who arrived at the Bulgarian capital in a more optimistic frame of mind. O'Beirne, together with the other Allied Ministers, knew that the Bulgarians placed the highest value on Macedonian acquisitions and were prepared to fight for them. It was also known that in Sofia the Bulgarians from Macedonia ran a highly effective political pressure group. On 17 July the Allies therefore threw in the portion of the 'uncontested zone' east of the Vardar river, in addition to their original May offer; finally, on 14 September 1915, the Allied Powers collectively guaranteed to Bulgaria the cession, in exchange for military co-operation, of the whole 'uncontested zone' at the close of the war.

Despite their tempting offers to Bulgaria, the Allies made little headway. They could not, much as they may have wanted to, make a promise that territory would change hands before the end of the war, and they were unable to induce the Serbs to approve offers made to Bulgaria. Looking back at the situation in August 1915, O'Beirne wrote:[40]

Unfortunately it was the feeling of Serbian military leaders and, I believe, of the Serbian people themselves, that they would sooner go under fighting than surrender the whole of the 'uncontested zone' to a hated foe.

The Bulgarians knew that differences existed between the Allies; the spring and summer of 1915 saw also an impressive and uninterrupted sequence of Austrian and German victories on the eastern front. On 5 August, the Austrians captured Ivangorod and the Germans entered Warsaw; on 17 August, Kovno (Kaunas) fell; on 25 August, Brest Litovsk was stormed. Toward the end of the month, the Allied Ministers knew that the military co-operation of Bulgaria was no longer obtainable, and they lowered their sights, trying to keep the country neutral.

When all else failed, only a thin hope in the effectiveness of bribery and corruption remained. In the words of Grey, 'There was nothing except dignity to be lost by trying at Sofia, and we all tried.'[41] The plots and counter-plots, the subsidies for the press and the politicians, the good-will missions and the speeches by prominent visitors – all these activities had been the undercurrent of diplomacy since the outbreak of the war. In this regard as well, the Central Powers had gained an advantage over the Allies. The Russians made a late start with their secret press fund in June 1915, after they had realized that almost all the news in the Bulgarian press from the eastern front came from Austrian and German sources.[42] A month later, a more ambitious Russian plan received French and British support. Since the harvest in 1914, Bulgaria had not been able to export corn; combined with the 1915 harvest, it was calculated that there would be some 900,000 tons available on the Sofia market. E. K. Grube, the President of the Siberian Bank, who had recently been engaged on a similar secret mission to Persia, suggested the purchase of surplus corn through the Bulgarian politicians, a plan which had the advantage of facilitating hidden bribery. Both France and Britain were interested in having the corn; the drawback of the scheme was that there existed no way of getting the purchase out of Bulgaria. The bribery side of the business being, however, more important, the expenses – some 262m. francs were needed – were to be shared among the three Entente Powers, and Des Closières, a French banker, was sent over to direct operations, for a fee of 500,000 francs. He started buying on 25 August 1915.

On the Bulgarian side, politicians were to purchase corn from the peasants, sell it to the Allied agent, and receive a commission according to their political influence. Genadiev, the former Foreign Minister, was to act as the main intermediary. The Allies could hardly have chosen a less suitable man: even for Sofia, where memories of scandals were short, Genadiev's reputation was too brutish. He was a friend of Vikenti Athanasov, the 'anarchistic philosopher' who had organized the bomb incident at the Sofia Casino in February 1914, when a number of prominent people were killed; Athanasov was known to have conspired to assassinate the King in order to bring about the reconstruction of the cabinet, with himself becoming Chief of Police, and his friend Premier. It was common knowledge in Sofia that Genadiev had embezzled moneys given him to influence the European press on the conclusion of the Balkan wars; his brother was notorious for having cornered the market in beans, cheese and cereal, in consequence of which prices rose sharply in the spring of 1915. When Genadiev began acting on behalf of the Allies, he had just been deposed, in May 1915, from the leadership of his own party.

The flaws in the crop-buying scheme soon became apparent. The Germans had been active in the market for some time, and it may well be that Grube's plan simply followed the German example: if Genadiev was to play a prominent part, in the summer of 1915, in an ambitious political plot, it was not likely to succeed. In any case, when the Allied agent bought the first lot of corn on 25 August, the Bulgarians were on the brink of committing themselves on the Central Powers' side. In mid-August, Colonel Ganchev arrived at the German General Headquarters at Pless (now Pszczyna) to discuss a military convention; at the end of the month, Duke John Albert of Mecklenburg, accompanied by a Wilhelmstrasse official, arrived in Sofia as the King's guests. The treaty and two conventions were signed on 6 September 1915. The Bulgarians agreed to take up arms against Serbia, and to fight Rumania and Greece, should either of them attack Germany. Bulgaria was promised the contested and the uncontested zones in Macedonia, a part of Serbia east of the Morava river and, if Rumania and Greece attacked, some territory in the Rumanian Dobruja and Greek Thrace. The territorial convention, of course, contained promises only, though they were much more far-reaching and definite than the Allied offers; the Central Powers, however, had an additional way of showing their good faith. Just as the Allies had to try to induce Serbia to surrender a part of Macedonia, so Germany had to induce Turkey to abandon a part of Thrace. The German diplomats succeeded where the Allies failed: on 6 September, the Turkish representative at Sofia signed an agreement under which Turkey ceded a strip of territory along the Maritsa river, which gave Bulgaria continuous railway connection with the Aegean, and the port of Dedéagach.[43] The protocol of transfer of the territory and railway was finally signed at Demotika on 21 September 1915; on the same day, Bulgaria mobilized.

The military convention which had been signed at Pless on 6 September had bound Austria-Hungary and Germany to attack Serbia with six divisions in thirty days, and Bulgaria to support the attack with four divisions in thirty-five days; it provided for, among other things, German financial assistance to Bulgaria; Field-Marshal von Mackensen was to command the whole operation.[44] On 4 October the Counsellor at the Russian Legation – the Minister, Savinski, having broken down under the strain – presented an ultimatum to Radoslavov, demanding that Bulgaria dismiss, within twenty-four hours, the German officers assisting in its military preparations, or demobilize. Radoslavov at once returned a negative reply. The Allied Ministers left Sofia, with assurances of a lasting Bulgarian friendship; they profited by Bulgaria's recent acquisition from Turkey, and left the country via the port of Dedéagach on the Aegean Sea. On 6 October, the Austro-German offensive against Serbia was launched, and the Bulgarians joined, as agreed, five days later. The fate of Serbia was now sealed: by the end of the year the whole country was under occupation by the Central Powers.

The Allies reacted swiftly to the loss of Bulgaria. A redoubled effort was now made to gain the co-operation of Rumania and, in order to bring Bucharest into the war, the British proposed to sign a military convention with Greece, send 200,000 'seasoned' troops to Salonika, and dispatch 500,000 rifles to Russia so that a 'strong and concerted action with Rumania in the southern theatre' would be launched.[45] The Russians were concerned at the prospect of military disaster in Serbia, and they were now prepared to go further than ever before in meeting Rumania's demands.

The Rumanians had demanded a high price for disloyalty to

their allies: their position closely resembled that of the Italians, only Bucharest was prepared to bargain even harder than Rome. Rumania was bound to Austria-Hungary, Germany and Italy by a treaty of defensive alliance, last renewed in 1913; on the outbreak of the war the Kaiser assumed that King Carol of Rumania, a member of the House of Hohenzollern, would actively support the Central Powers. Such confidence did not exist in Vienna. According to Count Czernin, the Austrian Minister to Bucharest, the impression in the Rumanian capital, after the ultimatum to Serbia, was that 'Austria had gone mad'.[46] The ultimatum startled the Rumanian King; at a dramatic meeting of the Crown Council on 3 August, in which past, present and future Premiers took part, the decision to remain neutral was taken. The scales were tipped, at the height of the discussion, by a telegram from Rome confirming Italy's neutrality.[47] Nevertheless, from the Allied point of view, Rumania's newly-found neutrality had a sting in its tail. The Crown Council decided to abandon the standpoint of the Treaty of Bucharest, hardly a year old at the time, and allow the intervention of Bulgaria against Serbia.

The Rumanians kept out of the war by breaking one treaty and interpreting another in a way that suited them best. It also became clear, at the Crown Council meeting, that King Carol, as long as he lived, was unlikely to join the Entente: he died on 12 October 1914. From then on, Rumania was on the open market, and the decisions of its rulers were to be dominated by the usual two considerations: the fortunes of the war, and the chances of territorial gain. Until Rumania's entry into the war in August 1916, Bratianu kept one eye on the eastern front, and the other on Transylvania. He was a cautious character, much better at short-term schemes than at long-term campaigns. At the Crown Council meeting on 3 August, Bratianu had said that 'the question of the Rumanians of Transylvania dominates the whole situation'. Some three million Rumanians lived in Transylvania, under the tough, unyielding rule of the Hungarian government; Tisza and his colleagues made no pretence at running the Hungarian part of the Habsburg dominions for the benefit of national minorities. The Rumanians in Transylvania had not developed – like the Serbs in Bosnia-Herzegovina – an irredentist movement before the war. The element of encouragement by Bucharest had been missing. Nevertheless, since the assassination of Franz Ferdinand, hopes for an amicable settlement of the Transylvanian problem had begun to fade in the Rumanian capital.

The Russian Foreign Minister, who had received indications before the war that Rumania was turning away from its old allies, was greatly encouraged by its declaration of neutrality. He made advances to Bucharest at once. His offer was suspect because he promised too much (not, of course, southern Bessarabia, a part of Russia, but all the Habsburg territories inhabited by the Rumanians) for too little (the maintenance of neutrality) at a time when King Carol was still alive. Bratianu was given his cue: it took some time before the Allies lived down the first rash offers by Russia. In the main, however, events in Bucharest developed according to the usual Balkan pattern. Bid and counter-bid followed each other in rapid succession; as in Sofia, the purchase of corn assumed the sinister significance of a political conspiracy. The intensified diplomatic activity in October 1915, after the entry of Bulgaria into the war, brought the Allies no rewards: their military situation was too bad for Bratianu to make a move. Finally, Rumanian intervention was offset by a Russian military victory. The Brusilov offensive in June 1916 was the last fling of the Tsarist army before the revolution: its success lasted long enough for the Rumanians to commit themselves to the Allied side. On 23 July 1916 the Rumanian Military Attaché in Paris signed the Chantilly convention: a Rumanian army of 150,000 troops, supported by the Russians, was to attack Bulgaria a week after the Allies had launched an offensive from Salonika.[48] But before Rumania entered the war, Bratianu evaded pressure from his allies till the last moment. He would commit no armed forces to an attack on Bulgaria, and he asked for the postponement of the date of Rumania's entry. Boris Stuermer, who had recently succeeded Sazonov as Russia's new Foreign Minister, had a draft treaty worked out, significantly, in the form of an ultimatum to Rumania. The territorial concessions – apart from Transylvania, Bukovina to the Prut river, the Banat, and a few Hungarian counties thrown in – sounded right to Bratianu. He did not, however, much care for the 'no separate peace' clause, and the French persuaded Stuermer to have it taken out. According to the new military convention, Rumania was to enter the war on 27 August 1916; by then, the Russian summer offensive had stalled. Rumania's performance in the war was disastrous. By the end of the year 1916 the Rumanian army had been broken and the Russians had some four hundred miles of additional front line to look after. The competition for allies in Europe was over.

It was not immediately apparent that the Central Powers had done better than their adversaries. We shall have occasion to remark on the way in which, a year later, the Italians proved a diplomatic and military liability to their allies; the Rumanians hardly helped the Russians at all. Most important, the Turkish alliance isolated Russia, to a great extent, from the rest of the world. With the Black Sea closed, Russian imports dropped by 95 per cent compared with the last year before the war, its exports by 98 per cent. Of the two remaining Russian outlets, Archangel was icebound for more than half of the year, and Vladivostok was some 8,000 miles away from the front. The new port of Murmansk, which had been constructed at a high cost of English capital and Russian labour, became operational only in 1917. For some of its supplies, especially medicaments, the Russian army depended on German trade, re-routed via the Scandinavian countries. Between August 1915 and July 1916, German exports to Russia amounted to the sum of 11,220,000 roubles.

Neither of the two belligerent sides gained a decisive preponderance in the war by the adherence of new allies. Except in the case of Turkey, whose rulers wanted protection by one of the Great Powers more than anything else, the ability, on the part of one alliance or the other, to satisfy the territorial ambitions of a new entrant into the war proved decisive. For the time being, all the attractive offers, apart from the cession by Turkey of western Thrace to Bulgaria, remained on paper. The promise of Constantinople to Russia was perhaps more illusory than any other undertaking given in the first two years of the war: it appealed to no one apart from the Russian politicians. They did not know that, when Turkey entered the war on the enemy's side, the ground was prepared for the victory of the Central Powers in the east.

3 Berlin

Soon after the outbreak of the war, Gottlieb von Jagow, the State Secretary in the Foreign Ministry, Bethmann Hollweg, the Chancellor, and the Kaiser moved from Berlin to the seat of General Headquarters. From there, they observed the failure of the Schlieffen plan, the grinding to a halt of a military machine, the fading of a vision. The swift and decisive victory in the west had not taken place. Now, in the middle of November 1914, the Chief-of-Staff thought:[1]

As long as Russia, France and England hold together, it will be impossible for us to inflict such a defeat on our enemies as to achieve a satisfactory peace. We shall rather be running the risk of our own slow exhaustion. Either Russia or France must be prised off. If we succeed in bringing Russia to terms, which should be our primary objective, we could then deal France and England so crushing a blow that we could dictate peace terms, even if the Japanese came across the sea to France, and England continued to put fresh reinforcements on the field. But if Russia made peace, there is every reason to expect that France also would give in. Then if England made any trouble, we could bring it to heel by blockade. . . .

The communication was addressed to Arthur Zimmermann, the Under Secretary of State, who had been left in charge of the Foreign Ministry in Berlin. He was well placed to influence the course of Germany's foreign policy: all the telegrams and directives to German missions abroad passed through his hands. He was then fifty years old, a 'very jolly large sort of German', square-headed, blue-eyed, bushy-moustached. He was an east Prussian but not a *Junker*; his origins were middle-class. After getting a law degree and a duelling scar at his university, he joined the consular service, the non-aristocratic part of Germany's foreign representation, in 1897. Five years later he was seconded to Tirpitz's naval staff, the turning-point of his career. He became a member of the political department of the Foreign Ministry in 1905, and in 1911 he was appointed the Under Secretary of State. He enjoyed the confidence of the Kaiser, who preferred dealing with Zimmermann to Jagow or Bethmann Hollweg.

Zimmermann knew well the lines on which the thinking at General Headquarters moved; his comprehensive memorandum of 27 November 1914[2] reflected Falkenhayn's arguments. In order to end the war with the kind of peace Germany wanted, 'I regard it as desirable that a wedge should be driven between our enemies, so that we may conclude an early separate peace with one or the other.'[3] But in one important regard the Under Secretary's argument differed from Falkenhayn's. France, not Russia, appeared to him the weakest member of the enemy alliance. He thought that the war was not popular with the French and that they carried on only because of English support and their faith in the effectiveness of Russian arms. Zimmermann estimated that the threat to Germany was equal from England and from Russia. Everyone in Germany was resolved to carry on the war against England to its bitter end: there were, on the other hand, rumours of a separate peace with the Tsarist Empire.

These rumours upset Zimmermann. In the first place peace with Russia could have no appeal for Vienna. The war had been started by the 'Panslav intrigues' of Russia aimed against Austria-Hungary. The Slavs in the Habsburg Empire were loyal to it; this, according to Zimmermann, could be explained partly by their devotion to the dynasty, and partly by the presence of a powerful ally, namely Germany. In any case, part of Galicia was occupied by the Russians, and the Central Powers would therefore not negotiate from a position of military strength. Another reason against peace with Russia was Turkey. It was a valuable ally for Berlin and Vienna, and would regard any move on their part toward an understanding with Russia as a betrayal. Moreover, an undefeated Russia would continue to exert pressure on Turkey and to threaten Germany's interests in the Near East. Zimmermann therefore suggested that 'in our own interest also an energetic struggle against Russia' should be carried on, and added: 'The Russian is not our friend.'[4]

Zimmermann realized that on this point he ran counter to the views held at General Headquarters. He knew that the military regarded the Franco-British alliance as the more difficult to beat and the more difficult to break up. And behind France the German war lords saw the brooding, powerful presence of Britain, resolutely hostile to Berlin. Britain was Germany's most implacable enemy. Zimmermann conceded that point in an afterthought concerning military matters. If Germany's military power, he hinted, were incapable of holding the western and pushing back the eastern front, only then should a separate peace with Russia rather than France be considered. In a telegram on 6 January 1915 the Chancellor put Zimmermann right in two terse sentences: 'The best thing for us would be the prising off of Russia from the alliance. England seems the least ready to give in.'[5] The idea of a separate peace helped the Germans keep up their faith in final victory.

While the leaders at General Headquarters were still discussing the ways of dealing with the failure of their military plans, an offer to mediate peace came from Copenhagen. A German and a Danish shipowner had won King Christian over to the idea of inquiring about the possibilities of peace in London and St Petersburg.[6] The Danish royal house had family connections with those of Russia and Great Britain, and proposed to put out feelers unofficially. Bethmann Hollweg treated the offer with great caution. Vienna would have to be informed, he thought, and Germany could not afford to show any desire for peace. To the enemy, as well as to the German people, that would only be proof of military weakness. On 30 November 1914, the German government agreed to mediation by the King of Denmark, on the understanding that a general peace conference was out of the question.[7]

Two days later, the two men from whom the original initiative had come met at the Hotel Esplanade in Berlin. One of them was Alfred Ballin, Director-General of the Hamburg-Amerika shipping line, and a close friend of Prince von Bülow; a self-taught and self-made man, resourceful, with a strong desire to please everyone. He had seen Bethmann Hollweg on 30 November and was briefed on the government's policy. His partner in the conversation was Hans-Niels Andersen, Director-General of the East Asia Company, a prosperous shipping and trading organization, which he had founded together with Princess Waldemar. Andersen was an intimate friend of the Danish royal family, with extensive business connections both in Britain and Germany.

Andersen said that he had been commanded by the King to set

out from Copenhagen as soon as possible. 'The king made it clear that it went utterly against his religious sense of duty to allow this noble mission to be delayed for a single day.'[8] Ballin then told Andersen of the Kaiser's surprise at the King of Denmark's offer to mediate, and proceeded to give the Dane the Kaiser's views on the nature of the war. It had been forced on Germany, and its continuation was necessary for the future peaceful development of the country. Nevertheless, out of the high regard Wilhelm II had for Christian X he could not turn down the offer. The King should rest assured that any suggestions from the Tsar or the King of England would be 'received with good will and examined with care'.[9] The Kaiser, being well aware of the King's wisdom, took it for granted that no proposals for any big peace conference would be made.

Andersen was pleased at Ballin's news, and assured the German shipowner that the Kaiser would certainly not be disappointed. Then he inquired what would be the best way of proceeding. Ballin had been briefed at General Headquarters, and he tried immediately to get over the most difficult hurdle. He said that, in his view, an understanding was much easier to achieve with Russia than with England, and that the King should approach Russia first. Andersen then told Ballin of the intrigues at the Tsar's court and about the King of Denmark's views on England. According to the King, England had passed the peak of her power and would have to be prepared to make big concessions to Germany. From his own conversations in London Andersen had formed the impression that the English no longer felt up to the task of policing the world on their own and were ready to share the task with Germany. Ballin replied that 'the perpetual threat from England and the underlying assumption that the balance of power in Europe is England's responsibility – these are things which Germany, once this war is over, will no longer tolerate'.[10] The war would therefore have to go on until the achievement of a 'guarantee of lasting peace', that is to say, the breaking of England's world power. After two hours the shipowners parted without having agreed on their objectives. Ballin expected Andersen to make a contribution to the cause of a separate peace with Russia; Andersen, on his part, had only a superficial knowledge of the Russian political scene, and fewer connections in St Petersburg than in London. He was unaware of the role for which his German friend had cast him. Whenever Andersen returned from London, he was full of optimism, whereas from St Petersburg he never had any good news. The confusion of aims at their meeting on 2 December 1914 led to the eventual disappearance of the Dane from the scene. The first doubts of his suitability emerged in Copenhagen early in July 1915. Scavenius, the pro-German Foreign Secretary of Denmark, was on very good terms with Brockdorff-Rantzau, the German Minister to Copenhagen, and was well aware – much more so than either the King or Andersen – of the true aims of German diplomacy. He put it to Rantzau that Andersen had not really the cause of a separate peace at heart, that he was therefore an unsuitable go-between, and that Germany must have other channels of communication with Russia at its disposal.[11] After his last visit to Petrograd in August 1915, Andersen was quickly dropped.

By then the German and Austro-Hungarian offensive had pushed back the Russian front and a new, more decisive diplomacy was to supplement military success. In the view of the Austrian Chief-of-Staff, the Central Powers could achieve their aim only if they

build golden bridges for separate peace with Russia, and clear the way for a lasting and complete understanding for all time between ourselves and Germany on the one hand, ourselves and Russia on the other. Moreover, we must above all firmly avoid any humiliation of Russia, and in the first place renounce without question any substantial territorial concessions on Russia's part.[12]

It was indeed ironical that the first hint of the policy of 'no annexations and no indemnities' was dropped in an exchange between the Austrian and German Chiefs-of-Staff. And not only that: St Petersburg would doubtless be interested in free passage in the Straits, and the German and Austrian Chiefs-of-Staff agreed that the Central Powers should put no obstacles in Russia's way. Conrad added:[13]

I am fully aware of the many kinds of difficulties in the way of such an attempt, and I grant that, despite our military successes, Russia may turn down flat the offers we are proposing. But I regard the declaration of our aims as so conclusive, and the present development of the military situation as so favourable for such a step, especially if, as seems likely, the present Italian offensive should be repulsed, that the attempt to arrive at a separate peace with Russia must certainly be made.

After pressure from his own and the Austrian military, Bethmann Hollweg said that he had been putting out feelers to Petrograd for many months, but without success. He could think of no remedy, apart from wondering whether it would not be a good idea to make a more or less official offer to Russia.[14]

At this point there was as yet no reason why the Chancellor should overhaul his whole strategy of separate peace. A few subtle changes were visible in the execution of the policy: in the summer of 1915, the scene shifted from Copenhagen to Stockholm; Warburg came to take the place of Ballin; Wallenberg, the Swedish Foreign Minister, that of Andersen. The difficulties, as far as Russia was concerned, began to emerge more clearly. Sazonov was a determined opponent of Germany and, as long as he remained in the government, peace between the two countries was out of the question. For a more accommodating government, Sergei Count Witte, the reforming ex-Minister of Finance and former Premier, was an obvious choice. His private secretary of long standing, a gentleman called Melnik, had been in Ballin's pay for many years; Witte himself had property and financial interests in Germany.[15] Nevertheless, shortly after the first moves had been made, Count Witte died on 12 March 1915. The ineffectiveness of the peace moves brought the policy to a halt. Between September 1915 and February 1916 no further attempts were made.

The reason for that inactivity was the existence of an alternative to the policy of separate peace. It was an attractive option. By encouraging national and social revolution in Russia, the Germans hoped to find themselves in a position where a new Russian regime, both revolutionary and weak, would be forced to make a peace with them. Andersen's peace feelers had not been expected to produce an easy peace. The alternative policy promised that the power of Russia would be broken, once and for all. It was a policy which brought the defeat of Russia, the release of the marginal territories from Russian domination, the long-term elimination of the threat from the east, within Germany's grasp. It did not mean, however, that the Germans dropped the policy of separate peace and took up the policy of subversion. Since the outbreak of the war, they had encouraged revolutions, a policy which was aimed at a variety of targets.

The first impulse to it in fact dated back to the last days of European peace, and it came from the highest quarter. On 30 July

1914, the Kaiser read a telegram from the Ambassador to St Petersburg, and a passage in it triggered off the Imperial fury. In a prophetic, sombre, incoherent marginal note Wilhelm II demanded that England should have the mask of the Christian peace-lover publicly torn from her face:[16]

our Consuls in Turkey and India, our political agents, etc. must inflame the whole Moslem world to a savage uprising against this hateful, devious, unscrupulous nation of shopkeepers; for if we are to bleed to death, then England shall at least lose India.

In that marginal note, the sentiment of the later slogan 'Gott strafe England' was contained, as well as a rudimentary programme of subversion.

The programme developed, soon after the outbreak of war, into an ambitious undertaking. It was aimed at the non-Russian peoples of the Tsarist Empire, from the Gulf of Finland to the Black Sea, as well as at the Moslems from Morocco to India. The policy was aimed at Russia and England, and Constantinople was its focal point. Indeed, Turkey and Constantinople played an important, threefold role in Germany's Near Eastern strategy: as a guardian of the Straits, severing the relations between Russia and its allies; as the starting-point for subversive activities in south Russia, from the Ukraine to the Caucasus; as the leader of the Holy War of the Moslems against the colonial Empires, especially that of England in Egypt and India.

The last policy had a long lineage behind it. From the turn of the century – there was the famous Damascus speech of November 1898 – the Kaiser had taken an increasingly benevolent interest in the Moslems. Wilhelm II showed it when he was irritated with England, with his grandmother, Queen Victoria, or with some other aspect of English life, rather than in his Anglophile periods. Nevertheless, Prince von Bülow, when still in office as Reich Chancellor, often had to remind the Kaiser that the foundations of British world power could not be so easily shaken.[17] The Kaiser made the speeches; the ideas came from Max von Oppenheim, scholar and diplomat. In a detailed memorandum written in September 1914, Oppenheim once again recommended Pan-Islamic propaganda and the Holy War as the most effective weapons for the incitement of the Moslems to a rising against their foreign masters.[18] Oppenheim ran the *Nachrichtenstelle für den Orient* in the Foreign Ministry, and he was shown, on Zimmermann's orders, all the relevant diplomatic correspondence. Oppenheim was assisted by Ernst Jäckh, Professor of Turkish history at the University of Berlin, a liberal journalist, who was a leading propagandist of Germany's eastern policy; he was very good at finding money for his various projects, and was known to his friends as *'König der Schnorrern'*. Together with Erzberger, Jäckh was a member of an organization, set up shortly after the outbreak of the war, for German propaganda abroad. He was a frequent guest at the Embassy in Constantinople and, as a member of the small Bethmann Hollweg circle, he gained occasional access to the Kaiser.

Despite the services of Oppenheim, Jäckh and other experts, Germany's Moslem policy never really got off the ground. The hopes set on it were high. A rising in India was naïvely expected to draw part of the Royal Navy away from the North Sea. The rising never took place. In the Indian venture, the Turks soon abandoned their German allies to their fate; they sent, on the other hand, 30,000 troops to Egypt. In Berlin, the expedition to the Suez Canal was regarded as 'a mortal blow at English supremacy'.[19] The advance of the Turkish troops, equipped with German arms and money, was expected to set off an uprising against English rule. Four million francs were put at the Khedive's disposal; Jäckh predicted that some 70,000 nomad Arabs would join in the revolt. The military target of the expedition was the closure of the Suez Canal, the destruction of the locks, railway bridges and harbour installations in Port Said and Alexandria. The Suez campaign, which had opened with bright promise, achieved neither its military nor its political objectives. There were disputes between Sanders, Enver and the Khedive for its leadership; the British forces were speedily augmented; the Egyptians themselves, remembering their former dependence, viewed the prospect of a Turkish invasion with mixed feelings.

None of the other plans for the Moslems succeeded. Contrary to the expectations of the German experts, the British Empire proved remarkably resilient. The memory of Turkish rule often cancelled out the ties of religious loyalty; the English usually bid higher than the German–Turkish allies for the Arab tribes, offering them complete independence. In this regard the German policy was amateur. The high hopes were disappointed; the *Weltpolitik* went wrong. The British fleet in the North Sea stayed undiminished; the Suez Canal remained unblocked. At best, the German and Turkish activities tied down some colonial troops who, in most cases, would have been stationed in the area anyway.

The policy of inciting the Moslems to an uprising also spilled over into the territory of the Tsarist Empire. In Transcaspia and in the Caucasus, the Turks attempted to influence the Moslem tribes, while the Germans interested themselves in the Christian Georgians. Again, as in Egypt, the success of the subversive activities was jeopardized by the military failure. The Turkish campaign in the Caucasus miscarried as early as November 1914.

The purely political part of the operation in the Caucasus was, in the long run, somewhat more successful. The Georgian independence movement dated back to the revolution of 1905, and the Russian authorities never quite succeeded in stamping it out. The first Georgians went into exile; soon after the outbreak of the war, Prince Matschabelli emerged as the leader of the Georgian committee in Berlin. He had at first supported the movement out of his own pocket, but gradually the Georgians became dependent on Germany. The Germans promised them the creation of an independent Georgian state after the war, and they made the Turks do the same: Prince Matschabelli, like Sir Roger Casement, was eventually transported in a German submarine, in his case to Batum. The Prince survived until the revolution in Russia in 1917, when independent states were formed in the Caucasus, following, in some respects, the plan he had first outlined in Berlin. By then, however, the military might of Russia had disappeared.

A similar situation developed in the north of the Russian Empire. A strong Finnish political emigration was based on Sweden, and the Reich government, from the first days of the war, intended to make use of the Finns against Russia. They held back, however, making no decisive move until after the November revolution in 1917.* The minority peoples of the Baltic provinces,the Lithuanians, Latvians and Estonians, on the other hand, received little encouragement from the Germans. They did not expect the

* See below, pp. 277 f.

Lithuanians to be interested in running their own national movement; in Livonia, Estonia and Kurland the German landowners' interest was strong, and the General Staff did not want to prejudice any future annexations by Germany: the name of Kurland came up early in the war. In Poland, the Austrians took the initiative. They had plans for merging Galicia with Russian Poland and then establishing some loose connection between the new state and Vienna. The Austrians got on well with the Poles under their rule. Galicia enjoyed administrative autonomy, and it supplied the Austrian government with some of its prominent members. The Berlin government, on the other hand, was not as popular among the Poles it ruled, and the attempts to win the Poles to its side lacked conviction.

For the Germans the Ukraine was the key to their policy on the Russian nationalities. In the nineteenth century, German students of Russia often paid special attention to the Ukraine. It was Russia's richest province, and, with its Black Sea coastline, it was easily accessible from Turkey. A number of Germans from the Baltic provinces – from the scholar Theodor Schiemann to the future Nazi leader Alfred Rosenberg – who supplied expert opinion on Russia, were inclined to believe that its frontiers should be pushed back to the limits of Muscovy before Peter the Great. They regarded the Ukraine as the area where pressure could be most successfully applied: in 1914, the German government shared that view. The policy enjoyed a broadly-based support, from the Pan-Germans, from the Catholic Centre party deputy Erzberger, even from the pacifists and the socialists. Nevertheless, in connection with the support by the Central Powers of the Ukrainian movement, the internal political developments in the Dual Monarchy were decisive. Vienna had sponsored the rise of Ukrainian nationality before the war. It needed an ally against the Poles inside the state and against Russian subversion from the outside. In the Habsburg Empire, the Ukrainians became aware of themselves for the first time as a separate political unit.

According to the original German strategic plan, after a short and sharp campaign in Belgium and France, the main thrust of the German army was to be directed against south Russia. But the victories did not materialize and the Ukrainian National Committee, based on Lwow in eastern Galicia, had to retreat with the Austrian armies early in the war. The Committee enjoyed support from the Uniate* Archbishop of Lwow; its propaganda was largely retrospective, recalling the past glories of an independent Ukraine. The 'Union for the Liberation of the Ukraine', a rival body, was highly critical of the National Committee's policy: the leaders of the Union maintained that the peasants would be moved, not by historical clichés, but by promises of land. They aimed at an independent and socialist Ukraine. They received generous support from Berlin and reluctant help from Vienna; the official interest in the Union sharply increased when, at the end of September 1914, its leaders put forward a proposal for military action in the Ukraine. Two of the leaders, Dr Leo Hankiewicz and Marian Basok-Melenevski, left for the Balkans and Constantinople in order to set up an advance base for the operation. In the Turkish capital, Melenevski at once set about recruiting a private army. Like a similar venture, based on Trebizond – Count Schulenburg's Georgian unit – the Ukrainian operation soon ran into trouble. The Turkish officials proved unco-operative; the organizers had no experience of partisan warfare, and instead of setting up flexible commando units, they thought in terms of regular armies. There were security leaks: the venture soon became known and, because of its obvious German connections, discredited among the Russian exiles. Neither the Georgian nor the Ukrainian private army ever became operational.

Indeed, in much the same way as the Moslem subversion plans, the schemes based on the employment of the minority peoples in the Tsarist Empire had produced, before the revolution in Russia, no tangible results. Only the political plans for the future were shaped and laid down in the course of those activities. The Ukrainian enterprise, however, had brought to the foreground another promising line of action. It was the encouragement of social revolution: the idea had been germinating for some time in the minds of Austrian and German politicians.

Lenin's presence on Austrian territory stirred the government in Vienna. The Bolshevik leader had lived near Cracow, the capital of Galicia, for two years; the last meeting of the party's central committee before the war had taken place there, in June 1914. In August, Galicia became an insecure domicile for a Russian: on 7 August the police searched Lenin's flat, and on the following

* Uniates are Catholics in union with the Holy See who nevertheless worship according to Orthodox rites.

day he was arrested. Jakob Fürstenberg, alias Kuba Hanecki, a Pole from Warsaw, a Bolshevik and Lenin's trusted friend, at once telegraphed the Austrian Social Democrat leader, Victor Adler, in Vienna. Adler assured Baron Heinold, the Minister of the Interior, that the Tsarist government had, in Lenin, the most determined enemy: on 19 August Lenin was released from prison. He packed his books, manuscripts and party correspondence, and left for Switzerland. He had to wait for the return journey until April 1917: when Heinold, who was then Governor of Moravia, heard that Lenin was on his way back to Russia via Germany, he told the German Consul General in Brno that, had it not been for his decision as Minister of the Interior in August 1914, Lenin would not be making the return trip in April 1917.*

The Lenin incident and the intervention of the Austrian Social Democrats drew the attention of the official quarters in Vienna to the Russian socialist revolutionaries. In October 1914, Romberg, the German Minister to Berne, hinted at the possibility of using them; on 26 December Bussche, the Minister to Bucharest, supported the idea.[20] Nevertheless, until the beginning of the following year, neither the Germans nor the Austrians did anything to encourage the Russian socialists. There were basic objections to that policy. Berchtold himself preferred the nationalist to the socialist Ukrainians. The Austrian Foreign Minister and his German colleague, Jagow, did not much care for the encouragement, anywhere, of social revolution. Berchtold had close personal connections with the Polish magnates, while Jagow saw in the problem a matter of principle. In contrast to the national ambitions of the minority peoples of the Tsarist Empire, social revolution was a weapon aimed at the very existence of the Tsarist regime, perhaps at the survival of the whole European order. In any case there seemed little point in using drastic measures, so long as there was a chance of concluding a separate peace with the established government in Russia.

Nevertheless, in the confusion after the failure of their military plans in the west, the German leaders soon added the policy of support of social revolution to the techniques of subversion. When Basok-Melenevski of the Ukrainian Union arrived in Constantinople, he visited an old friend, Alexander Helphand. He had first met Helphand, who was better known under his pen

* See below, pp. 229 f.

name 'Parvus', in Munich at the turn of the century. Helphand was then a Social Democrat journalist in Germany, well known for his writings on the country of his origin, Russia, as well as for his extreme revolutionary views. In 1900 he had been associated with Lenin and the editorial board of *Iskra*; five years later he returned to St Petersburg where he played, with his friend Trotsky, a prominent role in the Soviet formed in the course of the first Russian revolution. But his distinguished career as a socialist was marked by scandals of a vague and damaging kind: he left Germany for Turkey in 1910 and started trading there in corn, railway equipment and arms. He became wealthy and remained a socialist. He was undismayed by the outbreak of war and wanted to use it for the advancement of socialism.

After the arrival of Basok-Melenevski, Helphand's house in Constantinople became the meeting place of the revolutionaries – Ukrainians, Georgians, nationalists and socialists. They had one thing in common. Their activities, if successful, would result in the destruction of the Tsarist regime and the weakening of Russia's power. In their society Helphand first met Dr Max Zimmer, a gentleman farmer on the Black Sea who now supervised, on behalf of the German Embassy, the operations of subversion aimed against Russia. Early in January 1915, Zimmer introduced Helphand to the German Ambassador. Helphand made him an attractive offer. He told Wangenheim that[21]

Germany would not be completely successful if it were not possible to kindle a major revolution in Russia. . . . there would still be a danger to Germany from Russia, even after the war, if the Russian Empire were not divided into a number of separate parts. The interests of the German government were therefore identical with those of the Russian revolutionaries, who were already at work.

At the end of February 1915 Helphand was back in Germany, being interviewed by high officials at the Foreign Ministry. He elaborated on the plan he had originally put before the Ambassador in Constantinople.

For the first time in the war, the diplomats were treated to a comprehensive survey, in regard to Russia, of revolutionary strategy. With his socialist past, Helphand was a professional revolutionary who could be supremely useful to them. They had already caught a glimpse of his skill as a conspirator. Toward the end of 1914, one of the German socialist leaders was sent over to Bucharest, with official funds, to try to influence the Rumanian comrades. The mission was a failure. A few weeks later, Helphand, on his way from Constantinople to Berlin, found no difficulty in passing on the funds to his friend Christo Rakovsky, who was then editing a socialist newspaper in Bucharest.

Helphand's success with the diplomats was due partly to the fact that many of the elements of his plan were already present in Germany's wartime policy. The great attraction of his proposal was that it served two purposes: it promised, first, to eliminate Russia from the war; and second, to considerably reduce its power.

The combination of national and social revolution was to achieve precisely that aim. Social revolution, aimed at the core of the state, was expected to remove the regime bent on the continuation of the war, while national revolutions were to push back Russia's western frontier. Helphand agreed with expert opinion that the Ukrainians were placed in a key position for the latter purpose. He was not, however, very optimistic about the Caucasus: too many peoples lived there, and Helphand was not a man who liked mixing his politics with religion. He thought that the area would be best left to the care of the Turks. Wherever they existed, Helphand recommended the support of socialist parties among the minority peoples of the Tsarist Empire.

The diplomats had made arrangements for the support of the national movements on the periphery of the Tsarist Empire: it was in connection with Russian socialism that Helphand proved most useful to them. He drew their attention to the fact that Lenin and the Bolsheviks were opposed to the war and that they would therefore prove most useful. The Bolsheviks had a resolute leader who took an independent, and at that time unpopular, political line, and ran an effective revolutionary organization. The Bolsheviks, Helphand told the German diplomats, would assist them in bringing about the defeat of Russia: his policy formed a bold design for the victory of Germany and the revolution in Russia. It had a fierce dynamic quality:[22]

Agitation in the neutral states will have powerful repercussions on agitation in Russia, and vice versa. Further developments depend, to a large extent, on the course of the war. The jubilant mood that reigned in Russia in the first few days has already sobered considerably. Tsarism needs quick victories, while it is, in fact, suffering bloody reverses. Even if the Russian army merely remains pinned to its present positions throughout the winter, there will be grave dissatisfaction throughout the country. This mass mood will be exploited, deepened, extended, and spread in all directions by the apparatus for agitation sketched above. Strikes here and there, the risings produced by distress and the increase in political agitation will all embarrass the Tsarist government. If it takes reprisals, this will result in growing bitterness: if it shows indulgence, this will be interpreted as a sign of weakness and fan the flames of the revolutionary movement even more. Ample experience of this was gained in 1904 and 1905. If, on the other hand, the Russian army suffers a severe reverse, then the movement opposing the government may quickly assume undreamt-of proportions. . . .

Helphand wanted to act fast. As early as the spring of 1915, he suggested that a mass strike would cripple Russia; that the Tsarist regime would be forced to employ troops to suppress civil unrest and to protect the railways; 'the administrative apparatus will be thrown into confusion and will begin to disintegrate.' It is true that Helphand anticipated events in Russia by some two years. But his impatience was more than compensated for by his detailed knowledge of the Russian revolutionary movement. He had few illusions about the 'spontaneity' of a revolutionary situation: he knew that revolutionary mood could be used for political purposes and, in the right circumstances, deepened and extended. This was the crux of Helphand's thinking. The majority of his comrades who gave the matter consideration had no such conception of the mechanics of revolutionary action. Their belief in either the inevitability of the revolution, or in its spontaneity, sometimes blinded them to the facts of life; even a man of Lenin's calibre was surprised by every revolutionary outbreak in Russia.

On 11 March 1915, following a request from the Foreign Ministry, the Treasury in Berlin set aside 2m. gold marks for revolutionary propaganda in the Tsarist Empire. It was only a small part of a special secret fund. It was used for all the subversion enterprises: from the beginning of the war until 1 January 1918 the Germans spent 47m. in Rumania, 32m. in Persia, 10m. each in America, Italy and Spain. The budget for Russia was relatively modest: 41m. marks, out of a total of 382m., was allocated; out of this sum only 26m. was spent in the period until the end of January 1918.[23] Of the 2m. the Treasury parted with in March 1915, Helphand received 1m., plus the losses incurred in exchange in Copenhagen, Zurich and Bucharest. Contrary to the opinion of his personal and political enemies, there was no need for him to tuck the money away in numbered accounts in Switzerland. He was now a rich man, with perhaps an exaggerated faith in the effectiveness of money in politics. His revolutionary strategy was based on that faith, and there was no reason why he should have betrayed it.

Helphand's plan depended on the co-operation of the Bolshevik party. At a short meeting in Zurich in May 1915, Lenin turned the offer down, and Helphand set out to create his own organization in Russia. He was thinking in terms of a revolutionary action in Russia in January 1916. He had not much time to lose. Helphand made Copenhagen his base: for a number of decades the underground links between the exiles and the revolutionaries in Russia passed through Scandinavia; wartime business, espionage and diplomacy, the various links between Germany and Russia that had not been quite broken off after the outbreak of the war, centred on the Scandinavian capitals.

The German Minister to Copenhagen, Count Brockdorff-Rantzau, became one of Helphand's friends and, among the diplomats, his staunchest protector. Jagow, the State Secretary, liked neither Helphand nor his politics; Brockdorff-Rantzau, who after the war became the Ambassador to Moscow, was attracted to Helphand's world. He was far from being a part of it. A member of an old Holstein family related to the Danish royal house, Rantzau had served the Foreign Ministry in St Petersburg and elsewhere, becoming the Minister to Copenhagen in 1912, when he was forty-two years old. He was an intelligent, open-minded homosexual; he could be, and frequently was, icily reserved and elaborately polite. He had a liking for Helphand: not because of what he was – flamboyant, *nouveau riche*, in the company of big blondes – but because of what he stood for. Throughout the war, Rantzau advocated the achievement of a closer social cohesion in Germany. The sections of society that had stood aside before the war should now be incorporated into the body politic; it was a truly national war, and every German should regard it as his own. The socialists represented the most considerable group which had not quite belonged, and Helphand was the socialist Rantzau knew best. The Minister had not met many of them before and they could still alarm him:[24]

It *might perhaps* be risky to want to use the powers ranged behind Helphand, but it would *certainly* be an admission of our own weakness if we were to refuse their services out of fear of not being able to *direct* them.

After Lenin's refusal to co-operate, Helphand started at once recruiting Russian exiles for his own organization. Jakob Fürstenberg was Helphand's most valuable recruit. He had lived with Lenin in Cracow until the outbreak of the war and Lenin completely trusted him. He became Lenin's link with Helphand's organization. The Bolshevik leader wanted to know what Helphand was up to; Helphand, for his own part, wanted to keep open a channel of communication with the Bolsheviks. It was an arrangement that suited everybody quite well. There was no point in his trying to found a political party, an ambitious, comprehensive undertaking, covering a variety of activities, providing its members with a way of life. Such loyalty Helphand could not and did not want to command. Anyway, he had not enough time. He wanted a more limited as well as a more purposeful body: a group of conspirators associated for a specific purpose, behind some convenient, innocuous cover. In Switzerland, Helphand had started recruiting staff for a scientific, statistical institute; it was established in Copenhagen, under the name of the 'Institute for the Study of the Social Consequences of the War'. It acquired a building, a well-stocked library, and employed mainly Russian exiles. But it carried out no secret activities. It recruited revolutionaries, that was all. The Institute was in fact the cover for a cover organization. The revolutionary network was controlled by Helphand's trading company, *Handels og Eksportkompagniet*, also based in Copenhagen.

Early in August 1915, Dr Zimmer, Helphand's acquaintance from Turkey, arrived in Copenhagen to inspect Helphand's activities. He reported favourably to the Foreign Ministry on work in progress:[25]

The organization created by Parvus is now employing 8 people in Copenhagen and about 10 who travel in Russia. This work serves the purpose of contacting various personalities in Russia, as it is necessary to bring together the various disjointed movements. The centre in Copenhagen maintains an uninterrupted correspondence with the connexions made by the agents. Parvus has set aside a fund to cover the administrative costs of the organization, which is used very thriftily.

Till now it has been possible to run the whole affair so discreetly, that not even the gentlemen who work for this organization have realized that our government is behind it all.

By the end of August 1915, Helphand's organization was in operational order. The trading company started doing business, both ways, with Russia, and it could be used for political subsidies. At a time when the Bolshevik activities in Russia were severely impaired for lack of funds, Helphand launched his ambitious scheme.

It changed the course of German diplomacy in regard to Russia. The success of Helphand's preparations, the influence of Brockdorf-Rantzau, the ineffectiveness of the peace moves to date, combined to put a stop to the attempts to achieve a separate peace with the Tsarist regime. Andersen was dropped first; then a tentative exploration was made in Stockholm; finally, early in September 1915, feelers for a separate peace disappeared from the diplomatic scene altogether.

The decks were cleared for Helphand's policy: the value the German government placed on it had increased. Early in the war, the policy of subversion had, as we have seen, been no more than an extension of military tactics; as the hopes of victory faded, and the diplomats were entrusted with the task of reducing the extent of the war, the encouragement of revolution in Russia became an additional means of exerting pressure on the Petrograd government to conclude a separate peace with the Central Powers. Now, in the autumn of 1915, the policy of subversion was the only policy Germany pursued in regard to Russia. The summer offensive had put Warsaw and most of the Congress Kingdom of Poland into German hands; with the fall of Vilna, the capital of Lithuania, on 18 September 1915 and the Bulgarian mobilization three days later, military interest switched over from the Russian to the Serbian front. The Russians were to be harried by subversive activities; military defeat would facilitate anti-war propaganda; the government bent on further pursuit of war would be overthrown, and peace would be concluded with the revolutionaries. In this reckoning, there was no longer a place for the Tsarist government.

Helphand was the man who had raised and fed such hopes, and now bore a great responsibility. He had been too impatient. In his conversations in the Foreign Ministry toward the end of

February 1915, he had spoken of a 'political mass strike' that would take place in Russia in the same spring. After having recruited his own group of revolutionary agents, Helphand became more optimistic. He informed the diplomats in November:[26] 'The main thing is to stimulate the revolutionary mood. All this will have to be tackled vigorously, as according to every expectation, the revolutionary events will be concentrated around 22 January 1916.' The mass strike was upgraded to a revolution, which was to take place on the anniversary of Bloody Sunday (1905).

Throughout the autumn of 1915, Rantzau worked hard to further Helphand's plans. They were both haunted by the possibility of a separate peace with the Tsarist government, even after the danger had subsided in September 1915. Helphand feared that peace with the established regime would retard the course of the revolution; Rantzau did not like the prospect of the power of the Tsarist regime remaining unbroken on the conclusion of peace. In his report of 16 December 1915, Rantzau pleaded Helphand's cause with passion and eloquence. The Tsar, according to the Minister, was weak, insincere, corrupt, apart from bearing a frightful burden of historical guilt on his shoulders. The bond of sympathy between the Romanov and the Hohenzollern dynasties, if any still existed, must be severed once and for all. Germany, Rantzau argued, must behave like a Great Power: ruthlessly, unhindered by sentiment.

Victory and its reward, the first place in the world, will be ours if we succeed in instigating a revolution in Russia at the right time, thereby breaking up the *Entente*. After the conclusion of peace the internal collapse of Russia would be of little value to us, perhaps even undesirable.

It is certainly true that Dr. Helphand is neither a saint nor a welcome guest; he believes in his mission, however, and his competence was tested during the revolution after the Russo-Japanese war. I think we ought, therefore, to make use of him before it is too late. We should prepare ourselves for a policy with Russia which our grandchildren will, one day, call traditional, when, under the leadership of the House of Hohenzollern, the German nation has established a lasting friendship with the Russian *people*.

This goal will not be achieved until the Tsarist Empire is shocked out of its present condition. Dr. Helphand believes he can show the way, and he has made positive proposals which are based on twenty years' experience. In view of the present situation, I believe we must take the chance. The stakes are certainly high, and success not necessarily certain. Nor do I misjudge the repercussions on our internal political scene which this step can bring in its wake. If we are able to bring about a final military decision in our favour, this would be by all means preferable. Otherwise, I am convinced that all that remains is the attempt at this solution, because our existence as a Great Power is at stake—perhaps even more.[27]

Helphand received sustained support, the prominence of his plan in German strategy increased, and his responsibility was growing. He was not happy in that situation: toward the end of December 1915, he showed signs of strain. Perhaps, he told Brockdorff-Rantzau, the revolution would not take place in Russia after all; perhaps the unrest would not affect the whole country. The military should start getting ready for another winter campaign. But after the events of January 1916 he maintained that Russia would not regain its internal stability.

The strike movement in Russia early in 1916 put out of action a considerable amount of industrial plant, involved many tens of thousands of workers and at least three industrial centres engaged on the production of armaments. The Russian authorities suspected that the movement had been inspired by the enemy; there was no shortage of strike pay for the workers, and one of the factories in Nikolaev on the Black Sea had to be closed down because the workers were able to afford to stay out indefinitely. The strikes in January and February 1916 were a writing on the wall; in one country at least the civil truce had been broken on a large scale, for the first time since the wild popular enthusiasm for the war in the summer of 1914. The Allied Ambassadors to Russia were disturbed; Helphand had been right to argue that Russia would not regain stability. But no revolution had taken place.

The German government wanted quick, decisive results, and Helphand had not produced them. For over a year, from February 1916 till March 1917, the diplomats seem to have lost all interest in the millionaire Marxist and his ideas. In February 1916, they returned to exploring the possibilities of a separate peace. On 14 February, Lucius, the German Minister to Stockholm, reported on his conversation with the Swedish Foreign Minister.[28] The Minister's brother, Marcus Wallenberg, had recently visited

Petrograd; he talked to Sazonov, who looked 'moderately fresh', in contrast to the rest of the population. The Swedish Foreign Minister told Lucius that the question of peace had not been raised officially by the Russians, stressing the word 'officially', and then he went on to talk about the Straits. The Russians would achieve free passage sooner or later, he said, and it should be put to them that they could have 'peace and the Dardanelles, or the war goes on and you get nothing'. The English policy of trying to stop the expansion of Germany was as mistaken, the Swedish Minister thought, as the attempt to oppose the old Russian pressure in the direction of the Straits. In his view, Russia was the only country that could still be satisfied in a reasonable manner: there was no point in having conversations with England or France; both had 'lost their senses'. After the failure of Helphand's policy, the report from Stockholm was of exceptional interest to the Foreign Ministry. As soon as it arrived in Berlin, Jagow replied, inquiring whether the Russians had in fact put out peace feelers, whether Wallenberg could mediate, and what exactly his reference to the Dardanelles meant – possession by Russia, or only a guarantee of free passage. Turkey, Jagow added, would not agree to the former, but the latter might perhaps be achieved.[29] On the same day – 19 February 1916 – Lucius replied that, according to his impression, the Russians had not put out feelers yet, but that Wallenberg was prepared to sound them, through his brother. He told Lucius that it was in Sweden's interest to divert Russia's ambitions from the North to the Mediterranean.[30] The Swedes were too concerned with their own relations with Russia; the Wallenberg move soon lost its momentum. The businessman, Marcus Wallenberg, was then replaced by the industrial magnate, Hugo Stinnes. A modest, unassuming man and an amateur politician of extreme nationalist views, Stinnes controlled a coal, steel and shipping empire from his headquarters in the Ruhr.

Stinnes had had business contacts with Japan before the war, and knew Uchida, the Japanese Minister to Stockholm. The two men spent the evening of 30 March 1916 together. Japan was at war with Germany. It had been bound to Britain by the treaty of 1911, relating to the Far East only: on the outbreak of war in 1914, Sir Edward Grey thought that it would not be necessary for Japan to come in. The German Secretary of State was certain that Japan would come in on the German side, if only because Russia was with the Entente. He was prepared to meet most of Japan's wishes in the Far East. Though Sir Edward Grey tried hard to put them off, the Japanese were resolved to intervene on the Allied side. On 15 August 1914 they issued an ultimatum to Berlin; on 23 August, as they had received no reply, they declared war on Germany.

In March 1916 the Japanese Minister to Stockholm opened the conversation with Stinnes by remarking that Japan 'had settled its accounts with Germany for the interference in the first war against China', and that its attitude to Germany was now friendly.[31] His country, Uchida went on, had no interest whatever in the continuation of the war. He added that Japan was formally bound to Britain for four more years, but that other diplomatic combinations would be possible later; for a short while, the two men went on talking about the absence of hard feelings between Germany and Japan. Then there was raised a subject of absorbing interest to both parties: Russia. The Japanese knew of the German attempts to knock Russia out of the war, and they realized that the success of such a policy would have far-reaching repercussions on their diplomatic and military position.

Uchida told Stinnes that both Japan and Germany had a common interest in not standing in the way of Russian expansion in the Black Sea. It was a natural development and anyway, Uchida thought, Russia had too much land and could easily give some away: Poland certainly, perhaps Kurland as well. Stinnes was thinking in even bolder and more far-reaching terms. He expressed ideas on Germany's war aims which became current only in the last months of the war, and which originated in industrialist circles. He replied that the acquisitions Uchida had in mind would not be enough; they would not improve the food situation in the next war. He told the Japanese Minister that he was an industrialist, and that the German industrialists stood for the 'tough' (*stramm*) line. If Germany could not have a 'good' peace, it would rather go on fighting.

Our industrial and technical superiority was growing month by month, and if only every means is employed regardless of America, we should also in my opinion bring England to its knees. In this respect I am an advocate of the tough line, despite my great personal liking for the English.[32]

After that, the conversation between the German industrialist and the Japanese diplomat grew more animated. They agreed that their countries had the same problem in common: too little land and too many people; an alliance with Russia was indicated, after the conclusion of a separate peace. They assumed that it was easier to gain a victory over one's ally than over the enemy. Uchida told Stinnes that the Japanese Minister in Petrograd wanted Russia to carry on the war, because Japan had an interest '*in the weakening of Russia*'. The report on the conversation between Stinnes and Uchida raised a few eyebrows in the Wilhelmstrasse; Stinnes' views, however, incurred the wrath of the Secretary of State. 'That chap Stinnes', Jagow wrote to Lucius,[33]

is a high-handed type [*Gewaltmensch*] who would like to subordinate our politics entirely to his own interests. Hence an alliance with Russia, in order to bring us into fundamental opposition to the West. What can Russia offer us? First we must see what will happen to it *after* the war. Personally I am inclined to think that this time it cannot escape very serious internal revolutionary changes, and we have helpless allies enough on our hands!

Lucius then took over the negotiations from Stinnes. On 6 May 1916 the Minister to Stockholm reported that Germany would have to come to terms with Japan before Japan would approach Russia about peace; the German islands in the Pacific Ocean, now under Japanese occupation, were mentioned, as well as the cession of Tsingtau. Jagow replied that German concessions were conditional on Japan putting out feelers to Russia at once, and on the success of their action.[34] On the following day – 8 May – Arthur Kemnitz, Jagow's private secretary, began to draft the extremely complex list of concessions to be made by Germany, Japan and Russia, as well as by almost every other state involved in the war. It was one of the most elaborate and futile documents to come out of the war. On 17 May 1916, the day Kemnitz completed his labours in Berlin, Uchida told Lucius in Stockholm that his government had authorized him to say that Japan could do nothing until Tokio informed the other Entente countries of Germany's readiness to enter into negotiations. The telegram from Stockholm was forwarded to General Headquarters, where the Kaiser scribbled angrily on it:[35]

... makes not a scrap of difference. More would be achieved by thrashing! As *mediators* of a general peace, we have no need of them. W.

The Foreign Ministry, however, found it difficult to put Stinnes off. A month after the Japanese fiasco, on 17 June 1916, he sent Zimmermann a report on the negotiations between his agent in Scandinavia and Josef Kolyshko.[36] Kolyshko, a former Under Secretary of State in the Russian Ministry of Finance, and for some fifteen years Count Witte's private secretary, wanted to carry on the work that had been interrupted by Witte's death. Kolyshko was helped by his German wife, who lived in Stockholm during the war; he belonged to the ultra-conservative circle around Prince Meshchersky, the Tsar's *aide-de-camp*. Its members felt that Russia could no longer carry the burden of war, that peace would have to be concluded and followed by a *rapprochement* with Germany. They wanted to save the Tsar from himself. He did not realize how unpopular the war was becoming, he was unable to read the writing on the wall – the widespread strikes early in the year, shortage of food in the towns and of ammunition at the front, the consequences of Russia's isolation from the outside world. Stuermer, the Russian Prime Minister from January until November 1916, who in July of that year added the office of the Foreign Minister to his many cares, also belonged to the Meshchersky circle. He talked cautiously to Kolyshko (their two conversations took place early in May; Kolyshko arrived in Stockholm on 12 May 1916). Stuermer wanted to explore the ground for a possible understanding with Germany and find out who would be the most suitable negotiator. He had no objections against Kolyshko helping him, but gave him no specific commission.

In Stockholm Kolyshko discussed with Stinnes' agent the possibility of an understanding between Russia and Germany: Kolyshko mentioned some stiff conditions for a separate peace. Nevertheless, by the time Stinnes forwarded his report to the Wilhelmstrasse on 17 June 1916, the right moment for peace feelers had passed. General Brusilov's offensive on the eastern front had been launched on 4 June and affected a broad sector of the front line from Pripet in Poland to the Rumanian frontier.

Though Stinnes worked hard, he never succeeded in making a corner for himself in the 'separate peace' business. With Kolyshko's help, however, he achieved better results in a different field. When the Russian came to Stockholm in June 1915, for the first time during the war, he offered Lucius to conduct pro-German propaganda in Russia, in the *Russkoe Slavo* daily in particular. Rantzau from Copenhagen advised caution in regard to Kolyshko and his plans. Nothing came of them in the summer of 1915. In the following year, Kolyshko mentioned his plan again to Herr Bockelmann, a Foreign Ministry agent in Stockholm. Kolyshko was accompanied this time by Prince Bebutov, and the two Russians proposed setting up a publishing house in Petrograd which would specialize in pro-German propaganda. Max Warburg, the head of the Hamburg banking house, approved of the proposition, on patriotic as well as financial grounds. All these negotiations were taking place quite independently of Stinnes, who was rather cross at being left out. He kept on trying to take the initiative out of the hands of the diplomats; Lucius, however, insisted that Bockelmann was a more suitable contact with the Russians than Stinnes' agents. In the end, Stinnes was allowed to buy his way in, at a high price. He promised to lend Bockelmann 2m. roubles to finance a publishing house in Russia. On 14 August 1916 Jagow and Stinnes signed an agreement which gave the Foreign Ministry political control over the enterprise.[37] Stinnes was to have the profits, if any. The Foreign Ministry had no objection to spending Stinnes' money; for some time, the enterprise brought no visible political results. From the reports of Stinnes' agents that reached the Ministry after the revolution, in May 1917, it appeared that Kolyshko was subsidizing a newspaper called *Lutch*, and the agent suspected that some of the money had percolated to Maxim Gorky's newspaper, the *Novaya Zhizn*. He may well have been wrong. In the summer of 1917, the Russian Provisional Government arrested Kolyshko, and put an end to his doubtful usefulness for Stinnes and Berlin.

In July 1916, another hopeful start was made in Stockholm: by Fritz Warburg on the German side, and Count Olsufyev, a conservative member of the Russian Council of State, who was accompanied by Protopopov, the Vice-President of the Duma. The two Russian gentlemen – Protopopov a self-confident, fluent, worldly member of the middle class, Olsufyev a nervous aristocrat of ill-kept appearance – gave away nothing of importance. They nearly missed their train, and before they rushed off, Protopopov remarked that he hoped to see Warburg soon in peacetime while Olsufyev inquired how long Warburg was staying in

Sweden. Jagow was disappointed by the report; he wrote: 'Although the Russians brought Warburg out a lot in the conversations, they themselves in fact said nothing at all.'[38]

At the height of the summer, in July 1916, the diplomats took a short rest. The Allied offensives on the eastern and western fronts – the Italian offensive followed those in the main theatres of war – were in full swing; the Allied negotiations on Rumania's entry into the war were about to enter their concluding stage. Was it possible that the military stalemate would at last be broken? By the end of August, it was common knowledge (except in Bucharest: Rumania unwisely entered the war on 27 August) that the answer would, once again, be in the negative. On 15 August 1916, the Kaiser said that the failure of the offensives in the east and in the west would make the next few months decisive for the conclusion of peace with Russia. He asked the diplomats not to let any news concerning the negotiations with Petrograd leak out, in case a separate peace with Russia should be jeopardized.[39]

During a conversation with Grünau, the Foreign Ministry liaison officer at General Headquarters, the Kaiser revealed his ignorance of the development of German policy in regard to Russia. He said that it might be a good idea if the political leadership of the Reich established connections with Russia which could be, at a suitable military and psychological moment, used for the conclusion of peace. The most suitable people for this purpose, the Kaiser thought, would be the Jews; there was no shortage of money if winning over the right person in Petrograd to the idea of peace was at stake. Grünau replied that such people were already at hand, but that so far they had detected no inclination on the part of the Tsar's government to negotiate. The Kaiser then remarked that he had not meant his suggestion to sound as a rebuke, and that the Russian sense of solidarity with the Imperial idea – his idea – should also be appealed to. Grünau, however, felt that the Kaiser believed that peace with Russia could only follow military victory; he wrote to the Chancellor:[40]

I have the impression that his Majesty now takes the view which your Excellency has held for some time that Russia should be tackled on the field and forced out of the alliance, so that France will probably be dragged after it, and we shall have a free hand against England.

But, Grünau added, the Kaiser was not a very consistent person and, anyway, there existed little hope that troops would be available for transfer from the western to the eastern front.

Soon after he had heard the Kaiser's views, Bethmann Hollweg himself had an opportunity of discussing the problem with his Imperial Majesty.[41] The Kaiser had done some homework in the meanwhile, and was convinced that the psychological moment for peace with Russia had come. He had read a review, in a German newspaper, of a Russian book called *Why we are fighting*, and noted that the author had been unable to give any good reasons. There had also been news of a bad harvest in Russia. Expert opinion in the Foreign Ministry differed from the Kaiser's. There were conflicting reports on the harvest and in any case the Russians were used to partial famine. The German press was always avid for rumours of a separate peace; Stuermer was apparently not as fiercely dedicated to the pursuit of war as Sazonov had been, but if he tried to make a move toward peace, he still ran into difficulties with the Tsar and his court. Furthermore, Russia was bound to England and France by strong financial ties:* all in all, the Foreign Ministry did nothing to encourage the Kaiser in his belief that the Tsar might be influenced by feelings of dynastic loyalty, or that a separate peace could be concluded any time now, in the summer of 1916.[42] There was only a 'small glimmer of hope' of peace with Russia.[43]

In the autumn of 1916 that glimmer was maintained, without becoming much brighter, by the promise of a Bulgarian initiative. King Ferdinand of Bulgaria had visited the German General Headquarters in September, and on 23 October Bethmann Hollweg wrote him a letter saying that he would like to pursue further the ideas they had discussed during the King's visit.[44] They concerned peace, but no longer only a peace with Russia. The King and Bethmann had talked about reaching an agreement with the government of occupied Belgium; once again, the Belgians proved intractable because King Albert was 'watched over right and left by French and English troops, and opposed by his own government . . .' An understanding with France was, according to Bethmann, quite impossible to achieve.

Though bleeding from a thousand wounds, France is very much under English influence and in the grip of illusions nourished by its own leaders . . .

* See below, pp. 287 f.

Bethmann had, however, noted Ferdinand's hint that the King of Spain would be prepared to mediate. In England, it was useless to try. The German Chancellor complained that he could discern no great figure in the English government who could see 'beyond today into tomorrow, never mind the day after, and understand that bleeding Europe white can help only the yellow race and America'.

A general peace move, however, could be expected, Bethmann thought, from Washington. President Wilson was becoming more favourably disposed to the Central Powers, because 'in the dictionary which he uses for writing his Notes, President Wilson has found a few anti-English expressions', and he had taken a keen interest in the appointment of a new Austro-Hungarian Ambassador to Washington. Nevertheless, the presidential election was coming up on 8 November 1916, and Bethmann Hollweg found it difficult to tell where, for Wilson, electioneering stopped and any sense of responsibility for the future of the world began.

After having dutifully run through the various marginal possibilities, the Chancellor turned to the central issue. Much more than Wilson and America, Bethmann Hollweg told King Ferdinand,

> Russia remains for me the inscrutable Sphinx. Your Majesty knows how my repeated declaration of readiness to discuss peace aroused nothing but scorn and contempt on the banks of the Neva. Voices that reach me partly also through Sweden tend to indicate that the Russians are gradually growing weary of the pointless struggle.

They wanted to get Constantinople but now, Bethmann said, the situation had changed and they would have to think again. The last remaining route to Constantinople, across Rumania, had been cut off. The offensive by Bulgaria and its allies in the Dobruja and the advance of the Austro-German forces in east Rumania, as well as the battles on the Macedonian front, had closed that route, and buried the imperialist plans of Petrograd in the Balkans.

The Chancellor reassured the King of Bulgaria – he had made a similar remark in a Reichstag speech a month earlier, on 23 September – that his government did not want to appear to be fostering reaction in Russia. In any case, the Russian autocracy was weak, mainly because of the unbalanced character of the Tsar; moreover, the Russian autocracy had always operated on the principle that territorial expansion served as a safety-valve for discontent at home. For those two reasons the Russian liberals would have to be taken into consideration. At that point Bethmann got down to business. He said that he seemed to remember that Rizov, the Bulgarian diplomat who had been the Minister to Rome until 1915, and had then moved to Berlin, had very good connections with the Russian liberals. Would he be willing, the Chancellor inquired, to sound a few of his friends who were then visiting Scandinavia? Bethmann undertook in advance that he would do nothing without the King's agreement. On 11 November King Ferdinand let Bethmann know that he had requested Rizov, who had been spending a few days in Sofia, to do everything necessary in Scandinavia.[45] A week later, Jagow began to have doubts about the Russian liberals as well as about the suitability of Rizov as a negotiator. The liberals had included Constantinople among Russia's war aims, and as for Rizov, the first thing he did after his return from Sofia was to get in touch with 'Consul Marx', a banker from Mannheim, who had made some proposals on peace with Russia before, and who now repeated them, through Rizov.[46] The Bulgarian Minister left for Scandinavia on 1 February 1917, to find out from his Russian friends what the situation in their country was. The revolution broke out a few weeks later.

The last attempt at an understanding with Russia was made just when the fortunes of the war on the eastern front had turned in favour of the Central Powers. The letter from Bethmann Hollweg to King Ferdinand of Bulgaria on 23 October 1916 was in one sense misleading in that it gave the impression that peace with Russia was the Chancellor's main interest. In fact, this was not so. Some two months before Bethmann Hollweg wrote the letter, the policy of separate peace with Russia was no longer a top priority. It had not succeeded, and its failure, as well as new pressures from General Headquarters, made the Chancellor revise his views.

In the summer of 1916 the German military leaders launched behind the scenes a vigorous campaign for the declaration of unrestricted submarine warfare. It brought them into a sharp clash with Bethmann Hollweg and his supporters. The two parties to the controversy were on the whole agreed in their analysis of the overall military situation, but their proposed remedies were quite different. The military believed that the effort to stand fast on the western front was too costly and exhausting for Germany, that the effects of the blockade were beginning to make themselves felt and that the pressure would not abate, that the Allied strategy of attrition would force Germany to accept an unfavourable peace in the spring of 1917. Bethmann Hollweg's view of the situation may have been a shade more pessimistic, but it was basically similar.

The Austrians also found it difficult to maintain their customary cheerfulness. On 12 July 1916 Bussche, the German Minister to Bucharest, wrote to Zimmermann about the views on war and peace of his Austrian colleague, Ottokar Czernin, enclosing the Austrian's own memorandum. Rumania was then about to join the war on the Allied side and the Central Powers' representatives to Bucharest were deeply conscious of failure. Nevertheless, Czernin, who was soon to become Minister of Foreign Affairs, was in close touch with Vienna and with military developments on the eastern and south-eastern fronts. He was of the opinion that the human resources of Austria-Hungary would not last – he used the word '*Menschenmaterial*', one of the nastiest, in any language, to have come out of the First World War – and that the Central Powers were in every way worse placed than the Allies. He thought that 'England, the driving force behind the war, was getting off much too lightly to think of giving in and that English capital, with almost inexhaustible Russian reserves of human material as well as the supplies of the whole *world* at its disposal, can carry on this war for many years yet'.[47]

Without including the United States in his calculations, Czernin was convinced of 'the complete defeat of the central Powers with mathematical certainty'. The only question for Vienna and Berlin to ask themselves was what the most suitable moment would be for putting an end to their senseless exertions. And in order to achieve peace, so Czernin argued in July 1916, the Central Powers would have to renounce acquisitions of territory and reparations, and to show their readiness for financial sacrifice in connection with the restoration of Belgium. There must be a disarmament conference and agreements that would rule out the repetition of the First World War. It was the first time that the formula 'no annexations or indemnities' was clearly advanced in an official document of any of the belligerent countries. Though the memorandum from Bucharest was too far ahead of the thinking in Vienna or Berlin, it contributed to the pessimistic appreciation of the position of the Central Powers.

The German Chancellor, Bethmann Hollweg, was then turning away from the problems of separate to those of general peace, and Czernin's arguments, if not his conclusions, were at hand. On 16 August 1916 Bethmann informed the Kaiser that the Austrians, 'in dumb despair of their own power, are ready to accept the worst peace terms, but this does not stop them from living it up in the Wurstelprater in true Austrian style'.[48] The Chancellor painted the situation in Vienna and at Austrian General Headquarters in the darkest possible colours. At the same time, there seemed to be a good chance that President Wilson would make a peace initiative of his own. This was the way that Bethmann's thoughts turned. Bernstorff, the German Ambassador to Washington, kept on stressing in his reports that such an action might increase Wilson's, rather slim, chances in the presidential election in November 1916.

While the Chancellor was exploring the possibilities of peace through President Wilson's mediation, the intensity of the military campaign for the declaration of unrestricted submarine warfare was being stepped up. Indeed, in the second half of the year 1916 until January 1917 the two developments were so enmeshed as to be almost inseparable. President Wilson and the United States were the main links: the Chancellor and Bernstorff, the Ambassador to Washington, maintained that the declaration of submarine warfare would bring America into the war on the Allied side; the military were convinced that it would end the war before America intervened effectively.

The Germans had no separate command for their navy comparable with the British Admiralty, and decisions on naval policy were made at Supreme Headquarters. In that way Bethmann Hollweg and the politicians were placed at a disadvantage, and the German navy, the submarine arm in particular, became a pawn in the struggle between the political and military leadership. Like many other weapons used in the First World War, the submarine was almost untried. It had been used first, on a small scale and with moderate success, in the American civil war of 1861-5. It had to be used ruthlessly in order to be effective: in a way, it forced the hand of the men who employed it. It was highly vulnerable on the surface to the fire of even small calibre guns and therefore it had to operate stealthily, striking suddenly when submerged, without warning its victim. It was essentially a challenger's weapon, and the Germans, among other things, were challenging Britain's supremacy on the seas.

Nevertheless, as soon as the German military leaders raised their sights beyond the confines of the Continent, they were apt to lose their way. We have already noticed how they skimped their Moslem policy, how they expected inadequate means to produce extensive results. Though the discrepancy between the means employed and Berlin's expectations was not as striking in the case of the submarines, it nevertheless existed. In their strategic calculations, the Germans tended to overlook the tremendous advantage naval superiority gave the British, and they did not quite appreciate the skill and the resources behind it. By the end of the summer of 1916 the German military had convinced themselves that they were in a position to break England's naval supremacy.

When the war broke out in 1914 Great Britain had a fleet of 106 submarines, some of them still under construction; France had 70; Germany, 40. But many of the English submarines were old and small; the Germans had larger boats, displacing on the average 870 tons when submerged, and manned by crews some thirty-five strong. By 1914 standards most of the German submarines were large, and the outbreak of war further stimulated their construction. While the French and the British together built no more than 40 submarines during the war, the Germans added 320 boats to their fleet. It was tempting to believe that they could break the blockade of Germany, isolate Britain from the outside world and force her into submission.

As long as Bethmann Hollweg was able to prove that some hope of peace in the near future existed, he was also able to hold the military at bay. For some time, as we have seen, he relied on the readiness of President Wilson to mediate. But Bethmann was unaware of the fact that Wilson was resolved not to make foreign policy an issue in his election campaign: the controversy between Bethmann, Jagow, Bernstorff on the one side, and the Kaiser and the military on the other, was becoming sharper throughout the month of September. Then, in order to resolve the quarrel, the Emperor wrote a memorandum and ordered it to be dispatched to Washington. It was drafted in his idiosyncratic English (he maintained that nobody at the Foreign Ministry was capable of writing a simple sentence in that language); it contained the threat that if peace were not concluded soon Germany would make more use of the submarine arm. Fortunately, before the memorandum left Berlin, Bernstorff had been told, by Colonel House on 3 October 1916, that the President could do nothing for peace before the election. On the following day, by using all the powers of persuasion he possessed, Bethmann succeeded in postponing once more the declaration of submarine warfare. But time was running out for him.

The Kaiser was under the influence of the military and naval leaders at General Headquarters; Hindenburg and Ludendorff were authorized to choose their own time for a reappraisal of submarine warfare. On 7 November, President Wilson was re-elected and it took him a month before he gave the question of peace his attention. Moreover, on 24 November 1916, Jagow was replaced by Zimmermann as Secretary of State in the Foreign Ministry. From Bethmann's point of view, that was the worst omen so far. Jagow was sickly, retiring, unimpressive; he was disliked in the Reichstag, and even more by the journalists. In discussions with the military at General Headquarters, he could never hold his own. Yet he had a very good, subtle intelligence and, what was essential from Bethmann Hollweg's point of view, he was a resolute opponent of unrestricted submarine warfare. Zimmermann, on the other hand, was the very opposite of Jagow: soon after his appointment, he won a victory over Ludendorff on a minor issue of competence. But as to Zimmermann's soundness on major problems of policy, Bethmann was doubtful. Zimmermann was too ambitious, too keen to disguise his non-noble origin, too willing to oblige. Jagow, for his own part, realized that the advocates of ruthless submarine warfare would eventually win; he had been under fire from them, as well as from Prince von Bülow, who blamed Jagow for the failure of his Rome mission. Jagow felt no regrets when the time came for him to leave the Foreign Ministry.

Soon after the collapse of the Rumanian front and the fall of Bucharest on 6 December 1916, Germany's political leaders decided that they could no longer wait for a peace initiative to come from the United States, and they acceded to the Austrian suggestion that the peace offer should be made direct by the Central Powers. In a stark note of 8 December, Hindenburg agreed that 'the military situation is such that the political Reich leadership can make a peace offer',[49] on condition (1) that military and naval operations will continue as before; (2) that an army order to that effect will be published; (3) that the political leaders will bring about the kind of peace Germany needed. To his first condition Hindenburg added the rider that operations in Rumania should continue at least as far as the river Sereth, and that troops should be held in readiness for a security action against Denmark and Holland in connection with unrestricted submarine warfare, which was to be launched at the end of January 1917.

The Chancellor had no objections to the first two points; he thought the third too vague for him to comment on; he disapproved of the suggestion regarding the commencement of unrestricted submarine warfare. There were the assurances that Germany had given to the neutrals, and the Chancellor did not know whether they could be withdrawn by the end of January 1917. He did, however, agree that if the peace offer failed, surprise submarine attacks on armed merchantmen could take place, and that Washington would have to be informed beforehand of the German decision.[50] At that point, the weakness of Bethmann Hollweg's position lay revealed. He pursued peace not for its own sake alone, but also to keep the military at bay. He must have considered the possibility that, when the peace offer was formulated and made public, the Allied Powers would turn it down. In such an event Bethmann Hollweg was committed to agree to the launching of unrestricted submarine warfare.[51]

A few hours before the Chancellor announced the peace offer in the Reichstag on 12 December 1916, Zimmermann, his Secretary of State, had held a confidential press conference, at which he stated that Germany's action was intended to anticipate a similar move on the part of President Wilson. Zimmermann explained, after the war, that he said what he did in order to secure maximum support for the peace move at home. However that may be, neither the language nor the timing of the peace offer were right. President Wilson was then engaged on drafting his own Note, demanding a statement of war aims from the belligerents: he had intended to dispatch it to European capitals about the middle of the month.[52] The text of Bethmann's offer reflected the clash with the military behind the scenes: its language uneasily combined diplomatic restraint with the forthrightness of the German war lords.

The far-reaching military claims of the German peace offer jeopardized any chances of success it may have had. Its effectiveness as a piece of propaganda, though Bethmann never intended the offer to be that alone, was also reduced. It blandly stated that Germany and its allies had gained a considerable advantage over an enemy numerically and materially superior, that in fact there was no way of breaking their military strength. The document stated further that the war was a catastrophe for civilization, that Germany had been forced to take up arms to defend the justice and the freedom of national development, and that it wished now to put an end to the bloodshed. At the same time as the peace offer, the Kaiser issued an order to his forces:

Under the influence of the victory which you have gained by your bravery, I and the Monarchs of the three States in alliance with me have made an offer of peace to the enemy. It is uncertain whether the object to which this offer is aimed will be reached. You will have meanwhile, with God's help, to continue to resist and defeat the enemy.

Finally, the German government sent a simultaneous note to the Pope, asking that the efforts to secure peace might receive the support of the Holy See.

The offer was less popular abroad than in Germany. On the following day, 13 December, the *Times* leader-writer commented:

The Allies will of course be quite unmoved by all this parade of power and 'unctuous rectitude'; and so we imagine will all neutrals who have been at the pains to study the motives and the actions of Germany throughout the war. They will assign her newborn pity for the misery she has brought upon mankind, her horror of bloodshed and of the 'atrocities' of war, to very palpable causes of a wholly different order. She has been trying by all the means at her disposal to induce the United States to make a 'spontaneous' suggestion of mediation. The attempt has lamentably and conspicuously failed, and, as she does not judge that any other neutral could proffer mediation with much advantage, she falls back upon this indirect offer to the belligerents as a *pis aller*. It is in the first place, and above all things, a symptom of her conscious weakness, only because all her other hopes of hastening on the conclusion of a favourable peace before her strength has collapsed have utterly failed is she driven to this hypocritical pretence at humanity. She cherished strong hopes of a separate peace with Russia. The Tsar and his people have spurned her overtures. . . .

Lloyd George, who had recently formed a cabinet, said in a speech to the House of Commons that Germany had proclaimed itself the victor without mentioning the peace terms or agreeing to the conditions proposed by London on several occasions: full restitution and reparations and a guarantee against repetition of the war.

No one in London, Paris, Rome or Petrograd took Bethmann's offer for what it was: an action genuinely designed to put an end to the war, made in the teeth of fierce opposition at home and marred by compromises with its opponents. Instead of waiting for all the replies to come in, President Wilson made his own offer. It added little but confusion. His Note was on its way to the European capitals on the evening of 18 December; three days later, its text was generally known. It stated that it was in no way connected with the Central Powers' proposal, and that its chief purpose was to find out the belligerents' war aims.

The Kaiser spoke for all the opponents of peace in Germany when he uttered his suspicions of the American peace initiative in his usual succinct manner. He was convinced that the whole thing had been cooked up between London and Washington,[53] and wrote a long marginal note on the subject in his characteristic English style:[54]

Exclusion of Germany from the worlds trade, its destruction and partition has often enough been by every British statesmann declared as ultimate goal of the war! So that the President knows the british programm. The Powers that, like a bound of robbers, have made a surprise attack on Germany and Central Powers, with the avowed intention of its destruction, have been foiled, beaten off and crippled. They began the war, they have been beaten all along the line, they must state their intentions first. We, the party attacked, beeing on our defence purely, will state our proposals afterwards as victors and those who do not wish a recurrence of such a possibility of robbery with violence.

The German Emperor believed that the joint British-American plan was to organize a general conference with the participation of neutral states, and he thought that Wilson would then pass the German peace terms on to London. The Kaiser disliked the former possibility and abhorred the latter. The Berlin conservative newspapers went even further in interpreting the President's action as an attempt to save London from inevitable defeat. In the Wilhelmstrasse the view that Anglo-American collusion had taken place also prevailed. It was almost as if the Germans knew of the

agreement between Grey and Colonel House of 23 February 1916*
and confused it with the preparation of Wilson's peace note.

Bethmann Hollweg himself shared in the general attitude to the
American offer: this was a pitiful comedy of errors, on both sides.
The misunderstanding in Berlin of the nature of Wilson's offer
had far-reaching consequences. There were now signs that the
members of Bethmann's cabinet would be happier if the futile
attempts at general peace were abandoned and if the policy of
trying to break up the enemy alliance was rigorously continued.
A few days after Wilson's offer Zimmermann, Helfferich, the
Secretary in the Treasury, Solff, the Secretary for Colonies, and
Kühlmann, at that time Ambassador to Constantinople, met at
luncheon in Berlin. They agreed that Wilson must be stopped, by
every means, from mediating peace. They thought that it would be
impossible to come to terms with the Allied countries, and that
Germany must negotiate with its enemies directly and separately.
The disruption of the Entente was, in their view, Germany's most
important immediate aim in the war. Again, Russia was mentioned
as the main target for such a policy.[55]

The reply of the Central Powers to Wilson's Note on 26 December 1916 was drafted in the same spirit as their own peace offer.
The Germans and their allies agreed in principle that peace negotiations should be opened immediately at a neutral place. But they
were reticent as to peace terms: the Ambassador to Washington
was privately informed that Wilson's participation in the conference was out of the question.[56]

The quick reaction from Berlin made a brisker and sharper
Entente reply possible; the confusion created by the two peace
initiatives, from Berlin and from Washington, now became
apparent. The French Prime Minister, Briand, handed over to the
American Ambassador to Paris, on 30 December 1916, a note
which was in fact an answer to the Central Powers' offer of
12 December. The Allied governments refused to entertain a proposal 'without sincerity and without import' which appeared 'less
as an offer of peace than as a manœuvre of war'.[57] The Allied
answer to Wilson's offer was ready only on 10 January 1917. It
made a very bad impression in Berlin and especially in Vienna by
its ambiguous reference to the liberation of Italians, Rumanians,
Slavs and Czechoslovaks from foreign domination. From now on,

* See below, p. 185.

politicians in Vienna were convinced that the Allies desired the dismemberment of Austria-Hungary, though in fact this was not so.

More and more, Bethmann found it difficult to resist the combined forces of his opponents. Zimmermann was now fully committed to the military camp; Ludendorff thought that making conciliatory gestures to the enemy was incompatible with Germany's honour. In a letter from Bethmann Hollweg to Hindenburg, written on 4 January 1917, the two main strands of the Chancellor's foreign policy – separate and general peace – were hopelessly tangled up:[58]

... when we finally sit down with our enemies at a conference table, our main task, apart from achieving our war aims, will have to consist in using all those opportunities in the course of the negotiations which would lead to a split in the enemy coalition. ...

Five days later the declaration of unrestricted submarine warfare in the near future was decided upon, and the Chancellor's policies lay in ruins.

From November 1914, when the German war leaders realized the failure of their military plans, until September 1916, when their diplomatic initiative faded out, the actions of Bethmann Hollweg and of the German politicians aimed at helping the military. Encouragement of the Russian revolutionaries or separate peace with the Tsarist government, subversion and diplomacy, were expected to succeed where the soldiers had failed. The second half of the year 1916, however, witnessed a tragic race between Bethmann Hollweg, the German military, and President Wilson.

Bethmann Hollweg has often been criticized in Germany on the grounds that he opposed energetic action against England. It is true that he resisted the introduction of unrestricted submarine warfare because he wanted to avoid a fight to the death against the British Empire and because he did not want to provoke the neutral states, especially America. He held a pessimistic view of Germany's position in a global engagement and he genuinely wanted to bring about a general peace. But he diminished the small chances of achieving it because he used the promise of peace to restrain the military, and because he did not allow himself enough time for the execution of that policy.

4 Vienna

For three years of the war, from 1915 until 1917, the Austrians had a run of military success. They took no part in the technically accomplished but static fighting on the western front: the events in the eastern and the south-eastern theatres of war appeared more clear-cut, more decisive. Comparing the Allied progress in the West with that of the Central Powers elsewhere, Field-Marshal Sir Henry Wilson wrote in his diary: 'We take Bullecourt, they take Rumania; we take Messines, they take Russia; we don't take Paschendaele [sic], they take Italy.'[1] Year after year, the peoples of the Central Empires received the customary Christmas present from their armed forces. In 1915 the Russians were forced to abandon much of their territory east of the border with Germany, including a large part of Poland; the Austrians occupied Belgrade, and the Bulgarians began their advance into Serbia. In December 1915 Burián, the Foreign Minister, wrote to the Chief-of-Staff that the purpose of the war was to 'win the greatest possible increase in power and security'.[2] In 1916, after Rumania's entry into the war on the Allied side, Bucharest fell early in December, and soon the Austrian and German armies occupied most of the country's territory. It was in 1917, however, that the Central Powers achieved their most spectacular success in Russia as well as in Italy. In a sense, military success was a misfortune in disguise for the Austrians. It made them carry on the war too long.

After two years of total war, as the dull and bloody year of 1916 drew to its close, some change for the better was expected in all the belligerent countries. In the end, in London, Asquith's government gave way to Lloyd George's approximation to a dictatorship; in Russia the influence of Rasputin, 'the mad monk', was complemented by his assassins, who believed that they were clearing a path for political reform; in Vienna the death of the Emperor Franz Josef marked the end not only of a phase of the war, but of an historical era.

EAST AND SOUTH-EAST EURO

Victory in Rumania in December 1916 had the usual unsettling effect on the deliberations of the politicians in Vienna. Rumania's declaration of war in August of that year had brought to the fore the threat of starvation, especially in the industrial areas of Austria. The Allied blockade had begun to make itself felt, and now there was added to it the severance of food supplies from Rumania. Economic difficulties hit the Habsburg state in its most sensitive spot. The two meetings of the Council of Ministers for both Austria and Hungary in September and October 1916 dealt exclusively with the question of food supplies. The Austrians became convinced that the Magyar magnates in Budapest, who had the political power as well as the corn, were holding out on them: an Austrian remarked later that he could forgive the blockade by the enemy, but not by the Hungarians. It may be that the ties of a prosperous economy were strongest among the peoples of the Empire, and as the economy grew weaker, as it was transformed from an economy of plenty into one of scarcity, those ties were loosened. The peoples of the Empire found no appeal whatever in Hindenburg's grim slogan, '*Durchhalten!*' They were unwilling to go as far in making sacrifices as their German comrades in arms.

Since early in the war, when the thoughts of Germany's war leaders addressed themselves to peace, they thought of it largely in terms of a separate peace and its strategic advantages. The Austrians, on the other hand, did not begin giving the problem serious consideration until later, and their approach was different. On 5 November 1916 Burián wrote to Conrad, the Chief of General Staff:[3]

I am convinced that the key to the situation lies in the West. If Germany gives away France and Belgium and a bit more, then peace will come. The Chancellor has promised me, in strict confidence, to make the sacrifice. I cannot exercise pressure in that direction with any success if I make it clear to him at the same time that we intend to create every kind of difficulty for him in the East (Poland). Only if we concentrate on the Balkans and sell out Poland to Germany, can the idea of a partial cession of Alsace-Lorraine take shape.

Burián did not, however, carry the burden of office much longer. In Austria, the internal changes at the end of the year 1916 were more far-reaching than in the other belligerent countries. On 21 November, a few days before the sixty-eighth anniversary of his accession to the throne, Emperor Franz Josef died. His successor entered upon an unenviable inheritance. Emperor Karl's great-uncle had personified, for longer than most of his subjects could remember, the dignity and the power of the House of Habsburg. There had been a formidable, paternalistic aura about the late Emperor, the stuff of which personality cults are made of. Karl was twenty-nine years old, handsome and slight: when he was crowned King of Hungary in Budapest, the ancient Crown of St Stephen came down over his eyes, covering half of his face. Like the German Kaiser, Karl was fond of rapid changes from one splendid uniform into another.

Emperor Karl was impressionable, and for an estimate of a man's character he relied too much on other people's judgement, and on the judgement of his wife in particular. He had married Zita in 1911; she was the daughter of Duke Robert of Parma, who had lost his throne in his youth, during the unification of Italy. She was educated in Bavaria and on the Isle of Wight; she was a very pious Catholic: she was pretty, she had charm and she spoke several languages. Her gentleness sometimes deceived: on one occasion during the war she let a German Admiral feel the sharpness of her tongue. After he had carried on about 'sticking it out' and 'tightening the belt' at Zita's table one night, she put an end to these expressions by telling the Admiral that she disliked 'to hear talk of sticking it out at a well-laden table'.

As a member of a family with wide dynastic ramifications, Zita was something of a political liability. Her mother tongue was Italian; her two brothers, Prince Sixtus and Prince Francis Xavier, were officers in the Belgian army with distinguished service on the Flanders front to their credit. The Emperor's service on the Italian front had been his only important experience of the wider world of men and affairs. There were many politicians in Vienna who expected Karl to bring about far-reaching changes when he succeeded to the throne, and he was always rather anxious to please. In the ways that mattered most, the last two Habsburg Emperors were totally different. Franz Josef had had a great deal of political experience and no desire whatever to experiment: Karl was inexperienced, and enthusiastic about new, unorthodox ways of dealing with political affairs.

Vienna's relations with Berlin were the test case of Karl's political skill. In peacetime the German alliance had been, for nearly four decades, the king-pin of Franz Josef's policy; the war put it to a severe strain. Soon after the opening of the hostilities the Austrian army command became convinced that their German colleagues were wilfully neglecting the eastern front; then there were the differences that arose out of the Italian and Turkish negotiations and, more recently, sharp dissension on the future of Poland. The German Ambassador to Vienna frequently wrote in his dispatches of the 'spirit of Sadowa' that had survived in Austrian ruling circles since the Habsburg and Prussian armies last met on the battlefield in 1866. The Germans, moreover, had a nagging feeling that, with Austria for an ally, the chances of their victory were greatly diminished; while the Austrians feared being dragged into defeat and disaster by the Germans, who, they suspected, did not quite know when to stop.

Karl succeeded to the throne at a time of another crisis in the relations between the allies. Since the end of 1915, it had been generally assumed in Vienna that the Congress Kingdom – the former Russian Poland, now occupied by the German and Austrian armies – would become connected, by a personal union, with the Habsburg Empire. There had at first been no serious opposition to the idea in Berlin. The Germans accepted the Austrian plan, but no public announcement was made: as long as there was a chance of a separate peace with Russia, the *Auswärtiges Amt* refused to jeopardize it in any way. In the spring of 1916, however, it became apparent that the German military authorities in occupied Poland preferred a different solution. They envisaged an autonomous state, reaching as far east into Russian territory as possible, with frontier rectifications on the new state's western side in Germany's favour. The status of the Prussian and Austrian parts of Poland was not to be affected. In August 1916, the Austrians, without much enthusiasm, agreed to the German proposal; on 5 November 1916, the German and Austrian Emperors announced their intention of establishing an autonomous Polish state.

After having made the technical concession to Germany, the Austrians continued to hope for a high degree of influence on the new state. That was only a part of the misunderstanding. They had given way, in the first place, because the German Chancellor promised to make considerable sacrifices in the West. But the day before Burián informed the Chief-of-Staff of Austria's readiness to make sacrifices* Bethmann Hollweg drew up a catalogue of war aims that included the retention, by Germany, of the Longwy and Briey territory in France, a demand for far-reaching guarantees in Belgium, and possibly a strip of Belgian territory including Liége.[4] Finally, toward the end of 1916, the defeat of Rumania merely broadened the area of misunderstanding between Vienna and Berlin. The future of Rumania, viewed from Vienna, was an open question: the Austrians were not fully aware of the extent of German commercial commitment in that country. Whatever promises Bethmann Hollweg may have made to Burián, it did not look as if Germany was about to give up its ambitions in the west and turn to the east, for the sake of Austria and peace.

Emperor Karl's succession was marked by misunderstanding and friction with Berlin. A great deal was expected of him, and the choice of his new advisers indicated that Karl knew what it was. The Magyar influence on the foreign policy of the Empire gradually diminished: Burián left the Foreign Ministry in December 1916 and, a few months later, Tisza, the tough defender of Magyar supremacy, was dislodged as the Hungarian Premier. Two members of high Bohemian aristocracy were raised to positions of prominence: Ottokar Czernin succeeded Burián and Clam-Martinitz was asked to form a new Austrian government.

Czernin, the former Austrian Minister at Bucharest, had had little to do since Rumania's declaration of war; his name had been connected with the examination of the chances of peace at a time when no one in Vienna was much concerned about it. A Habsburg aristocrat, Czernin felt no need to identify himself with any particular nationality; he had a conviction that men of his class and background were best suited to assist the Habsburgs in ruling their dominions. He was an experienced diplomat who saw the international scene more comprehensively and clearly than either Berchtold or Burián had done. He was acutely aware of the weaknesses of Austria's internal situation; peace was for him not a tactical move but a necessity dictated by the inconclusive development of the war. Czernin understood a lot but changed little. He was an excitable man, usually overworked, and always nervous. He got on badly with those who worked for him: he found it difficult to make friends and impossible to retain them. He had been a member of Archduke Franz Ferdinand's circle – after the

* See above, p. 123.

Sarajevo assassination he said: 'My sun went down with the Archduke' – but his acquaintance with Karl was only superficial. As long as he remained in office, Czernin failed to establish a relationship of trust with Karl and his family.

Their understanding of the need for peace was the strongest tie between the Emperor and his Foreign Minister. At the first meeting of the Austro-Hungarian Council of Ministers at which Karl took the chair, on 12 January 1917, he raised the question of war aims and with that, the question of peace.[5] The Emperor suggested that there existed two ways of looking at the problem of war aims. The maximum demands, by Austria, would include the incorporation of Poland and of Montenegro, 'rectifications' of the frontier in Transylvania, the replacement of the Karadjordjević dynasty in Serbia by another. The minimum demands, on the other hand, would be confined to the preservation of the 'full integrity of the territory' of the monarchy, the acquisition of Mount Lovchen, commanding the Bay of Cattaro, the biggest Austrian naval base in the Adriatic, and the change of the dynasty in Serbia (the Karadjordjević princes had deeply annoyed the Austrians before the war).

Conrad, the Chief-of-Staff, was present at the meeting and it may have been for his benefit that Czernin said that Austria was engaged in a defensive war and that in any case the achievement of total victory was improbable and therefore peace would have to be one of compromise. In the circumstances, Czernin pointed out, the preservation of the Empire's territorial integrity would be a considerable achievement. Military considerations would of course, he added, come into play at the time of the conclusion of peace. Austria would have to have Mount Lovchen, an improvement of its frontier in the region of the Iron Gates on the Danube, as well as at Braşov in Transylvania. The Entente, Czernin went on, could hardly allow a complete disruption of the smaller Balkan states; they might put up with an extensive carving up of Rumania (its allies, he thought, had as low an opinion of Rumania as its enemies), in the course of which Russia would take Moldavia, but no more than that. In the new circumstances, Austria and Russia might well improve their relations after the war.

Czernin made his most important point, however, when he dealt with the problem of reparations. He said that in the interest of an early peace it should be suggested to the Entente, and especially to England, that there will be neither victors nor vanquished in the war. That would rule out reparations, as they could be collected only from a truly defeated country. Czernin's formula of little annexations and no indemnities anticipated a demand that was yet to come; he in fact advanced the idea on which President Wilson was to elaborate ten days later. In his speech to Congress on 22 January 1917, President Wilson said:[6]

It must be a peace without victory. . . . I am seeking only to face realities and to face them without soft concealment. Victory would mean peace forced upon the loser, a victor's terms imposed upon the vanquished. It would be accepted in humiliation, under duress, at an intolerable sacrifice, and would leave a sting, a resentment, a bitter memory upon which terms of peace would rest, not permanently, but only as upon quicksand. Only a peace between equals can last.

For the Austrians, peace was the logical conclusion of a war which brought them economic privations and internal stress, sometimes defeats, more often victories of doubtful political value. The general agreement on the necessity of peace which existed in Vienna at the outset of the year 1917 was reciprocated, as we shall see, in two Allied capitals at least.

The Austrian peace offensive of 1917 opened with a skirmish in Scandinavia. On 10 January 1917 the British Foreign Office received a telegram from the British Minister at Christiania about a visit he had had from Axel Christiansen, a merchant and a pioneer of the Danish film industry. The Dane had information, from Austrian sources, about the possibility of peace between the Entente and the Habsburg monarchy. His Austrian contacts – Baron Franz, a Counsellor at the Austrian Legation to Copenhagen, and Herr Ernst Westfried, who manufactured dynamite in Austria and owned landed property in Hungary – indicated that Czernin, the Minister of Foreign Affairs, was ready to send a representative to Denmark, to meet his British counterpart. It appeared that Austria was in severe straits and Christiansen was also given to understand that Germany must know nothing of the negotiations, which should be pushed forward as fast as possible.

In London on 18 January, six days after the meeting of the joint Austro-Hungarian cabinet in Vienna, Balfour brought the matter before the War Cabinet. He said that Emperor Karl's recent choice of Ministers pointed to his desire to emancipate himself from the influence of Berlin, and that the forthcoming changes in Austrian representation at The Hague and Berne were also significant. There were indications, he thought, that Austria was anxious to negotiate peace. That it was a separate peace that Austria wanted appears to have been taken for granted by the War Cabinet. The Chief of the Imperial General Staff was of the opinion that such a peace would be an advantage from the military point of view, as it would eliminate 47 Austro-Hungarian divisions on the eastern front, leaving 149 Russian divisions to deal with 78 German divisions. The War Cabinet in the end agreed that the Secretary of State for Foreign Affairs should let the Allied Ambassadors in London know that he proposed to respond to the Austrian peace feelers in order to find out whether any real offer was intended. Balfour did not wish to take anyone by surprise. He wanted to know whether any of the Ambassadors had objections to make to his proposed course of action, and he offered to consult them before entering on negotiations.[7]

On the following day, 19 January 1917, the Foreign Office informed the Minister at Christiania that the War Cabinet were sceptical as to the credentials of Messrs Christiansen & Co., but that they had decided to investigate the matter. On 1 February, Sir Francis Hopwood left London on a tour of the Scandinavian capitals. He was following a faint trail: apart from the Christiania telegrams, there had been no other traces of an Austrian desire for peace. Sir Francis Hopwood was not a happy choice for a mission of that kind. He was a civil servant and an accomplished chairman of committees; his experience of international negotiations derived largely from conferences on railways. He was not an easy man to know. The Austrians had occasion to find this out: when Sir Francis arrived in Norway he made no move. He disliked the way Sir Mansfeldt Findlay, the British Minister, pressed for a meeting with a prominent Austrian and he disapproved of the fact that Sir Mansfeldt was on good terms with the Austrians. Moreover, a noticeable increase in the activity of German agents in Scandinavia soon after Sir Francis's arrival in Bergen on a Norwegian torpedo-boat – the Norwegians had not allowed the Royal Navy destroyer to take Hopwood all the way to Bergen – indicated that caution was necessary. It was possible, Sir Francis thought, that the Germans had got wind of their ally's intentions; in any case, German agents were keeping a close watch on the movements of the Austrians.[8]

In the end, Balfour's special emissary left Christiania as soon as he conveniently could. The British Minister there was convinced of the Austrians' good faith, but he failed to bring them and Sir Francis together. Hopwood's brief was to establish what the Austrians were up to, but he had no powers to negotiate with them. The Minister telegraphed to London asking that Lord Milner should be sent over to Christiania as negotiator; Sir Francis left the Norwegian capital for Copenhagen, and from there he advised the Foreign Office to await his *bona fide* report before going any further. On arriving in Copenhagen Sir Francis at once got in touch with the Austrian agents. But Christiansen and Westfried produced neither credentials nor an official from the Austrian Legation, though an Austrian diplomat was found lurking in the bushes near the villa that was a possible place of assignation. There were other incidents that further annoyed Sir Francis. Count Albert Mensdorff-Pouilly-Dietrichstein, the former Ambassador to London and one of the ablest members of the Austrian diplomatic service, arrived in Scandinavia about the same time as Hopwood. Rumours began to circulate, and a Danish lady told the British Minister at dinner that at luncheon on that very day the Austrian Minister had assured her that 'Austria would have peace in two months, and that something was now going on in Copenhagen'.

It remained a pious hope. At times it appeared as if Sir Francis Hopwood was doing his best to jeopardize the success of his mission; from beginning to end there was a tragi-comic element about it. Sir Francis, together with the British Minister to Copenhagen, met Hans-Niels Andersen on at least two occasions. There was no surer way of letting Berlin know that the official explanation for Sir Francis's Scandinavian trip – the discussion of commercial and blockade matters with the British Ministers – was only a cover. Andersen, who had acted as Ballin's partner in the 1914–15 negotiations with Germany, had enough time, between his meetings with Sir Francis, to visit Berlin and talk to the Chancellor and other German politicians, and return to Copenhagen with an offer from the German government that they would send a representative to the Danish capital at once, to discuss peace with the English emissary. Later in the month, the German offer and its rejection by the British government ruled out a meeting between Hopwood and Mensdorff, and on their subsequent

Scandinavian travels the two men did their best to avoid each other. Apart from a formal promise by the King of Denmark to mediate, if need be, a general peace, and the opinion that Austria's endeavour was serious, though clumsy, Sir Francis brought nothing back with him from his mission.

While Sir Francis Hopwood was travelling unprofitably in Scandinavia, the French established a promising contact with Vienna. The family of the Empress Zita had been divided by the war. Two of her brothers had joined the Austrian army, while the elder two Princes – Sixtus and Francis Xavier – had thought it more fitting, for descendants of the Bourbon Kings, to fight on the Allied side. They became the *dramatis personae* in a new Austrian peace move. It was one of many similar moves across the board of European diplomacy in that year; it became the most famous because of its delayed effect: a year later, Clemenceau's revelations discredited the young Emperor, caused an internal crisis in Austria-Hungary, deepened Vienna's dependence on Berlin, and shattered any lingering hopes of peace that might still have existed in the Habsburg capital.

In 1917, however, the two brothers had the confidence of the French government because of their distinguished service in Flanders; in Vienna, they had an easy entry into the highest court and political circles. Their basic loyalty belonged to their family. If they succeeded in mediating peace, they knew their family would benefit: it would become united, retaining one throne and perhaps gaining others.

While the Bourbon-Parma Princes were trying to help Karl to achieve peace, the extent was revealed to which the Emperor was under the influence of his wife and her strong-minded family. Toward the end of January 1917, Princes Sixtus and Xavier went on leave from the Belgian army to Switzerland, where they visited their mother. She had urgent news from her daughter, the Empress Zita, so urgent in fact that the Princes at first considered going to Vienna straightaway. In the end, however, they wisely decided to get an agreement to their journey into enemy territory from the French authorities.

By 17 February 1917 the Princes had returned to Switzerland for a meeting with their childhood friend and representative of Emperor Karl, Count Erdödy.[9] The opening moves were so promising that a month later the two Princes set out, with the knowledge of the French government, on a very secret mission. Their destination was the Imperial castle of Laxenburg; there they met their sister and her husband as well as Czernin. The Foreign Minister introduced a certain element of discord into the family reunion. Sixtus thought Czernin 'tall, thin, chilly', his conversation 'glacial'. The following day, Sixtus met the Foreign Minister again, at Count Erdödy's house in Vienna, without a marked rise in temperature. The reason for this was the two divergent – and on one side, not precisely formulated – attitudes to the question of peace. Czernin resolutely opposed the idea of a separate peace: the Imperial family, on the other hand, were quite ready to consider it. In Czernin diplomatic experience engendered caution, even pessimism; the Emperor acted under no such restraint. On 24 March 1917, he drafted the notorious 'Sixtus letter'. The following is the official Foreign Office translation:

My dear Sixtus,

The third year of this war that has brought the world so much mourning and sorrow is coming to an end. All the peoples of my Empire are united more closely than ever in a common will: to preserve the integrity of the Monarchy even at the cost of the heaviest sacrifices. Thanks to their unity, thanks to the generous co-operation of all the nationalities of my Empire, the Monarchy has been able to withstand, it will soon be three years, the most severe assaults. Nobody can deny the achievements won by my armies, especially in the Balkan theatre of war.

France has also shown magnificent power of resistance and dash. We all admire, without reservation, the traditional bravery of her army, and the spirit of dedication of the whole French people.

Although we are enemies at the present moment, I note with special pleasure that my Empire is not divided from France by any real clashes of interest, and that my lively sympathies for France, shared by the whole Monarchy, justify my hope that it will be possible to avoid in the future the repetition of the war for which I am not responsible. Therefore, so that I can prove precisely the sincerity of my feelings, I beg you to let the President of the French Republic, M. Poincaré, know in a secret and unofficial way that I shall support the just claims of France to Alsace-Lorraine in every way and with all my personal influence.

Belgium must be re-established as a sovereign state, retaining all its African possessions, notwithstanding the compensations she may receive for the losses inflicted upon her. The sovereignty of Serbia will be re-established and, as a token of our good-will, we are inclined to guarantee her an equitable and natural access to the Adriatic, and far-reaching economic concessions. Austria-Hungary, on the other hand, will demand as indispensable condition that the Kingdom of Serbia disassociates itself from, and suppresses the tendency for the disintegration of the Monarchy, especially the *Narodna Odbrana*,* that it shall faithfully and by all means in its power stop that kind of agitation in Serbia and outside her frontiers, and that it will make a pledge to that effect under the guarantee of the Entente Powers.

The recent events in Russia oblige me to withhold comment on that subject until the final formation of a legal government.

After having disclosed my ideas to you, I should like to ask you to let me know, after a previous consultation with the two Powers, the views of France and England, so that a basis for official and mutually satisfactory negotiations may be laid.

Hoping that in this way we shall soon be able, on both sides, to put an end to the suffering of so many millions of men and of so many families that live in sorrow and anxiety.

I beg you to believe in my kindest and most fraternal regards,

Karl.

Emperor Karl had little French, and was unable to write a long letter in that language. He drafted the original in German, and then had it translated, rather freely, by Sixtus. The translation was the first link in a fateful concatenation of blunders. It now appears that Czernin, although he met the Bourbon Princes and had taken a part in the negotiations, knew nothing of the letter or of the absence of any reference in it to Berlin. Had he known of this, he would not have referred to the negotiations in a public speech a year later. The Emperor did not seem to appreciate fully the difficulties involved in the conclusion of a separate peace, nor did he realize that for such an enterprise the support of his Foreign Minister was even more essential than the approval of his family. He lightheartedly broke faith with his Minister as well as with the constitution.

Neither was the timing of the letter right. The French were just about to launch their offensive on the western front; Emperor Karl's reference to 'the recent events in Russia' was a euphemism for the revolution; on 2 April 1917, President Wilson declared war on Germany (though not yet on Austria); a week later, Lenin

* lit. 'National Defence': an anti-Austrian organization based on Belgrade which specialized in cultural propaganda. The Austrian authorities were unaware of the existence of the 'Black Hand', the secret terrorist organization which was responsible for the assassination of Archduke Franz Ferdinand.

boarded the train in Zurich that took him across Germany, back to Russia.

It was not until 11 April that Lloyd George heard of the letter from the Emperor Karl. On that day, Alexandre Ribot, the Premier who was his own Foreign Minister and who had replaced Briand's cabinet three weeks earlier, was met by Lloyd George on Folkestone Quay. In the falling rain, urgently, the Prime Minister was told of the offer from Vienna: 'That means peace' was his immediate reaction. His second thought was that the Italians – but not the Russians – must be consulted. At their Folkestone meeting, when Lloyd George was given a copy of Emperor Karl's letter, nobody apart from the two Premiers was present. Lloyd George was bound by a personal pledge of secrecy which made it impossible for him to inform his cabinet; he did, however, stipulate that he must be allowed to inform the King. A few days after the meeting, Lloyd George told his colleagues that he had arranged to attend a conference with Ribot and Sonnino on the Italian frontier on Saturday 21 April. Newspaper reports in circulation at the time about an offer of peace by Austria to Russia made it possible for Lloyd George to discuss the matter, in a general way, in the cabinet before his departure. Once again, the War Cabinet agreed that the withdrawal of Austria from the war would be beneficial from the military point of view.

On the day of the cabinet meeting, 17 April, Lloyd George left for the Continent, accompanied by the Director of Military Intelligence and the Secretary of the War Cabinet. At the Hotel Crillon in Paris, the Prime Minister received a visit from Prince Sixtus. No record of their conversation was made; it is very likely that Lloyd George asked questions about the terms of the Austrian offer, and that Prince Sixtus inquired about the Italians' attitude, and sought reassurance as to the secrecy of the proceedings. He had shown concern about these two subjects before, and Cambon tried to put the Prince's mind at rest. He told Sixtus that Sonnino was entirely trustworthy because he had a Scottish mother. The Prince may have continued to have doubts about the Italian Foreign Minister; it was impossible for the French and the English Premiers to maintain an absolute and exclusive secrecy. The circle of the people who knew of the Austrian offer grew slowly, but dangerously. Before the meeting with Sonnino, Jules Cambon, the Secretary-General at the Quai d'Orsay, had seen Prince Sixtus;

on the train from Paris to the Italian frontier, Lloyd George told the Secretary to the War Cabinet, Sir Maurice Hankey, 'in case anything happened to me', of the existence of the letter from the Habsburg Emperor.

In a railway carriage at St-Jean-de-Maurienne, the Prime Ministers discussed with Baron Sonnino the question of peace with Austria. But – possibly as a result of the intervention, in Paris, by Prince Sixtus – the Italian Foreign Minister was told nothing about the letter from Emperor Karl. And as far as peace with Austria was concerned, Sonnino was very much against it. He would not move from that position even when reminded by Lloyd George of the rumours then in circulation about peace between Austria and Russia and of the considerable Austrian forces that would be transferred, in the event of the conclusion of peace, from the Russian to the Italian front. After lunch, the conversation turned to subjects of greater interest to Baron Sonnino: Italian aspirations in Asia Minor and Greece. Nevertheless, toward the end of the day and of the conference, the subject of Austria came up again. Sonnino told his allies that the Italians could be induced to fight no other war than that against Austria, and warned them that offers of a separate peace were aimed only at dividing the alliance.

After further discussions between the French Premier and Prince Sixtus in Paris, Emperor Karl, having been told of the difficulties made by the Italians, wrote, on 9 May 1917, another letter. The same routine was probably followed as in March, and the Emperor copied a draft of it made by his brother-in-law. In its first paragraph, the letter contained an ill-considered, almost gratuitous, lie. The letter began, again in the official Foreign Office translation:

My dear Sixtus,

I write with satisfaction that France and England share my views on what I believe is the essential basis for a European peace: they will however not have peace without the participation of Italy. But Italy has offered me peace with the Monarchy, giving up all the impossible claims to the South Slav territory she had been making up to now. She confines her demands to the Italian Trentino alone. I have postponed the examination of this demand until I hear from you the answer from Britain and France to my peace feelers. . . .

Sonnino had not offered Austria peace. There are two explanations possible for Emperor Karl's clumsy attempt to deceive. He was resolved, at the time of the first meeting with Sixtus at Laxenburg in March, not to let Berlin know about the negotiations; nevertheless, after pressure from his Foreign Minister, he allowed Czernin to inform the German Chancellor. Soon after the Bourbon Princes left for Paris, Bethmann Hollweg arrived in Vienna; Czernin told the Chancellor about the negotiations without going into any detail. (In fact the news of the negotiations was known in Berlin a fortnight before it reached London.) He had been forbidden by Emperor Karl to give away the names of the people involved: it should not have been difficult for Bethmann to guess. On 3 April, Karl, Zita and Czernin visited the Kaiser at Bad Homburg, and again the problem of peace was raised. Indeed, since February 1917, the Germans knew that the Austrians were bent on negotiating peace, and that they had taken steps to that end. It has been suggested[10] that the opening paragraph of Karl's letter of 9 May 1917 had been inspired by Berlin: an intrigue aimed at dividing the Allies, which Sonnino had all along suspected the Austrians of hoping to do. The theory of collusion between Berlin and Karl is, however, difficult to uphold. It attributes more cunning to Karl than he naturally possessed, and it would have made unnecessary his Canossa in May 1918 when, after Clemenceau made his March letter public, Karl had to go and make his supplication before the Kaiser at the German General Headquarters.

The simpler explanation of the reference to Italy's peace offer is the more likely. When Karl made a statement quickly or under stress, the truth of it was sometimes questionable. His Foreign Minister remembered a number of such occasions, and the last one forced him to resign.

But to return to London and Paris. Here, in May 1917, a new apprehension made the western Allies take another look at their strategy. On 9 May, the day Karl wrote his second letter, the War Cabinet considered, for the first time, the situation which would arise if Russia made a separate peace. Lloyd George pointed to the effect such an event would have on the blockade and on the western front, where great German forces would be transferred from the East, and went on:[11]

In such circumstances, the best chance for the Allies would appear to lie in a separate peace with Austria, in which Italy might be compelled to acquiesce. If we failed to induce Austria to make a separate peace,

I can see no hope of the sort of victory in the War that we desired. In these circumstances, it might be necessary to make a bargain with Germany for evacuating Belgium and for the restoration of her colonies . . .

The meeting concluded that 'our diplomacy should, if possible, be used to assist the military situation' and that if Russia were to go out of the war every possible effort should be made to secure a separate peace with Austria. But the flaw in such a policy, the cabinet realized, was that

if the Central Powers considered that the withdrawal of Russia rendered victory to them probable, it would be difficult to secure a separate peace unless their exhaustion and general desire for peace outweighed their hopes of victory.

The discussion at the cabinet meeting on 9 May 1917 had anticipated Lord Curzon's consideration of the subject of a possible Russian defection in a memorandum he was then writing. Lord Curzon, who had consulted the memoranda by the First Sea Lord and the Chief of the Imperial General Staff, saw no reason why either Austria or Turkey or Bulgaria should

sever themselves from an Alliance which has already proved to be so successful in so far as its main objects in Eastern and Central Europe are concerned, and from which they are more likely to derive advantage in the future, even at the expense of German domination, than from anything which we are at present in a position to offer them.

The only brighter feature in the situation was the fact that

Austria, Bulgaria, and Turkey are nearing the brink of exhaustion, and as soon as the present menace from Russia disappears, Germany will not be able to get more than a moderate degree of military exertion out of any of them during the remainder of the war.

In the spring of 1917, politicians and soldiers on both belligerent sides were faced with difficult strategic problems. It was not yet possible to assess the effects either of unrestricted submarine warfare or of America's entry into the war; the positions of both Russia and Austria within their respective alliances were uncertain, though Russia was more out of line than Austria. In all those cases, success depended on winning the race against time. As far as doubtful allies were concerned, it was apparent that Austria would be more difficult, perhaps impossible, to detach from Germany after the defection of Russia.

After the conference at St-Jean-de-Maurienne, Lloyd George, who had said that with allies it was difficult to win the war, may well have reflected that allies might make it impossible for him to end it. Neither he nor the French Prime Minister were satisfied with the results of their meeting with Sonnino, and a new suggestion was therefore put forward by the French on 25 May for a meeting between the Kings of England and Italy and the President of France. Once again, Baron Sonnino sabotaged the project. At first he argued that the moment was ill-chosen because Russia, who would have to be left out, would become suspicious, and because American opinion also had to be taken into account. On 31 May 1917, the Foreign Office was resolved to go ahead with the plan despite Sonnino's objections, 'in view of important special information affecting the Russian Revolution'. Sonnino was, however, insistent. He would not expose the Italian monarchy, he argued, to any criticism at a time when it was becoming fashionable to criticize monarchies. The French government dropped the invitation to the two Kings.

Baron Sonnino's political predicament was generally understood in London and Paris. He was unable to make peace on Austrian terms because Giolitti would have achieved the same results without fighting – but that made no contribution to Sonnino's popularity in Allied capitals. The failure of Nivelle's offensive on the western front contributed to keeping the hope of peace with Austria alive in Paris and London. On 8 June, when the English War Cabinet discussed the Austrian problem, it reached the conclusion that

the Austrian approach ought to be pursued. Although not unmindful of the risk that the conclusion of a separate peace with Austria might produce an atmosphere of peace in which the crushing of Germany might become difficult, and while fully conscious of the importance of not being drawn into a trap designed to secure the release of the 2,000,000 Austrian prisoners with a view to a subsequent resumption of hostilities, the War Cabinet were of the opinion that, if properly handled, these negotiations might result in the isolation of Germany and a general peace on the terms sought by the Entente Powers. . . .

The Foreign Office then put forward an alternative to the French plan for a summit conference: the French, British and Italian Prime Ministers, or Foreign Ministers, were invited to meet. The object of the meeting, the British Government stated, was to be that Italy might have no reason to complain later that information so vitally affecting the Allied cause, and the interests of Italy in particular, had been withheld from her. But Sonnino still did not want to listen to such information. When Sir Rennell Rodd told him of the proposed conference, the Italian Foreign Minister said at once that, in view of current rumours, 'if there were any question of separate peace with Austria, he could not be expected to agree to that'; a few days later Sonnino told the French Ambassador that in no circumstances would he discuss the question of a separate peace with Austria.

The Austrians and Prince Sixtus were aware of the difficulties Italy was causing, and of the fact that they might prove insuperable. In a final attempt to save the negotiations, as well, perhaps, as to put them on a different footing, the Bourbon Princes came over to London at the beginning of June. They lunched at 10 Downing Street, and had a number of conversations at the Foreign Office. They told their hosts that Emperor Karl and Empress Zita were entirely pro-French and pro-English, and that they detested the Kaiser and Prince Rupprecht on political as well as personal grounds. The Kaiser had apparently insulted Zita in her youth; Rupprecht, the Crown Prince of Bavaria, was a Prussianized and coarse oaf with a tendency to bully the Emperor and his wife. Karl himself was not, as some people believed, a colourless young man. On the contrary, he was 'full of character and autocratic'. True, Sixtus said, Karl took advice from his wife, a very intelligent woman, but he was in no way under her thumb. In fact, Karl was his own master, determined to carry out the political programme of the late Archduke Franz Ferdinand, his murdered uncle, which centred on the solution of the national programme by satisfying the political ambitions of the Slavs, thereby breaking the power of Berlin as well as of the Magyars.

When Prince Sixtus came to the actual purpose of his visit to London – a separate peace – it became apparent that the Austrian attitude had undergone a subtle change. He told his English hosts that the Emperor Karl was still in principle keen to make a peace with France and England, but that there existed two obvious obstacles. The Russian revolution, in the first place, had changed the Austrians' approach to the war: they thought the Central Empires had now a very good chance of winning it. And secondly, Sixtus said, the Habsburg monarchy could hardly be expected to make a separate peace on the basis of its own liquidation, a demand which had been made by France and England in the Italian and Rumanian agreements, as well as in their note of 10 January 1917 to President Wilson.

In view of those diplomatic undertakings, the Bourbon brothers hinted, the Emperor Karl had no incentive to make, or accept, advances to or from England and France. The Italian nationality question could perhaps be adjusted, but the Austrians could not be expected to give up the vital port of Trieste: more than anything else, Italy stood in the way of peace. But a drastic political change in Italy – perhaps a republican revolution – could transform the situation. The Habsburg Emperor would then be able to make another overture to the Allies; he would do so chiefly because he was determined to shake off the domination of Berlin. In this regard, the Allies would have to assist Austria: German military units would have to be drawn away from Austro-Hungarian territory. If Austria concluded peace, there was little doubt that Bulgaria would follow. Prince Sixtus added that from Karl's point of view, the danger of a 'socialist peace' was an incentive to come to an agreement with England. The Princes then told their hosts in London that they would remain available if the need for a secret communication with the Austrian Emperor arose.

Their offer was never taken up. The attitude of Sonnino, as well as the new strategic perspectives opened up by the Russian revolution, first slowed down, and ultimately ruled out a negotiated separate peace with Austria. In the summer of 1917, no further proposals came from the Court in Vienna. As the diplomats had been unable to help the soldiers, the soldiers might be able to aid the diplomats. At its meeting on 8 June 1917, the British cabinet had set up a Committee on War Policy: in the following two months this Committee met twenty-one times, as well as twice informally, over dinner. Its most important task was to consider whether the forthcoming offensive should be directed against the German line in Flanders, as Field-Marshal Haig and General Robertson urged, or whether the Allies should remain on the defensive in the west, and concentrate on the Italian front, so as to deliver a stroke against Austria which would force Vienna to conclude peace. At the first meeting of the Committee General Robertson described a conversation with General Foch, in the course of which they had agreed that the position in Russia was very unsatisfactory, but that Austria was very weak, and might perhaps be hit hard by the Italian offensive. General Foch also thought he had information that Austria would make a separate peace if she had a decent excuse. The general conclusion which he and General Foch reached was that they should see General Cadorna as soon as possible, and that the three Generals should send a joint telegram to General Brusiloff.[12]

Robertson did not reveal the purpose of all the consultation at general officers' level, and it never took place. The Flanders plan received Robertson's full support, and it was in connection with this plan that Lloyd George had very strong misgivings indeed. At the tenth meeting of the Committee, the Prime Minister summed up the whole question for the benefit of Haig and Robertson. He said that it would be a great responsibility for the Committee to take the strategy out of the hands of military advisers; the implication was that the Committee could do so. After having engaged the soldiers' attention in that way, Lloyd George begged them to listen, very carefully. He said that the alternative to Flanders

was to undertake an operation which was, in the first place, military, and, in the second, diplomatic, with the object of detaching Austria from Germany, namely, an attack on the Austrian front.

Lloyd George felt that the fatal error which had been committed in the war had been always to attack where the enemy was strongest: it was a mistake, the Prime Minister thought, to strike with the sword against the thickest part of the enemy's armour. It was a hard fact, and not a matter of conjecture, that Austria wanted to be out of the war; it would not pay the price demanded by the Allies, but if a heavy blow was struck against it, Austria might change its attitude. The internal position in the Habsburg Empire, Lloyd George went on, was desperate; 'the nation was sulky.' The opportunity was there, and 'the prize was far the biggest in sight. If Austria could be forced out of the war, Bulgaria and Turkey would have to follow.' The vital link binding the Central Alliance together would be severed. In the following year, the Allied forces locked up at Salonika, Mesopotamia and Egypt would be set free for operations on the western front. There would be an added advantage in such a policy: Italy would have to support France and England, because it would not be aided by them against Austria unless Rome agreed that, after the reduction of Austria, Italy would remain in the war against Germany. Lloyd George was convinced that Trieste alone stood between Italy and separate peace with Austria, and the question was whether there was a way of capturing the port.

Perhaps the most important point in connection with the Austrian operation was the effect it would have on Russia. It was the Prime Minister's opinion that

> if Russia went out of the War while Austria still remained in, we could not win. If the Eastern armies of Germany were released we should have no chance of eventual victory. The United States of America might in time place half a million men in the field, but if Russia had gone out of the War, Germany could bring $1\frac{1}{2}$ million men to the Western front. The Allies could not bring so large a force from anywhere. We should then have an inferiority both in men and guns in the West, and this means defeat.

Lloyd George put forward his case with force and conviction, but it failed to make an impression in the right quarters. Haig and Robertson, supported by Admiral Jellicoe, laid the utmost stress on the danger to the navy of allowing Ostend and Zeebrugge to remain in enemy hands, and the Committee sanctioned the Flanders offensive. Lloyd George's Italian plan was to be kept in reserve,

> on the cessation of the Flanders offensive, if it is not too late, and subject, of course, to the general conditions then prevailing, there should be a rapid transfer of heavy guns to the Italian front.

At the Allied conference in Paris on 25–26 July 1917, the question of peace with Austria was discussed, on the highest level and privately, on several occasions. The suggestion that it should be a negotiated peace was never made: the conversation centred on a knock-out blow against Austria. The defection of Russia from the Allied side was also considered, and its possibility was no longer regarded as remote; Lloyd George argued that the Allied blow against Austria could achieve a great part of the Italian desiderata. And it was more than ever important, as well as considerably easier, to give the Italians what they wanted:

> if the Russians collapse, Rumania's collapse was also inevitable, and in such circumstances it would be very difficult to exact the claims of the

Entente's Eastern Allies against Austria. This rendered it the more desirable to concentrate on the claims of Italy.

And then Lloyd George went on to point out that

if the whole of the Russian, Rumanian, and Serbian claims against Austria were realised in their entirety, the break-up of the Austrian Empire was involved, but that the Italian claims could be exacted without any such break-up.

The internal difficulties of the Habsburg Empire, the Prime Minister went on, were considerable. It was both exhausted and divided against itself; in the population of some fifty million 'something like thirty million consisted of disaffected races'. If the strategy were successful, and Austria were knocked out of the war, Lloyd George asked, would then Italy continue to support its Allies? Sonnino said that it would. In that case, Lloyd George hinted, the Entente Powers should show more anticipation. They had been too slow-footed: they should now take swift action, and 'convert a possible defeat into a possible victory'. The military document presented to the conference spelled one word only and that word was disaster. For the Allies, 'holding our own' was really not good enough: 'Germany is in possession of Belgium, North France, Serbia, and the mistress of a great part of the Ottoman Empire. Merely to hold on is, therefore, to face a disastrous peace.'

In one way or another, the Allies had incurred many obligations, and in order to fulfil them, they would have to acquire a lot of territory. Lloyd George confined himself to mentioning a few of them: 'Galicia, Bukowina, Banat, Temesvár, Transylvania', but he did not bother to enumerate either the Italian or the Serbian claims, and made no reference to Constantinople. He finished by asking his colleagues to consent to an effort being made to detach 'Germany's Eastern Allies with the object of concentrating all our efforts on our main aim in the war, namely the defeat of Prussian autocracy'.

For reasons that were obvious to everyone present – Lloyd George's plan involved military assistance to Italy on a large scale – Sonnino supported the English Premier: French military opinion, on the other hand, was dead against his proposal, and no decision on any problems connected with the Austrian peace was taken.

Another Allied conference followed in London on 7–8
August 1917: it was attended by most members of the British
War Cabinet, by the Secretary of State for Foreign Affairs, by four
members of the French Cabinet – Ribot, Painlevé, Thierry and
Thomas – by Baron Sonnino, Generals Robertson, Foch and
Albrieti. On this occasion, Lloyd George was even more outspoken than before. He contrasted the method of the Central
Powers in pooling their resources which made it possible for them
to deal successfully with great armies (Lloyd George had the
eastern front in mind), driving them back and breaking them up;
whereas the gallant Allied effort 'only chipped a few bits off a
granite block'. He said that his view had always been that for
three years Allied diplomacy and Allied strategy had been kept
apart. When soldiers met they discussed the best place at which to
fight a battle. They were suspicious of the statesmen, who, in
their turn, did not trust the soldiers; in consequence, military
action could never be fitted to diplomacy. After the Russian revolution early in the spring, the Allies should have considered
whether they could defeat all their enemies. If not, they should
have decided which enemy they should concentrate their forces
upon, and which enemy they should try to detach. Had the whole
ground been treated as one, Lloyd George believed, the Allies
would already have won the war.

Again Sonnino supported the British Premier throughout, and
again the French had objections to make. Ribot and Painlevé
considered it impossible to change plans for 1917, and they were
inclined to shelve the whole unpleasant subject. They had taken
the advice of French and British generals, who would not change
their current plans and argued that Austria could be knocked out
only by continuing the attack on the German forces on the
western front and by attacking Austria simultaneously on the
Russian and Italian fronts. Any other plan, said General Foch,
would make it necessary for the Allied troops either to cross the
Alps and go forward to Vienna, which would involve a great
military effort, or to aim lower – at the occupation of Trieste, for
instance – which might not produce the desired result. In the end,
the three Allied governments directed their General Staffs to consult as to the best way of striking at Austria. For the second time
in 1917, Lloyd George failed to achieve his objective in regard to
Austria, or to secure the Allies' approval of his grand strategy;

for the second time, he failed to convince them that a separate peace with Austria was essential for the successful conduct of the war on Germany.

But in the summer of 1917, as the idea of 'peace' was growing more and more popular, many meanings became attached to it. In June, socialists of most of the belligerent countries met in Stockholm, in an attempt to restore the peaceful days of the Second International; on 14 August 1917, the Pope invited heads of states to consider the reduction of armaments, the freedom of the seas, and other controversial subjects. Underneath the public activity, politicians were trying to make partial peace for strategic advantages. They had ceased regarding their business as the art of the possible, and they took lightheartedly the lengthening of the odds against them. Increasingly, the voice of reason could be identified with the voice of dissent. The popular enthusiasm for the war, at the time of its outbreak, was nothing but a faded memory; even the formal political unity – *Burgfrieden, union sacré* – in most of the belligerent states was no longer what it had been. In Russia, the March revolution opened the floodgates of freedom, and made further conduct of the war almost impossible; in Vienna, the reopening of the Reichsrat in May 1917 revealed profound political differences that had had time to mature in the provincial capitals of the Empire since the beginning of the war. In the parliaments in Paris and in Rome, the socialists harassed their governments, and Italian republicans were becoming more than an acute embarrassment for the cabinet and the King. It so happened that the two most resolute antagonists, England and Germany, maintained, in contrast to their allies, the steadiest political fronts.

The English blockade of Germany was, however, proving more effective than Germany's unrestricted submarine warfare, launched in February 1917 with the ambitious aim of defeating England in six months. At the end of July, while the Germans were facing starvation, England was still undefeated. And there were signs, since the fierce controversy on the declaration of unrestricted submarine warfare, that all was not well on the German home front. In March 1917 it was suggested, in a Reichstag committee, that the generals should come under the control of the civilian government; the generals as well as the Kaiser expressed their displeasure in no uncertain terms. The Social Democrat organization, creaking and cracking under the stresses of war, found it impossible to justify patriotic policy to the majority of its members who had accepted that policy in the summer of 1914. In July 1917, the majority socialist leaders doubted if they could vote for the war credits and wanted an assurance that their country was fighting a defensive war. On 6 July, Erzberger, the Catholic Centre party deputy, made an impressive speech to the Reichstag, giving a sombre analysis of Germany's military future.

The preceding months had been marked for Erzberger by sharp clashes with the officials: his unquestioning co-operation with the Foreign Ministry in the Italian negotiations in the spring of 1915 was very much a thing of the past. He was convinced that the declaration of submarine warfare would be less effective than was assumed by the naval experts, and the entry of the United States into the war on the Allied side more effective than was expected by the soldiers. In addition, Erzberger maintained his connections with Vienna, and the influence from that quarter strongly coloured his views of the war. From the Habsburg capital no consolation was forthcoming.

On 23 April 1917 the Emperor Karl granted Erzberger an unusually long audience at Laxenburg, and gave his German visitor a report by Czernin. It was dated 12 April 1917 and it radiated gloom. The Austro-Hungarian Foreign Minister was convinced that 'our military strength is coming to an end', and that the 'dull despair that pervades all classes owing to under-nourishment makes further endurance of the suffering caused by the war impossible'.[13] Another winter campaign was therefore entirely out of the question: 'it will be most important to begin peace negotiations at the moment when the enemy has not yet grasped the fact of our waning strength'. But at the heart of the matter, there lay one consideration alone. Czernin pointed to the danger of revolution that was threatening the whole of Europe; he suspected that England welcomed that sinister development. The established order everywhere in Europe was in danger; there was the amazing ease of the dynastic collapse in Russia. 'The world is no longer what it was three years ago.' The revolution in Russia, Czernin went on, influenced the Slavs more than the Germans of the Habsburg Empire.

As to Austria's ally, Czernin did not think that 'the internal situation in Germany is widely different from what it is here. I am only afraid that the military circles in Berlin are deceiving themselves in certain matters.' Like most of the well-informed pessimists in Vienna and Berlin – still rather small groups in both the capitals – Czernin regarded America's entry into the war as an aggravating event more than as a happening on the margin of the world scene, comparable to, say, the declaration of war by Venezuela.

It may be many months before America can throw any noteworthy forces into the field, but the moral fact, the fact that the Entente has the hope of fresh forces, brings the situation to an unfavourable stage for us, because our enemies have more time before them than we have . . .

And parallel to Czernin's line on America, there ran his conviction that 'Germany places great hopes on the U-boat warfare. I consider such hopes are deceptive.'[14]

Such were the arguments that convinced Erzberger of the pointlessness of the war of attrition and of the sombre prospects before the Central Powers at the end of it. In his speech on 6 July 1917 – it caused panic throughout Germany – Erzberger called on the Reichstag to oppose annexations as the first step on the way to a negotiated peace.

The day after Erzberger's Reichstag speech, excitement in Berlin grew more intense when it became known that Ludendorff, who sensed a political crisis in the air, had arrived in the capital, with the express purpose of toppling the Chancellor from power. Although the Kaiser ordered Ludendorff to return to his post at General Headquarters, Ludendorff left a friend of his behind in Berlin to look after his political interests. A week later, he issued an ultimatum that either he or Bethmann Hollweg must go. The Chancellor went, and was replaced by Georg Michaelis, a man of no consequence, who had been previously responsible for Prussian food supplies.

The fact that the Kaiser had not consulted the Reichstag when he was considering the appointment of the new Chancellor annoyed its members; it was another incentive for hurrying Erzberger's peace resolution through and in that way asserting their authority. In addition, Erzberger knew that the Pope would make a peace offer in the following month, and he wanted to prepare the ground for it.[15] When the resolution was passed on 19 July, it bore the marks of Erzberger's sponsorship. It pleased the extremists on neither side of the house; 126 of them voted against it. The Conservatives and National Liberals argued that it was cowardly in renouncing territorial gains; the passage to which they objected read:

The *Reichstag* strives for a peace of understanding and the permanent reconciliation of peoples. Forced territorial acquisitions and political, economic, and financial oppressions are irreconcilable with such a peace.

The Independent Socialists, on the other hand, objected that the resolution did not renounce annexations and indemnities, that it was too fainthearted to accept a clear, unambiguous formula. The resolution was indeed open to differing interpretations; when he endorsed it the Chancellor added the qualification, 'as I understand it'. The Reichstag peace resolution passed almost unnoticed abroad, but it aggravated public controversy and sharpened political divisions in Berlin. Some of the annexationists, in their belief that they had to close their ranks, founded the Fatherland Party. They identified the 'will to victory' with bold plans of annexation.

Soon after the passage of the resolution in the Reichstag, Cardinal Pacelli, who later became Pope Pius XII, came to Berlin. He had discussed peace with Bethmann, and he now intended to continue the conversation with Michaelis. Pacelli put forward proposals that became the basis of the Papal peace note: arbitration, disarmament, freedom of the seas, evacuation of occupied France, Belgium and German colonies, friendly settlement of territorial disputes between Germany and France and between Italy and Austria-Hungary, and the restoration of Serbia, Rumania, Montenegro and Poland. The Germans took a long time over replying to the Papal note. The leaders of the majority parties in the Reichstag discovered that the Chancellor did not see eye to eye with them on their earlier peace resolution, and they ran into difficulties with the new Foreign Secretary, Richard von Kühlmann, who had replaced Zimmermann in July 1917.

Born in Constantinople, a Bavarian and a Catholic, Kühlmann was an astute man of the world. He had a fondness for the good things of life, a certain playfulness and detachment from every problem before him. The dedicated severity of Prussia was not for Kühlmann. He had already had a distinguished diplomatic career, at Tangiers, in London and then, during the war, at The Hague and at Constantinople. The German parliamentarians thought that Kühlmann was opposed to annexations and they took it for his greatest asset.

The first reaction to the Papal note came from London on 23 August 1917, when Balfour instructed the Minister to the Vatican that the British government would have to wait until the Germans revealed their plans in regard to Belgium. A week later, Pacelli let Michaelis know how important it was for Germany to renounce Belgium. On the same day, 30 August, President Wilson wrote to Benedict xv, accepting most of the Papal proposals, but adding that the abdication of the Kaiser and the breaking of Germany's military power should take place before any negotiations with Berlin.

The Foreign Secretary met the Reichstag leaders on 10 September and asked them not to 'sell the Belgian horse. It is for me to decide that. At present the horse is not for sale.' He added that he was quite ready to resign if his views were not accepted. The deputies did not want to antagonize Kühlmann, and he met them half-way by agreeing to make a specific reference, in his reply to the Pope, to the Reichstag resolution. The deputies assumed that this meant the renunciation, by their government, of annexations in the west. They, of course, knew more about the intentions behind their resolution than anyone else, but such knowledge was not common outside Germany. On 19 September they agreed to Kühlmann's answer to the Pope's note. It was drafted in very general terms and made no specific mention of Belgium.

The bland way in which Michaelis thought of himself as Ludendorff's nominee, plus his incompetence, soon removed the Chancellor from the political limelight. On 28 October 1917 he was replaced by Count Hertling, the seventy-four-year-old politician who had made his name in Bavaria as a leader of the Catholic Centre party. Hertling, again, was appointed by the Kaiser without consulting the parliamentary parties. Not that the new Chancellor disapproved. As a Bavarian, Hertling was a federalist. As an aristocrat, he had no fondness for the parliamentary system. The thought of a central representative body was quite abhorrent to him. He treasured his quaint views and at his stage of life was unlikely to give them up. He discerned, for instance, a strong link between economic evils and original sin; he thought the state useful for the protection of certain basic human rights, such as the right to Sunday rest.[16] He was almost blind and had to reduce his working hours to an absolute minimum. He stayed in power until September 1918, when the war was lost.

In the memorandum of 12 April 1917, of which Erzberger, as we have seen, made so much use, the Austrian Foreign Minister had written:

> Your Majesty has rejected the repeated attempts of our enemies to separate us from our allies, in which step I took the responsibility because Your Majesty is incapable of any dishonourable action.

The truth of the matter was that when Czernin wrote the memorandum, the Emperor was engaged in just such an action: that was the sense in which the negotiations were understood in London and Paris.

At the same time, however, in the spring of 1917, explorations of the possibility of peace were made by representatives of Czernin and the Ballhausplatz who had instructions that Austria could not separate itself from its allies, and that peace could ultimately be concluded only on behalf of the whole group of the Central Powers.[17] Early in April 1917, Count Mensdorff arrived in Switzerland, where he talked with a representative of the British Minister to Berne; in August, Count Revertera, an Austrian diplomat on the retired list, carried on the conversation with a French friend of his, Count Armand, who was then serving in the military intelligence. Quite apart from the difficulty of devising peace terms acceptable to Vienna, and the fact that on the French side the military and not the diplomats were in charge of the negotiations, such contacts were eroded by a basic misunderstanding. Paris and London were interested only in a separate peace with Austria and it was known – only, of course, on the highest level – that similar inclinations existed in Vienna. The Armand–Revertera talks were not yet concluded when Clemenceau became Prime Minister and Minister of War on 15 November 1917; when he was told of them he advised that Armand should merely listen, and say nothing: just in case the proposal of a separate peace were made.

It never was. By the end of August 1917 the diplomats in Paris and London had become convinced that Czernin's main objective was to act as broker between the two Great Powers in the west and Germany, and that it would be impossible to limit the discussion of the conditions of peace to Austria only.[18] The prevalent Foreign Office opinion was that 'now that it is evident that there is no chance of detaching Austria from Germany and that she only appears in the role of a broker, we must be more careful than ever as to how we proceed'.

In the autumn of 1917, the cause of peace was moving at a snail's pace, but without coming to a complete standstill. It was the job of agents, on both sides, in the neutral countries to feed information to their masters on the latest Austrian moves. In Vienna, neither the Emperor nor Czernin ever quite lost interest in the negotiations. But then, late in the autumn of 1917, two events occurred which affected the perspectives of war and peace.

Toward the end of August 1917, news had been received in London and Paris of the remarkable success of General Cadorna's offensive in the Carso, the eastern part of the Italian front. After the failure of the Russian and French offensives, the news from Italy was a much-needed tonic, and both the French and the British governments grasped the opportunity of exploiting the Italian success. The British had dispatched heavy artillery equipment to Italy before; now, late in the summer of 1917, one hundred heavy French guns were released for service in Italy. By the time they arrived there at the end of September 1917, however, General Cadorna had decided not to press his attack further. A few days later, the withdrawal from Italy of all British and French heavy artillery had begun. Early in October, the Austrians began to counter-attack; on 24 October the Austrian and German armies broke through the Italian lines at several points on the eastern sector of a front twenty miles long. The attack soon became a rout; five days later, the Austrians captured the former Italian headquarters at Udine. By 7 November 1917, the Austrian and German armies had captured 2,300 guns and some quarter of a million Italian troops. On the same day, Lenin and the Bolsheviks moved in to take over power in Petrograd.

At first, the events in Petrograd offered no clear indication of the future position of Russia in the war. Communications with the Russian capital became even more difficult than they had been at any time during the revolution, telegrams taking up to five days to reach the western European capitals. On 8 November *The Times* announced a 'Maximalist Sedition in Petrograd'. The news on the following day was still of anarchy and confusion; when Nabokov, the Provisional Government's representative in London, met Balfour in the evening, he had had no direct news from the capital, and he told Balfour that he assumed that the Provisional Government had not gone out of existence. On 12 November, Kerensky was apparently marching on Petrograd, and the *Times* headline read: 'The Bolsheviks Wavering'. It was not until 23 November that the newspaper had a long leader on the meaning of Lenin's victory.

The Russian Bolshevists have ordered the soldiers at the front to begin formal *pourparlers* for peace with the enemy. During Tuesday [20 November] night they instructed the Commander-in-Chief to 'offer an armistice' to all the belligerents.

Nevertheless, the Allies knew that

the Maximalists are a band of anarchists and fanatics who have seized power for the moment, owing to the paralysis of the national life which a series of attempts to govern by speechification has inflicted upon all classes, with the exception of the Cossacks. They know that Lenin and several of his confederates are adventurers of German-Jewish blood and in German pay, whose sole object is to exploit the ignorant masses in the interest of their own employers in Berlin. But while the Allies are confident that sooner or later the instincts of patriotism and of national preservation will bring about the downfall of this travesty of a Government, they cannot shut their eyes to the grave character of its acts.

While the Bolshevists, the 'wild political amateurs', remained at the head of affairs, the *Times* leader-writer warned the Russians, 'Allied help to Russia is out of the question'. By the end of November 1917 it had become apparent that Germany and Austria wanted, and would soon have, an armistice on the Russian front.

Such were the circumstances in which the last round of peace negotiations opened. Count Mensdorff, who had been travelling around Europe since the beginning of the year in search of a suitably prominent opposite number with whom to open the talks, at last achieved his aim. On 18 December 1917, in a quiet suburb on the outskirts of Geneva, Count Mensdorff met Jan Smuts, the former Boer General and a member of the British War Cabinet. The two men spent most of the day together; Smuts conceived of the objects of his mission as first, to instil into the minds of the Austrians that in case they freed themselves from German domination and made a fresh start in sympathy with the British Empire they would have our full sympathy and support; and secondly, to gather as much information as possible while declining to enter into a general discussion of peace terms as far as the Germans were concerned. . . . A third object which I had in mind was, if possible, to induce the Austrians to conclude a separate peace; but the subject was from many points of view a risky one to open, as I was anxious to avoid laying ourselves open to this charge in future of having intrigued with the Austrians for a separate peace.[19]

On the last point, Mensdorff was helpful. The Austrian declared straightaway that a separate peace was out of the question, that it would be madness for Austria to entertain such an idea, and that Austria would do nothing treacherous or dishonourable. He made the same point toward the close of the conversation: Mensdorff's impression was, quite correctly, that Smuts had come to Geneva to discuss a separate peace.

Smuts, for his part, told Mensdorff that he had come in response to numerous unofficial overtures from Vienna, that the friendly feelings toward Austria which the British had entertained before the war had not disappeared, and that Austria, far from being Britain's main antagonist, had been 'used by Germany both in the policy which led to the War, as well as during the course of the War'.[20] The Russian breakdown, Smuts said, had created fresh anxiety for the political future of Europe. Some new counterweight, he intimated, would have to be placed against the power of Germany on the Continent, and he politely inquired whether Mensdorff thought Austria might become such a counter-weight. If the answer were Yes, the Entente would do everything 'to uphold and strengthen her [Austria] and to assist her economic reconstruction'.[21]

Mensdorff replied that he was very gratified to hear this, especially since, in the last word of the Entente upon the matter in reply to President Wilson's Note on 10 January 1917, the break-up of the Habsburg Empire had been foreshadowed as one of the principal Allied war aims. Smuts denied that the note had had any such intention and said that

its object, and still more our object now, was to assist Austria to give the greatest freedom and autonomy to her subject nationalities. The best way to strengthen the bonds of sympathy between the British and Austro-Hungarian people was to liberalise as much as possible the

local institutions of Austria-Hungary. We had no intention of interfering in her internal affairs, but we recognised that if Austria could
become a really liberal Empire in which her subject peoples would, as
far as possible, be satisfied and content, she would become for Central
Europe very much what the British Empire had become for the rest
of the world.[22]

Mensdorff listened while Smuts went on painting a bright future
for the Habsburg state. As a man who had fought against the
British Empire and then made his peace with it, Smuts thought
that his views carried a special authority. But scattered among the
eloquent periods on the benefits of liberalism and freedom, there
were the shorter inquiries, more to the point: would the new
Austria dissociate itself entirely from the old military dictatorship, the German Empire?

Mensdorff replied that the views Smuts had expressed would
appeal very deeply to Austria's rulers, but that the new policy
could not be initiated during the war, nor could Austria break
with Germany. For the time being, however, London could do
something to lighten the task of Czernin and his Emperor. The
Foreign Minister, said Mensdorff, taking a view that would have
sounded very strange from a senior diplomat earlier in that revolutionary year, 1917, was not 'a diplomat of the old school, but
a young statesman descended from the ancient Royal House of
Bohemia, full of lofty political idealism'.[23] He had expressed himself, very often and very strongly, in favour of general disarmament and a league of nations to safeguard the public order of
Europe. Mensdorff regretted that no word of sympathy had come
from London for Czernin's policy; instead, there were only the
sneers of the press.

Smuts replied that his government was known to be in favour
of such a league, and that leading British statesmen had expressed
their agreement with President Wilson in that regard. But such
a league must be founded, he pointed out, on a satisfactory peace,
not on a peace based on Germany's hegemony on the Continent.
Otherwise, the states of Europe would continue arming as before,
because no one would really feel safe: 'It was therefore essential
for a League of Nations that the German military domination
should be broken in this war.'[24]

But Germany, Mensdorff objected, was making its own arrangements for a new order. The German parliament had more power

than ever before, and it was impossible to form a government without a Reichstag majority. That was the real meaning, Mensdorff quite rightly told Smuts, of the obscure crisis that had recently shaken Berlin. If the Allies expected more than that, if they were waiting for a revolution in Germany, they were greatly mistaken. The German workers were either loyal or fighting in the front line; far-reaching political changes would take place, but not till after the war. When Smuts observed that the German civil government seemed to have lost ground to the General Staff during the war, Mensdorff brushed the suggestion aside, with a contemptuous gesture.

He then returned to the main purpose of his mission, the discussion of general peace terms. In line with Czernin's ideas, Mensdorff said that in his opinion the time had come to open informal discussions between Great Britain and Germany, and that Austria would gladly mediate. Smuts declined the offer politely, saying that 'neither the British public nor the British Government were in a temper to discuss peace with the German Government, and that our conversations should be confined entirely to questions affecting Austria-Hungary'.[25] Mensdorff agreed, regretfully.

After the preliminary skirmishes, when both men had established that they were not prepared to play each other's game, they moved on to discuss territorial questions. Mensdorff said that Poland had 'rather a Western than an Eastern orientation', to which Smuts replied that it should not have a German orientation. Mensdorff's view was that there existed little danger of that because of the liberal policy Austria had pursued toward the Poles; their future state would naturally incline more to Vienna than to Berlin. Smuts then reminded Mensdorff that the Allies were committed to an independent state of Poland, but if Austria really broke away from Germany the possibility of a link between Austria and Poland would not be excluded.

If Vienna obtained satisfaction in Poland, Smuts went on, would it then make concessions to the claims, based on Allied pledges, of Serbia, Rumania and Italy? Mensdorff replied that Serbia presented no difficulty: the Austrians had no liking for the Karadjordjević dynasty, which was founded on assassination – Mensdorff had in mind the gory palace revolution in Belgrade in 1903 – and they would welcome guarantees which would once and for all stop Serbia being the centre of anti-Austrian intrigue. He was of the opinion that Bulgaria would want to hold on to its own parts of Serbia, and that it should be allowed to do so. In that case, Smuts objected, Serbia would have to be compensated, and Bosnia-Herzegovina, with its access to the sea, would be the most suitable compensation. It might then be possible to bring the new, greater Serbia into a more friendly relationship with Vienna. Russia would no longer be there, Smuts added later, to foment anti-Austrian feeling among the southern Slavs. When Rumania was mentioned, Mensdorff became agitated and said that this treacherous state was finished, and that Austria-Hungary would refuse to surrender an inch of territory to it. His brother-in-law, Count Appyoni, had told him that Hungary would fight Rumanian claims to the last ditch and that, in any case, only a fringe of Transylvania was inhabited by the Rumanians. But Smuts could hold his own in the Austro-Hungarian nationality stakes: he pointed out in reply that large parts of Bukovina and Bessarabia had a mainly Rumanian population, and that, as Bulgaria was claiming a large part of the Dobruja, the problem of bringing the Rumanians together in one state deserved Vienna's serious consideration. Mensdorff opposed Smuts's suggestion on Bukovina, but suggested that Austria was not directly concerned with the question of Bessarabia.

Smuts had made much play with the principle of nationality: 'it seemed to me essential if the foundations of a future peaceful Europe were to be laid that rearrangements on a national basis should as far as possible be effected.'[26] When the problem of Italy came up for discussion, Mensdorff asked Smuts how the Allies could defend such a principle and yet at the same time make the promises they had made to Italy in the Balkans. Were the Allies really so favourably disposed to Austria? If they were, why did they want to cut off its access to the sea, and plant Italy on both shores of the Adriatic? Austria would never agree to Trieste being wrenched away, said Mensdorff. Smuts did not want to discuss these questions; he was not fully conversant with them. But it seemed to him essential from every point of view that the Trentino should be ceded to Italy. Mensdorff referred to Italian treachery and the disinclination in Vienna to make concessions; nevertheless, Smuts felt that Austria would be prepared for a deal in this connection. On the whole, in territorial questions, Smuts gained the impression that 'the Austrian mind was in an accommodating mood';[27] he did not go any further with the discussion because he felt that neither the War Cabinet nor Britain's allies had definitely made their minds up on all those problems.

Smuts and Mensdorff then discontinued their conversation, but met again in the evening. The ice had now been broken, and the two men said what was on their minds. Their talk that evening, 18 December 1917, was probably the most open exchange of views that took place between senior representatives of any two sides opposed in the war. Again, Mensdorff explored the possibility of discussing general peace: when Smuts would have none of that, Mensdorff exclaimed: 'In that case there is no peace in sight, and this horrible war must go on!' Europe, he said, was dying at the centre; America was becoming the leading financial and economic power in the world while, at the other end, Japan was engaged in gathering immense influence and resources, as well as the trade of the whole of Asia. Why did the Allies go on fighting, Mensdorff asked, and answered the question himself. The British Prime Minister had said that he 'must have victory';[28] Asquith had said that Prussian militarism must be crushed. If the war continued for another year, Europe would be destroyed beyond repair. What kind of victory had the Allies in view? How would they know when it was achieved? 'Do you want the Hohenzollerns to go?' Mensdorff asked Smuts, adding that such an aim could not justify the destruction of European civilization and that, in any event, political revolution in Germany would follow, not precede, the peace. Or perhaps the break-up of the German army was the Allied aim? or the occupation of Belgium?

Smuts replied that the British people were deeply impressed

with the dangers to the future political system of Europe, if Germany survived as a sort of military dictator, and that we meant to continue the War until either victory had been achieved or the dark forces of revolution had done their work in Germany as they had already done in Russia.

He then explained to Mensdorff that the Allies were in a good position to go on.

America was coming in with resources far greater and more real than any we had lost through the defection of Russia. France had suffered but little this year, and her Army had a very high morale and quite sufficient reserves for next year; while our full resources in mechanical and man-power were only now being mobilised for the decisive phases of the War. I explained to him how the submarine and shipping situation had altered since last spring, and that we were now in a position, if necessary, to go on indefinitely as we had done during the Napoleonic Wars. The menace of Germany was no less grave than the menace of Napoleon, and was meeting with an even more determined temper on the part of the British people.[29]

Mensdorff did not stop to consider whether Smuts's historical analogy was appropriate; he simply said that 'that would indeed be the end of Europe',[30] and asked again what this vague victory was, for which all these immeasurable sacrifices had to be made. If the Central Powers accepted their terms, the Allies would have won; if not, the Allies would have to go on until they forced the enemy to accept their terms: Mensdorff pleaded for reasonable terms. He again offered Smuts mediation by Vienna, outlining the attitude Germany was likely to take. There would be no difficulty, he thought, in evacuating Belgium, so long as German economic and industrial interests there – they had been considerable before the war – were not injured. He did not believe Berlin intended to annex any of the occupied parts of Russia; he knew the difficulties about Alsace-Lorraine, but he asked whether France wanted 'the whole' of Alsace-Lorraine back. The Germans, he continued, were very keen to get their colonies, or some of them, back, and he thought they would claim heavy compensation if England declined to return them. Above all, Mensdorff added, the Germans would resent a post-war economic hostility that would mean their boycott in the markets of the world.

Smuts was doing most of the listening. In his record of the conversation with Mensdorff that evening Smuts wrote:[31]

I did not enter into a discussion of these general questions, and the Count went on to say with obvious sincerity that the two greatest peoples on earth, the two greatest peoples that had ever existed, were the British and the Germans, that the future of the world depended on both of them and on their co-operation, that it was not in the interest of the world that either of them should be utterly defeated, even if that were possible, and that such a defeat would become the source of fresh calamities for the future of mankind. He hoped most earnestly that reason would prevail.

Smuts told the Austrian flatly that

we did not wish to leave the root of the evil to survive and to grow afresh in the future. It was not from any warlike spirit but because of our horror of war that we were prepared to endure its evils longer . . .[32]

After that, the two men said goodbye; Smuts, at any rate, regarded the incident as closed. On the following morning, 19 January, Mensdorff sent the South African a message asking whether he might have another interview. They met in the afternoon, and Mensdorff told Smuts that he wanted to make quite sure that Smuts was clear on certain points. He said that Austria was prepared to go to any lengths with London in pressing on Berlin a policy of disarmament; he was deeply grateful for the sympathy Smuts had expressed for the Habsburg Empire, and 'when in future they took a line of their own independent of Germany they would count on our support'. Finally, Mensdorff told Smuts that he trusted that at the peace conference the English would use their influence with their friends to make the terms moderate.

Smuts replied that Austria now had a great opportunity to show the highest statesmanship and help the world toward an early, satisfactory, and lasting settlement. He again urged it upon Mensdorff that Austria-Hungary should sever its relationship with Berlin. Later on in the conversation, Mensdorff returned to the subject of victory, a subject which was so much on his mind and, in a way, puzzled him. He said that

it was misleading to talk of victory, for while the Germans had been successful in Central Europe, the British Empire had gained far more lasting and far-reaching victories over the whole world, and was now in complete control of everything outside Central Europe. The victory was already ours [Britain's] in a very important sense, . . .[33]

But Mensdorff's main concern was that the lines of communication from one belligerent camp to the other – he knew well how difficult they were to establish – should not be cut off. He felt sure, Mensdorff said, that Count Czernin would come to the discussion if London wanted someone who could speak with greater authority.

But neither Mensdorff nor his Foreign Minister had occasion to travel abroad on a peace mission. The close of the year 1917 put an end to Austrian peace feelers. Only Count Armand met Count Revertera again, in February 1918: a futile occasion.

All the efforts of professional and amateur diplomats throughout the year 1917 to give Austria some kind of peace had failed. Although the Hopwood–Mensdorff chase in Scandinavia early in the year was both comic and unnecessary, the fault did not lie with the emissaries alone. The objectives of the two parties coincided for a short time only; the onlooker at the greater part of the negotiations feels as if he is suffering from an acute attack of double vision. On the Austrian side, a separate peace was seriously considered only in the case of the Sixtus negotiations, and then only by the Emperor, not by his Foreign Minister. Karl's political inexperience, his lack of steadfastness under stress, did much to jeopardize Vienna's chances of knowing what it wanted, and getting it. Czernin, on the other hand, underestimated the degree of hostility that existed between Britain and Germany; London disregarded his attempts to arrange a negotiated peace with Berlin. The Allies wanted a separate peace with Austria, but the Sixtus offer was not repeated. It was a hazardous idea for the Emperor to have entertained in the first place, and then, by the end of the summer of 1917, there were signs that the fortunes of war were going in favour of the Central Powers. By the middle of November, the offensive against Italy was in full swing, and a 'defeatist' government was in power in Petrograd. In such circumstances, the Emperor Karl would of course not press for a separate peace; Czernin, on the other hand, pursued his former policy and sent Mensdorff to Geneva in the middle of December 1917. In view of their internal situation, it was not surprising that the Austrians still wanted to negotiate; but what was said by Mensdorff to Smuts was remarkable. Even under the first impact of the Central Powers' good fortune, Mensdorff did not lose sight of the wider issues in the war. A lone voice, he knew that there was more to the war than just Central Europe; he contrasted the cabbage patch that absorbed the attention of German and Austrian politicians and generals with the wide, open spaces outside, and found the former lacking. After all, the whole of the Habsburg dominions could be put down, very comfortably, on the territory of Texas alone. Mensdorff had preserved his reason intact; he was mistaken in expecting the same of other people.

By the end of 1917, there had appeared further ominous signs for the Austrians to note. Their relations with the United States had been unsettled since early in the war: in September 1915, the Austrian Ambassador to Washington was asked to leave because of his complicity in plots to sabotage the production of ammunition. A replacement for Dumba arrived only in February 1917, but he was given no opportunity to present his credentials, because Austria did not dissociate itself from the German policy of unrestricted submarine warfare. When America's declaration of war on Germany was followed by the severance of diplomatic relations between Vienna and Washington the United States did not declare war on Austria-Hungary. The situation remained unchanged so long as there existed a chance of peace with Austria. On 7 December 1917 President Wilson announced the existence of a state of war between the two countries. The year 1918 held out the promise neither of a separate peace nor of the survival of the Habsburg Empire.

5 Washington

On 2 April 1917 President Wilson appeared before Congress and asked for a declaration of war on Germany. The request was approved by an overwhelming majority four days later.

The way that took the United States into the war has often been explored. A mass of documents is available on a problem that has exercised the ingenuity of many historians. Yet, in the opinion of one writer, 'We still do not know, at any level that really matters, why Wilson took the fateful decision to bring the United States into the First World War.'[1] It is a history of two great protagonists, Wilson and America, whose reasons for going into the war were not identical.

On America's entry into the war Woodrow Wilson, the twenty-eighth President, was sixty years old. He had the kind of face that conceals emotion – angular features, a strong jaw, but his eyes sometimes betrayed the feelings that 'lay close under the skin'. He was always impeccably dressed in the severe style of nineteenth-century teachers and preachers; he was of middle height, his bearing rather stiff, always straight. On his family Wilson depended for encouragement, and he sought a purely intellectual understanding from a number of women; his friends thought his personality very attractive, and he impressed those who admired him from afar. But to the people he distrusted or disliked, Wilson seemed cold, distant, prejudiced, deceitful.

He was 'descended from a long line of Presbyterians' with the Scottish strain 'predominant in his ancestry'.[2] His early years were 'coloured by an atmosphere of academic interest and intense piety': he was educated at Princeton, Virginia, and Johns Hopkins universities. When he was twenty-six, he started and soon gave up a law practice, without clients. He taught at a number of colleges and universities before becoming, in 1890, Professor of Jurisprudence and Political Economy at Princeton; twelve years later, he was elected President of the university. As a scholar, he followed academic fashion: English and American constitutional history were his main interest. In 1885 he published *Congressional Government*, his first, and possibly his most important, book: he got married in the same year. As a writer and teacher Wilson had no taste for intensive and detailed research; he insisted rather on intellectual curiosity, breadth of reading, elegance of expression.

At Princeton, Wilson was a reforming President, following the English rather than the German university pattern. But he believed that the function of a university was to train the intellect rather than the character or the body. That belief, combined with his views on the physical shape of the university (his 'quad plan'), brought him into conflict with the powerful clubs and with the older members of the faculty just at the time when the Democratic party was looking for candidates in the coming elections. Wilson resigned at Princeton in October 1910 and in the following month he was elected Governor of New Jersey. A year later, he met Colonel House, who had been closely associated with successive Governors of Texas, for the first time: this was the beginning of what Sir Horace Plunkett called 'the strangest and most fruitful personal alliance in human history'. House was convinced that Wilson would make a very good President of the United States. On 5 November 1912 Wilson was elected to the highest office.

He had embarked on a vigorous programme of reform as a Governor; as the President, he tried to maintain the pace. One liberal manifesto followed another, all of them bearing the message, 'Live and let live': in practical terms, Wilson's legislation tried to do away with monopoly, with some of the abuses of the industrial system; it was designed to protect, as far as possible, the 'small man'. His work was, however, impeded by the inexperience of the Democrat leaders, who had been kept out of power for sixteen years, and by the industrial depression in the two years before the outbreak of the European war. After less than two years in office, Wilson started to run into severe criticism of the kind that tended to recur in his career. He was, his critics maintained, too impatient and impetuous; he wanted to go too fast.

By taste and by background Wilson was not a high-powered, tough politician. In the end, political life broke him. He had been very happy when he was still a university teacher. Yet, in a way, his academic interests and qualifications smoothed Wilson's transfer from university to political life. He was an admirer of Gladstone, an impressive lecturer, a reforming administrator. Oratory was Wilson's chief strength as a politician; he remained an academic lecturer who did away with the qualifying clauses. His speeches were often inspired by such moral fervour that they were described as 'political sermons'. A religious man, Wilson 'claimed an intimacy with the designs of Providence that could scarcely be justified'. To foreign observers, he often looked like the 'quintessential prig'.

He was not very sensitive to the articulate criticism of his peers. Although he had aristocratic personal tastes, he ultimately relied on the sanction of public opinion, on the democratic verdict. He expected his sincerity to command mass appeal. It did so as long as he was riding the crest of the wave.

Wilson regarded himself as being qualified to deal with internal American politics, but he wrote to a friend that it would be an irony of fate if he were forced to deal chiefly with foreign affairs.[3] He was forced to do precisely that. The United States' entanglement in Mexico had been a rehearsal for the great test: the outbreak of the First World War. Wilson did not understand the recurrent crisis that shook Europe in the decade before 1914, nor was he interested in doing so. It is true that earlier in 1901, he made an attempt to explore America's changed international position.[4] He argued that the Americans were living in a new and dangerous age which made the concept of security through isolation meaningless. They would have to learn to be 'neighbours to the world'.

That was as far as Wilson's thinking on foreign affairs had gone before he became President of the United States. In the absence of other equipment, he had to fall back on first principles. The universe in which men as well as nations lived was a moral, God-directed environment, in which Americans had a unique role to play. There were good reasons, Wilson was convinced, for his belief in the uniqueness of the Americans. They had succeeded in constructing a federal system which bound together a vast country and a hundred million people into a unit that might one day become the pattern for a world organization. The Americans were a new mixed people who carried the torch of equality and justice, of the belief in the perfectibility of life itself: they had turned their backs on the caste- and class-ridden societies of Europe and Asia. (Wilson believed that the inequalities of American life were either easily removable or insignificant.)

From such principles, a diplomatic practice followed. Wilson tended to assume that relations among states consisted only of civilized intercourse between gentlemen, regulated by universal moral standards and by enlightened public opinion.[5] His academic studies convinced him that the President's powers in regard to foreign affairs were extensive; his personal predilections led him to believe that he himself had better motives and a better intellect than other politicians, at home or abroad. Diplomats in Washington knew that there was little point in seeing the Secretary of State; on urgent matters he always had to wait for instructions from the President.

In his conduct of foreign affairs Wilson rarely sought or received any assistance. He usually ignored the advice of his Secretaries of State as well as that of Colonel House. Party considerations had forced Wilson to appoint William Jennings Bryan Secretary of State, but the President never came to trust him; nor did he later make use of Robert Lansing's experience and knowledge of international law. And it seems that the men who were associated with the President in the conduct of foreign policy repaid his detachment by acts of disloyalty.[6] Nor was Wilson very fortunate in his choice of Ambassadors. He thought that only 'the best man' would do, and that posts abroad should not go to men who deserved them from the party. That practice was not the only reason why Wilson disapproved of American diplomatic personnel. Toward the end of his first year in office, he wrote:[7]

. . . those who have been occupying the legations and embassies have been habituated to a point of view which is very different, indeed, from the point of view of the present administration. They have had the material interests of individuals in the United States very much more in mind than the moral and public considerations which it seems to us ought to control. They have been so bred in a different school that we have found, in several instances, that it was difficult for them to comprehend our point of view and purpose.

Nevertheless, there is no evidence that Wilson had succeeded in introducing a new type of diplomat into the service before the outbreak of the war.

, In no sense could Wilson and his country be said to be prepared for the war in the summer of 1914; while the international crisis ran its course, Wilson had been caught up in a private tragedy: his first wife, the mother of his three daughters, was dying. Wilson issued a formal appeal to the belligerents and offered his services in the cause of mediation. On that point, an American historian later wrote:[8]

All that the strongest, richest, most peaceful nation in the world could do was to stand aside while Europe slipped into anarchy, and declare that it would take no part in the tragedy.

Almost for three years, America stood aside. The dramatic development of the attitude of Washington to war revealed, most clearly, the global, the very modern, nature of the contest. It involved world-wide communications, the flow of trade as well as of information and ideas and it concerned the neutral and the belligerent countries alike.

A state of war existed between Germany and England from midnight on 4 August, and a few hours later, H.M.S. *Telconia* arrived at a spot in the North Sea near Emden, on the Dutch–German frontier. *Telconia*'s mission was to cut the five German transatlantic cables. Soon, the first British naval action of the war was successfully accomplished; in order to make quite certain, *Telconia* returned after a few days, to wind up the cut cables on her drums. After that only one cable remained open to the Germans: it connected Liberia in West Africa and Brazil, and the Americans owned most of it. This clumsy, roundabout route functioned for a few weeks, until the American company agreed to British requests, and closed it to the Germans. From then on, the Germans had to rely, for communication with overseas countries, on the powerful Nauen wireless station outside Berlin. Its disadvantage, of course, was that all wireless messages could be picked up by the enemy, and that a telegram from Washington took about four days to reach Berlin.[9]

As far as communications were concerned, the British held America in the palm of their hand; they also ran a very able publicity. In September 1914 the Prime Minister invited a member of the cabinet, Charles Masterman, to take charge of propaganda. The operation had a high security rating. Masterman was the chairman of the national insurance commission at Wellington

House, and he set up inconspicuous propaganda headquarters at the same address. He had been a don at Cambridge whose best-known book was *The Condition of England*, published in 1909. He became a Member of Parliament in 1906, a junior Minister two years later, and Chancellor of the Duchy of Lancaster in February 1914. He was a high-minded, high-church person lacking the common touch: he found the winning and retaining of parliamentary seats a constant trial. As a publicist, however, he was first-rate.

The mystery surrounding the covert activities at Wellington House soon aroused public interest, and rumours were by no means quashed by a statement to the House of Commons that Masterman was receiving a compensation of £1,200 from the Secret Service funds.[10] The production of pamphlets and books was the hard core of the Wellington House activities, the best-known of them being the Bryce report on the conduct of the Germans in Belgium, published in over thirty languages five days after the sinking of the *Lusitania*. (The largest ship of the British merchant navy, the Cunard liner *Lusitania*, was sunk south-west of Queenstown Harbour on 9 May 1915. The German submarine fired two torpedoes without warning: 1,198 lives were lost. At the inquest at Kinsale the jury, reflecting the anger that had swept through the country, returned a verdict of wholesale and wilful murder against the officers of the submarine as well as against the Emperor and government of Germany. The Germans telegraphed their sympathy to Washington at the loss of American lives. They added that the *Lusitania* had carried large quantities of war material on previous occasions and that, on the day it was sunk, it had on board 4,500 cases of ammunition.) But to return to Wellington House: apart from literary productions, it made propaganda films, which were released by the Home or the Foreign Office. As long as Asquith remained in power and the value of propaganda was suspect, Masterman was able to carry on his work undisturbed.

The only serious blunder committed by English publicity in the United States followed the dramatic events of the spring of 1916: the arrival, off the coast of Ireland, of Sir Roger Casement in a German submarine and his subsequent capture; the Easter Rising in Dublin; its suppression and the execution of its leaders. In consequence, it was feared in London, Irish America was irretrievably lost. .... The bad effect on American public opinion was not so much due to the fact of an Irish rebellion taking place, nor to the suppression of the rebellion, nor even to the punishment of the leaders of the rebellion, but to some quite avoidable accidents of publicity.[11]

To begin with, reports in the American press of Casement's unsuccessful landing and of the Dublin rebellion created a musical comedy atmosphere; it reminded the Americans and their cartoonists of similar events in Latin America. But then, suddenly, the executions were made known. No charges had been specified against individual leaders, no trial announced or reported. The stark news items brought about a sharp change in the tone of the American press. Animosity against England swelled up and affected many more Americans than those of Irish origin.

This blunder coincided with the opening of the attack, in London, on Masterman's monopoly position. By the end of the summer of 1916 a number of government departments had acquired their own information services and in November, Asquith, who was Masterman's friend and protector, fell. Lloyd George then formed the Department of Information, with Colonel John Buchan at its head. Masterman remained in charge at Wellington House, which was to specialize in the production of books and pamphlets for home and neutral countries. There was also a 'film and entertainment of foreign visitors' department; a political intelligence department; a news department. An advisory committee consisting of Northcliffe, Burnham, Robert Donald, C.P.Scott – they were joined by Beaverbrook later in the year – was formed to assist Colonel Buchan, who was responsible direct to the War Cabinet and the Prime Minister. Nevertheless, the old frictions continued, and after some additional readjustments, the Department of Information was abolished and, early in 1918, Lord Beaverbook was put in charge of the Ministry of Information. By that time, Masterman's originally modest enterprise had developed into a big government industry. Lloyd George talked about 'our propaganda, costing I dare not tell the House how much . . .' In fact, Lord Beaverbrook, by getting rid of Wellington House, was able to cut the proposed budget of his Ministry from £1,800,000 to £1,200,000.[12]

As long as Masterman was in charge of British propaganda, it was aimed mainly at the United States. It made a later and better start than German publicity. There were of course the natural advantages: the common language as well as the similar under-current of attitudes and ideals. The Americans knew their Shakespeare but they did not know their Goethe; they thought that the battle of Waterloo was won by the Duke of Wellington, not by Blücher. An American scholar wrote that, in 1914, the British viewpoint

stood an excellent chance of infecting America, for American public opinion has often been a cockle-shell, floating helplessly and un-consciously in the wake of the British man-of-war.[13]

When, late in the autumn of 1914, 367 American newspaper proprietors were asked, 'Which side in the European struggle has your sympathies?', 105 replies favoured the Allies; 20 were for the Central Powers, and 242 proprietors had no preference.[14] In Paris, a former American Ambassador told a French historian early in 1915:[15]

In the United States there are at present perhaps 50,000 persons who feel that the nation should immediately intervene in the war on your side. But there are 100,000,000 Americans who do not so think. Our duty is to reverse these figures so that 50,000 may become 100,000,000.

Though sympathy for the Allied cause and the decision to inter-vene in the war were two quite separate things, the publicists in London worked to strengthen the former, and prepare the ground for active intervention.

The Allies were fortunate in that the Germans had committed a number of basic blunders. Dr Dernburg, the head of the German propaganda outfit in New York, made no attempt to conceal his official connections with Berlin; he used the sledge-hammer type of appeal, and it is doubtful whether he had a clear view of the audience he was aiming at. Masterman's answer to the German effort was much crisper. It was based on the inspired motto of 'Hands Across the Sea'; its tone was restrained, and it always had the personal touch. The place of origin of the propaganda material was carefully concealed; one of the first things the staff at Wellington House were instructed to do was to make a careful analysis of the opinion of the American press and of university teachers and students on the war; by the middle of December 1914 there existed at Wellington House a comprehensive mailing list for the propaganda material destined for the United States. Until America's entry into the war, the flood of books and pamphlets continued to grow, their tone becoming gradually less restrained. The Germans themselves supplied the dramatic incidents and around them the propagandists spun their yarn. The bestiality of the enemy was packaged and sold under the labels 'Lusitania', 'Captain Fryatt', 'Edith Cavell'; the accusing finger always pointed to the perpetrators of these horrors, the Germans. When America at last entered the war, the emotions of many of her citizens had been whipped up to a frenzy of hatred.

We hated with a common hate that was exhilarating. [I remember] attending a great meeting in New England, held under the auspices of a Christian church. . . . A speaker demanded that the Kaiser, when captured, be boiled in oil, and the entire audience stood on the chairs to scream its hysterical approval. This was the mood we were in. This was the kind of madness that had seized us.[16]

The fact that the Americans were ready for the war in the spring of 1917 was decisive for the President, who would never have made a move of such importance as the declaration of war on Germany without the sanction of public opinion. The sympathy for the Allied cause, the feeling of community of interests, we have seen, had been there; the hatred for Germany, the readiness and acceptance of the war, had to be created. Allied, and especially British, propaganda in the United States had a professional touch about it, and available evidence points to the fact that it was highly effective.

The German failure in America, on the other hand, was not merely a matter of severed cable communications. The German political and strategic thinking was cramped inside continental confines. France and Russia, Turkey and the Balkans, the territory of the Habsburg monarchy of course and Italy: in that area the Germans were more or less at ease, their armies in the Great War moving across the familiar rivers and mountain ranges with as much assurance as their strategic thinking had done before the war. But elsewhere, the Germans lost their sureness of touch. We have seen how high expectations accompanied low investment in their Moslem Holy War venture. In regard to the United States, the German ignorance was even more striking, and ultimately more costly. (Between the wars the Germans themselves detected, and tried to correct, this flaw in their political thinking. The science of 'geopolitics' was expected to put their *Weltpolitik* on a scientific basis. Although many Nazi leaders sympathized with the new 'science' it does not seem to have helped them very much. In spite of geopolitics, their horizons were even more limited than those of the politicians of the imperial era.)

In 1915, German banknotes had printed on them the super-imposed sentence '*Gott strafe England und Amerika*'. In the same year, American shipyards produced twenty submarines, sent them in parts to Canada where they were assembled, then crossing the Atlantic under their own power. A year later, the Germans sent their submarine *Deutschland* on a good-will mission to the United States. They gave this feat tremendous publicity, speaking of it as something quite unprecedented in naval history. There was no way in which German submarines could be made popular in the United States, even if it could be proved that they were toys of peace made of marzipan and run on lager beer. There was also the more serious failure of German intelligence, which seemed to have been unaware of the earlier journey of American submarines, in the opposite direction. In this instance, as in many others, the Germans underestimated the level of American technical achievement. Their calculations involving the American factor had a haphazard appearance, and the decisions based on them were disastrous. As far as we know, there was a single isolated voice of warning. Soon after America's entry into the war, the Hamburg shipowner, Alfred Ballin, remarked:[17]

We are mad; we have done a disastrous thing, a thing which will throw its shadow over our economic life for a generation. How are we to resume our foreign trade in the face of an Anglo-Saxondom which loathes and must loathe our presence among them? All the military victories and all the wild will-of-the-wisps about Hamburg to Bagdad will not help us.

The Allies, and England in particular, had of course had much stronger commercial connections with America and they did not diminish after August 1914. On the contrary; a long time before American troops gave the Allies a decisive military superiority, American agriculture, industry and finance aided the Allied war effort. In the process, the economic and financial predominance of the old world was destroyed. After two years' warfare, the

United States ceased to be a debtor state, and instead had Europe deeply in their debt.[18] America had lent foreign governments close on $2,000m. and investment brokers in New York still complained that they could not find enough securities for their customers. It was the reverse of the situation before the war. American securities valued at $4,000m. had then been held in London and Paris; two years later, the amount was reduced to $1,000m., of which $300m. were pledged as securities for loans, while the rest was earmarked for similar uses. American holdings of gold went up sharply as well: from $1,887m. on the outbreak of the war to $2,563m. on 1 December 1917.

The war constricted the operations of European financial centres and opened up new horizons before the Americans. On 3 August 1914 the Kaiser's ultimatum to St Petersburg set off a rush of European investments to the London market; the Stock Exchange, in order to avert panic, closed down. The markets all over Europe as well as in Latin America followed suit. New York was undecided. On Monday morning, 3 August 1914, the brokers gathered on the floor as usual. At about 9.45 the messenger who rang the gong, announcing the opening of the day's business, was standing at his post. The excitement mounted. Almost every broker on the floor had been ordered to sell vast quantities of stock and had no idea if the market could take the strain. At 9.55 a clerk of the Exchange walked into the middle of the floor, and read the official notice. It announced that the market would close down for an indefinite period of time. A cheer went up, and the brokers started dispersing.

They stayed away for four months. Restricted trading was started again in New York on 28 November 1914: all the European markets were still closed. European investors started selling large quantities of the $4,000m. of American securities they had held at the outbreak of war: the economic and financial prestige of the United States was greatly enhanced.

Early in 1915, Asquith's cabinet asked the City bankers to use their resources for war purposes only; the scope of London banking activities became severely limited, and New York was now ready to take over international trade. Until August 1914, Wall Street had played little part in financing foreign governments. There had been the London loan of $200m. at the time of the South African war, and another loan of $50m. to Tokio at the time of the Russian-Japanese war, but little else. There had existed no public market for foreign securities in America on the pre-war European scale; early in the war Morgan's was cautioned by the State Department that 'loans by American bankers to any foreign nation which is at war are inconsistent with the true spirit of neutrality'.[19] The situation changed in the course of the year 1915. At first, London and Paris tried to pay for American supplies in cash, but the volume of trade was so big that such primitive financial methods had to be abandoned. In September 1915, a distinguished Anglo-French delegation, led by Lord Reading, arrived in New York in order to float an Allied loan. The sum of £200m. was at first suggested, and it so amazed the American bankers that it was cut down by a half, and successfully disposed of. The proceeds of the loan were to be spent in the United States; when it was used up the Allies went on borrowing, usually pledging American securities in their possession. By the time the United States entered the war, New York had taken over from London much of the burden of financing the Allied war effort.

The war was insatiable in regard to money and material. Allied agents soon started combing the United States for supplies; the timing of the Allied demand was perfect. The closure of the Dardanelles had, as we have seen, cut off the Russian wheat producers from the world markets just at a time when the American farmers had brought home a record harvest. At first, soon after the outbreak of the war, the American farmers panicked. Wheat and barley began to pile up on the wharves; Democratic politicians saw the South, with its one-crop economy, faced with immediate ruin. But it did not take long before brisk bidding for American food supplies brought about a sharp increase in United States' export statistics.

In the long run, however, the war affected industry much more than agriculture. Since the first months of Wilson's administration, the country had been going through an economic depression, and the outbreak of the war aroused fears that the situation would get worse. On 23 November 1914, in a letter to Wilson, Andrew Carnegie was still pessimistic, though he could see a glimmer of hope for the future:[20]

The present Financial and Industrial situations are very distressing. I have never known such conditions, such pressing calls upon debtors to pay, and especially to reduce mortgages. Saturday morning last my Secretary reported forty-five appeals to me to meet such calls in one delivery – today he tells me that we shall have a hundred or more *at least*. This may change slowly, the Allies purchases from us from Horses down, are certain to be great.

They were great, and American industry did everything to meet them. Soon after the outbreak of the war, the Allied agents who looked in the United States for caches of guns and ammunition were disappointed: there was little for them to buy. But the skills and the raw materials were there. The House of Morgan, which had always been on confidential terms with the London banking houses, took over the task of mobilizing American industry for the war, placing European orders in the right quarters. A special agency was set up under Edward R. Stettinius, the American match-king, who got together an organization of 175 men, most of them buyers. It became known as SOS (the Slaves of Stettinius), and it was soon buying supplies for the Allies at the rate of $10m. a day. The purchasing operation was conducted against a sophisticated financial background. By the end of August 1917 J. Pierpont Morgan's firm had bought more than $3,000m. of merchandise for the Allies, marketing at the same time well over $2,000m. American securities formerly held in Europe. Another American link was established by Kitchener soon after he became the Minister of War. He asked Charles M. Schwab of the Bethlehem Steel Company to come over to London, and together they worked out the Allied requirements that could be met by Schwab's company. Schwab pledged the whole of its capacity, and he agreed not to sell out to anyone – this really meant German interests – as long as British contracts were under way.

The stimulus to American industry was great. In 1916 the production of steel in the United States shot up to 43 million tons, by far out-distancing Great Britain with her 9 million tons.[21] The value of steel and iron products exported from America in the month of March 1915 was $1,363,693 and in November of the same year $10,776,183. The Allied demand for ammunition was insatiable. The total value of the exports of munitions for the year 1916 was calculated at the figure of $1,290,000,000.[22]

There was a high price to pay for American war supplies, yet from time to time such nervousness overcame the English about the position of the United States in the war that they considered raising the price even higher. On 15 July 1915 Sir Cecil Spring-Rice, the British Ambassador to Washington, telegraphed the Foreign Office:[23]

> Situation here is growing very serious. We are dependent for at least a year and a half on this country for war supplies. A campaign, supported by various organizations, some of them not in sympathy with Germany though acting on parallel lines, is being conducted against the export of munitions of war, and movement is growing in strength.
>
> In the circumstances it is essential that we take what action is possible, to conciliate public opinion where this is possible through material interests.
>
> Cotton interests, which dominate the South and the Administration, meat interests, which dominate the Central States and Standard Oil Combines, which have great power in New York, are, as an eminent personage [?informed me], in sympathy with us. But rightly or wrongly they think that their interests have been disregarded.
>
> I beg to remind you that Crawford, of whose zeal and great ability there can be no question, was sent out as adviser to you in these questions. His opinion entirely coincides with my own, and with that of all our sympathizers here, namely: that something ought to be done, and done soon even at a great sacrifice, to conciliate the powerful interests that think themselves aggrieved. In succeeding telegrams, I will submit detailed suggestions.
>
> With the greatest earnestness I beg that you will take these matters into your most serious consideration, and lay them before the Cabinet.

The Ambassador then proposed that Great Britain should subsidize the price of American cotton: it could be put on the contraband list without fear of further offending the growers. They had been accustomed to Germany and Austria taking about 2,700,000 bales yearly, and in 1915 the growers had a surplus, from the previous year's crop, of some two million bales. The Ambassador suggested that they be bought up by a syndicate of London banks, acting through Morgan.

Foreign Office opinion concurred with the Ambassador's views: the English diplomats knew that cotton interests were more vital for America than, say, the Manchester cotton trade had been for England half a century before. In the American South everything, from the grower's wife's new hat to the wages of the plantation labour, depended on the price of cotton. If the cotton market were a complete wash-out, it was quite possible that somebody like Senator Hoke Smith would manage to get together two hundred votes in Congress for an embargo on the export of arms.

Such a movement was growing in July 1915: desire for the imposition of an embargo on the export of arms and ammunition went hand in hand with the complaints of other American exporters – cotton-growers, meat-packers, oilmen – that British wartime measures disrupted the usual pattern of their trade. A delegation of meat-packers called on Lansing in the summer of 1915 because their business with the neutral states had been destroyed and they were left with goods valued at 3m. sterling on their hands. Lansing instructed Page, the Ambassador to London, to make strong representations to the British government.

Nevertheless, the Allies needed America more than the other way round, and the losses following the disruption of peacetime trade were soon offset by the new requirements of war. At the height of the crisis in the relations between the United States and Britain in the summer of 1915, an optimistic view of the situation was put forward in the Foreign Office:[24]

Throughout the war, as before it, we have been nervous about the United States to the point of periodically considering a revision of our attitude. I believe that this nervousness is quite unjustified. We have to face unpleasantness in the United States, but they are wholly calculable and are none the more serious because they are shouted at us through a megaphone in our own language. We are fighting for our existence and one of the stakes we have to play is the friendship of the United States. I am prepared to back that stake to the end, subject only to that respect for vital interests which one has to show in dealing with every nation.

Nevertheless, President Wilson knew little about the ways of big business, and the American manufacturers had enough to do whether their country was in the war or not. It is unlikely that economic pressure made Wilson consider the possibility of war. There were, however, political consequences of America's commerce that the President could hardly overlook.

The United States traded in war supplies with the Allied side only: the Central Powers were self-supporting as far as arms and ammunition were concerned. The one-sidedness of the trade did not escape the notice of the German government. On 4 April 1915, Bernstorff, the German Ambassador to Washington, presented the State Department with a memorandum that gave the

German view of American trade with the Allies. The main weight
of the German complaint lay in the fact that the other neutral
countries had put an embargo on the export of war supplies to the
belligerents: the American Secretary of State delayed his reply for
over a fortnight, and even then he avoided dealing with the point
Berlin had made. He confined himself to stating that to place an
embargo on the sale of war supplies to the belligerents would be
'an unjustifiable departure from the principle of strict neutrality'.
Again, on 29 June 1915, the Americans received a note protesting
against the trade in war supplies, this time from the Austrian
Ministry of Foreign Affairs. After some disagreement between the
President and the Secretary of State – on that occasion Wilson
showed how much he disliked the way in which America's
immediate economic interests cut across his long-term pursuit of
peace – the reply was sent to Vienna on 12 August 1915. After the
preamble which contained an involved legal argument in favour
of the trade in war materials, the Note got down to a more
practical level:[25]

It has never been the policy of this country to maintain in time of
peace a large military establishment or stores of arms and ammunition
sufficient to repel invasion by a well-equipped and powerful enemy. . . .
In consequence of this standing policy the United States would, in the
event of attack by a foreign power, be at the outset of the war, seriously
. . . embarrassed by the lack of arms and ammunition. . . . The United
States has always depended upon the right and power to purchase arms
and ammunition from neutral nations in case of foreign attack. This
right, which it claims for itself, it can not deny to others.

As an afterthought a week later, the State Department asked its
representatives in the neutral countries in Europe to describe the
way those countries put their neutrality into practice. According
to the Secretary of State, the replies established the fact that
Spain, Italy, Denmark, Sweden, Norway and Holland had forbidden exports of war supplies, so they all said, 'to conserve their
supplies for their own use'. In any case they could have sold such
materials in negligible quantities; the crux of the matter, Lansing
wrote, was that

It is not possible to ascertain whether the real ground for embargoes
was, in some cases, that of conservation or really to avoid the enmity
of the belligerents, to retaliate against some vexatious measure of the
belligerents or to maintain a strict neutrality.[26]

The uncertainties, the hesitations of the Americans were understood neither in Berlin nor in Vienna. The munitions trade created hostility to the United States among the peoples of the Central Powers while their governments, long before America actually entered the war, thought of it as firmly committed to the Allied side. The scarcity of munitions and other equipment in Britain and France, instead of losing the war for them, in the end contributed to their winning it.

In February 1915, the Germans declared the seas around the British Isles a war zone. The submarine threat forced the English to arm their merchant vessels, and the Americans, in their turn, started making difficulties about admitting armed merchantmen to their ports. The question was in the end settled to the satisfaction of the British government, but it remained a sensitive spot in the relations between the two countries. Much later, in November 1916, Lord Crewe made a passing reference in Parliament to armed merchantmen sinking submarines at sight. He received a reproving note from the Foreign Secretary:[27]

There is a real danger that the U.S. Government may deny use of their ports to defensively armed merchantmen on the ground that their armament is really for offence. The Admiralty have had to guard their instructions most carefully on this account and if any words are used which suggest that a merchant vessel might sink an American submarine our armed merchant vessels will be treated as war vessels and will be unable to trade to United States ports. This would be disastrous. . . . It is only this year and after much trouble that we have got the U.S. Government to let our defensively armed merchantmen trade to their ports, and I live in dread of the question being reopened.

The command of the high seas by the Royal Navy made trade with the United States possible. Though at times it annoyed the Americans – an American historian wrote that it 'did not touch our pockets so much as our pride'[28] – British naval measures involved property only, while German activities often resulted in the loss of human lives. On the whole, the Royal Navy was used in a way that harmed the enemy without antagonizing the neutral countries. The first lists of contraband were issued in London on 4 August 1914. They included war supplies only; on 27 October Sir Edward Grey reminded the Ambassador to Paris:[29]

In our history we have always contended that foodstuffs and raw materials destined for the civil population are not contraband of war. . . .

Over and over again, we have laid this down as a doctrine of international law; and our Prize Courts would not act on any other.

The employment of the submarine by the Germans and pressure from Paris for a more ruthless conduct of economic warfare caused the British government to review its customary attitude. They gave their reply to the German move on 18 February, when the seas around Britain were declared a war zone, in an Order in Council on 11 March 1915. It announced that the fleet had instituted a blockade 'effectively controlling by cruiser cordon all passage to and from Germany by sea'. No merchant ship was to be allowed to proceed on her voyage to any German port, nor was a vessel allowed to leave a German port.[30] The blockade aimed to deprive Germany of

certain raw materials essential for the manufacture or use of munitions of war, such as cotton, copper, rubber and lubricating oil, to cut off her food and other necessaries and to weaken her economic position.[31]

The blockade was a cruder and more effective method of conducting economic warfare than the contraband policy. In July 1915 the British Foreign Secretary argued that it

was adopted as a measure of reprisal against the illegal warfare on merchant shipping pursued by German submarines, as a means of exerting pressure on the enemy of which the effect, comparatively small at first, gradually becomes greater. It has barely commenced as yet to be seriously inconvenient to Germany, whilst, on the other hand, the German submarines' depradations have, from the start, been steadily destructive of British shipping, together with the lives of non-combatants, including women and children, and valuable cargoes, nearly 300,000 tons of British shipping, exclusive of fishing vessels, having been destroyed since 18 February last. It is accordingly unreasonable to expect His Majesty's Government to acquiesce in this destruction of British life and wealth by discontinuing their means of retaliation almost before the enemy has commenced to feel its effects, and they could not contemplate such a relaxation of their policy unless the German government first paid compensation for the consequences of their illegal submarine warfare.[32]

By the end of the year 1915, the English blockade policy had become so important and so complex that it had to be organized on completely new lines. Too many different people and offices were responsible for it: there were the Contraband and Foreign Trade

Departments in the Foreign Office; the Contraband Committee and the Enemy Exports Committee; the War Trade Department and several committees sitting under it; the Board of Trade with its Coal, Tin and Rubber Committees; the Trade Department at the Admiralty and finally the Trade Advisory Committee, presided over by Lord Crewe. The last committee was meant to be a clearing-house of all the departments concerned, but it was too numerous to be of much practical value. On 12 January 1916, Lord Robert Cecil drafted a minute for the Prime Minister concerning the difficulties in the execution of the blockade policy; he went on to argue that

the German resources available for purchase from abroad are now very limited, and that it may well be that we should aim at, among other things, inducing her to spend those resources in the least valuable way that we can secure.

Questions of this kind are not really fit to be decided by any of the Departments of the Foreign Office, or, I think, of any other of the offices mentioned, nor do I regard the War Trade Advisory Committee as a satisfactory body for their determination.[33]

Cecil made his point, and became the Minister of Blockade.

Under his supervision the blockade policy was tightened up in the course of the year 1916, a process facilitated by the internal situation in the United States. This was the only country capable of exercising effective pressure on the decisions of the London government, and for the best part of the year it was in the throes of a presidential campaign. At a time devoted to settling the paramount problem of domestic politics, Americans had not much time for doing anything else. And there was the danger that a decisive action would give some opponent a handle – the reason why Congress, as well as the President, were habitually inclined to do as little as they could get away with in presidential years. Expert opinion in the Foreign Office took the situation in the United States into account:[34]

... we need not be deterred from any development in our blockade policy by the fear of an embargo or other hostile action by the United States in this year. Of course no gift of prophecy enables me to say what may happen a year hence when the dust of the Presidential election has cleared away, but the danger of any hostile action even then is so remote that it can safely be disregarded.

The ruthless prosecution of the blockade policy prevented, for instance, the American Red Cross from shipping medical supplies to Germany. When, however, the commerce of the neutral states was in any way injured, the Foreign Office took great pains over negotiating agreements on compensations. By the end of the year 1916 all blockade measures were in good working order, and were starting to show results.

They were not yet very striking: the ultimate goal of disabling the industry and starving the people of the Central Powers was still far distant.[35] The German and the Austrian armies were well equipped. The production of guns and ammunition was unaffected by the shortage of manganese, as a substitute for the steel-hardening ingredient was found; substitutes for wool and leather were also developed. Whereas the armed forces had, until the end of 1916, survived the blockade unharmed, the civil population was not cosseted to the same extent. Shortages of milk and meat were becoming acute, and they pressed especially hard on the poor sections of the town population. In Berlin and Vienna, in Constantinople and Sofia, food rationing was introduced toward the end of 1916.

American trade with the Allies and Wilson's unwillingness to place an embargo on the export of war supplies helped the Germans to decide on the launching of unrestricted submarine warfare. They assumed that, whatever they did, the Americans were hostile to the Central Powers anyway. The decision was made in Berlin soon after the Presidential election, when Wilson was once again free to look to events outside the United States.* The British had been able to put the blockade into operation comparatively undisturbed in the course of the year 1916; now the Germans were trying to reverse that development at a less propitious time.

Yet the argument that 'the sole factor that could have driven Wilson from neutrality in the spring of 1917 was the resumption of the submarine campaign'[36] has a deceptive simplicity about it. Concern on the part of the President that Germany would gain supremacy on the high seas would have been understandable, but it does not seem to have been much on his mind. Nor did Wilson see himself as the head of a powerful industrial state who was in duty bound to look after its economic welfare. The two elements –

* See above, pp. 113f.

control of the high seas and America's trade in war supplies – were closely linked. Yet on their own, they do not provide a satisfactory explanation for Wilson's decision to take his country into the war. There were also Wilson's disappointments in his role of peacemaker. A thankless task, it satisfied the practical politician and the idealist in Wilson. He knew that if he failed he might be unable to keep his country out of the war. He was convinced that there was no one else apart from himself who could restore peace to a world gone mad. While Wilson was free to negotiate peace none of the European Great Powers wanted it. And when they began to turn their minds to peace, the President was no longer free to negotiate it.

As a peacemaker, Wilson was either ill-used or badly regarded in Europe. The Allies, and the English especially, never took Wilson very seriously in his chosen role. They saw him as a Don Quixote tilting at windmills, and they were convinced that he did not really understand any of the issues at stake in the war. We have seen how the German Chancellor tried to use Wilson and peace in a rearguard action against the German military. Bethmann Hollweg's attempt failed, casting a long shadow over the Chancellor's political future, as well as over the cause of peace.

The President was convinced that it was his and his country's duty to lead the quest for international understanding. It was an idea which Bryan, Wilson's first Secretary of State, had outlined a long time before the outbreak of the war:[37]

> Behold a Republic, increasing in population, in wealth, in strength and in influence, solving the problems of civilization and hastening the coming of universal brotherhood, a Republic which makes thrones and dissolves aristocracies by its silent example and gives light to those who sit in darkness. Behold a Republic gradually and surely becoming the supreme moral factor in disputes.

Though Bryan had concluded a record number of arbitration treaties, neither he nor his successor Lansing were called on by the President to help him carry out the peace programme. Colonel House was Wilson's choice.

The son of a Texan merchant and shipowner who had made a fortune blockade-running in the civil war, House gave all his adult life, apart from three years spent in promoting a new railway line, to the pursuit of politics and politicians, 'advising and helping wherever I might'. He was influential in his home state, and on the national level he became one of the architects of the Democratic revival, as well as Wilson's chief promoter. His appearance had nothing memorable about it apart from an air of having just emerged from a confidential, high-level conference. This was very often the case. Immensely self-centred, he was capable of writing such a sentence as 'Another curious thing is the number of people desiring to cross the ocean on the same ship with me, believing that safety is thereby ensured'[38] without a word of explanation. House was so ambitious that he often thought that there was no point in trying to satisfy his ambition. He could be snobbish, innocent, idealistic, in rapid succession; he was always discreet and persuasive. One winter shortly before the outbreak of the war, House wrote a political fantasy;[39] its motto came from Mazzini:

No war of classes, no hostility to existing wealth, no wanton or unjust violation of the rights of property, but a constant disposition to ameliorate the condition of the classes least favored by fortune.

and it was dedicated by House

To the unhappy many who have lived and died lacking opportunity, because, in the starting, the world-wide social structure was wrongly begun.

House was for Wilson 'my second personality. He is my independent self. His thoughts and mine are one.' House's health and ambition prevented him from accepting an office in Wilson's administration: instead, he became the President's representative at large.

It was a powerful position, and it suited Colonel House well; politicians outside the United States were puzzled by it, uncertain of the Colonel's official standing. The English treated him with courtesy, at the highest level; the Germans took him for a real colonel and treated him to various military entertainments.

House admired the unhurried, aristocratic approach to politics of the English; he got on well with Grey. On 10 February 1916, the Foreign Secretary set aside the whole morning for a conference with House. An unusual agreement then began to take shape. It would have suited Britain best if the United States entered the war on the submarine issue, without in any way interfering with the promises that the Allies had made to one another during the war. House told Grey that America would not enter the war, at least not for the time being, and that the best thing would be if Wilson demanded a conference of the belligerents for the discussion of peace terms. Grey promised that the Allies would agree to such a conference; House for his own part said that if the Germans refused to come 'we will throw in all our weight in order to bring her to terms'.⁴⁰ The following day House lunched at 33 Eccleston Square with Grey, Asquith and Balfour. He was wrong if he thought that the question of English and Allied agreement to the idea of a peace conference had been settled: in order to make it seem more attractive, he had to use two arguments for all their worth.

House maintained that Russia could not be expected to take the strain of the war much longer and that if the Allies came too near defeat they would be wrong if they thought the United States would come in, at the last moment, in order to reverse the result.

In these circumstances we would probably create a large army and navy, and retire entirely from European affairs and depend upon ourselves.⁴¹

But the Colonel took it that the Germans would decline the invitation to the conference. During his conversations in London, House more than hinted what the reward for agreement would be; he wrote in his diary:⁴²

If my plan was adopted, I believed it would inevitably lead to an alliance between the United States and Great Britain, France, and Italy, the democracies of the world.

The Ambassador to London, Page, took no part in any of the unofficial meetings: Colonel House's position made it possible for him to be outspoken, and pursue peace in unorthodox ways. Three days after the lunch at Grey's town house, in the evening of 14 February 1916, Asquith, Balfour, Grey and Lloyd George met Colonel House at dinner. The Lord Chief Justice, Lord Reading, who had successfully negotiated the largest loan in America's history, was their host. Apart from House, nobody really wanted to talk about peace and how President Wilson could bring it about. Even if we allow for the custom that developed during the war of not discussing important problems in the presence of the servants, House had to hold back too long and in the end brought up the subject himself.

The setting of the conference could be, say, The Hague, and the President would be in the chair: House opened the conversation. But it was steered round to more general topics:

The nationalization [*sic*] of Poland was discussed at great length. . . . We all cheerfully divided up Turkey, both in Asia and Europe. The discussion hung for a long while around the fate of Constantinople. George and Balfour were not enthusiastic over giving it into the hands of Russia, Grey and Asquith thinking if this were not done material for another war would always be at hand.[43]

Lloyd George later remembered that 'an outlet to the sea' for Russia was discussed:[44] no one told House that the Allies had undertaken, some eleven months ago, to give the Straits and Constantinople to the Russians. Shortly before the dinner-party broke up at midnight, Asquith had asked House what he thought would be the proper time for approaching the other Allies with the conference plan. House replied that the Allies should try to make some impression on the German battle-lines first, in order to create the right psychological moment; he added that such an offensive should not be too successful, so as not to over-excite Allied public opinion.

On 23 February 1916, two days before Colonel House sailed for New York, Sir Edward Grey had given him a copy of his memorandum, the outcome of the Colonel's work in London. It stated that President Wilson was ready, on hearing from France and England, to propose that a conference should be summoned to put an end to the war:[45]

Should the Allies accept this proposal, and should Germany refuse it, the United States would probably enter the war against Germany.

It went on to state that

Colonel House expressed the opinion that, if such a conference met, it would secure peace on terms not unfavourable to the Allies; and, if it failed to secure peace, the United States would leave the conference as a belligerent on the side of the Allies, if Germany was unreasonable.[46]

After having made specific references to the 'not unfavourable' terms, Grey pointed out that the British cabinet would have to inform their allies about the President's offer, and that the present moment was not suitable for doing so.

It was one of the more unusual agreements in the annals of European diplomacy, and it was bound to become an object of controversy and misunderstanding. The President, who was very pleased about the outcome of the Colonel's trip, added the word 'probably' between the words 'would' and 'leave', so that the sentence read: 'the United States would probably leave the conference as a belligerent on the side of the Allies . . .' There were two ways of looking at the President's insertion of the word. The Americans have tended to regard it as a conventional covering expression, common in diplomatic practice; the phrase now corresponded more closely to similar passages above and below. The English, and Lloyd George in particular, took it for an expression of doubt by the President. Lloyd George wrote in his memoirs:[47]

Sir Edward Grey's view was that this completely changed the character of the proposal, and, therefore, he did not think it worth while to communicate the purport of the negotiations to the Allies. . . . The real explanation probably is that President Wilson was afraid of public opinion in the U.S.A. and Sir Edward Grey was frightened of our Allies.

Nevertheless, Grey let Briand know of the proposal, very briefly, and without recommending it because, in his own words, 'Both France and Russia had up to this time suffered more heavily in the war than we had. We could never be the first to recommend peace to them.'[48] The agreement clearly revealed the extent to which Wilson and House expected more sense to be forthcoming, on the question of peace, from London than from Berlin. In February 1916, therefore, there lay an important decision before Grey. Was he to risk a conference with Wilson in the chair and the remote possibility that peace might break out? The idea somehow seemed so wrong to him that even the promise of the United States coming into the war on the Allied side was not enough of a compensation. Colonel House made no similar proposal when, toward the end of January 1916, he visited Berlin.

After Wilson's re-election in November 1916 and the formation, a month later, of Lloyd George's War Cabinet, House made an effort to revive his agreement with Grey. But early in December 1916, Wilson's mind was moving on different lines. Instead of an early peace conference, Wilson now wanted a clear definition by the belligerent countries of their war aims.[49]

We have seen the way in which President Wilson's and Beth-mann Hollweg's peace initiatives crossed in December 1916, and the confusion that resulted. We have also noted that Zimmermann made an indiscreet and, as it also happened, untrue remark about the German offer being meant to anticipate President Wilson's initiative. Like Bethmann, Wilson was not really helped by his Secretary of State. On the day the Note was handed over to Zimmermann in Berlin, Lansing in Washington told the press that the President acted because America was 'growing nearer the verge of war' and for that reason was trying to find out what the various states wanted to get out of the war, so that 'we may regulate our conduct in the future'.[50] Wilson made Lansing with-draw his statement in public and say that the United States had no intention of departing from the policy of neutrality and that he, the Secretary of State, gave his wholehearted support to the President's peace policy. Despite Lansing's public recantation, the incident left a bitter after-taste in Berlin, and strengthened the suspicions of those Germans who opposed American mediation.

In Berlin at the close of the year 1916 the cause of peace seemed all but lost. Bethmann might still grasp at straws, and he had Bernstorff in Washington to feed his optimism. But the Secretary of State, Zimmermann, was committed to support the military, and so was the Kaiser. They were ready to stake everything on the effectiveness of the submarine weapon, a gamble that had been first suggested in the summer of 1916, under the influence of a gloomy military prospect. The situation had improved a little since, but the declaration of unrestricted submarine warfare had lost no support, rather the contrary. In London, a pessimistic view also prevailed. Lloyd George's cabinet were convinced that the war would be lost unless America joined the Allies soon.[51] But gloom as to their chances in war did not turn the minds of most politicians and soldiers to peace.

President Wilson was unaware of the situation in London and Berlin, and perhaps it was his ignorance that made it possible for him to carry on the policy of peace. There were Colonel House and Count Bernstorff to help him. The son of an Ambassador, the holder of at least five American honorary degrees, Bernstorff knew the Washington scene well. He saw it as his personal mission to prevent a war between Germany and the United States: it was not for lack of trying that he ultimately failed. Some of the strength was taken out of his arguments by the distance between Washington and Berlin. It had grown considerably, we have seen, soon after the outbreak of the war, and was now making a mockery of wartime urgency. Especially at times when speed was essential, communications between the two capitals seemed to move at a pace belonging to another century. Sending reports by diplomatic bag was out of the question, and telegrams in either direction were taking eighty hours at least. They kept on crossing each other as did the intentions of Zimmermann and his Ambassador to Washington. The last glimmers of a hope of peace were extinguished somewhere on that roundabout telegraphic route, Washington–Buenos Aires–Stockholm–Berlin.

In the evening of 27 December 1916 Bernstorff called on Colonel House at his New York flat. The Ambassador was told that the President had come to regard a peace conference without some preliminary secret talks as impracticable. The Allied Powers, House said, would either refuse to attend the conference or they would make conditions before accepting the invitation. There may have been a note of resentment against the Allies in what House said. Anyway, Bernstorff was encouraged to redouble his efforts. He reported to Berlin that Wilson and House, in contrast to other Americans, could keep a secret, and that the President had never been really interested in the territorial side of the peace settlement. 'Guarantees for the future' were his hobby-horses: disarmament, freedom of the seas, arbitration, a league of nations.[52] On the following day Bernstorff returned to Washington and drafted the telegram. It was dispatched on 29 December and it reached Berlin on 3 January 1917, at 2.30 p.m. Telegraphic messages between the Wilhelmstrasse and Supreme Headquarters at Pless in Silesia took only about twenty minutes, but it seems that Bernstorff's telegram, with the American offer of secret negotiations, was never actually forwarded to Pless.

The decision to declare unrestricted submarine warfare in the near future was taken at Supreme Headquarters on 9 January 1917, when instructions for Bernstorff were on their way from Berlin. The Ambassador to Washington was informed that the President's mediation at the actual peace conference was thoroughly undesirable. The President's offer of secret negotiations was simply disregarded. Everything had to be done, the Secretary of State went on, to avoid giving the impression that the peace offer had been made by the Germans because their situation was untenable. The Ambassador was told that

We are convinced that we can bring the war to a victorious end both from the military and the economic points of view. The question of communicating our peace terms can therefore be handled by your Excellency with deliberation.[53]

Zimmermann then explained to the Ambassador that the experiences of the past two years of war showed that America would place an embargo neither on war nor on food supplies, and that only if it did so might the German government decide against unrestricted submarine warfare. The tone, if not the actual text, of the second part of Zimmermann's instructions for Bernstorff contradicted that of the first. It was conciliatory and made a few concrete proposals; it stated that the German government would like to co-operate with President Wilson on matters of arbitration, a league of nations, the examination of disarmament and the freedom of the seas:[54]

In principle we are ready to give any guarantee, which would be agreed on in detail by a general conference, after a conference of the belligerents had brought about a preliminary peace. . . . We beg Your Excellency to let the President know this and ask him to work out a programme for a conference for the securing of world peace.

From now on, the exchanges between the Embassy to Washington and the Wilhelmstrasse have the weird quality of a conversation between two deaf people. Bernstorff did not know how deeply dispirited was his one ally in Berlin, Bethmann Hollweg. As soon as the Chancellor received, on Wednesday 3 January, Bernstorff's telegram containing the American offer of secret mediation, he drafted instructions accepting the offer, together with a statement on Germany's peace conditions.[55] But then Bethmann Hollweg decided against sending his own instructions to Washington; Zimmermann's draft, which began by deliberately disregarding the American offer, was dispatched on 7 January instead. When he received it, Bernstorff interpreted it in his own way.

The Ambassador called on Colonel House again on 15 January. He said nothing about the main, discouraging part of Zimmermann's instructions; full of enthusiasm, he concentrated on the positive side of the message. House reported on the conversation to the President:[56]

Bernstorff said he believed that if Lloyd George had stated that there should be *mutual* restoration, reparation and indemnity, his Government would have agreed to enter negotiations on those terms. . . . To my mind [added House] this is the most important communication we have had since the war began and gives a real basis for negotiations and for peace.

The five days between 16 and 20 January 1917 were decisive for Bernstorff and the policy he was then pursuing. The Ambassador's optimism made a great impression in Washington. House was enthusiastic about the opportunity, though he was not quite certain how to use it to the best advantage; Wilson was at first cautious, but then gave in to House's enthusiasm. The Colonel thought that the English would see reason because they knew that it was impossible to secure a military decision. As to Berlin, House was aided by a popular misconception current at the time. This was the belief that the 'liberal element' everywhere was peace-loving and that if liberal politicians came into power, the path to peace would be clear. When he was in charge of the Foreign Ministry, Jagow had believed that the Russian liberals would conclude peace with Germany; now, in January 1917, Colonel House was convinced that the liberals had gained the upper hand in Berlin, and that they were likely to be reasonable in regard to peace.

Two days after their meeting, on 17 January, House asked for a confirmation of what Bernstorff had told him, especially of the request that the President should prepare the programme for a peace conference.[57] Bernstorff must have had second thoughts by the time he received House's request. On 19 January, at the very time when President Wilson had abandoned caution in regard to the German proposal, Bernstorff's reply reached the Colonel. The Ambassador repeated that his government would support the President's guarantees for the future, but he pointed out, in terms of the instructions dispatched from Berlin on 7 January, that a conference of the belligerents only would have to meet first, before a big post-war conference in which the Americans would participate.[58]

By following his instructions more closely, the Ambassador succeeded in vexing House. The Colonel wrote to him again at once, inquiring about the terms the Germans would propose and about their attitude to submarine warfare. But when the second letter reached him, Bernstorff's optimism had vanished: he had just received a telegram from Berlin, dated 16 January 1917, informing him of the decision on unrestricted submarine warfare against shipping in a broad zone around Britain and France, and instructing him on the measures to be taken in case America broke off relations with Berlin. Bernstorff's reply to the Colonel proved to him how slippery the Germans were.[59] The lag in the communications between Berlin and Washington continued to complicate the situation. On 16 January 1917, the day on which the telegram on unrestricted submarine warfare was drafted in Berlin, one of the more cheerful messages was sent from Washington. Bernstorff dismissed Zimmermann's inquiry about embargoes on American exports in one sentence:

It is as yet difficult to say whether an embargo on *all* exports will really come about; perhaps the threat of it will be enough to push our enemies to the conference table.

And addressing himself to German suspicions of Wilson's policies and their motives, Bernstorff wrote: 'It will sound strange to German ears that Wilson is generally regarded here as pro-German.' But the main part of the telegram concerned the President and his peace plans:[60]

All that is certain is that the President at the moment is concerned only with bringing about peace, and is seeking to carry through this purpose with the utmost energy and by every means at his disposal. Very soon a further declaration from Wilson, possibly in the form of a message to Congress, is to be expected. He apparently means to ask the American people to help him in achieving peace; ...

The President had started working on the address toward the end of the first week of January; it was ready on 12 January and dispatched to the American Embassies in the belligerent countries on Monday 15 January. A week later, the President delivered it to the Senate, and it was simultaneously released abroad. It was an epoch-making speech. It received the highest praise from a wide variety of persons, from the Pope to the Tsarist Russian Foreign Minister. It was seen as an attempt to restore peace rather than as a criticism of the European political system.

Quietly, quite conventionally, the President began to survey the replies to his Note of 18 December. To the Allies he awarded the higher marks:[61]

The Central Powers united in a reply which stated merely that they were ready to meet their antagonists in conference to discuss terms of peace. The Entente Powers have replied much more definitely, and have stated, in general terms, indeed, but with sufficient definiteness to imply details, the arrangements, guarantees and acts of reparation which they deem to be the indispensable conditions of a satisfactory settlement.

The replies, President Wilson said, had brought nearer a discussion of peace and at that point he started to outline his vision of the new world. Discussion of peace implied a discussion of future arrangements to prevent the recurrence of the disaster. Such work was essential, and the United States would have to take part in it. But it could do so only on certain conditions.

The present war would have to be ended first of all, and it would make a 'great deal of difference in what way and upon what terms'. Though America would have no say in working out those terms, the belligerents must establish a peace worth guaranteeing. In other words the United States would take an interest in the new international order only if the peace, established without its participation, met with its approval. And no international order – this was the next step in the President's argument – in which America did not participate was really worth having.

The question upon which the whole future peace and policy of the world depends is this: is the present war a struggle for a just and secure peace, or only for a new balance of power? If it be only a struggle for a new balance of power, who will guarantee, who can guarantee, the stable equilibrium of the new arrangement? Only a tranquil Europe can be a stable Europe. There must be, not a balance of power, but a community of power; not organized rivalries, but an organized common peace.[62]

The President believed that the belligerent Powers did not wish to destroy each other.

Victory would mean peace forced upon the loser, a victor's terms imposed upon the vanquished. It would be accepted in humiliation, under duress, at an intolerable sacrifice, and would leave a sting, a resentment, a bitter memory upon which terms of peace would rest, not permanently, but only as upon quicksand. Only a peace between equals can last. . . .[63]

In Wilson's world, small nations would exist side by side with the Great Powers:

no nation should seek to extend its polity over any other nation or people, but ... every people should be left free to determine its own polity, its own way of development, unhindered, unthreatened, unafraid, the little along with the great and powerful.[64]

In such a world, the 'paths of the sea' would be free, and every nation would, as far as possible, have access to them. The President then proposed that

all nations henceforth avoid entangling alliances which would draw them into competitions of power, catch them in a net of intrigue and selfish rivalry, and disturb their own affairs with influences intruded from without. There is no entangling alliance in a concert of power. When all unite to act in the same sense and with the same purpose all act in the common interest and are free to live their own lives under a common protection.[65]

The President further proposed

government by the consent of the governed; that freedom of the seas which in international conference after conference representatives of the United States have urged with the eloquence of those who are the convinced disciples of liberty; and that moderation of armaments which makes of armies and navies a power for order merely, not an instrument of aggression. . . . [66]

Such were the American principles, but they were also upheld by all forward-looking men and women everywhere; earlier in his speech, the President had made a moving reference to the

silent mass of mankind everywhere who have as yet had no place or opportunity to speak their real hearts out concerning the death and ruin they see to have come already upon the persons and the homes they hold most dear.

Wilson spoke on their behalf. He had not witnessed the wild enthusiasm with which in all the capitals of belligerent Europe this 'mass of mankind' welcomed the outbreak of the war in the summer of 1914. After more than two years of warfare, they may have become more muted. *The Times*, in an otherwise appreciative leader, hinted that the President had misunderstood the intentions of the governments and the peoples alike:

The Allies, it is enough to say, believe a 'victory peace' to be as essential as Mr Lincoln believed it to be essential in the Civil War.[67]

In Paris, Anatole France compared Wilson's formula of 'peace without victory' to a 'town without a brothel'.

The *Times* leader-writer suggested that Wilson's address to the Senate contained a project no less ambitious and splendid than

the establishment of a perpetual and universal reign of peace. That has been the dream of many thinkers for a great number of centuries. Mr Wilson, we believe, is the first head of a mighty State who has proposed it as a scheme of practical politics. . . .

Politicians had in fact made similar proposals before, but perhaps none of them was as ready as President Wilson in his address to the Senate to commit himself to the principle of peace through a 'universal union' in more than the most general terms. As early as May 1916 Wilson had said that the war advanced the thinking of statesmen everywhere 'by a whole age' and that the principle of public right must take precedence over the individual interests of particular nations, that they must somehow come together to see that right prevails against selfish aggression. And the President indicated that the tradition of the American people gave them a special right and duty to share in the work of laying 'afresh and upon a new plan the foundations of peace among nations'.[68] Then, in November 1916, a cablegram from Sir Edward Grey was read at a banquet given by the American League to Enforce Peace. The Foreign Secretary supported the objects of the League, adding: 'I sincerely desire to see a league of nations formed to secure peace after the war'. And a long time before Grey, shortly after the outbreak of the war, Asquith had made a speech in Dublin based on Gladstone's words that 'the greatest triumph of our time would be the enthronement of the idea of public right as the governing idea of European politics'. Asquith said that it meant

the substitution for force, for the clash of competing ambition, for the groupings and alliances and a precarious equipoise, of a real European partnership, based on the recognition of equal rights and established and enforced by a common will.[69]

But more than anything else the President's January 1917 address resembled the suggestions made more than a century before by another great outsider about to be admitted, with his country, among the Great Powers – Alexander 1 of Russia. It mattered little that in the one case the plan was designed to protect conservative, in the other progressive, interests. Even the words of their proposals were similar. The two rulers believed in the particular untainted character of their people and their special mission in the world; their countries had lived in some isolation from Europe and they were on the point of getting involved in European affairs for the first time. Like Alexander I, Wilson felt that there existed a simple remedy for that sickness of Europe which Europeans themselves had been unable to discover and cure. Wilson had a much larger audience than Alexander I, and a much broader popular response to his plans. This response distracted, on important occasions, the attention of politicians from the many concrete problems that had to be solved before Wilson's Utopia could be established: in Berlin in the winter of 1916–17 the men who wanted to carry on the war to a victorious end were relieved to note that the President was more interested in 'guarantees' of the future than in any immediate territorial settlement. Though the President had little intention of disguising, like Alexander, 'under the language of evangelical self-abnegation schemes of far-reaching ambition', his proposals did little to stimulate a rational discussion of European problems.

The day after the President had delivered his address to the Senate, Bernstorff informed the Wilhelmstrasse that the speech was generally approved of, 'only our wildest opponents are again attacking the President as pro-German'. Once again, the Ambassador insisted:[70]

The proposed unrestricted submarine warfare will probably bring the peace movement completely to a halt. On the other hand, it is possible that Wilson may redouble his peace effort if he is given time. I should like to leave nothing untried, to avoid war with the United States. Presumably the reason for our refusal to announce peace terms is that public opinion on our side would consider them too moderate. Might it not be possible, before the beginning of unrestricted U-boat warfare, to announce peace terms which we would circulate at our proposed peace conference, saying at the same time that since our enemies' shameless refusal of them we can no longer stick to these lenient conditions? It should thereupon be indicated that as victors we would demand an independent Ireland. Such a declaration would win over public opinion here, so far as that is possible, and also perhaps pacify our own people.

In a way the President's speech brought out the worst in the Germans. Bernstorff's rushed, unusually uncouth communication of 23 January 1917 was followed, four days later, by Zimmermann's telegram to Washington. In broad outlines, the Secretary of State let the Ambassador know, the government agreed with the President's address to the Senate, especially with

the right of self-determination and the equality of all nations; in acknowledging this principle Germany would welcome it if such peoples as the Irish and the Indians, who do not enjoy the blessings of political independence, were now granted their freedom.

The enemy, on the other hand,

making great show of the principle of national rights, have at the same time revealed their aim of the break-up and degradation of Germany, Austria-Hungary, Turkey and Bulgaria. They meet the spirit of conciliation with a will bent upon destruction. They want war to the bitter end.[71]

A new situation, Zimmermann argued, had therefore arisen which forced Germany to make new decisions. For two and a half years England had been misusing her fleet in an attempt to subdue Germany through starving it out. He requested the Ambassador to hand over the note on the use of submarines to the American government in the evening of 31 January 1917.

On the day of the dispatch of Zimmermann's instructions, 27 January, Bernstorff was drafting the most urgent message to Berlin, on the President's latest move.[72] The day after he had delivered his Senate address, Wilson had been pleased, even flattered, by the reception of his message abroad. But his main interest was what the Germans were thinking. 'If Germany really wants peace she can get it, and get it soon, *if she will but confide in me and let me have a chance*', the President wrote to Colonel House on 24 January 1917, asking him to see Bernstorff at once.[73] Two days later, on 26 January, the two men met at House's flat in New York. The Ambassador opened the conversation by telling House that the military leaders had taken over the control of Germany, and that an intensified submarine campaign would be launched at the beginning of the spring operations. House then told the Ambassador of the President's request. Bernstorff returned to Washington and immediately drafted his message to Berlin. It read:

House asked me spontaneously on Wilson's behalf [*sic*] to call on him and he told me the following officially on the President's behalf:

Wilson in the first place offers confidentially, peace mediation based on his address to the Senate, i.e. without interference in territorial peace conditions. His simultaneous request to us for information of our peace conditions Wilson regards as *not* confidential.

House developed for me the President's reasoning as follows: our enemies had publicly announced their impossible peace conditions. The President had thereupon announced his programme in direct opposition to theirs. We also now are morally bound to state our conditions, because otherwise our intentions in regard to peace could be thought dishonourable. After Your Excellency had let Mr Wilson know that our peace conditions were moderate, and that we were willing to enter the second peace conference, the President believed that his address to the Senate corresponded to our intentions. Wilson hoped that we should inform him of peace conditions that could be published here and in Germany, so that they would become known in the whole world. If we would only trust him, the President was convinced that he could bring about both peace conferences. He would be especially pleased if at the same time Your Excellency would be willing to say that we were ready to enter the conference on the basis of his address to the Senate. We could explain the reason for our declaration by the fact that Wilson had now asked directly for our peace conditions. The President thought that the Entente note to him was a bluff and need not be taken into consideration. He was convinced that he was able to bring about the peace conferences, and so soon that the unnecessary bloodshed of the spring offensives would be prevented.

It is impossible to tell from here how far Your Excellency is willing or able to meet Wilson. Meanwhile I urgently beg your leave to make the following suggestion. If the submarine war were commenced straightaway the President will regard this as a slap in the face and war with the United States will be inevitable. The war party here will gain the upper hand and, in my opinion, it will be impossible to tell when the war will end, since the resources of the United States, whatever may be said to the contrary, are very great. If, on the other hand, we accept Wilson's proposal, and these plans then come to nothing because of the obstinacy of our opponents, it will be very difficult for the President to enter the war against us, even if we then launch unrestricted submarine warfare. A brief respite is therefore needed for the time being, in order to improve our diplomatic position. At all events I hold the view that we can now get a better peace by conferences than if the United States join our enemies.

Since cablegrams always take more days, I beg for an immediate advice by wireless if the telegraphic instructions 157 [Telegram of 16 January 1917 that unrestricted submarine warfare would begin on 1 February.] are not to be carried out on 1 February.[74]

Bernstorff's telegram was sent by the State Department wire and reached Berlin on Sunday 28 January 1917, at 4.30 p.m. Bethmann was excited when he read it, and drafted a reply immediately. It gave him new hope that war with America might be avoided and peace somehow achieved. There was one snag. Bethmann could do nothing about the Ambassador's inquiry as to the start of submarine warfare. It was a question the Chancellor knew could not be reopened with the military and in any case the submarines had already set out for their action stations to the west of Ireland. They could no longer be reached by wireless.[75] Soon after he had perused the telegram Bethmann forwarded it to Supreme Headquarters at Pless; after his talk with Helfferich, the Chancellor met Zimmermann at the station, where a special train was waiting to take them to Pless.

The way in which the telegram was received at Supreme Head-quarters was in sharp contrast to Bethmann's badly controlled enthusiasm. The Kaiser was furious when he heard that the Chancellor and the Secretary of State were on their way to Pless; as to the contents of the Washington telegram, he was convinced that President Wilson was only trying to delay German submarine action in order to save England from starvation and certain defeat. On the following day, 29 January 1917, a conference met at Supreme Headquarters to discuss the instructions Bethmann had drafted on Sunday. There were no serious objections to them because the military knew that their contest with the Chancellor had already been decided in their favour. Hindenburg had no comment to make, and the Kaiser confined himself to saying that it must be made quite clear to Bernstorff that he, the Kaiser, would not have Wilson mediate or America take part in the peace conference.[76]

There was nothing the Chancellor could do about Zimmermann's earlier instructions to Washington, nor did he try to do anything. Bernstorff had the two memoranda for Lansing at hand, one of them stating that, from 1 February 1917, submarines would sink all ships without warning in a zone surrounding Britain, France, Italy and in the eastern Mediterranean. There was to be a short period of grace for neutral ships on their way at the time, and one American passenger ship, properly marked with red and white stripes and carrying no contraband, was to be allowed to ply its trade between New York and Falmouth once a week. On

that topic, in his telegram dispatched to Washington on his return
to Berlin from Pless in the evening of 29 January, the Chancellor
remarked:[77]

As the instructions on intensified submarine warfare indicate, we are
always ready to meet America's requirements as far as possible. We
nevertheless beg the President to take up or continue his efforts and we
declare ourselves quite ready to suspend the intensified submarine warfare as soon as we are certain that the efforts of the President will lead
to a peace acceptable to us.

The end of the telegram to Washington, quoted above, cancelled
the expressions of good will in its opening part. That was why at
Pless, Hindenburg could agree without difficulty to Bethmann's
draft; the military were convinced that an occasion to suspend
submarine warfare would not arise. But Hindenburg was unaware of the fact that the Chancellor's peace conditions, in the
telegram, were milder than those Bethmann had set down earlier
in the month. (They were filed away, undispatched and unread, in
the Foreign Ministry: we have seen that Zimmermann's instructions instead were sent to Washington on 7 January.[78]) At the
end of the month of January, when hope of a successful American
intervention was all but lost, Bethmann Hollweg put forward what
he had regarded as especially attractive proposals. Unfortunately
nobody apart from the Chancellor knew that.

On 29 January Bethmann Hollweg went to great lengths to
introduce his conditions in an ingenious manner. He asked
Bernstorff to inform the President that the conditions he was
about to enumerate were the very same

under which we *would have been* willing to enter peace negotiations had
the Entente accepted our peace proposal of 12 December last year.

He knew that it was quite untrue. The Chancellor had not put
down his thoughts on peace proposals until 4 January 1917, and
when he did so they were more explicit and tougher than those he
sent to Washington later in the month. As far as colonies were
concerned, for instance, Bethmann Hollweg wanted, on
4 January, 'a restitution of colonies in the form of a closed
[*geschlossen*] colonial empire, secured by naval bases'. And on
29 January, the Chancellor wrote of

Colonial restitution in the form of an understanding which would
assure Germany of colonies appropriate to its population and importance of its economic interests.

Point after point, the Chancellor took the edge off his earlier demands; some of them disappeared altogether. He now asked for the part of upper Alsace occupied by France; a frontier in the east which would protect Germany and Poland – the two Emperors' manifesto of 6 November 1916 had proposed a new Polish state – against Russia; an economic and financial adjustment on the basis of an exchange of territory occupied by the two sides, which was to be returned on the conclusion of peace; compensation for German business and private interests injured by the war; the renunciation of measures and arguments which would interfere with the free flow of trade in peacetime. Bethmann left out his earlier mention of the annexation, by Germany, of Briey and Liége and the detachment, from Russia, of Kurland and Lithuania as well as the annexation by Austria and Bulgaria of Serbian, Rumanian and Montenegrin territory. Bethmann was prepared to concede the restoration of Belgium 'under certain guarantees assuring Germany's safety', as well as the return of most of the French territory occupied by the Germans. As a special inducement for the President, Bethmann added the demand for the freedom of the seas, and Germany's readiness to attend the international conference proposed by Wilson.

Bernstorff received the Chancellor's message on 30 January 1917, recast it in the form of a letter from himself to Colonel House, and, early in the morning of 31 January, asked an *aide* to take the letter over to New York. After that, the Ambassador requested an interview with Lansing, who received him at 4.10 in the afternoon. Bernstorff handed over the two documents from Berlin announcing the commencement, on the following day, of unrestricted submarine warfare.[79]

Instead of a reply to the President's Senate address, a declaration of war: such was the opinion of the vast majority of English-language newspapers published in America. The President had believed that a good chance of peace existed; now, on 1 February 1917, he was more under the impression of the contents of the German memoranda than of Bernstorff's paraphrase of the Chancellor's message. The President's peace policy had run into a cul-de-sac. Quite apart from the fact that Bethmann could be clearly seen as a two-faced deceiver, a sharp distinction emerged between the two communications. One of them was open to public comment, the other hidden from public view. Nobody in

Germany appreciated the importance of that difference: Beth-mann, to his disadvantage; Hindenburg and his associates, in their favour. Nobody foresaw the reaction of the American press, and nobody remembered how sensitive President Wilson was to the movements of public opinion.

But it was largely the bland tone and the undiscriminating nature of the German declaration, the threat to all American and neutral shipping over a wide area, that amazed the President, more perhaps than any other event so far in the war.[80] Wilson decided on severing diplomatic relations with Germany, and waiting to see what Berlin would do to implement its threat. On 3 February 1917 Bernstorff and his staff were handed their passports, and the President informed a joint sitting of Congress of his action. He said that he hoped the Germans would not translate their threats into deeds, but if they did,

> I shall take the liberty of coming again before Congress to ask that authority be given to me to use any means that may be necessary for the protection of our seamen and our people in the prosecution of their peaceful, legitimate errands on the high seas.[81]

Only the convinced interventionists – and there were not many of them in Washington – saw the diplomatic break with Germany as inevitably leading to a declaration of war.

The President, however, held different views, and asked Lansing to pass them on to the Ambassador to London, who would then inform the 'leading members of the Government rather than of the Foreign Office'.[82] Frederick C. Penfield, the United States Ambassador to Vienna, had kept Washington well informed on the developments in the Habsburg Empire; at the time when the first explorations of peace, by the Austrians, were taking place in Scandinavia, President Wilson argued that peace was

> intensely desired by the Teutonic powers and much more by Austria than by any of her allies because the situation is becoming for many reasons much graver for her than for the others.

The President was trying to

> avoid breaking with Austria in order to keep the channels of official intercourse with her open so that he may use her for peace. The chief if not the only obstacle is the threat apparently contained in the peace

terms recently stated by the Entente Allies that in case they succeeded they would insist upon a virtual dismemberment of the Austro Hungarian Empire.

Wilson insisted that 'the effort of this government will be constantly for peace even should it become itself involved . . .'

On 10 February 1917 Page spent most of the afternoon with Lloyd George, discussing with him the President's views. The Prime Minister, in his crafty way, told the Ambassador that he was aware of Vienna's desire for peace, and that negotiations were in fact in progress. But the Allies, he said, would rather have Austria-Hungary in the war because it was a heavy liability to Berlin. (If the Prime Minister really held that view we know that he soon changed it.) During the conversation Lloyd George showed that he understood the ways in which President Wilson's mind moved, perhaps better than the President himself. He invited Wilson to come and play the Great Powers' game, on Wilson's own terms:[83]

We want him to come into the war not so much for help in the war as for help with peace. My reason is not mainly the military nor naval nor economic nor financial pressure that the American government and people might exert in their own way against Germany; grateful as this would be [sic] I have a loftier reason. American participation is necessary for the complete expression of the moral judgement of the world on the most important subject ever presented to the civilized nations.

The Germans, even when they were trying to please Wilson, would hedge on the question of his participation in the peace conference: in contrast, there was the warmth and the flattery of Lloyd George's invitation:

The President's presence at the peace conference is necessary for the proper organization of the world which must follow peace. I mean that he himself must be there in person. If he sits in the conference that makes peace he will exert the greatest influence that any man has ever exerted in expressing the moral value of free government.

Soon after that conversation, the English were able to pass on to Washington news of great interest. Their Naval Intelligence had cracked the German diplomatic code, and reconstructed the notorious 'Zimmermann Telegram' of 16 January 1917: they obtained copies of it from three other sources, one of them from their agent in Mexico City. Balfour then gave Page a transcript of the telegram, and it reached Washington on 24 February. The message was to the German Minister in Mexico, Heinrich von Eckhart, informing him of the imminent declaration of unrestricted submarine warfare and of the intention to keep America neutral:[84]

In case we should not be successful in this, we propose Mexico an alliance on the following terms: joint conduct of the war; joint conclusion of peace; ample financial support and an agreement on our part that Mexico shall gain back by conquest the territory lost by her at a prior period in Texas, New Mexico and Arizona. Arrangements as to details is entrusted to Your Excellency.

Your Excellency will make the above known to the President [of Mexico, Venustiano Carranza] in strict confidence at the moment that war breaks out with the United States, and you will add the suggestion that Japan be requested to take part at once and that he simultaneously mediate between ourselves and Japan.

The Zimmermann Telegram was nothing out of the ordinary: the Wilhelmstrasse files were full of messages of that kind. Its extraordinary importance lay in the effect on the United States. Its timing was important. After the President had read it, he was furious and wanted to make the telegram public at once. He may well have remembered that the day before the telegram left Berlin, on 15 January 1917, House had talked to Bernstorff in New York, and on that occasion the Ambassador was more encouraging and optimistic about peace than at any other time. Wilson believed what Colonel House told him about Germany's intentions: now, just over a month later, he had the proof of German dishonesty before his eyes. He was in the end persuaded to delay the publication of the telegram until Lansing returned from the short holiday he was taking at White Sulphur Springs.[85] The two men discussed the publication on 28 February, and on the following morning American newspapers printed the telegram in full.

It was the first time in the war that a secret diplomatic communication was published, and it started something of a wartime fashion. In regard to American public opinion, it was immensely effective. The various events on the high seas, though they had received full treatment in the newspapers, may have convinced the Americans that the Germans were barbaric, but they contained no proof of their hostility to America itself. The Zimmermann

Telegram was different. It engaged not humanitarian emotions but the deepest instincts of self-preservation and fear.[86] In Washington, the atmosphere of panic affected the House of Representatives, where the armed merchantmen bill was passed by 403 votes to 13, after a session in which emotional expressions of patriotism almost obliterated the business on hand. There was some questioning, especially by German Americans, of the authenticity of the message to Mexico, but on 3 March Zimmermann put a stop to that by his statement that the telegram was quite genuine.

It had made a deep but transitory impression on the President himself. He did not regard the threat by Mexico, even when backed by Germany, to the southern states as serious; he had meant to ask Congress for powers to arm American merchantmen before the Zimmerman news broke. When the excitement had died down, the first American shipping casualties were reported. They were indeed slight when compared with the losses sustained by the British: the removal of restrictions on submarines about doubled their powers of destruction. (Up to December 1916, losses averaged about 100,000 tons; in December 1916 and January 1917 they went up to 250,000 tons for each month; in February they shot up to 500,000 tons. The most sudden increase in British losses took place in the third week of April 1917, after America's entry into the war.[87]) It was not until 12 March 1917 that the American steamer *Algonquin* became the first casualty of the intensified submarine warfare: it was sunk by shell-fire and without any loss of life. On 16 March *Vigilancia* was torpedoed without warning, and fifteen members of the crew were drowned. Then the *City of Memphis* was sunk on the following day after warning, and on 18 March the *Illinois*, without warning; in neither case was there any loss of life. The rapid succession of these sinkings added to their impact on public opinion: in view of the total amount of neutral shipping engaged in trade with Britain – some 3,000,000 tons – it was an insignificant loss.

And yet, by the end of March 1917, President Wilson had made up his mind. When the new Congress reassembled on 2 April 1917 the President asked it for an immediate declaration of war on Germany. Wilson said that the 'present German warfare against commerce is warfare against mankind'. America could no longer confine itself to the policy of armed neutrality.

With a profound sense of the solemn and even tragical character of the step I am taking and of the grave responsibilities which it involves, but in unhesitating obedience to what I deem my constitutional duty, I advise that the Congress declare the recent course of the Imperial German Government to be in fact nothing less than war against the Government and the people of the United States; that it formally accept the status of belligerent which has thus been thrust upon it; and that it take immediate steps not only to put the country in a more thorough state of defense, but also to exert all its power and employ all its resources to bring the Government of the German Empire to terms and end the war.[88]

The Senate passed the motion two days later; the Lower House in the early hours of the morning of 6 April 1917, after a debate lasting seventeen hours.

The United States did not declare war on Austria-Hungary and it did not formally join the Allied Powers. America became 'associated' with the Allies: it was with them, but not one of them. On the whole, the United States were unprepared for the war. The Council for National Defence was summoned to meet by Wilson on 23 March, and a new army bill was submitted by the Secretary for War a week later. Though the sympathies of the American public were on the side of the Allies, and the blows of the Zimmermann Telegram and of the sinking of four merchant vessels followed each other in rapid succession, there was no overwhelming public demand for war. Only the American war industries were working at full capacity, but they would have done that anyway. Britain and France depended on them and without their contribution the Allies would have found fighting the war more difficult. At any rate, in March 1917, the fortunes of the war were going against them.

The submarine campaign was then being quite successful and if the rate of destruction of merchant ships had been kept up, Britain would have run into serious difficulties early in 1918. The morale of the French army was dangerously low, and the French were drawing on their last reserves of manpower. Rumania's defeat left the Russians in charge of a new part of the battle-line. And in the middle of March there was news of revolutionary interest in Russia. The Americans tended to see it, at first, as a happy event, as the disappearance of the last obstacle so that the war in Europe would become a straight contest between Democracy and Absolutism. Washington lost no time in recognizing Prince Lvov's provisional government.

It seems that nobody in Washington realized how difficult the position of the Allies was. Early in January, the President had been convinced that the war was in its final stage. It is unlikely that, at the end of March, he gave much weight to the thought, if it occurred to him at all, that by bringing his country in he would prolong the war. He was convinced that American participation would speed up the coming of peace and facilitate the construction of a new international community under his and America's leadership. The Germans, with their unfortunate knack of making themselves look deceitful when they were merely trying to behave in the way they thought other people behaved, had largely themselves to blame for bringing upon themselves Wilson's displeasure. They suspected the President of being anti-German when in fact he was not, and in the end they proved themselves unworthy to help him and America in their great task. Unrestricted submarine warfare was more important as a proof of German duplicity than as a threat to American merchant shipping. His own vision of peace was the President's most treasured political programme, and he was prepared to go to war for it. No matter what the technical term was, whether America was an 'associated' Power or not, Wilson brought his country into what had been, up to April 1917, largely a European civil war. For almost three years, America had stood aside, a mere onlooker. Now it took its place in the ranks of the Great Powers. President Wilson believed that he and his country had a special contribution to make.

6 Petrograd

A month before America came into the war the revolution had broken out in Russia. A progressive paralysis gripped the eastern front. The Russian troops began deserting as the first small American contingents were arriving in France.

Russia had suffered in the war at the hands of friend and foe alike. For thirty-two months before the outbreak of the revolution in March 1917 the army had been battered along a front of over 1,100 miles. The adherence of Turkey to the Central Powers in November 1914 had isolated Russia from the outside world. Though its western Allies themselves were hard pressed for war supplies, it was difficult to get the spare oddments to the Russian front: the Italian front was usually given priority. In the spring of 1915 Paris and London secured the alliance of Italy, partly at the expense of Serbia's aspirations in the Adriatic. Russia's prestige in the Balkans suffered a setback in consequence. Even a diplomatic victory, in Bucharest in the summer of 1916, added, after Rumania's defeat in the autumn, some 400 miles to the Russian front line. But there was always the promise of Constantinople at the end of the road and a few Russian politicians held on to that promise for more than it was worth.

The memory of Russia's *union sacré*, of the national unity proclaimed by the Duma meeting on 26 July 1914, had grown dim over the years; the political truce that had united Russia in face of the enemy a few days before the outbreak of the war had broken down. The first widespread strikes began to affect Russia's industry as early in the war as January 1916: the bread riots in Petrograd in March 1917 appeared harmless enough at first. Neither the Tsar and his advisers, nor the revolutionaries themselves, expected a revolution. But when it came, everybody agreed that far-reaching political changes would inevitably take place.

Four days after the outbreak of popular unrest in Petrograd, a provisional government was formed on 12 March; on 15 March the Tsar abdicated, renouncing the right of his son to the succession. On the same day, the composition of the provisional government was announced. It was to be a caretaker cabinet, until the proposed elections to the new Constituent Assembly, and it contained some reluctant revolutionaries. Prince Lvov became Prime Minister. He had behind him a career of devotion to a variety of liberal causes; he was a thoughtful man, with a reputation of being too soft, too yielding. That was why his candidature for the premiership was promoted by Professor Paul Milyukov, a distinguished historian. In 1905 Milyukov had been one of the founders of the Kadet – Constitutional Democrat – party, which became the dominant political organization in the Duma. Constitutional reform had been its chief objective; under Milyukov's leadership, the party became increasingly nationalist and expansionist. Milyukov, the strongest personality in the revolutionary provisional government, was its Foreign Minister; he possessed a remarkable self-confidence that no adversity could shake. Many years later, in exile in a small town in southern France, at eighty-two years of age, Milyukov complained of being unable to pursue his usual interests: journalism, politics, scholarship. He started writing his memoirs: 'Therefore, I feel no guilt in occupying my unwanted leisure with recollections of my own past. By so doing, I do not deprive anybody of anything.'[1]

On 17 March 1917, Milyukov visited the Foreign Ministry for the first time. Its dignified building was half-deserted; otherwise, it appeared untouched by the revolution. The new Minister talked briefly to Pokrovsky, his predecessor; he consulted the First and the Second Assistant Ministers, Neratov and Polovtsev. He asked them to carry on their duties, and reminded them that victory in the war remained Russia's foremost aim. There was little Milyukov did, or indeed could do, about the depleted state of the missions abroad, and the unsatisfactory quality of the information that was reaching Petrograd. The monarchist Ambassador to Washington, George Bakhmetev, resigned as soon as he received the news of the revolution; there was no Ambassador in London at the time; in May, Izvolsky resigned his Paris post. Owing to staff shortages at the top level, the standard of diplomatic reporting was usually low. The press was often Milyukov's main source of information.

In the Allied capitals the question that received the most serious consideration was the effect of the revolution on Russia's war effort. At first, there was no lack of optimism in London, Paris and Washington. The revolution was expected to release a new wave of patriotism, remove corrupt pro-German officials in the administration, and much else besides: the overall outcome would be a greatly improved conduct of the war. And if there existed any doubts as to the strain imposed on Russia by war and revolution, Mikhail Rodzianko, the affable President of the Duma, would allay them. He told General Knox, the head of the British Military Mission to Russia:[2] 'My dear Knox, you must be easy. Everything is going on all right. Russia is a big country, and can wage a war and manage a revolution at the same time.'

Milyukov was, like most of his colleagues, not revolutionary by choice. They had little intention of leading, exploiting or in any way deepening the revolutionary mood. They were rather surprised and frightened by it. Paul Milyukov, therefore, had no revolutionary foreign policy. He believed that the events in Russia had changed the country's internal, not its foreign policy. He wrote in his party newspaper, *Rech*, on 23 March 1917: 'In diplomacy, such a sharp revolution as in internal affairs is of course impossible.' He argued that the revolution would bring Russia closer to its Allies, an argument in line with his basic historical and political views. He admired the west and believed that Russia's historical development would follow the same path. Nor did he see why his country should sever the ties of mutual obligation that bound it to its Allies. He had not a word of condemnation for the expansionist policy of his predecessors: he only wanted to carry it out more effectively.

In the first place, Russia had to stay in the war: its government had pledged itself not to conclude a separate peace by the secret Declaration of London in September 1914. In March 1917 there was no difficulty about that; the revolutionaries in Petrograd were agreed that their country would have to carry on the struggle. The rest of Russia's treaties with its Allies were in fact promissory notes, to be honoured only in the case of total victory. By a series of agreements made between March 1915 and February 1917, Russia's Allies conceded to it Constantinople, as well as the Bosporus, the Sea of Marmara and the Dardanelles with some hinterland, and the islands Imbros and Tenedos. Another agreement concerned Russia and France alone: neither London nor

Rome knew anything about it, although it was concluded in January 1917, while the Allied conference was meeting in Petrograd. It gave Russia a free hand to redraw its western frontier, in exchange for allowing France to do the same on its eastern frontier.[3]

In contrast with the grim present, the secret treaties held out a bright promise before Russia. Milyukov wanted to preserve that promise, and while doing so, he came sharply up against other revolutionaries who held entirely different views.

Whether the proverbial 'duality of power' – that elusive, shifting division of political power between the provisional government and the Soviet – existed or not in fact, there can be no question that the members of the Soviet took a truly revolutionary view of foreign policy. It was sharply opposed to that of Milyukov. The members of the Soviet were elected by the workers and the soldiers: a system of direct representation, which had first been evolved in Petrograd during the revolution of 1905. In a way, the Soviet was complementary to the Duma, which had a more orderly, but also a more rigid and class-ridden system of representation. The Soviet sometimes co-operated with the provisional government, at other times the two bodies came into sharp conflict. In the Soviet, every shade of Russian socialism was to be found, and among the socialists, many forms of criticism of traditional diplomacy were then in circulation.

This was so everywhere in Europe. At the outbreak of the war most of the socialists had taken part in the political truce. Nevertheless, they were the most volatile element in the compound thus produced. The length of the war, the demands for continued sacrifice that were at their shrillest and most senseless when they were aimed at the broad masses of population, and now a deep crisis in Russia – those factors were working as a solvent of the political truce. It was amazing that the truce had survived more than two years of warfare; a process was now set in motion that revived the various pacifist and internationalist movements that had been silenced by the political truce and by popular patriotic fervour.[4]

Apart from their desire for total victory, the Great Powers had entered the total war with their objectives undefined. If the aims of the European Powers were to be discovered at all, they could be found in the secret treaties. These were a record of those aims, but one deformed by pressures from the Allies, by their conflict-ing desires, by the fortunes of war. Although the treaties were often far-reaching within their diplomatic context, they were too specific and too secret to inspire a front-line soldier to greater effort, or indeed to make him stay in the front line. The effective-ness of such treaties could make itself felt only within a very small circle, in the case of people like Milyukov, of patriots with access to official secrets.

Traditional diplomacy held good as long as political truce held good. In the spring of 1917, when revolutionary unrest ushered a strong ideological element into the struggle, traditional diplo-macy became the revolutionaries' favourite whipping boy. It came to be blamed for many things: the outbreak of the war, its viciousness, its length; the diplomats were seen as weak and remote from the lives of common humanity, or as sinister and grasping, or simply as 'gold-plated gentlemen'. *Izvestia*, the official organ of the Soviet, put it thus:[5]

Secret diplomacy is the natural offspring of autocracy. It is afraid of light and prefers to hatch its dirty plots in darkness. . . . You cannot pour new wine into old bottles. The new power, created by the revolu-tion, must also make a decisive break with the traditions of men like Izvolski and Stuermer in the realm of foreign policy. But it will only be able to practice the new methods of diplomacy openly before the whole world if it remains as the traditional policy of conquest. . . . Only on the foundation of a new foreign policy can a new diplomatic system be built, answering to the principles of freedom. . . .

Though there was a long way to go from the expression of a sentiment – it was by no means a new one – to the formulation of a policy, such a sentiment doubtless ran counter to the ideas of Russia's first revolutionary Foreign Minister. It did not take the members of the Soviet long to formulate their views on foreign policy; they were aided by the influx of revolutionary talent into the capital. Those revolutionaries who had been ex-pelled by the Tsarist authorities to Siberia returned first: Irakli Tsereteli was among them. A Georgian and a Menshevik leader, Tsereteli had been the head of the Social Democrat delegation to the Second Duma; after the dissolution of the Duma in 1907, he was exiled to Siberia, where he remained for ten years. He was always a convincing speaker who occasionally rose to inspiring oratory; he was highly esteemed for his integrity as well as for his thoughtful, intelligent approach to politics. He quickly became the leading personality in the Soviet and had a decisive influence on the formulation of its foreign policy.

In the same way as many other members of the Soviet, Tsereteli thought mainly in terms of peace. Peace was his point of departure as well as his ultimate aim; it was the magic word that the Soviet used against Milyukov, in the same way as Lenin and the Bolsheviks were later to use it against the Soviet. Although the idea of peace dominated Tsereteli's thinking, he was not, and in the political circumstances of the early weeks of the revolution could not be, as single-minded about putting it into practice as Lenin was later in 1917. Tsereteli wanted to avoid the pitfalls of support for the war without any reservations on the one hand and of Lenin's stark 'defeatism' on the other. He saw international socialist action as an obvious way out of the impasse – an action that would aim to bring about a peace of conciliation, not one of military victory. But until the achievement of that aim, Russia would have to go on defending itself against the enemy. Tsereteli and many of his colleagues in the Soviet hoped that the example of the revolution in Russia would move their comrades abroad to act in favour of peace. Their hope had a messianic element in it:[6]

Conscious of its revolutionary power, the Russian democracy has announced that it will, by every means, resist the policy of conquest of its ruling classes, and it calls upon the peoples of Europe for concerted, decisive action in favour of peace.

In this way, the revolutionary foreign policy of the Soviet majority involved itself in a fatal contradiction. It was committed to the defence of Russia while it waited for a socialist peace: it had to encourage the soldiers to fight while agitating for peace. A foreign policy based on such conflicting principles was open, in practice, to more than one interpretation. Its military aspect could be stressed at the expense of peace, or vice versa. It made co-operation of the Soviet with the provisional government possible while opening the door to every kind of misunderstanding.

In the fullness of time every one of them occurred. Every newspaper attack, and there were many of them, on the 'imperialist' character of the war was also an attack on the Foreign Minister and on his policy: in the meanwhile, Milyukov went on making public references to the glorious moment, in the not-so-distant future, when Constantinople would be Russian. The campaign against Milyukov gathered momentum when the exiles from western Europe began returning to Russia. Viktor Chernov, the founder and leader of the Social Revolutionary party, a man with a sharp tongue but little political sense, launched into a fierce attack on the Foreign Minister as soon as he came back to Petrograd. He usually referred to Milyukov as 'Dardanelski'.

The Foreign Minister's declaration of 9 April 1917 was an uneasy compromise between the policy of the provisional government and the views held by the majority in the Soviet. Milyukov drafted it unwillingly, under pressure. It stated that 'the aim of free Russia is not domination over other nations, or seizure of their national possessions, or forcible occupation of foreign territories' – not a sentence the Foreign Minister could have enjoyed drafting, but it added that the rights of the fatherland would be defended, 'fully observing at the same time all obligations assumed toward our Allies.'[7] The clash of views between the Foreign Minister and the Soviet during the negotiations before the publication of the manifesto overshadowed the differences inside the cabinet itself. Milyukov disliked the idea of any such pronouncement, but had to give way to pressure from his colleagues, Kerensky and Tereshchenko in particular.

At the time of the revolution Aleksandr Kerensky was thirty-four years old, thin, pale and ubiquitous. He had made a name for himself as a defence lawyer in political trials; during the revolution he emerged as an accomplished mob orator. He had a good line in theatrical gestures, flashing eyes, a gift for dominating his audience. Kerensky could sway his audience, and also himself; when he spoke in public, he believed everything he said. His weakness lay in his inability to plan and carry out a consistent, determined line of political action; he was easily influenced by outside pressures. There were too many of them. As a member of a small socialist party, the Trudoviki, he derived much of his prestige from the fact that he was a member of the Soviet and its Vice-President. In the provisional government – first as Minister of Justice, then of War and finally as Prime Minister – Kerensky claimed to be the sole representative of 'revolutionary democracy'. But he disliked the restraints imposed on him by the Soviet, and he freed himself from them; he was an individualist who wanted to go his own way and who tried, as Premier, to remain above the parties. He succeeded to such an extent that when it came to the final trial of strength with the Bolsheviks in November 1917, Kerensky was on his own. As an orator, he was in the same class as, say, Trotsky: as a politician, he was no match for Lenin.

From the beginning, Kerensky had a staunch admirer in the provisional government. This was Mikhail Tereshchenko, a man, even younger than himself, who became Minister of Finance at twenty-nine. Tereshchenko was a multi-millionaire from the Ukraine, who dealt in sugar, a very profitable commodity in Tsarist Russia; when his name was announced on the formation of the provisional government, it caused surprise; it was utterly unknown, except to a few people. He had done some voluntary work in the provinces before the revolution; although he had no party affiliations, he owed his rise to prominence to his familiarity with conspiratorial circles. He was competent, intelligent and fluent in French and English. His facility as a linguist stood him in good stead when he succeeded Milyukov as Foreign Minister. He was often able to convince Allied Ambassadors to Petrograd that the political situation in Russia was not as bad as it seemed; because he thought so himself. It was indeed surprising that someone as able and intelligent as Tereshchenko should have had such blind faith in Kerensky and therefore be so optimistic about the political developments in Russia. Tereshchenko's youth and Kerensky's oratory must doubtless bear part of the blame.

For some little while before the 9 April declaration on foreign policy by the provisional government, Milyukov's off-the-cuff public pronouncements had been getting more and more outspoken. He described the formula of 'peace without annexations' as a 'German formula that they are trying to pass off as an international socialist one'; on another occasion he expressed the view that the Turks were an alien element in Constantinople. At the cabinet meeting on 6 April, Kerensky accused Milyukov of conducting personal diplomacy in the same way as the Tsar had done. Milyukov replied that he thought that he was conducting foreign policy on behalf of the provisional government, and if the cabinet disagreed with his policy, it should say so. Lvov then told Milyukov that his policy was in fact the policy of the cabinet, and Kerensky was forced to withdraw his charge. He retreated, but not for long.

The tension increased again early in May, when Milyukov forwarded the provisional government's declaration of 9 April, together with his own covering note, to the Allied capitals. Milyukov, of course, interpreted the declaration to suit himself: he disregarded the renunciation of annexations and indemnities in his note, and stressed the sections of the declaration which dealt with the defence of Russia and the validity of the existing treaties. When Tsereteli and several other members of the executive committee of the Soviet received Milyukov's declaration in the evening of 2 May 1917, they were stunned by what it contained. A meeting of the committee was summoned at once, and consultations between the Soviet and the government took place the same night. When an agreement was reached at five o'clock the following morning, Milyukov regarded it as his victory. The crisis was explained away as a misunderstanding.

Nevertheless it was a danger signal. Foreign policy, embracing questions of war and peace, was the key issue before the provisional government. Milyukov had almost as little control over it as the government had over the situation in the streets of Petrograd. With the threat of popular unrest ever present, it was possible to argue that the maintenance of the precarious cooperation between the Soviet and the government was possible only if the composition of the latter was drastically revised. At the cabinet meeting on 11 May 1917 Kerensky and Tereshchenko sharply attacked Milyukov in his absence. Guchkov, the Minister of War, defended his colleague: when he saw the impression his defence made, he resigned. Three days later, Lvov, the Prime Minister, made another appeal for the formation of a coalition government in which the Soviet would participate. The negotiations dragged on until 18 May, and the question of foreign policy and of the Foreign Minister played an important role in them. Lvov finally agreed to accept the Soviet formula of 'no annexations or indemnities' as the basis of the new government's policy. There was now no question of Milyukov carrying on as the Minister of Foreign Affairs; he was offered the Ministry of Education but refused. The choice of his successor was not difficult: all parties were agreed that the post should not go to a socialist, who would have frightened the western Allies while making it impossible for the Kadets to remain in the government. Tereshchenko was the obvious choice; Kerensky became Minister of

War. Altogether, the Soviet sent six ministers to the new cabinet. The contradictions of the foreign policy of the Soviet were not resolved when it became the official policy of the government. Peace, on the basis of no annexations or indemnities, now came to be referred to, by Prince Lvov, in the same breath as an offensive on the eastern front. On the latter point, Lvov thought that the virtual armistice on the eastern front 'must cease. The country must express its imperative will and send its army into combat.' Lvov gave in to the unceasing Allied pressure on the provisional government to play a more active part in the war effort. Nevertheless, the revolution put additional strains on the relations between Russia and its western allies. There had been indications, while Milyukov was still in power, that neither London nor Paris would oppose the renunciation of the Straits by Petrograd. No Russians were invited to the inter-Allied talks either at Folkestone or at St-Jean-de-Maurienne in April 1917. Milyukov knew nothing of the discussion that took place there of a separate peace with Austria, and believed that the meetings were concerned only with the future of Asia Minor. The misunderstanding as to the agenda of the two meetings arose because Ribot, the French Foreign Minister, felt that Petrograd was due some kind of an explanation. He let the Russian Ambassador, Izvolsky, see the minutes concerning the discussions on Asia Minor, adding that Sonnino had demanded the whole Smyrna province, partly in the Russian sphere of influence. But Ribot assured the Ambassador that he himself and Lloyd George had told Sonnino that they could make no move without Russian consent.[8]

Even on that point, Ribot misled Izvolsky. At St-Jean-de-Maurienne, the main object of French and English diplomacy was to persuade the Italians to reduce their demands on Austrian territory, the main obstacle to an understanding with Vienna; the French were also trying to divert the Italians' attention from their own territorial claims in Asia Minor. Sonnino was given to understand that the Russians would probably not be in a position to press their claims very actively, and that Italy could have Smyrna. Although in this case, as well as in a number of others, the obligatory reference was made to the 'consent of the Russian government', the western Powers in fact paid less and less attention to their Russian ally. In the Austrian negotiations, no notice whatever was taken of Petrograd; when Ribot again leaked the news to Milyukov, the Russian Foreign Minister was a little wiser and much sadder.

In any case, Milyukov and the party he represented were not very popular with the Allies. From April until July, London and Paris supported the interests of the moderate socialists. Delegations of prominent socialists from France, Britain and Belgium were a common sight in Petrograd in those days; Albert Thomas, the leader of the French socialist party and Minister of Munitions, who arrived in Petrograd on 13 April 1917, relieved Paléologue, the Ambassador who had done nothing to hide his aristocratic sympathies after the outbreak of the revolution. Thomas stayed in Petrograd for two months, as a *ministre en mission*; his presence strengthened Kerensky's hand in his struggle with Milyukov. But most of all, Allied influence made itself felt in the sifting of the exiles who were returning to Russia after the revolution. Milyukov made no objection when the Canadian authorities detained Lev Trotsky, on his way home from the United States. Trotsky spent a month at a prisoner-of-war camp in Canada, passing the time of day in making converts among his fellow prisoners, mainly German sailors.

The Soviet soon came to object to the policy of discrimination which was being carried out against the internationalist exiles. *Izvestia* was puzzled by the strange fact that shipping problems arose whenever the exiles who were in favour of peace were to be transported. At first, the Russians abroad were entirely dependent on Allied shipping and had no other way of getting back to Russia; the British and French policy forced the exiles to look for an alternative form of transport. Lenin in the end found it, and the first 'sealed train' left the central Zurich railway station on the morning of 9 April 1917. Soon after their monopoly in the transport of Russian exiles was broken, the Allies became more accommodating to men who held a wider range of revolutionary views. But it was in this connection that the first hint was made of a more violent quarrel yet to come. When Sir George Buchanan, the British Ambassador to Petrograd, gave the official explanation for Trotsky's detention, he said that his government was in possession of information indicating that Trotsky was one of the men involved in a German conspiracy against the provisional government.

The western Allies, and especially the British because they

controlled a global network of communications, became involved in both the controversies that concerned the traffic in and out of Russia. After his abdication on 15 March 1917, the question of the future of the former Tsar and his family arose. Nicholas II first returned to General Headquarters at Mogilev, but his presence there threatened to complicate relations between the army and the provisional government. The government therefore welcomed General Alekseev's suggestion, on 17 March, that Nicholas II and his family should be allowed to go to Murmansk, before going abroad. The Soviet, however, disapproved; the socialists demanded his arrest and trial, and many of them feared a revival of the monarchy. On 20 March, Kerensky offered to accompany the Tsar to Murmansk, where he would embark on a ship bound for England. There was a dramatic flurry of activity: the Soviet ordered troops to occupy all the railway stations through which the Tsar's and Kerensky's train was to pass. In the end, however, Nicholas went the other way, to Tsarskoe Selo, where his children were sick with measles.

The Tsar was a cousin of King George V, and the day after Kerensky's abortive attempt to start him off on the way abroad, Sir George Buchanan inquired at the Foreign Ministry about the Tsar's reported arrest. At that point, the question of Nicholas' asylum came up for the first time: would England be prepared to have him? On 23 March 1917 a telegram reached the British Embassy in Petrograd, granting asylum to the Imperial family; arrangements were then made with the German government, via Copenhagen, to let the cruiser carrying the exiles pass safely on its way to England. But nothing happened. The former Tsar and his family remained in Russia, shunted about from one place to another by a nervous government before finally being murdered by the Bolsheviks in a house in Siberia. Did London withdraw the offer to Nicholas? Sir George Buchanan as well as Lloyd George answered the question in the negative: the Ambassador's daughter, however, wrote that the British government did in fact withdraw its offer.

On 10 April 1917, the Ambassador's return for luncheon was delayed by the arrival of an urgent telegram from London. When he eventually came in, he said in a flat, lifeless voice, 'I have had news from England. They refuse to let the Emperor come over!' After a moment he added:[9]

They say that it is wiser to discourage the idea of the Imperial family coming to England. The Government are nervous of any interior unrest leading to strikes in the shipyards, the coal-mines or munition factories. There has been a certain amount of revolutionary talk in Hyde Park, the Labour Party declare that they will make the workmen down tools if the Emperor is allowed to land. . . .

Apparently Lloyd George had warned the King that feeling in the country was violently against the Russian Imperial family, and that the Labour politicians were out to make trouble. Milyukov's evidence also supports the view that the British offer was withdrawn, at least temporarily. Soon after 10 April, Buchanan apparently told Milyukov that Nicholas and his family would be welcome in England after the end of the war.

The French, who took pride in their special relationship with Petrograd, fared no better than the British in the early weeks of the revolution. Soon after its outbreak, Paléologue told a Russian revolutionary that

the war is my main concern of course, so I want the effects of the revolution to be kept down as much as possible and order to be restored at the earliest moment. Don't forget that the French army is making preparations for a great offensive and that the Russian army is bound in honour to do its share.[10]

The French military went ahead with their plans for a spring offensive in the west as if nothing had happened in the east; the result was Nivelle's disastrous campaign, widespread mutinies in the French army, and further deterioration in the relations with the Russians. At a time when their country was going through the greatest political upheaval in its history, the Russians resented the 'business as usual' attitude of their western Allies. They resented being told what to do, and being ignored when invitations to inter-Allied conferences were sent out. By the time Milyukov had left the provisional government, it was clear that those politicians who had hoped that the revolution would bring Russia closer to the western Allies would be disappointed. Ramsay MacDonald once said that 'Russia in arms with us to free Europe from an autocracy whether political or military is a grim joke'. But when the revolution at last removed the offending regime, Russia remained as remote as it had always been. If the conservative politicians in the Allied countries were suspicious of the Russian revolutionaries, such feelings were reciprocated in Russia. The front-line soldier easily accepted the view that the Allies were prepared to fight to the last drop of Russian blood; when members of the Duma inspected the army at the front in April 1917, they were struck by the suspicion, among the troops, of the Allies and their 'imperialist' aims.[11]

In a way, the Allied support for the moderate socialists limited the socialists' freedom of action without strengthening their political position. They were committed to carrying on the war, and they never examined the reasons carefully enough. Tsereteli was concerned with Russia's loyalty to its allies less than with the protection of the gains of the revolution against foreign enemies. While the Russians went on fighting to defend their revolution, their politicians set out to work for peace.

After the formation of the coalition government on 18 May 1917 Russian peace policy was based on two quite separate initiatives. The Soviet was committed to rallying public opinion in the belligerent countries behind the idea of a negotiated peace and to organizing a conference that would discuss its terms. The provisional government, on the other hand, intended to organize an inter-Allied conference which would review war aims as well as peace terms.

The idea of a conference had been current, since the outbreak of war, in socialist circles in the neutral countries, and among minority socialists in the belligerent countries. On 27 April 1917, Borbjerg, the Danish socialist leader, arrived in Petrograd with an invitation to the Russian socialists to attend a conference organized by a joint Dutch-Scandinavian committee. Borbjerg also had a message with him from the German party – that Germany was willing to negotiate peace, and that no military offensive would be undertaken against revolutionary Russia. The Dane at first discussed the proposals with the socialist leaders in Petrograd and then, on 5 May, put his proposal before the executive committee of the Soviet. The invitation of the Dutch and the Scandinavians was welcome, but not so the message from Berlin, with its too obvious identification of the majority socialists with German official policy. It was unwise of the Germans to make promises to their Russian comrades concerning decisions of a purely military nature. Nevertheless, on the question of the socialist conference there were discordant voices in the executive committee of the Soviet as well. The Bolsheviks argued that only those parties which had consistently opposed the war and the internal political truce should be invited; the majority of the committee, however, overruled that suggestion, opting for the representation of all the socialist parties. It had also become clear that the Russian socialists, conscious as they were of the prestige that a successful revolution had given them, were disinclined to play second fiddle to their Dutch and Scandinavian comrades. The Russians agreed that the conference should take place in Stockholm but no more. Vandervelde, the Belgian socialist who came to Petrograd soon after Borbjerg, thought that the Russians were convinced that their revolutionary prestige would make it possible for them to impose their own peace formula on all the other socialist parties in Europe. On 15 May 1917, at the height of the Milyukov crisis, the Soviet took matters in its own hands, and issued an appeal for a conference.

The Russian revolution, the revolution of the toilers, workers, and soldiers, is not only a revolt against the terrors of the world butchery. It is the first outcry of indignation, from one of the detachments of the international army of labour, against the crisis of international imperialism. It is not only a national revolution – it is the first stage of world revolution, which will end the baseness of war and will bring peace to mankind. . . . The Russian Revolutionary Democracy appeals first to you, Socialists of all the Allied countries. You must not permit that the voice of the Provisional Government should remain a lone voice among the Allies. You must force your Governments to state definitely and clearly that the platform of peace without annexations or indemnities, on the basis of self-determination of peoples, is also their platform. . . . The Russian Revolutionary Democracy appeals to you, Socialists of the Austro-German alliance: you cannot allow the armies of your Governments to become executioners of Russian liberty. . . .

After an appeal to socialists in neutral countries, the Soviet declaration went on:

In order to unite these efforts [for peace] the Petrograd Soviet of Workers' and Soldiers' Deputies has decided to take the initiative in calling for an international conference of all the Socialist parties and factions in every country. Whatever may be the differences of opinion which have disrupted socialism for a period of three years of war, not a single faction of the Proletariat should refuse to participate in the struggle for peace, which is on the programme of Russian revolution.[12]

From the beginning, there was little doubt that the various minority factions in all European countries would support the initiative of the Soviet. The majority socialists were more of a problem. They were known to have no sympathy for the idea of a socialist conference. The French party had rejected the invitation from the Dutch-Scandinavian committee. But the effect of the revolution was powerful: two leaders of the French majority socialists, Cachin and Moutet, who visited Petrograd in May, left it as convinced supporters of the idea of a conference. They promised to win over their party and to demand that their government revise its war aims on the basis of the principles of the Russian revolution. On 16 May 1917 Moutet, who left Petrograd for Paris on the same train as Paléologue, told the Ambassador: 'Fundamentally, the Russian revolution is right...'– a remark that opened a long conversation. Albert Thomas was, however, not so easy to convince. On the day before Paléologue's departure, Thomas telegraphed the Prime Minister in Paris that French socialists should decline the invitation and insist that they could not attend any meeting in which the Germans took part. But Thomas too yielded. A week later he warned his government against an intransigent attitude, and soon after that he wrote to Lloyd George that he thought it necessary to attend the conference, even without having laid down any conditions beforehand. In London, Arthur Henderson, the Labour leader, was even more resolute: 'If my Government concurs, I have decided to go to Stockholm at any cost.'[13]

Although Moutet and Cachin had succeeded in swinging their executive over to the idea of the Stockholm conference – when the decision was announced to the crowds waiting outside the party headquarters, the Internationale was heard in the streets of Paris for the first time since the outbreak of the war – on 1 June 1917 the French government announced that it would not issue passports to socialists for the conference. Lloyd George, who was not hostile to the plan, waited for further developments. The government in Washington had anticipated the French by refusing to let American socialists have passports; but they had no political influence, and their numbers were insignificant. More than from the difficulties made for them by their respective governments, the socialists suffered from dissensions in their own ranks. For almost three years, there had been little contact between them, and they now started finding out how difficult it was to revive the habits of internationalism, how deeply the war had divided them.

They all applauded the revolution in Russia; they all gave their approval to the Soviet peace formula; they all meant to attend the conference in Stockholm. Yet every attempt to agree on the conference agenda failed. Apart from the hotly disputed question whether the decisions of the conference should be binding on all the participants, the socialists argued about the liquidation of the political truce, as well as the question of responsibility for the war and the disruption of the International on its outbreak. The Allied socialists, and the French in particular, wanted to put the war guilt of Germany and of the German socialists as the first point on the agenda. The Soviet opposed the French suggestion on practical grounds, because it would ruin the conference; their theoretical explanation of the causes of the war was that it had been brought about by the imperialist rivalry of all the capitalist governments. Again, the Allied socialists demanded that their German comrades renounce the *Burgfrieden* before they come to Stockholm. Again, the Soviet objected. The Russians argued that the renunciation of the civil truce should take place at the conference, simultaneously by all the socialist parties.

With these controversies still unsettled, the Soviet issued, on 2 June 1917, an invitation to all the socialist parties. The conference was to take place in Stockholm, and it would open some time between 28 June and 8 July.[14] It was not a popular move among the majority of the Allied socialists. They asked why the Russians had acted independently; why did they not want to join an inter-Allied conference in the first place? On 4 June 1917 Thomas, Henderson and Vandervelde – they were all still present in Petrograd – drafted a letter of protest to the executive committee of the Soviet. They accused the committee of issuing the invitation when the negotiations of the Allied socialists were still going on; they insisted that the Germans should repudiate their civil truce. At first, Tsereteli replied that the reconciliation of the two blocks still remained the intention of the Soviet, and that if the Soviet acted as a member of one or the other, the prestige of the Russian revolution, its influence toward the ending of the war, would be lost.[15]

On 12 June the executive committee replied to the Thomas–

Henderson–Vandervelde letter. It pointed out that socialists everywhere could accept the Soviet peace formula as a basis for negotiations at the conference; it contained a sharp hint that mutual distrust between socialists derived from their being duped by the imperialists, and that the conference could succeed only if the socialists regarded themselves as representatives of the universal brotherhood of the proletariat rather than of the warring coalitions. The executive committee of the Soviet went on to attack the demand of their western comrades that conditions for attendance should be laid down; they insisted that, as far as they were concerned, good faith and recognition of working class internationalism were the only conditions.

On 16 June 1917, the all-Russian Congress of the Soviets met in Petrograd; the question of war and peace was the most controversial issue before it. Like the Petrograd Soviet, the Congress was dominated by the moderate Social Revolutionary–Menshevik coalition; the Bolsheviks and the internationalist wings of the Social Revolutionaries and of the Mensheviks were in opposition. Fyodor Dan, a Menshevik leader and Tsereteli's friend, read the main report. He argued that the revolution must end the war bfore the war destroyed the revolution. The Soviet resolution in the main reflected Dan's arguments: it rejected both a separate peace and a complete victory by one side or the other, because these would intensify rather than remove the conditions that had made the war possible in the first place. The resolution also recommended the government to re-examine the treaties so that the policy of conquest could be fully abandoned: Russian diplomatic personnel should be changed to facilitate such a change of policy. And all the time, the army must be ready for action.[16]

The resolution of the Congress indeed gave the impression that the moderate Russian socialists were abandoning the high hopes they had entertained for the Stockholm conference. There was not enough support for it in the west, and apart from that, the governments in Paris, Rome and Washington maintained their refusal to issue passports. The Congress decided to send a delegation abroad; it arrived in Stockholm on 5 July 1917, when a Russian–Dutch–Scandinavian committee was formed to carry on the good work; a part of the Russian delegation travelled on, to western Europe. There was, however, no way of resolving the differences between the Russian and the western European socialists. At the very centre of their dispute there lay the hard fact that the Russians were the only nation who had broken their civil truce. It was impossible to ask anyone else to follow the same course, without calling for an internal revolution. In the flush of their recent revolutionary successes the Russians did not fully understand that. They simply continued to grow more and more exasperated with their comrades in the western countries. At one point, for instance, the usually moderate *Delo Naroda* suggested that Russia might find it best to break with the Allies and conclude peace with the Central Powers.

It may have also occurred to some members of the Soviet that now, when hopes of peace were diminishing, the revolution needed the protection and prestige which only military victory could give. In June 1917, the provisional government and especially its Minister of War, Aleksandr Kerensky, were absorbed in preparing an offensive at the front. The visiting Allied socialists also did their best to help: soon after the delegation led by Vandervelde arrived at Petrograd on 18 May 1917, the Belgians, accompanied by Albert Thomas, left for the front. We have little evidence on the impact they made but we may assume that those respectable, well-dressed, well-fed foreign gentlemen made less than a passing impression on the Russian troops in the front line.

About the same time, the army commanders reported in Petrograd on the situation at the front. Their reports were deeply pessimistic. General Dragomirov said that 'from the famous phrase about peace without annexations our troops caught only the word peace'. General Brusilov, who commanded the important south-western front, spoke about the way the soldiers misunderstood the revolutionary slogans. One of them told Brusilov: 'It has been said, No annexations, then why do we need that hilltop?'[17] Brusilov regarded the notion that peace could come without victory on the battlefield as nothing but a delusion.

It appeared that the revolution had caused a deep rift between the troops and their officers. There were only a few officers who subscribed to the Soviet ideas on the central issues of war and peace: most of the troops did. When the front commanders met in the capital, at the time when the coalition government was being constructed, the British Ambassador reported to London that the new cabinet offers us the last and almost forlorn hope of saving the military situation on this front. Kerensky, who assumes charge of both the War Office and the Admiralty, is not an ideal War Minister, but he hopes, by going to the front and making passionate appeals to the patriotism of the soldiers, to be able to galvanize the army into new life. He is the only man who can do it if it can be done.[18]

On 1 July 1917, the offensive was launched on a fifty-mile-long sector of the front in eastern Galicia. The offensive was in no way on the grand scale. On a small part of an Austrian-held line, the Russians had to be reinforced by the newly formed Czechoslovak brigade, with many of its troops recruited in the prisoner-of-war camps;* although a victory against heavy odds was won by the Czechs and the Slovaks at Zborov, it failed to inspire the Russians. Many of them never reached the front-line trenches, and of those who did many refused to go over the top. Kerensky's impassioned oratory failed also: by the time he succeeded Prince Lvov as Prime Minister on 22 July 1917, the summer offensive had collapsed. And added to failure at the front, a government crisis, accompanied by popular unrest, was running its course in the capital. On 15 July the Kadet members of the government, who had never really felt at ease with their socialist colleagues, resigned over a disagreement on policy toward the non-Russian peoplss of the Empire, the Ukrainians in particular. On the following day, demonstrations by pro-Bolshevik troops took place, which were directed against the Menshevik and Social Revolutionary leaders of the Soviet rather than against the provisional government. The demonstrations quickly assumed threatening proportions; they subsided equally quickly, however, after the Ministry of Justice released information that the Bolsheviks were being supported by the German government.

The opinion, widely held by its allies, that Russia was ceasing to be a factor in the military struggle proved correct; the French General Staff submitted a memorandum to the Allied conference in Paris on 24–6 July 1917 on military strategy to be followed if Russia left the war and large numbers of German troops were transferred to the western front.[19] The Russians had of course not been asked to that conference. Soon afterwards, a similar meeting took place in London. When Konstantin Nabokov, the Russian Chargé d'Affaires, called at the Foreign Office to arrange an

* See below, pp. 301, 311.

interview with Balfour, he was told that the Foreign Secretary was not available because he was attending an inter-Allied conference: Nabokov observed that Russia was an Allied country as well; he received an invitation within a few minutes.

Nabokov's presence at the second and last day of the conference did not much improve Russia's standing in the eyes of her allies. They were of course still interested in maintaining the illusion of a Russian front for the benefit of the enemy. The conference in Paris had gone as far as promising new military, naval and transport missions: the French were to reorganize the army, the British the navy, the Americans were to take care of transport. The French sent a mission, and it was discovered that the Americans already had a number of railway experts in Russia, but no practical improvements followed. None could really be expected; the relations between the western Allies and the Russians were now beyond repair.

The end of the revolutionary episode in the relations between Russia and its western allies was marked by an informal meeting in Petrograd, which was organized by Colonel Thompson, the head of the American Red Cross mission. Generals Niessel and Knox, of the French and British military missions, General Neslukhovski, the Russian Minister of War, David Soskice, Kerensky's private secretary, Thompson and his assistant, Raymond Robins, were present. Knox at once fiercely attacked the Russian government and the army, concluding his diatribe by describing the Russian troops as cowardly dogs. The Russians then left the meeting, and Knox went on to say that he was not at all interested in stabilizing Kerensky's government, and that the establishment of a military dictatorship was what Russia needed. The meeting took place on 2 November 1917, five days before the Bolshevik revolution.[20]

The Russians, for their own part, could be as suspicious, and as remote, as the Allies. After July, they were too preoccupied with their internal affairs to be able to attend to foreign policy: Tereshchenko, who had given up hopes for a negotiated peace on the lines proposed by the Soviet, pursued a policy that came to resemble, more and more, the foreign policy of Milyukov. Although he made no public pronouncements about Russia's need for glory abroad, in private conversation Tereshchenko showed no wish to forgo any of the promises that had been made by the

Allies to his predecessors. But there were few Russians who had so much sympathy for the Allies as Tereshchenko had. Maxim Gorky's newspaper *Novaya Zhizn* printed articles so insulting to France and Britain that the government asked the Minister of Justice to draft a law forbidding insults in the press against the Allied states and their diplomatic representatives. The draft became law on 23 August 1917, but it made little difference. In the middle of September, for instance, a drunk soldier member of the Soviet arrested, in a tram, two members of the Rumanian military mission because they were speaking French.

In the meanwhile, there was a turn for the better in the fortunes of the Bolshevik party. On 6 September General Kornilov, the Commander-in-Chief of the army whom Kerensky himself had appointed, ordered his troops to march on Petrograd, declaring that he would make short shrift of the revolution and the revolutionaries. Kerensky had to find protection against Kornilov wherever he could; by the most ironic twist of the revolution, the Bolsheviks, the same men whom the government had suppressed in July, now came into their own as the saviours of that very same government. Bolshevik agitation, rather than the Red Guard, defeated Kornilov. By the middle of September, the Bolsheviks had a majority in the Petrograd and Moscow Soviets: Trotsky, who had joined their party shortly before, was elected chairman of the Soviet in Petrograd on 23 September. A month later, Lenin returned from his hiding place in Finland and immediately began to plan the Bolshevik take-over of power. Its success was made possible by an efficient, disciplined party organization and by Lenin's ruthless simplification of foreign policy. But without Lenin's policy, the Bolshevik organization would have remained a blunt, useless tool.

In March 1917, when the revolution broke out, Lenin was living with his wife, Nadezhda Krupskaya, in a sub-let room in Spiegelgasse 14 in Zurich. The winter of 1916–17 had been the most depressing of their wartime exile: their connections with Russia had been cut off; there was no news, they received neither letters nor visitors. The things that used to keep the revolutionaries going were no longer happening, and it seemed as if they would never happen again. There were only the usual libraries to visit, the customary cheap eating-houses; Lenin and his wife rarely sought out the company of their fellow exiles for its own sake. He had an essay on imperialism to finish; from time to time, he gave a talk to foreign and Swiss workers or to a socialist youth organization. At one of them, he told his audience: 'We of the older generation may not live to see the decisive battles of this coming revolution.'[21] The winter in Zurich in 1916–17 provided a suitable background for gloomy thoughts; Lenin described his life then as 'slow' and 'poky'.

But the revolution came, and for Lenin the decisive battle was about to begin. He was impatient, wanting to get back to Petrograd as soon as possible. There was, we have already seen, no chance of the western Allied governments assisting his passage. His wife later wrote:[22]

As there were no legal ways of travelling, illegal ways would have to be used. But what ways? From the moment the news of the revolution was received, Ilyich had no sleep. His nights were spent building the most improbable plans. We could fly over by plane. But such an idea could only be thought of in a waking dream. Put into words, its unreality became at once obvious. The thing was to obtain the passport of some foreigner from a neutral country, best of all a Swede, who was less likely to arouse suspicion. A Swedish passport could be obtained through the Swedish comrades, but ignorance of the language was an obstacle to using it. Perhaps just a little Swedish would do? You might easily give yourself away, though. 'Imagine yourself falling asleep and dreaming of Mensheviks, which will start you off swearing juicily in Russian! Where will your disguise be then?' I said with a laugh.

Nevertheless Ilyich wrote to Hanecki enquiring whether there was any way of getting into the country through Germany.

For more than a week after the outbreak of the revolution Lenin was agitated, restless: he did not know that in Berlin, ground had been prepared for his trip across Germany. Yet in spite of his excitement and insomnia, his readiness to make a deal with the devil himself, Lenin's customary prudence did not desert him. At first, a false move was made. In Copenhagen, Alexander Helphand – we came across him at the beginning of 1915, when he first got into touch with the German Ambassador to Constantinople* – shared in Lenin's impatience, but he had none of Lenin's caution. While the Foreign Ministry were still discussing technical details of transporting Russian revolutionaries across Germany, Helphand obtained a permit from the General Staff for the transit

* See above, pp. 94 f.

of two leading Bolsheviks only – Lenin and Zinoviev. Hanecki (alias Jakob Fürstenberg), employee of one of Helphand's trading companies in Scandinavia and the contact man between Lenin and Helphand, let Lenin know that the trip across Germany had been arranged; Georg Sklarz, another German businessman in Scandinavia, travelled to Zurich to accompany the two Bolsheviks on their journey, and pay their fares. Before Sklarz reached Zurich, Lenin had telegraphed Hanecki, asking for more details about the offer; when Sklarz arrived, Lenin at once broke off negotiations.

A trip of a large group of revolutionaries across enemy territory in wartime, with the aid of the enemy government, was taking a serious enough risk; an individual trip, arranged by some backstairs deal and paid for by a person of Sklarz's dubious reputation, would have meant political suicide. Lenin knew that, if he travelled across Germany, the arrangements on his own side at least would have to be above board and quite irreproachable. A Committee for the Return of Russian Political Exiles in Switzerland was organized and at first Lenin came under its wing. Robert Grimm, the editor of the Social Democrat *Berner Tagwacht*, was asked to travel to Petrograd on behalf of the Committee. But Grimm had had differences with Lenin earlier in that year, when Lenin had accused him of being a 'social chauvinist'; now, in April 1917, Grimm sided with the Mensheviks, who maintained that the Russian exiles should wait for the consent of the provisional government before they travelled across Germany.

Lenin could not stand the delay. He had a few close contacts among the Swiss Social Democrats, and Fritz Platten was the most suitable to ask on his behalf. Of working-class origins, Platten was a self-taught man, and personally dedicated to Lenin. He made the arrangements with the German mission in Berne for Lenin and his group of fellow-travellers.

On the morning of 3 April 1917 Platten was asked to come and lunch with Lenin. A little party was waiting for him at the table: apart from Lenin, Karl Radek, a Jew from Austrian Galicia, who later became one of the leading Soviet publicists, and Willi Münzenberg, who built up, after the war, a powerful communist publishing empire in western Europe. Lenin at once asked Platten whether he would act on his behalf in the matter of the journey across Germany, and whether he would accompany the party on its trip. Platten hesitated a moment: he knew that his future as the

Secretary of the Swiss party was at stake. Nevertheless he also knew that Lenin's return to Russia was more important than his own career in the Swiss party.[23] Immediately after lunch, the company boarded the three o'clock train to Berne. Platten let Robert Grimm know by telegraph of their imminent arrival.

The conversation between Grimm and his visitors was short and somewhat sharp: there was nothing much to be said. Grimm told them that he regarded Platten's interference with the job in hand as undesirable, that 'Fritz is a good revolutionary but a bad diplomat' and that in his own opinion he would make a mess of things. Lenin disregarded what Grimm said and simply told him that Platten was asking Baron Romberg, the German Minister to Berne, for an audience on the following day. The details of the conditions that were to be put to Romberg were worked out the same evening in Lenin's bedroom. The main question was on whose behalf Platten was to negotiate; Lenin allowed him to tell the Germans that he himself and Zinoviev would travel with the first group of exiles. The remaining conditions were set down in writing and their chief purpose was to protect Lenin against any possible accusations in the future. The document that Platten put before Romberg was cautious and naïve, and admirably served its purpose. Platten undertook to accompany his friends 'bearing full responsibility and personal liability at all times'. He would buy the tickets at 'the normal tariffs', and would undertake 'all communication with German organizations'. The carriage was to enjoy extra-territorial rights; 'as far as possible the journey shall be made without stops and in a through train.'[24] Romberg remarked how unusual it was for travellers to propose conditions to the government of the country through which they intended to travel, and he forwarded the document to Berlin. The conditions were approved two days later, with the exception of point 2, which made Platten a go-between for the exiles and the German organizations. The Germans were to have direct access to Lenin and his fellow exiles after all; Jansson, the trade union leader, was to travel with them because the 'proposal for journey was agreed after request from German Trades Unions'.[25] When Romberg told Platten of the message from Berlin, Platten objected. The German Minister then told him not to make too much fuss about it, 'not to make it a matter of principle', because if he telegraphed Berlin with another inquiry, the railway arrangements would have to be cancelled. 'I remained silent', Platten remembered.[26] The train was to leave on 9 April 1917.

The news that Lenin was to travel through Germany created a sensation in Zurich. Newspaper correspondents, artists, writers, expatriates, were amazed by his daring and foolhardiness. Salomon Grumbach, a correspondent of *L'Humanité*, with considerable knowledge of Russian emigration – he occasionally let the French and the British missions in Berne have the benefit of his knowledge – complained of the treachery that would help the Germans to prolong the war. He said that he would bring the whole thing into the open in a public debate he was to have with Lenin the following evening, but the debate never took place. Franz Werfel and Stefan Zweig, who were also sitting in the Pfauen café when the news broke, disapproved of Lenin's action; in another corner of the café Romain Rolland, who was usually remote and dignified, joined in the general discussion and disapproval. James Joyce thought the arrangement some kind of practical joke. 'It's just like the Trojan horse to me', he said, adding, 'I suppose Ludendorff must be pretty desperate. Lenin and Ludendorff?'[27] Lenin, for his own part, had no illusions about the arrangement or the motives behind the German decision to help him. He was resolved to get back to Russia as quickly as he could because he knew, from his experience of the revolution in 1905, that failure was the price paid for delay.

Soon after eleven on the morning of 9 April 1917, the Russian exiles started arriving at an inn called the Zähringer Hof. They had a lot of luggage with them, and enough food for ten days. When the party assembled at last, it was a small, rather subdued, slightly shabby company of just over thirty people. There was nothing exceptional about them; without the piles of luggage, baskets and bundles they could have been a party from a Zurich suburb setting out on a day's excursion to a remote part of the lake. Most of the revolutionaries were wearing ties, waistcoats and bowler hats, and carrying umbrellas. Others did not bother; there were a few children about. They finished their lunch and at 2.30 they slowly moved off, carrying their own luggage, toward the railway station.

The journey, with Platten taking good care of his charges, went according to plan. At the German frontier station of Gottmadingen the travellers boarded a second- and third-class carriage; the women and children moved into the second-class compartments with upholstered seats, the men sat on the wooden benches of the third. Three of the doors of the carriage were then sealed, the fourth left open. The two German officers who accompanied the Russians had the compartment nearest the open door; there was a mark in chalk across the corridor that separated the Russian from the German part of the carriage. Mannheim–Frankfurt–Stuttgart–Berlin–Sassnitz. In Frankfurt the carriage was slightly delayed, having missed its connection; in Stuttgart, Jansson boarded the train and asked to see Platten. The two men had met before; Jansson told Platten that he wanted to greet the travellers on behalf of the General Committee of the German Trade Unions, and that he wished to speak with the Russians personally. Platten refused to let Jansson enter the 'extra-territorial' part of the carriage, and the German trade union leader left for another part of the train. The Russians did not return the greetings, and the following morning Platten told Jansson that they thanked the German trade unions for their kind message. Jansson then left, this time for good. In Berlin, the German authorities provided the children with milk; in Sassnitz, there was a boat waiting to take the party to Malmö, and from there to Stockholm.

The Russians arrived in Sweden on 12 April, and at no point of their long, exhausting journey were they aware of the drama that kept the diplomatic wires busy on their behalf. In their anxiety to arrange the journey as soon as possible, neither Lenin nor Platten realized that they would have to cross Sweden, and that they would need Swedish visas. Fortunately, Romberg in Berne remembered just in time, when the Russians were having lunch at the Zähringer Hof in Zurich before their departure, and he at once telegraphed the Wilhelmstrasse.[28] Twenty-four hours later, permission was secured in Stockholm for the Russians to travel through Sweden; the news of it had not, however, reached General Headquarters by the morning of 12 April. At breakfast on that day the Kaiser, talking about the transit of the partly sealed carriage across Germany, said that the Russians should be given German political literature and that, if they were refused entry into Sweden, the Army High Command would get them into Russia through the German lines.[29]

Apart from the Jansson incident, the trip across Germany was uneventful; Lenin read most of the time while, in the compartment next door, Radek told his friends almost every anecdote he knew. The passage through Sweden was shorter but more eventful. At Trelleborg, Kuba Hanecki, Lenin's friend and Helphand's employee, gave the whole group a very good dinner; on the following morning in Stockholm there were journalists, photographers, Swedish socialists waiting for the arrival of the Russians at the railway station. Breakfast with the Lord Mayor followed. Helphand came to Stockholm and tried to get in touch with Lenin on behalf of the executive committee of the German Social Democrat party. Lenin refused to see him. The Bolshevik leader knew that 'Parvus' was a potential source of trouble for him, and, to make doubly certain, he asked his comrades to draft and sign a protocol about his refusal to see 'Parvus' in Stockholm. Nevertheless, two of the three men who signed the protocol – Hanecki and Radek – were themselves in touch with 'Parvus'.

After eleven years, for the first time since he had fled abroad on the failure of the revolution in 1905, Lenin crossed the Russian frontier. He had spent most of his political career, some seventeen years in all, abroad. In six days' time, on 22 April 1917, he was to be forty-seven years old. As the train approached the Russian frontier he wondered whether he would be arrested in Petrograd: he knew that he had taken a risk. But instead of prison and obscurity, a triumphant welcome awaited Lenin at the Finland station. Large crowds of people had collected there; the executive committee of the Soviet sent a delegation. The train was late and the politicians had enough time to talk over the wisdom of Lenin's decision to travel across Germany: there could be no agreement on that question. Finally, the band on the platform struck up the 'Marseillaise' and a few minutes later Lenin walked into the room, wearing the sober, dark suit that Hanecki had bought for him in Stockholm, and carrying an incongruous bunch of flowers. Chkeidze greeted him in the name of the Soviet – a lukewarm welcome, containing an implied warning that Lenin had better not make trouble in the revolutionary camp. Lenin was restless while the speech lasted, looking at the people around him, at the ceiling, at his bunch of flowers. He turned away from Chkeidze and his men when he spoke, beginning 'Dear comrades, soldiers, sailors and workers!' He told them that the general imperialist war would be reduced to a number of civil wars, and that capitalism would crash: he ended his short speech with the exclamation,

'Long live the world-wide socialist revolution!' The people out-side were trying to break down the glass doors; when Lenin walked out of the station and started getting into a car he was stopped by the crowd. He mounted the bonnet of the car and made another speech; after that he transferred to an armoured car which kept on stopping, at crossroads, wherever the crowd thickened, to allow him to say a few words. It took a long time before he reached the palace of ballerina Kshesinskaya, now the Bolshevik headquarters. All the lights inside the palace were burning: most of the party leaders were already waiting there when Lenin arrived, and nobody bothered much that night about sleep.[30]

In spite of his frequent pronouncements, in the past, on ques-tions of war and peace, the Bolsheviks who came to welcome Lenin on 16 April 1917 were uncertain as to what the future party line would be. Since the outbreak of the revolution, at a time when it was essential that the party spoke to the Russians with a steady, single voice, its policy was showing considerable fluctua-tions. In its first issues *Pravda*, the Bolshevik organ, had made a forceful attack on the provisional government. Other Bolsheviks, including Stalin, were affected by revolutionary enthusiasm, after their return from exile in Siberia. When they took over the management of *Pravda*'s editorial policy they not only advocated unity between the Bolsheviks and the left Mensheviks, but went so far as to take a conciliatory attitude toward the provisional government. Such a policy had implications for much more than Russia's internal affairs. Conciliation with the provisional govern-ment implied at least some degree of approval of its foreign policy, and the editorial board of *Pravda* did indeed condemn the defeatist, anti-war slogans that were then circulated by some Bolsheviks in Petrograd.

At the time of this vacillating policy on the part of the Bolshevik party newspaper, Lenin, still in Switzerland, looking for a way of getting back to Russia as soon as possible, wrote his *Letters from Afar* to *Pravda*. Lenin wrote the first letter on 20 March 1917, and it appeared on 3 April. (It was sent first to Hanecki, who for-warded it to Lenin's sister Maria in Petrograd.) It stood in sharp opposition to the policy of the editorial board. Lenin looked at the situation in Russia from the outside: his distance from the confusion, from the enthusiasm of the early days of the revolution, gave his policy a detachment and a firmness that was lacking in men more immediately involved. He argued that the ease with which the Romanov dynasty was swept away was due to a

conspiracy of Anglo-French imperialists who pushed Milyukov, Guchkov and Co. to seize power in order to prolong the imperialist war, in order to wage it more ferociously and tenaciously, in order to slay fresh millions of Russian workers and peasants, so as to obtain possession of Constantinople for Guchkov, Syria for the French, and Mesopotamia . . . for the British capitalists.

In the letter written five days later, on 25 March, Lenin called for the repudiation of the Russian treaties with the western Allies, for the publication of all secret diplomatic agreements, for the liberation of all colonies, and for the proclamation of new peace terms. At the same time, he appealed to the Russian proletariat to form a militia, and to the working classes everywhere to set up their own Soviets.

To the *Pravda* letters Lenin added one to the Swiss workers.[31] He told them that the Bolsheviks remained faithful to the policy that had been first formulated in the party newspaper, the *Sotsialdemokrat*, on 13 October 1915. It was stated there, Lenin went on, that if the revolution was victorious in Russia and a republican government came to power, and if that government wanted to carry on the imperialist war in alliance with the capitalist middle classes of England and France, the Bolsheviks would oppose it with every means at their disposal. This was precisely the situation that came about. Such a revolutionary government, Lenin argued, intended to betray the workers. The slogan 'The Germans should overthrow the Kaiser!' was part of the deceit. Why don't they add, Lenin asked, that the 'Italians and the English should overthrow their kings, the Russians their monarchists, Lvov and Guchkov'? The socialists who maintained that 'as long as the Kaiser remains on the throne our war is a war of defence' were talking sheer nonsense.

The answer, according to Lenin, was that the provisional government should receive no support at all. 'Whoever maintains that this support is necessary in the fight against the restoration of Tsarism is lying.' In the same issue of the *Sotsialdemokrat*, Lenin told the Swiss comrades, the Bolsheviks had stated what they would do if their party got to power:

1. We shall offer peace at once to all belligerent nations.
2. We shall put forward the following peace conditions:
   (*a*) immediate liberation of all colonies;
   (*b*) immediate liberation of oppressed nations deprived of their rights.
3. We shall at once begin with the liberation of the peoples oppressed by the Great Russians.
4. We have no doubt that the conditions will be unacceptable, not only to the monarchist, but also to the republican bourgeoisie of Germany, and not only of Germany but also to the capitalist governments of England and France.

If point 4 proved correct, then the Russians would have to carry on a revolutionary war against Germany: 'We are no pacifists', Lenin wrote. But it would be preferable to stop the wholesale slaughter, the destruction of European culture, by putting power in every civilized country into the hands of the revolutionary proletariat. The Russian working class was entrusted with the great task of beginning a series of revolutions, which will be created 'with objective necessity' by the imperialist war. But Lenin did not regard the Russian proletariat as the chosen instrument of historical necessity:

We know very well that the organization of the Russian proletariat is weaker and that it is spiritually less prepared than the working classes of other countries. No special qualities, but special historical circumstances have put the Russian proletariat into the forefront, possibly for a short time, of the revolutionary proletariat of the whole world. Russia is an agrarian country, one of the most backward in the whole of Europe. Socialism cannot be victorious in Russia immediately: but the agrarian character of the country may, in view of the large feudal landed property, as the experience of the year 1905 has shown, give the bourgeois-democratic revolution a powerful impetus, and make it an overture, an introduction, to the socialist world revolution.

From the Russian situation Lenin turned to the conditions in Germany. 'The pot of the proletarian masses is already cooking in Germany', Lenin wrote with conviction and without elegance, and he added: 'The German proletariat is the most loyal and reliable ally of the Russian and international proletarian revolution.'

The corner-stones of Lenin's policy were to be found throughout his letters and in the speeches he had made before arriving at the Bolshevik headquarters on the night of 16 April 1917. In exile in Switzerland, in the dark, hopeless years of the war, Lenin had given these matters much thought. There were still a few ill-defined, blurred concepts in his argument – they were revealed especially in the inconsistencies between his references to the arrival of socialism on the one hand, and to that of socialist revolution on the other – but the main elements of his policy, whether they were part of a reasoned argument or merely the high-lighted contents of a slogan, fitted all in together. Lenin's reasoning moved, in the main, on the lines of Trotsky's and Helphand's theory of permanent revolution, which was based on the lessons of the unsuccessful revolution of 1905. Indeed, the intellectual accord between Lenin and Trotsky at this point was near-perfect, and it smoothed Trotsky's entry into the Bolshevik organization later that year.

After the long, exhausting trip, the uncertainties of its last stages, and then the triumphal welcome at the Finland Station, there was no question of Lenin retiring for the night. When he reached the Bolshevik headquarters at the Kshesinskaya Palace he talked to a few people, had a snack, and then addressed a large delegation of party workers in the reception room of the palace. When he spoke,

> It seemed as though all the elements had risen from their abodes, and the spirit of universal destruction, knowing neither barriers nor doubts, neither human difficulties nor human calculations, was hovering around Kshesinskaya's reception-room above the heads of the bewitched disciples.
> Lenin was in general a very good orator – not an orator of the consummate, rounded phrase, or of the luminous image, or of absorbing pathos, or of the pointed witticism, but an orator of enormous impact and power, breaking down complicated systems into the simplest and most generally accessible elements, and hammering, hammering, hammering them into the heads of his audience until he took them captive.[32]

On that occasion, when the day was breaking on 17 April 1917, Lenin spoke for some two hours to the Bolsheviks; later on, he addressed the last joint session ever to be held of all the Social Democrats, Mensheviks, Bolsheviks and those who belonged to neither of the two major factions. The gist of the two speeches was similar, but they were made to different audiences. In the first instance, he had a rapt group of dedicated disciples before him; in the second, a meeting largely consisting of highly critical adversaries. The latter noted the fact that Lenin insisted on sharply differentiating his position from the rest of the socialists, that he came in no spirit of conciliation; one opinion expressed at the meeting was that 'Lenin's new words echo something old—the superannuated truths of primitive anarchism'.[33] The feeling at the last Social Democrat meeting ran strongly against Lenin because he was ready once again to jeopardize the cause of unity and introduced a harsh note of dissent into the Soviet camp. But he could not be accused of not having made his position clear.

On 20 April *Pravda* printed Lenin's April Thesis, a summary of his views on war and peace since the outbreak of the revolution. There was to be no defence of the revolution before the proletariat seized power: the Soviet was to be converted to Lenin's way of thinking; not a parliamentary republic, but a republic of Soviets was to be established. The bureaucracy, the police, were to disappear: instead of the army, Lenin envisaged universal arming of the people. There were to be separate peasants' Soviets; all private lands were to be confiscated. All the banks in Russia were to be merged into one nationalized colossus. The party was to have a convention, change its programme and its name; the International, that had been broken up on the outbreak of the war, was to be reconstituted.[34]

The revolution, commented *Rabochaya Gazeta*, can be threatened not only from the right, but also from the left: Lenin has now rendered a service to the reaction by disregarding the natural limits of the revolution.[35] Chernov, the leader of the Social Revolutionary party, described Lenin as the poor man's Antichrist: a symbol of the thing the common man fears most of all, of the disaster just around the corner. Lenin was, Chernov thought, tremendously dangerous: a man who had elaborated a jargon that could offend the most insensitive ear, whose 'settling of accounts with opponents makes a crunchy screech like iron over glass', but at the bottom of whose impulses was always a grain of some 'unquestionably vital and political truth'. Lenin, in Chernov's view, possessed an

imposing wholeness. He seems to be made of one chunk of granite. And he is all round and polished like a billiard ball. There is nothing you can get hold of him by. He rolls with irrepressible speed. . . .

a man with a powerful mind and tremendous reserves of energy, a single-minded devotion to the revolutionary cause whom, nevertheless, the new Russian life must break, and not the other way round. Chernov was 'amused by the fears that the reverse will occur, that he will destroy the new Russian life'.[36]

The immediate reaction to Lenin's programme was largely one of fury and amazement, while its acceptance by the Bolsheviks owed a lot to party discipline. What its adversaries failed to perceive was the strength, the resilience in the programme. It had, in the first place, strong links with those traditions of European socialism abandoned on the outbreak of the war. The doctrine of the international brotherhood of the working classes, propagated and embodied in the Second International; pacifism; the refusal of the socialists to co-operate with the established order: such views and policies had all had to be abandoned for the sake of the civil truce. It is true that they were not powerful enough to sway the decisions of the leaders of the great European socialist parties in the summer of 1914; but they were never completely discarded or forgotten. They were there, ready to be taken up again in new circumstances. Such circumstances came about in 1917. The support, by the majority of socialists, of their respective national governments after the outbreak of the war had given the governments of the Great Powers a considerable length of rope. It was not so much that they were wholly ignorant, or incompetent, or inhuman. Like the socialist leaders, the politicians in the belligerent countries accepted, whether consciously or not, the fact that on the outbreak of the war the whole nation would have to be committed to the war effort, that there would be no place for open political dissent, that it was both possible and necessary to forge a perfect unity of the nation. The civil truce was to make total war possible, and total war made the civil truce necessary.

We have noted earlier that in August 1914 the socialist leaders readily gave up the internationalist ornaments of their political beliefs. Not so Lenin. He was one of the small band of men who could, throughout the war, claim the discarded inheritance of pre-war socialism. He was there, unknown and unyielding, poised for action. Lenin struck at the time when the civil truce had broken down in Russia, and when it was showing signs of stress elsewhere.

If the words, 'deepening of the revolution', so often heard in

Petrograd at the time, had any meaning at all, they referred to the interaction between the revolutionary policies and the desire for peace. There can be no doubt that such a desire existed in Russia. It was first used by the leaders of the Soviet, the Mensheviks and Social Revolutionaries, in their contest against Milyukov; later, with poetic justice, by the Bolsheviks against the leaders of the Soviet. The attitude to peace and war determined a man's political place in revolutionary Russia. Reluctant revolutionaries, men like Milyukov, who had no intention of disturbing anyone or anything very much, never came to grips properly with the problem of peace. Milyukov himself did not feel that the war was a bad thing for Russia and the Russians. On one occasion, indeed, he told a friend that the war held everything together and that without it everything would fall apart. Though subsequent coalition governments never quite returned to Milyukov's simple formula of 'war until victory at any cost', they were neither very interested in a negotiated peace nor did they know how to bring it about, and they were incapable of overcoming the aversion to it of Russia's allies. There was a feeling in the provisional government that, because of the length of the war, it would be difficult to return to the *status quo ante*.

The length of the war, however, convinced other people that it was time hostilities were brought to an end. For Tsereteli and his comrades in the Soviet, the idea of peace was at the very centre of their thinking, yet they were incapable of translating their formula into effective political action. It was not an easy operation. There was, in the first place, a sharp contrast between the 'peace' part of the Soviet programme and the 'defence of the revolution' part. It really meant the continuation of the same war for different reasons until the socialists of the belligerent Powers forced their governments to make peace. As regards the latter, the moderate members of the Soviet overestimated the international authority that their successful revolution gave them just as much as they misjudged the influence foreign socialists were capable of exerting on their governments. They disregarded the determination of these governments to achieve a decisive victory.

On one important point, however, the Soviet leaders were agreed with the provisional government. It was that separate peace with the enemy was out of the question. The rejection of a separate peace by both parties was so much taken for granted that the issue was hardly ever raised during the months of the revolution. The members of the Soviet as well as those of the provisional government thought a separate peace dishonourable; many years later, talking about 1917, Mr Kerensky told the present author that he did not for a moment consider a separate peace. Apart from the sympathy many Russian revolutionaries had for the democratic west, there was another reason why separate peace appeared disadvantageous in the circumstances. If Berlin won in the west by transferring troops from the front in the east after the conclusion of peace, there would be nothing to stop the Germans from turning, with all their might, against Russia. Nevertheless, there was something slightly quixotic in the attitude of these Russians, and they were soon proved wrong.

Failure marked the foreign policy of the provisional government as well as that of the Soviet. The provisional government in the end acquiesced in the Allied sabotage of a negotiated general peace: the Soviet, relying heavily on the help of European public opinion, was outraged at the gradual destruction of their programme. It was this failure that opened the door to Lenin's success.

Lenin and the Bolsheviks recognized no treaties or obligations, nor, until November 1917, were they limited by any ties of political power. Their rise was watched with satisfaction in Berlin since the German leaders expected Lenin and the Bolsheviks to help them to achieve the elusive objective of a separate peace. But between Lenin and the Germans there were no bonds either of sympathy or of contract. By the time Lenin came to power Russia was no longer capable of prosecuting the war. The Bolshevik revolution, as we shall have more than one occasion to note, affected rulers and people everywhere in diverse ways.

Lenin's peace programme had two distinct facets. There was its international content, with its call to the poor to refuse any longer to be used for purposes not their own, and to make war on the rich. In the specifically Russian context, the Bolsheviks stripped down Lenin's programme to the bare bones of the slogan 'Peace, Bread, and Land'. Lenin himself was prepared, more than any other politician in Russia, to use and deepen the desire of the Russians for peace. Once in power, Lenin did not for one moment hesitate to discard the treaties that bound Russia to its allies and to take it out of the war.

7 Brest Litovsk

On the eastern front thousands of square miles of territory changed hands in the course of sweeping offensives. Cavalry was much used and no tanks took advantage of the plain north of the Carpathian mountains; a few precious aircraft flew on occasional solitary reconnaissance sorties. Sturdy Maxim machine guns, mounted on little iron wheels, their crews pulling the guns behind them like some clumsy toys, proved one of the most effective weapons the Russians had. But they never had enough of them. The 'Russian steamroller', the ponderous but invincible army of the fond imagination of western politicians and journalists, proved unreliable. Yet the comparative technical backwardness of the armies in the east – the Germans kept their most up-to-date equipment for the west – made their war more mobile, and not as pointless as the western war of attrition. In France, the latest products of the great arms manufacturers of western Europe created a military stalemate: in Russia, the possibility of a knockout blow never quite disappeared from military calculations.

After the revolution of March 1917 a virtual armistice descended on the Russian front. It was broken by the Russians in June, but their few initial successes were soon reversed by the Austro-German armies. At the end of July Galicia and Bukovina were cleared of Russian troops, and the line was established which remained until the conclusion of the official armistice in December 1917. It began on the Baltic about forty miles north-east of Riga and continued south-west to a point where it cut across the main Moscow–Warsaw railway about fifty miles west of Minsk; further south, the line all but disappeared into the Pripet marshes. South of Pripet, the Austro-Hungarians, reinforced by German, Bulgarian and Turkish troops, took over. Their line ran along the left bank of a small river, the Stochód, met the frontier of Galicia and then more or less followed the frontier between Austria and

Russia all the way south to Rumania, where it cut across the whole country, running a few miles south-west of the river Sereth. Dobruja, the Rumanian province between the Danube and the Black Sea, had been occupied by the Germans and the Bulgarians in the autumn of 1916.

In three years of war, the Russian army had suffered severe punishment. Of the 15,500,000 men mobilized, a tenth of the total population of the country, the Germans had taken more than 1,250,000 prisoners and the Austrians over 870,000 before the beginning of June 1917: in the same period the Russians suffered some 5,400,000 casualties.[1] The losses in men and territory were, however, less surprising than the manner in which the army melted away in the course of 1917. At a critical point during the summer offensive a few regiments refused to go into action near the Galician village of Zborov and from there the infection spread. In July the Army Committee of the south-western front reported:[2]

> Some elements voluntarily evacuate their positions without even waiting for the approach of the enemy. Cases are on record in which an order given to proceed with all haste to such-and-such a spot to assist comrades in distress has been discussed for several hours at meetings, and the reinforcements were consequently delayed. These elements, at the first shots fired by the enemy, abandon their positions. For a distance of several hundred versts long files of deserters, both armed and unarmed, men who are in good health and robust, who have lost all shame and feel that they can act altogether with impunity, are proceeding to the rear of the army. Frequently entire units desert in this manner.

Though the troops at the front were under a double pressure – the revolutionary agitation from the rear was reinforced by peace propaganda from the German lines – the disintegration of the Russian army had not started at its most exposed and vulnerable points. In the same way as in France in 1917 and in Germany in 1918, the Russian troops not engaged in fighting were more susceptible to revolutionary agitation than the front-line soldier. The Petrograd garrison became the driving power of the revolution and in consequence the northern front, with the capital behind it, was the least stable; another revolutionary centre, Moscow, undermined the stability of the western front. The armies in Rumania, on the other hand, furthest removed from the focus of the revolution, stationed in a foreign country and there-fore, to some extent, out of touch with the local population, main-tained a high morale, unaffected by revolutionary agitation.[3] In Petrograd, the revolutionaries, especially those of the Soviet, had a difficult choice before them. They could treat the army as sacrosanct because it was defending the country against a foreign enemy, and therefore run the risk of the army being used against them. They could, on the other hand, try to destroy it and thus expose the revolution to the mercy of the Germans. Goldenberg, the Menshevik editor of the *Novaya Zhizn* put the dilemma, and its solution, this way:[4]

On the first day of the Revolution we understood that, if we did not destroy the old army, the latter would crush the Revolution. We had to choose between the army and the Revolution. We did not hesitate. We took a decision in favor of the Revolution and we used, I declare it boldly, the proper means.

By the time of the Bolshevik victory on 7 November 1917, most of the front had melted away and Russia was at the mercy of the enemy. Such was the compelling background of Lenin's foreign policy in the early months of the Soviet state. He had himself contributed to bringing that situation about and now had to deal with it. He had a small party – there were about 115,000 Bolsheviks at the beginning of 1918 – and his political skill to help him.

Like most European socialists, Lenin had regarded the Tsarist regime as the main obstacle to international revolution. Remove that obstacle and the path of the revolution would be clear: Lenin's 'defeatist' policy during the war was founded on that proposition. If the Tsarist regime were victorious in the war, the socialist movement would be condemned to insignificance for many years to come. The defeat of Tsarism and the victory of the revolution would move the Russian workers to the vanguard of the international proletarian movement: in Lenin's view – it was shared by many of his comrades – there was no one else in Russia, certainly not the middle-class parties, who was revolutionary enough to accomplish the revolution successfully.

Another socialist who had noticed long before the war the revolutionary deficiency of the Russian middle class was Lev Trotsky. The discovery became the corner-stone of his theory of 'permanent revolution'. Trotsky argued that the Russian revolu-tion, led by the working class, would have to be protected and reinforced by simultaneous revolutions in the western countries. Revolution in one country could not, in Trotsky's view, survive. There were points of contact between Trotsky's theory and Lenin's wartime policy. Lenin agitated for the transformation of the 'imperialist' war – one country pitted against another – into a number of civil engagements, in which the people would rise against their rulers.

The similarities between their views brought the two men together, resulting in a formidable partnership combining political sense and revolutionary zeal. In November 1917, their kind of revolution, a socialist revolution, was victorious, and now it was to be followed by workers' revolutions in the west. As the Commissar of Foreign Affairs, Trotsky thought that he would issue a few revolutionary proclamations and then 'close down the shop', that is, his Ministry. Signs of revolutionary unrest abroad were Lenin's main interest in the first weeks of his rule in Russia. When he talked of peace he meant a peace concluded by revolutionary governments.

Lenin's theories made him overlook the realities of wartime socialism outside Russia. For someone as interested in party organization, as practical and hardheaded a politician as Lenin, he showed, in regard to foreign parties, a certain lack of perception. He knew that most European socialists had supported, since the beginning of the war, their own governments; he knew that some were in prison; he had met those few who could come to the 'internationalist' conferences in Switzerland. The war, it is true, had lasted more than three years. There were, however, no signs yet that the majority socialists were becoming converted to Lenin's views.

From the first day in power, Lenin and Trotsky set themselves to promote revolution abroad. They made a bid to exploit the differences between the peoples of Europe and their governments; the Soviet Commissariat of Foreign Affairs, under Trotsky set up a department of foreign propaganda under the ubiquitous and fluent Karl Radek. In November 1917, Lenin and Trotsky were confident of the success of their revolutionary policy. Trotsky said, 'Our future dealings will be with the German peasants and workers clad in soldiers' coats. There, in their midst, grows our future popular soldiers' diplomacy.' And he added that socialist principles will make it possible for the Soviets to 'defeat the enemy in an all-proletarian battle against the imperialists, not only the German ones; but also against Messrs Clemenceau, Lloyd George, and others, we shall win or die.'[5]

Whereas Trotsky was willing to stake 'almost everything on the potential or actual antagonism between the rulers and ruled',[6] Lenin never went quite as far as that. He was spreading his risks, protecting himself on every side. Most of all he needed time for the consolidation of his regime. When he addressed the Congress of Soviets on peace late in the evening of 8 November 1917 he had just emerged from several tense, busy days and nights first of planning, and then of seeing through, the take-over of power. When the Bolshevik leaders entered the Assembly Hall at the Smolny Institute, formerly a school for Russian gentlewomen and now the seat of the Soviet and of the Bolshevik government, they looked tired, shabby, unsmiling. They knew that their bid for power could still turn against them. On entering the Assembly Hall Lenin was cheered for several minutes; when he finished the 'Decree of Peace' speech there were more ovations, the Internationale was sung, then a funeral march in memory of the martyrs of the war; the delegates shouted and flung their caps in the air.[7] Lenin's statement, the Decree of Peace, appealed to the belligerent peoples, and especially to the workers of the 'three most advanced nations of mankind', Great Britain, France and Germany, to 'help us to bring to a successful conclusion the course of peace'. Lenin said that his government 'considers it the greatest crime against humanity to continue this war for the sake of dividing among the powerful and wealthy nations the weaker nationalities they have conquered'. There should be neither annexations nor indemnities, and from now on the diplomats were to work in public, before the eyes of the whole world. Peace negotiations therefore were to start immediately, and Lenin proposed a general armistice lasting three months. Nevertheless, the Decree of Peace was addressed to the existing governments.[8] The revolutionary solvent would make itself felt later: Lenin was convinced that ultimately he would not have to sign peace with any of the capitalist states.

The Peace Decree itself was another step toward the consolidation of Lenin's power. It met the desire for peace in Russia that should have been satisfied some months ago. Lenin did not offend his comrades by referring either to a separate peace or to a peace concluded with the bourgeois governments. Lenin knew that Russia could not be successfully defended and that he would have to conclude peace.

Russia's allies did not at first react to Lenin's offer. Between 10 and 13 November 1917 their press carried instead news of the imminent downfall of the Bolshevik regime. Berlin also was marking time, wanting to make certain that the Bolsheviks could maintain themselves in power. But the Germans were well-informed about the situation in Russia and anxious to make no move that could harm the Bolsheviks. On 8 November, a few hours before Lenin made his peace speech to the Congress of Soviets, Lucius, the Minister to Stockholm, telegraphed the Wilhelmstrasse:[9]

I urgently recommend that all public announcements of amicable agreement with Russia be avoided in German and Austrian press. Amicable agreement with imperial states cannot possibly be accepted as a watchword by the Bolsheviks. They can only justify peace with Germany by citing the will of the people and Russia's desperate position. Moreover, I am assured from all sides that, in view of their present position, the Russians would only be able to explain friendly words from Germany [*two words garbled*] the weakness of our position in face of the English. It would be advisable for the press to exercise moderation, especially as the extent of the Bolsheviks' victory is not yet certain, since they control the Telegraph Agency.

The mistrust of the Bolsheviks expressed in the last sentence of Lucius' telegram was more than compensated for by the concern with their welfare in the opening words. Apart from the desire not to aggravate the position of the Bolsheviks, there was an additional complication for Berlin. Now, when his policy of support for the Bolsheviks was at last rewarded by success, Alexander Helphand, the chief adviser on Russian affairs to the Wilhelmstrasse, was not to be found anywhere. On the day of the Bolshevik take-over of power Helphand was in Vienna: when the diplomats in Berlin started testing their connections with the new rulers of Russia, Helphand became unusually elusive. The socialist revolution in Russia was victorious: Helphand calculated that he would no longer need the assistance of the diplomats. He thought that socialists (perhaps with himself as the representative of German Social Democracy) would meet in a neutral town, say, Stockholm, and conclude peace with their Russian comrades. It appears that the Bolshevik representatives in Stockholm, Radek among them, fell in with the idea: certainly a sharp clash of wills between the diplomats and Helphand took place.

As soon as his whereabouts were established, Helphand was put under official surveillance. His every move was watched, his every telegram scrutinized. Nor did he get any support from Lenin, who disliked and distrusted the ambitious schemer. Though the plan for a socialist peace conference misfired, it added to the delay in the opening of the official negotiations.

Lenin waited for almost two weeks. On 21 November 1917 he instructed General Dukhonin, the Commander-in-Chief, to begin direct armistice negotiations at the front. Dukhonin did no such thing and was dismissed at once. He nevertheless stayed on at the Stavka, the General Headquarters at Mogilev, writing leaflets and issuing proclamations to the troops. He had the support of the Allied governments: they ignored Lenin and his Commissars and appealed, through their military missions, to Dukhonin direct, not to break the terms of the treaty of alliance of September 1914 and not to conclude a separate armistice. The Allied governments hinted that the most serious consequences would result, and they left it to the Russians to interpret the threat as a Japanese attack on their country from the east.[10]

Though the Allies had treated the Stavka as a rival government, the contest between Dukhonin and the Bolsheviks was soon resolved. As on many other occasions in the early days of their rule, the Bolsheviks had to show their opponents at home, as well as 'the routine-ridden mind of bourgeois Europe', that they meant business. In that endeavour they disregarded the feelings of their friends as much as the lives of their enemies. Ensign Krylenko, a Bolshevik who had held a commission in the Tsarist army, was appointed to command the Russian land forces. On 28 November 1917, Krylenko ordered 'firing to cease immediately and fraternization to begin on all fronts', and the Soviet government addressed a wireless message to 'all the belligerent peoples and governments' to open negotiations for a general armistice. On 2 December Dukhonin and his staff were arrested at the Stavka by the garrison troops; on 3 December Krylenko and his retinue of Bolshevik sailors arrived at Mogilev. Dukhonin was beaten by the mob and shot dead by one of the sailors, in spite of Krylenko's attempt to protect him. On the same day, armistice negotiations between the Russians and the Germans opened at Brest Litovsk.

Apart from the fortress, there was not much left of the town of Brest Litovsk, the seat of the German Headquarters in the east. The Russians had burnt the town when they evacuated it in July 1916; the German military had lived there uncomfortably, in a train on the sidings of the local railway station, until the fortress was ready for them to move into. It was a bleak place even in summer; now, at the beginning of winter, its barrenness was haunting. The great north European plain was like some vast, frozen ocean; below and above the horizon the predominant colour was grey. High winds whipped large, ragged clouds across the sky, and in November they started bringing with them sleet and snow. About 110 miles east of Warsaw, Brest Litovsk was 80 miles away from the nearest point of the silent, snow-bound front line.

The German delegation at the armistice talks was led by General Max Hoffmann, the commander on the eastern front. As an expert on Russian affairs in the General Staff before the war, Hoffmann had worked under von Schlieffen and, as an observer during the Russo-Japanese war, created at least one international incident. He had a clean-shaven skull, an incongruous rosebud mouth, and he plucked his eyebrows to grow level and then curve upwards at the far ends. Very fond of large quantities of simple food and drink, Hoffmann was astute, courageous, even-tempered. He would think his opposite numbers at the negotiations humorous rather than formidable. Hoffmann knew nothing about the Foreign Ministry's policy in regard to the Bolsheviks; his military assistants at the negotiations were Major Brinckmann from General Headquarters and a cavalry lieutenant, Bernhard von Bülow, a nephew of Prince von Bülow, the former Chancellor and Ambassador Extraordinary to Rome in 1914. Baron von Rosenberg was there on behalf of the Foreign Ministry; Austria-Hungary, Turkey and Bulgaria were also represented on the armistice delegation.

For the Bolsheviks, on the other hand, getting the delegation together was no mere matter of routine. There were no diplomats among their ranks. When Trotsky, on his second day in office as the Commissar of Foreign Affairs, went to the Foreign Ministry and asked for Lenin's Decree of Peace to be translated, some six hundred officials walked out. When Lenin decided to fulfil his promise to publish the secret treaties of the Tsarist government, Trotsky sent a Bolshevik over to the Ministry to collect them. He was manhandled by the archivists, and in the end Trotsky had to arrest a few high-ranking diplomats before the treaties were handed over to him for publication. In the early weeks of Soviet rule, the Foreign Ministry was virtually deserted; the situation at the Russian embassies and legations abroad was no better. The Bolshevik mission to Stockholm, which originally consisted of Radek, Vorovsky and Hanecki, was the only direct contact the new government had with the outside world.

The delegation that left Petrograd for Brest Litovsk on the last day of November 1917 could hardly be mistaken for a group of diplomats. There was the bearded, long-haired, scholarly Adolf Abramovich Ioffe, wearing a bowler-hat as the one concession to convention; a Bolshevik party worker of long standing, a friend of Trotsky, Ioffe later became the first Soviet Ambassador to Berlin. He was accompanied by Lev Kamenev, Trotsky's brother-in-law, a moderate Bolshevik, and the kind of person, according to a friend of his, who easily gets himself assassinated.[11] Leo Karakhan, who acted as the secretary to the delegation, had a remarkable facility at changing swiftly from a state of suspended animation to noisy activity, and back. The young, 29-year-old Grigori Yakovlevich Sokolnikov, who later became the Commissar for Finance and Ambassador to London, added a more ordinary element to the delegation. It was almost cancelled out by the presence of Anastasia Bitsenko, the distinguished Social Revolutionary terrorist and assassin. The rest of the delegation consisted of what the Bolshevik leaders regarded as representative types of their revolutionary democracy, and their function was purely decorative. A gnarled, tongue-tied old soldier; a handsome young sailor; a Petrograd worker who enjoyed himself hugely; a peasant who was press-ganged to serve on the delegation and who apparently began to see the joke only later.

In spite of the obvious differences between the two delegations there was no reason why they should have found agreement difficult. The Russians were unable to defend their country and the Germans had other tasks in hand than further punishing Russia with the final knock-out blow. Ludendorff and the German military wanted to reduce the war to a manageable, one-front engagement: they had been trying to do that for three years now, since November 1914. Their chief interest therefore was the transfer of troops from the east to the west; their abiding hope was the decision they were about to seek on the western front; their main concern was whether their troops would arrive in France before the Americans began landing there in bulk. Ludendorff meant Brest Litovsk to 'clarify' the situation in the east.

After having made a preliminary propaganda gesture Ioffe proposed an armistice of three months' duration and the evacuation by the Germans of Moon Island in the Gulf of Riga. He also asked for an undertaking that no troops from the east would be transferred to any other front. General Hoffmann offered the Russians twenty-eight days' armistice that would be extended automatically or cancelled at a week's notice. He thought it was silly of the Russians to try to dictate to the Germans what territory to evacuate, and he said so, and he found a way round the proposal about the transfer of troops. He agreed that no troops would leave the front during the armistice apart from those that were being transferred or had received their orders to leave. Nevertheless, Hoffmann did not push the Bolsheviks beyond the point of endurance. When, a few days later, the Russians announced that they in fact were aiming at an armistice on all fronts, Hoffmann asked who gave them the authority to speak on behalf of their allies. In the end, the formula that the members of the Brest Litovsk conference should pass on to their governments 'the proposal made by the Russian delegation to invite all belligerents to take part in the negotiations'[12] saved the Bolsheviks a lot of embarrassment.

On 6 December 1917, Trotsky informed the Allied representatives in Petrograd that the Brest Litovsk negotiations had been suspended for a week so that 'the peoples and Governments of the Allied countries' could be informed of the course they had taken. (Ioffe did not know whether he could accept the terms without consulting Trotsky first: another reason for the break in the negotiations.) The last paragraph of Trotsky's communication resembled an ultimatum more than anything else:[13]

Thus, between the Soviet Government's first decree on peace and the time when the peace negotiations will be resumed, more than a month will have passed. This time limit, even with the present disorganized means of international communication, is considered quite

sufficient to give the Governments of the Allied countries an opportunity to define their attitude to the peace negotiations—that is, to
express their readiness or their refusal to take part in the negotiations
for an armistice and peace, and in the case of a refusal to state openly
before all mankind, clearly, exactly, and definitely, in the name of what
aims must the peoples of Europe shed their blood in the fourth year
of war.

Trotsky may have been right that the Allies had had enough
time to make their attitude to the armistice talks known. But the
Commissar for Foreign Affairs was over-optimistic if he really
believed that his appeals would move the Allies to declare their
readiness to negotiate peace. He knew little about the previous
offers of a separate or general peace and about the reasons why it
had been impossible to break down the reluctance to bring the
hostilities to an end. On no occasion in the past did the military
of any of the Great Powers admit defeat or even irreparable
weakness: in Petrograd, when the army had virtually ceased to
exist, it may have been hard to realize that elsewhere military
considerations went on playing a major role in the making of
policy.

Once more, there were no replies from any of the Allied capitals. On 12 December 1917 the Russians returned to Brest Litovsk,
and two days later, in the evening of 14 December, rumours began
to circulate in Petrograd that armistice terms had been agreed on.
The news was officially released on Sunday 16 December: the
armistice was to start on the following day and continue until
14 January 1918. In Trotsky's appeal to the 'toiling, oppressed,
and exhausted peoples of Europe' on 19 December it was
described as a 'tremendous victory for humanity'. He nevertheless pointed out:[14]

A truly democratic people's peace will still have to be fought for.
The first round in this struggle finds in power, everywhere except in
Russia, the old monarchist and capitalist Governments which were
responsible for the present war, and which have not yet accounted to
their duped peoples for the waste of blood and treasure.

Neither Trotsky's appeal, nor the earlier note to the Allied
governments, contained of course the slightest hint that, in the
matter of the transfer of troops from the eastern front, the
Germans could do as they liked.

The terms of the armistice provided for an early start of negotiations for peace. The situation on the eastern front was well on
the way to being clarified, as Ludendorff had wished. The
Germans were given their last opportunity of bringing the war
to a victorious conclusion. The submarines had been unleashed
against Allied and neutral shipping without bringing victory any
nearer. By the end of the year 1917, the convoy system had become effective and the British shipbuilders had begun to catch up
with the losses inflicted by the Germans. England had not, after
all, been defeated in six months.

When Germany entered the negotiations at Brest Litovsk, the
conflicts that had caused the political crisis in Berlin in the summer of 1917* were still unresolved. The Reichstag was still dis-
satisfied with its share of political power and a weaker Chancellor
than Bethmann was in office. The political surface in the Reich
looked calmer, and the new Secretary of State tougher, but that
was all. Both the open and the secret diplomatic peace moves had
failed. General Ludendorff was undismayed, and ready to dictate
terms in the east.

The peace conference at Brest Litovsk opened officially on
22 December 1917. Some 400 people, the delegates and their
technical staff, had to be fitted somehow in the ruined fortress
town. The peace talks attracted more distinguished men than the
armistice negotiations had. Austria was represented by Count
Czernin, the Foreign Minister, and Germany by Kühlmann, the
Secretary of State; Popoff and Nessimi Bey led the Bulgarian and
Turkish delegations until the arrival of Radoslavov, the Prime
Minister, and Talaat Pasha, the Grand Vizier. The Soviet delegation, containing the 'representatives of revolutionary democracy',
was again led by Ioffe and reinforced by Pokrovsky, the historian.
The Germans were good hosts. They provided official cars for the
delegates although, apart from the few muddy roads striking out
across flat fields, there was nowhere to go.

On the evening of 20 December, all the delegates sat down at a
common table; the dinner was given by Prince Leopold of
Bavaria, the Commander-in-Chief of the German armies in the
East. Ioffe sat on his right, between the Prince and Czernin, and
the Russian and the Austrian had a long talk about the self-
determination of peoples. It was concluded by Ioffe's remark,

* See above, pp. 147f.

made in a kindly, imploring voice: 'Still, I hope we may yet be able to raise the revolution in your country too.'[15]

The instructions for the Soviet delegates to Brest Litovsk were contained in Lenin's peace speech on 8 December 1917 and in the 'outline programme for peace negotiations with Germany'. This was agreed on at the meeting of the Council of Soviet Commissars on 10 December, and set down, hesitantly by Lenin and decisively by Stalin, in the same document. On 22 December Ioffe, after having read long passages from Lenin's peace decree, put six points before the delegates of the Central Powers, still on the assumption that a general peace was being negotiated. All the key proposals advanced by Ioffe had been made before; they were now comprehensively presented in six paragraphs:

1. Not to allow any forcible annexation of territory seized during the war. Troops occupying these territories to be withdrawn in the shortest possible time.

2. To restore in full the political independence of those nations deprived of their independence during the present war.

3. National groups not enjoying political independence before the war to be guaranteed an opportunity to decide freely by means of a referendum whether to adhere to any given state or to be an independent state. This referendum to be so organized as to guarantee complete freedom of voting for the entire population of the given territory, not excluding emigrants and refugees.

4. In regard to territories inhabited by several nationalities, the right of minorities to be protected by special laws, guaranteeing them cultural national independence, and, so far as is practicable, administrative autonomy.

5. None of the belligerent countries to be bound to pay other countries so-called 'war costs'; indemnities already paid to be returned. Private individuals who have incurred losses owing to the war to be compensated from a special fund, raised by proportional levies on all the belligerent countries.

6. Colonial questions to be decided on the lines laid down in points 1, 2, 3 and 4.

It took Czernin and Kühlmann two days to work out the reply to Ioffe's conditions. They agreed to accept them, though Kühlmann believed that Kurland and Latvia could pass under German rule, in spite of the 'no annexations' clause. The Bulgarians took a lot of convincing before they decided to go along with their allies. Nor was General Hoffmann pleased with the

Foreign Ministers' policy. He thought it deceitful, founded on a lie. Nevertheless, he told the Russians that, though forcible annexations were to be disapproved of, there was nothing to stop them giving up, of their own free will, say, Kurland, Latvia and Poland. Ioffe was amazed at the suggestion. Pokrovsky, the historian, shedding tears of anger, declared that to take some eighteen provinces away from the Russian Empire was incompatible with a peace without annexations.[16] On 24 December, the night before he delivered the Central Powers' reply to Ioffe, Czernin wrote in his diary:[17]

If the great victories which the German generals are hoping for on the Western front should be realised, there will be no bounds to their demands, and the difficulty of all negotiations will be still further increased.

The negotiations were going too slowly for the German High Command. Sometimes, one or the other party was not quite ready to discuss a particular point; at others, someone had lost the thread of the conversation. Mme Bitsenko, the lady assassin, regarded the details of the proceedings with indifference, coming to life only when one of the great revolutionary principles was mentioned. The question of withdrawal by the Central Powers from occupied territories caused a lot of trouble. The Russians were stalling; Ludendorff was on the telephone all the time. Czernin threatened to conclude a separate peace with the Russians if Berlin refused to negotiate. In the end, the delegates decided to go home and report to their governments. They gave the Entente the chance, between 28 December and 5 January 1918, to make up its mind about the events in Brest Litovsk.

Kühlmann and Hoffmann returned to Berlin to a quarrel with Ludendorff about annexations; Czernin, to two long audiences with the Emperor; Ioffe and the Russians went back to confer with Lenin and Trotsky.

In Berlin, Ludendorff thought Germany's military position so good that there was no need for Kühlmann's involved negotiating tactics. The Kaiser showed such lack of resolution that Ludendorff felt free to shout at him at a meeting of the Crown Council. In the exchanges between the Kaiser, the High Command and the Chancellor, another attempt was made to define responsibility for the conduct of the war. Though, on paper, the outcome went in the Chancellor's favour, the disposition of power in effect changed even more to Ludendorff's advantage. The Quartermaster General said at the time that 'the German people value me more highly than the person of the Kaiser'.[18]

In Petrograd, on the day the delegation returned from Brest Litovsk, Trotsky issued another long and impassioned appeal to the Allied governments as well as the workers. He argued that Germany, by accepting the formula of 'no annexations', had in fact promised withdrawal from occupied France and Belgium, from Serbia, Montenegro and Rumania, and from Poland, Lithuania and Kurland. There was therefore no foundation for the Entente claim that it was fighting for the liberation of those countries. Trotsky then paraded the bogy of a separate peace between Russia and Germany before the Allies, and threatened them with their own working classes:[19]

If the Allied Governments, in the blind stubbornness which characterizes decadent and perishing classes, once more refuse to participate in the negotiations, then the working class will be confronted by the iron necessity of taking the power out of the hands of those who cannot or will not give the people peace.

In the same way, Trotsky did little to endear himself to the Germans. The resolution of the central executive committee of the Soviet on 1 January 1918 addressed itself to

the peoples of Germany, Austria-Hungary, Bulgaria, and Turkey. Under your pressure your Governments have been forced in words to appropriate our motto: 'No annexations or indemnities', but in fact they are trying to carry on the old policy of annexations. Remember: the conclusion of a speedy and really democratic peace is now more than ever in your hands.[20]

On the following day, 2 January, Trotsky said in a press interview that it was unlikely that peace negotiations would be resumed at Brest Litovsk: 'In many respects we consider it most appropriate, at the stage which the negotiations have now reached, to continue them in a neutral country.'[21]

A few weeks before, the German diplomats had taken a lot of trouble in putting down a similar proposal, and they had not changed their minds. After a trip through deserted Russian lines, Trotsky came to Brest Litovsk on 8 January 1918. With his arrival, the forced friendliness that had marked the December negotiations disappeared. Trotsky put an end to fraternization between the delegates, and confined his comrades to their quarters at mealtimes. When he was approached by a member of another delegation, Trotsky would have no back-slapping *bonhomie*. Any attempt at it made him wince and bristle. His peace, if it were achieved at all, was going to be a very cold one.

It took Trotsky little time to succeed in thoroughly irritating the Germans. He represented a Power that had been, as far as the Germans were concerned, defeated in a straight fight. Yet Trotsky did not behave like the emissary of a vanquished state. Very much to the contrary. He was convinced that the revolutionary weapons, appeals to the sanity of the proletariat, were more powerful than all the arsenals of the world combined, and that, especially if they opposed the universal desire for peace, governments would be swept away on the rising tide of the revolution. Trotsky saw no reason why he should feel inferior to the German politicians and military, and made no secret of it. He went to Brest Litovsk to spin out the negotiations as long as he could, so as to give Bolshevik revolutionary agitation a chance of making itself felt outside Russia.

When the negotiations at Brest Litovsk reopened on 9 January 1918, Kühlmann stated that the Central Powers had accepted the formula 'peace without annexations or indemnities' only in case of general peace. On the following day, Trotsky addressed the conference. Czernin thought him a 'clever and very dangerous adversary'; Trotsky, on his part, made a tactical error in regarding General Hoffmann as the authentic voice of the Supreme Command.[22]

So as not to be drawn into a squabble with the Ukrainian delegates, Trotsky made no objection to their participation in the conference. They represented the Rada, a government based on Kiev, the outcome of the exercise of the right to self-determination by the Ukrainians immediately after the Bolshevik take-over of power. The three delegates were very young: Czernin disliked the thought of having to negotiate with school-boys. Not subject to the discipline imposed by Trotsky on the Russians, the Ukrainians mixed freely with the Germans and the Austrians.

Trotsky treated the other side with contempt. He refused to

apologize for Soviet revolutionary propaganda, and charged the Germans with insincerity because they had refused to be bound by the formula of 'peace without annexations'. He insisted that the negotiations be conducted in public throughout. When the German draft treaty was put before the Russians on 12 January 1918 Trotsky disputed its form as well as its intention. The argument on self-determination between two masters of logic, Trotsky and Kühlmann, went on for days. Its fine subtlety took the edge off the propaganda value of the public proceedings. Czernin, the Austrian Foreign Minister, became impatient with the inconclusive 'spiritual wrestling match', and his relations with Kühlmann became very strained. On 18 January, Trotsky asked for a break in the conference.

Still no sign of revolution in any of the belligerent countries.

In February 1917, a few weeks before the outbreak of the Russian revolution, Lenin had been doubtful whether he would see that event happen in his lifetime. The revolutionary year gave him new hope. At its end, Lenin was convinced that the situation was ripe for a world revolution. Together with Trotsky, he anxiously scanned the horizon for signs of working-class rebellion. There were distant sparks of anger and frustration, but no more. They were set off in Austria and Hungary, especially in their German and Magyar areas. In the week before Trotsky had asked for a break at Brest Litovsk, starting on Monday 14 January 1918, there were widespread strikes and demonstrations in German Austria, triggered off by reductions in food rations, with their epicentre at Wiener Neustadt and the Daimler motor works. On 16 January the Social Democrat *Arbeiter Zeitung* published an appeal by the party to the 'workmen and women of Austria' not to allow the war to go on 'merely for the sake of extending the power of Germany and Austria-Hungary over foreign lands'. References to the grave economic situation were scrapped by the censor: on the same day, the *Neue Freie Presse* explained why news on food supplies was blanked out by severe censorship. Such news apparently affected adversely the prospects of a separate peace with Russia, especially the Ukraine. On Sunday 20 January, a mass meeting in Vienna approved a resolution which stated:

The workers demand with the most passionate positiveness universal peace; they regard the speeches of Mr Lloyd George, and especially

President Wilson's peace programme, as tokens that the hostile governments, also under pressure of the proletariat, have already begun to
restrict their Imperialist war aims.

It was ironic that the initial workers' rebellion in Austria-
Hungary, the most promising movement so far for Lenin and
Trotsky, was put down partly by troops released from the
Russian front. The mutiny of the Fifth Austrian Fleet in the
Adriatic Gulf of Kotor, which opened with a shot from the flag-
ship at noon on 1 February 1918, ended a few days later with
salvoes fired by the execution squad. Five sailors, including their
Bohemian leader, were sentenced to death. Nevertheless, in the
Slav parts of the Empire, especially in the Czech lands, industrial
unrest rarely assumed that wildcat quality it had in and around
Vienna, and even more so in Budapest, where workers' Soviets
emerged at several factories. The Czech Social Democrat leaders
on the whole remained in control of the popular movement,
behaving as if they were saving the workers and themselves for
something more important, later.

Support for the war, the strain produced by the continuation of
that support, had divided the Socialist Party of Germany. Soon
after August 1914 a small anti-war group appeared which included
Franz Mehring, Karl Liebknecht and Rosa Luxemburg, and it
continued to strive to 'love internationally and hate at home', or in
the words of Liebknecht, 'the main enemy is at home.'[23] After
forty-two years' existence as a united party, in the same town
which had seen its unification, and under the chairmanship of the
same man, the Socialist Party split, with the USPD (*Unabhängige
Sozialdemokratische Partei Deutschlands*) going into opposition. Its
members – there were among them some illustrious names of
pre-war socialism, such as Karl Kautsky and Eduard Bernstein –
disapproved of the alliance between the majority socialists and the
imperial establishment, but otherwise there were profound ideological differences among them, especially in their attitudes toward revolution. Franz Mehring, a USPD member, opened his
maiden speech to the Prussian Diet on 19 January 1918 with a sharp
criticism of the announcement by the Minister of Finance that the
American 'great army beyond the water can neither swim nor
fly: it will not come'. Mehring asked the Minister on what
grounds he based his prophecy, and went on to say that, at Brest
Litovsk, the Russian revolutionaries alone showed intelligence

and honourable intentions. Turning to domestic affairs, Mehring said that the state of siege, censorship and preventive arrest, were as desolating to the intellectual domain as the unbridled greed for gain to the economic sphere.

Shortly before Mehring's speech to the Diet, news of the Austrian strikes had reached Berlin, despite strict military censorship on both sides of the frontier. Shop stewards asked the USPD to declare a general strike, but the party executive hesitated, and left the initiative to the workers themselves.[24] On 27 January 1918 a meeting of Berlin shop stewards called for a general strike. Though it affected large areas of industrial Germany, the strike did not become general, and it lacked specific aims. The strikers' main antagonist, Ludendorff, was then at the height of his power; the discipline of the army was unimpaired. By 4 February industrial unrest in Germany had been suppressed, with more ease than in Austria.

On the other side of the battle-line, Entente countries did not remain unaffected in the aftermath of the Russian revolution. The political truce in France had been broken by a mutiny of the troops and a simultaneous strike in May 1917 of engineering workers in Paris. One hundred and fifty soldiers were sentenced to death, of whom twenty-three were executed. At the end of 1917, the French Socialist party came to be controlled by the *minoritaires*, led by Karl Marx's grandson, Jean Longuet, and decided to withdraw the party's representatives from the government. In January 1918, the strike movement was renewed, in response to Soviet appeals. But it was weaker than in either Austria or Germany, and soon fizzled out.

In Britain, the impact of the Russian revolution was even weaker. On 17 January 1918 there was a working-class demonstration in Manchester, caused by food shortages. Six days later, on 23 January, a special meeting of the delegates to the Labour Party conference opened at Nottingham. The party chairman, W. F. Purdy, presided over a large and enthusiastic gathering, which began by singing the 'Red Flag' and giving cheers for the International and the Russian revolution. The chairman then welcomed Huysmans, secretary of the International Socialist Bureau; Vandervelde, leader of the Belgian socialists; Litvinov, the Soviet representative to Britain. At the extraordinary conference in London in February, the party proclaimed itself to be 'socialist', approved a new constitution, and declared that its aim was to reform society 'on the basis of the common ownership of the means of production'.[25]

Neither in Berlin nor in Vienna did the government put forward, or accept, any of the radical demands in circulation at the time. Czernin wanted peace in the East and bread for the starving population in Austrian towns; Kühlmann wanted to keep up appearances; Ludendorff wanted annexations. Their response to the new situation in their own countries and abroad was negative, totally lacking the political flexibility displayed by Lloyd George and President Wilson.

Soon after the publication of the secret diplomatic treaties by the Bolsheviks,* the Labour Party executive and the Trades Union Congress agreed on a statement of war aims. It was the most comprehensive statement on the subject made in London during the war, and it advanced all the points which the Union of Democratic Control, an organization which concerned itself with making foreign policy more open and less of an aristocratic occupation, had been putting forward since the beginning of the war.[26] In his speech to trade union leaders on 5 January 1918, Lloyd George endorsed them, in his own way. He was trying to satisfy Labour because he wanted more manpower to be released from the factories, and at the same time he was replying to Lord Lansdowne's recent appeal for a negotiated peace.

Lloyd George said that the Straits would be 'internationalized and neutralized' and that 'Arabia, Armenia, Mesopotamia, Syria and Palestine' were entitled to emerge as separate states. He implied that Germany would lose its colonies. There would also have to be reparations and independence for Belgium: 'the great wrong of 1871', i.e. the detachment of Alsace-Lorraine, would have to be made good. But apart from these measures aimed at the strengthening of the international position of the two western Powers, the Prime Minister's speech showed the extent to which he had assimilated the ideas of dissent. Even in regard to Germany, there was a conciliatory tone in his speech: 'We are not fighting a war of aggression against the German people . . .'; Austria-Hungary was not to be destroyed – there was some hope that the Smuts–Mensdorff conversations might be resumed – nor was Turkey to be deprived of its capital. A new Poland would have to be formed

* See above, p. 251.

and the peoples of the Habsburg Empire would have to receive 'genuine self-government on true democratic principles'. And there was to be an international organization – the only new demand that neither the German nor the Austrian politicians found it difficult to accept – to look after the emergent order.

The speech by Lloyd George to the trade unionists anticipated President Wilson's Fourteen Points by three days. But it was Wilson's programme, communicated to Congress in a message on 8 January 1918, that made the important impact on the peoples of Europe: it was strong in western Europe; while in central Europe, especially in Austria-Hungary, it was often impossible to say whether the origin of the new slogans was American or Bolshevik.

The Fourteen Points formulated, in a comprehensive manner, the dissenting views on foreign policy that had been in circulation, in one belligerent country or another, since the beginning of the war. They were illuminated by President Wilson's visionary conception of international community and in parts informed by America's national interest. The President's enumeration of American aims in the war was set off by the negotiations in Brest Litovsk: he believed he owed that duty to the sorely stricken Russian people. He said that it was impossible to know whether the Central Powers' delegations spoke for the liberal majorities in the parliaments or for the militarist minorities in Berlin and Vienna. The President suggested that the general principles had been formulated by the liberals but that the military were dictating their practical application. He said that the programme of the world's peace was America's programme and then went on to give its details, in fourteen paragraphs:[27]

I. Open covenants of peace openly arrived at, after which there shall be no private international understandings of any kind, but diplomacy shall proceed always frankly and in the public view.

II. Absolute freedom of navigation upon the seas outside territorial waters alike in peace and in war except as the seas may be closed in whole or in part by international action for the enforcement of international covenants.

III. The removal, so far as possible, of all economic barriers, and the establishment of an equality of trade conditions among all the nations consenting to the peace and associating themselves for its maintenance.

IV. Adequate guarantees given and taken that national armaments will be reduced to the lowest point consistent with domestic safety.

V. A free, open-minded, and absolutely impartial adjustment of all colonial claims based upon a strict observance of the principle that in determining all such questions of sovereignty the interests of the populations concerned must have equal weight with the equitable claims of the Government whose title is to be determined.

VI. The evacuation of all Russian territory, and such a settlement of all questions affecting Russia as will secure the best and freest co-operation of the other nations of the world in obtaining for her an unhampered and unembarrassed opportunity for the independent determination of her own political development and national policy, and assure her of a sincere welcome into the society of free nations under institutions of her own choosing; and, more than a welcome, assistance also of every kind that she may need and may herself desire. The treatment accorded Russia by her sister nations in the months to come will be the acid test of their goodwill, of their comprehension of her needs as distinguished from their own interests, and of their intelligent and unselfish sympathy.

VII. Belgium, the whole world will agree, must be evacuated and restored without any attempt to limit the sovereignty which she enjoys in common with all other free nations. No other single act will serve as this will serve to restore confidence among the nations in the laws which they have themselves set and determined for the government of their relations with one another. Without this healing act the whole structure and validity of international law is for ever impaired.

VIII. All French territory should be freed, and the invaded portions restored, and the wrong done to France by Prussia in 1871 in the matter of Alsace-Lorraine, which has unsettled the peace of the world for nearly fifty years, should be righted in order that peace may once more be made secure in the interest of all.

IX. A readjustment of the frontiers of Italy should be effected along clearly recognisable lines of nationality.

X. The peoples of Austria-Hungary, whose place among the nations we wish to see safeguarded and assured, should be accorded the freest opportunity of autonomous development.

XI. Rumania, Serbia, and Montenegro should be evacuated, occupied territories restored, Serbia accorded free and secure access to the sea, and the relations of the several Balkan States to one another determined by friendly counsel along historically established lines of allegiance and nationality, and international guarantees of the political and economic independence and territorial integrity of the several Balkan States should be entered into.

XII. The Turkish portions of the present Ottoman Empire should be assured a secure sovereignty, but the other nationalities which are now under Turkish rule should be assured an undoubted security of life and an absolutely unmolested opportunity of autonomous development, and the Dardanelles should be permanently opened as a free passage to the ships and commerce of all nations under international guarantees.

XIII. An independent Polish State should be erected which should include the territories inhabited by indisputably Polish populations, which should be assured a free and secure access to the sea, and whose political and economic independence and territorial integrity should be guaranteed by international covenant.

XIV. A general association of nations must be formed under specific covenants for the purpose of affording mutual guarantees of political independence and territorial integrity to great and small States alike.

There were points of contact between the President's and the Bolshevik programmes. They both regarded themselves as not bound by traditional diplomatic usage. On their entry into the war, the United States had not formally become one of the 'Allied' states. The publication of the secret treaties by the new Russian government in 1917 did not affect the Americans in the same way as it affected the other Great Powers. President Wilson had consistently refused to acknowledge the secret treaties, though he was aware of their contents. Most important, the doctrine of self-determination of nations, a sharp weapon poised over old Europe, had two powerful advocates: Lenin and Wilson.

But there were differences between the Americans and the Russians, from the very beginning of the existence of the Soviet state. They derived from the vastly different positions of the two governments. On the one hand, there was a revolutionary regime with only a rudimentary apparatus of state power, intent on shedding obligations rather than on taking up new ones: on the other hand, a stable government, a President to whom the war gave both prestige and increased executive powers, taking the initiative abroad. Early in 1917 President Wilson had coined the phrase 'peace without victory'. It had passed into Bolshevik usage but, by the time Lenin came to power in Russia, Wilson's thinking on problems of war and peace had moved away from that proposition. When he addressed Congress on 8 January 1918, Wilson believed in a victorious peace. He saw it as a way of realizing the democratization of Germany without which, he thought, a lasting peace was out of the question. It meant that the war would go on.

Lenin took over a defeated country, incapable of waging war. Peace was a necessity for the Soviet state. But, after the break in the Brest Litovsk negotiations on 20 January, the question before the Bolsheviks was what kind of peace did they want. The 'peoples' peace', concluded by revolutionary governments, was out of the question, as far as Lenin was concerned. He now concentrated on retaining and consolidating power in the hands of the Bolsheviks; he no longer believed in the proximity of revolutions in Europe. On 20 January 1918 Lenin wrote:[28]

... it would be a mistake to base the tactics of the Russian Socialist Government on an attempt to determine whether the European, and especially the German, Socialist revolution will take place in the next six months. ...

Lenin saw the Russians as being confronted with a German ultimatum: either the continuation of war or an annexationist peace. His government therefore had to make a stark choice; there were no further alternatives.

At the meeting of the Bolshevik central committee on 24 January 1918 Lenin summed up the outcome of the meeting three days before, on 21 January, when a vote was taken on three proposals. These were – (his own suggestion) that separate peace should be signed immediately; that the revolutionary war should be carried on; that the army should be demobilized and the peace not signed.

The last policy of 'neither war nor peace', advanced by Trotsky, advocated the freezing of the Brest Litovsk negotiations at their inconclusive stage, and allowing inactivity and revolutionary propaganda to do their work among the German and Austrian troops. Trotsky had been encouraged by reports of working class unrest in Germany and Austria; he had by no means given up his belief in its corrosive effect. His proposal had received, at the meeting on 21 January, sixteen votes as against fifteen for Lenin's policy. Nevertheless, with thirty-two votes, the resumption of revolutionary war was the most popular programme.[29]

The controversy about peace continued at the meeting on 24 January 1918. Bukharin and other members of the central committee accused Lenin of betraying the revolution, stabbing the German and Austrian proletariat in the back, looking at the whole problem from a 'narrow Russian and not from an international standpoint'. Lenin restated his position. He told the committee that the Russians were helpless in face of a German advance; the Germans were so strongly entrenched on the Baltic Sea islands that they could take Reval (Estonian: Tallin) and Petrograd 'with their bare hands'. German imperialism would be strengthened if the war went on. The peace would be horrible, but it would give the Bolsheviks a breathing space to consolidate their position. Otherwise the Soviet government would be swept away and its successor would be compelled to conclude an even more onerous peace.

Lenin's cool appraisal of the situation failed to carry the day. Most of his comrades were amazed at his flexibility, and deeply resented it. At a time of grave danger to the new Soviet state, they were unable to give up their dream of international revolution. Trotsky finally put forward his formula: 'We interrupt the war, do not sign the peace, demobilize the army.'[30] It was passed by nine to seven votes, and it worked out as something Trotsky had never intended it to be: a compromise solution. It postponed the conclusion of peace and made resumption of hostilities unnecessary. Thus, before returning on 29 January 1918, Trotsky obtained a mandate from the central committee to pursue his policy at Brest Litovsk.

It was at least partly shaped by Trotsky's desire to lift from the Bolsheviks the stigma of the accusation that they were agents of the Kaiser's Germany.[31] The charge had been made by Milyukov, the Foreign Minister in the first provisional government, when Lenin reached Petrograd again after his journey through Germany; it was put forward again on 22 July 1917 by the Public Prosecutor at the Petrograd Court of Appeals. Lenin fled the capital, disguised as an engine driver; Trotsky was arrested. On the one side, the willingness of the Germans to help the Bolsheviks was at the root of the 'great slander'; on the other, the charges appeared slanderous to Lenin and his friends because they were indeed pursuing the goal of a socialist revolution, and not that of Germany's victory.

Trotsky was especially sensitive to the charges because the name of his former friend, Alexander Helphand, had come up many times in connection with them. He was therefore inclined to harass the Germans at Brest Litovsk as much as he could; he was distant and very formal with them. His 'open diplomacy' avoided any appearance of a secret understanding with them. These motives, in addition to his propensity for international revolution – he placed very high value on the wave of strikes then in progress in Austria – made Trotsky oppose the policy of an immediate separate peace.

Lenin's flexibility, on the other hand, was combined with toughness, and he allowed no ideological considerations to obscure his view of the hard facts of Russia's political and military position. In addition, he had no great liking for Helphand and always kept his distance from him. When Helphand asked Lenin, ten days after the Bolshevik victory in November 1917, to be allowed to return to Russia and help to build the Soviet state, the answer was a firm No.[32] In that way Karl Radek, then the head of the Soviet mission in Scandinavia, who personally brought Helphand's message to Lenin, lost his main contact and source of information on Germany's policy and strategy. Whether that loss in any way affected Lenin's policy is a matter of speculation.

Before Trotsky left for Brest Litovsk at the end of January 1918, he made a private arrangement with Lenin. The Bolshevik leader was concerned with what would happen if the Germans resumed hostilities, and Trotsky promised to adopt Lenin's policy and sign the peace in such an event. The agreement was not quite clear. Lenin believed that Trotsky undertook to abandon his policy when he was confronted with the threat of an offensive, or with an ultimatum; Trotsky assumed that the agreement was to become operative only after the launching of the offensive, and that he could then accept only the terms the Germans had already offered.[33] Waiting for Trotsky's arrival at Brest Litovsk, the delegates of the Central Powers knew that the Soviet government had succeeded in consolidating its position in Russia. On 24 January 1918 Count Mirbach, the representative of the German Foreign Ministry in Petrograd, wrote that 'the power of the Bolsheviks seems to have secured itself to some extent during the last few days'. A week later Helphand told the diplomats in Berlin that the 'Bolsheviks' ideas will spread still further in Russia and that the [Ukrainian] Rada will not last much longer'. He said that 'nobody would be able to drive out the Bolsheviks, now that they had occupied the Donetz basin and Kharkov, the centre of the industrial Ukraine, except with the help of German troops'.[34]

When the Brest Litovsk negotiations reopened at the end of

January, the Central Powers' delegates were concerned to conclude peace with the Ukrainian Rada as soon as possible. In the first round of the negotiations Trotsky had made no objections to the presence of the youthful Rada delegates. Indeed, on 12 January he had recognized them as the representatives of the Ukrainians. Self-determination of peoples was part of the Bolshevik policy. Yet Trotsky himself, born in the Ukraine, found it difficult to regard the Ukrainians as a separate people, especially when they were represented by the Rada. In a contest between the demands of the socialist revolution and self-determination, there was no doubt which side Trotsky would take.

When the second round of the negotiations opened, Trotsky had with him, as a member of the Soviet delegation, Medvedev, president of the executive committee of the Ukrainian Soviet, then based on Kharkov, and Satarisky, the commissar for education, and General Shakhrai. They came into sharp conflict with the Ukrainian Rada while the Germans and the Austrians looked on, with interest and not without malice. Alexander Sevriuk, the 25-year-old head of the Rada delegation, asked Trotsky and his Ukrainians why there was no one among them representing Moldavia, Siberia, the Crimean Tartars and the Don Cossacks, all peoples who did not recognize the authority of the Bolshevik government in Petrograd. He added that, in spite of the opposition to the Bolsheviks in Petrograd, the Rada did not follow the example set by Trotsky and challenge the Bolshevik right to rule the Russians.[35]

Trotsky then accused the Ukrainians of wanting to opt out of a federal Russian state. He was right. The Ukrainian parties, because of their desire to federate or separate from a particular system of government in Russia, had switched their policies. The federalists before November 1917 became separatists, and the other way round. The acrimonious exchange between the Russians and the Rada Ukrainians went on for three days. It brought peace with the Russians no nearer – Czernin thought that it might – and delayed its conclusion with the Rada.

On 3 February 1918, the last day of this pointless discussion, Czernin declared that the Central Powers recognized 'immediately the Ukrainian People's Republic as an independent, free and sovereign State, which is able to enter into international agreements independently'.[36] This was nothing new. The Central

Powers, and Vienna especially, had supported the Ukrainian movement throughout the war and now they expected their efforts to bear fruit. In January 1918 the Austrians were convinced that without Ukrainian corn they would starve. They had negotiated with the Rada independently, without Bolshevik participation. At the meeting on 16 January 1918, which followed private consultations between the Austrians and the Ukrainians, the disputed Kholm province was at the top of the agenda. It had been set up after a Duma decision in 1912 and contained, according to official Russian statistics, 52 per cent Ukrainians, 29 per cent Poles, 15 per cent Jews and 3 per cent Germans.

The meeting did not get off to a good start. The Ukrainians were using a different map of the district from the one before the Germans and the Austrians. Czernin said that he wanted to make no settlements concerning the territory of the historical Polish kingdom over the heads of the Poles, but that he was by no means opposed to the wishes of the Ukrainians. Kühlmann thought that it was essential to consult the population of the province first. Vsevolod Holubovich, the Ukrainian leader, told Czernin and Kühlmann that the Ukrainians wanted to know what the frontiers of their state would be before they signed the peace treaty. Sevriuk then touched on a very sensitive spot. After having remarked on the necessity of non-interference in the affairs of other states, he asked Czernin flatly what would happen to the Ukrainians in the Habsburg state, in Bukovina and eastern Galicia. 'This is not the time or the place', Sevriuk said,[37]

for me to describe the long struggle of our nation in Austria. . . . Ukrainian territory in Austria was the spring-board for our national movement, and I imagine it is no secret to those present here what a stubborn fight the Ukrainian people of Austria have waged against their Slav neighbours. Now, when the situation in the East in regard to the establishment of new states has changed, and the Austro-Hungarian monarchy will have common frontiers with the new Ukrainian state, we sincerely hope with all our heart, that the future will reveal no dark features that will do anything to jeopardize the friendly relations between the two states. It is our firm conviction that this can only come about if the cultural and political rights of our people are properly guaranteed. The rumours of the possibility of an incorporation of the Austro-Hungarian territory inhabited by our people into Poland are no mere newspaper items, and Count Czernin knows the colossal wave of anger stirred up by this rumour . . .

Count Czernin, the Austro-Hungarian Foreign Minister, told the Ukrainians that it was none of their business, that though two friendly countries might exchange views on their internal affairs, there was no guarantee that the peace talks would not break down and the Ukraine turn into an enemy again. But Czernin could not go on being tough for long. Three days later, on 19 January, the Central Powers agreed to give the Kholm province to the Ukrainians, as well as undertaking to set up a special crown possession (*Kronland*) for them in eastern and northern Galicia. In return, they demanded the conclusion of the peace treaty by 30 January 1918, the start of the demobilization of the Ukrainian army on 1 February, and the exchange of goods to begin immediately after the conclusion of peace. In addition, the Ukrainians were to guarantee the Poles minority rights in their new Republic.[38]

The economic details of the 'bread peace', the *Brotfrieden*, were considered by a special commission of experts, and settled before the deliberations of the full conference were resumed. While arguments about self-determination were tossed back and forth at Brest Litovsk, and Karl Radek, the Bolshevik publicist of great versatility, emerged as an expert on Polish affairs, Bolshevik troops drove the Rada out of Kiev, on 5 February 1918. There was no time to lose. At 2 o'clock on the morning of 9 February, the delegates, brightly flood-lit, film camera crews and their unusual equipment getting in their way, signed the first peace treaty of the war.

It did not have a pacifying effect. Czernin telegraphed Vienna and von Ugron, the Foreign Ministry's representative to the Polish Regents' Council at Warsaw, explaining why he was in such a hurry at Brest Litovsk:[39]

The catastrophic food supply situation as well as the growth of the forces of subversion in the hinterland have made the earliest possible conclusion [of peace] with the Ukraine, the only possible source of food supplies, a categorical imperative. This necessarily swift conclusion was to be achieved only by handing over the Kholm province to the Ukraine . . .

After von Ugron had told two members of the Regents' Council, Prince Lubomirski and Josef Ostrowski, of the Kholm decision, he wrote:[40]

The impression made by my words is difficult to describe. They were both as if struck down. Prince Lubomirski shook all over and could scarcely find words to express his disappointment. He spoke of the fourth partition of Poland . . .

It was the first of many diplomatic blunders committed by Vienna in the course of 1918. The Kholm decision antagonized the Poles inside and outside the Empire, and put an end to any hopes of an 'Austro-Polish' solution which should cast Vienna in the role of protector of the Poles. On the following day, 10 February 1918, Trotsky put an end to the negotiations: 'We are leaving the war, but we find it necessary to forgo the signing of a peace treaty.'[41]

Kühlmann had tried hard to keep the negotiations going. He had trimmed down the territorial demands made by the military: he had risked his resignation. But to no avail. Trotsky would not be reconciled.

It seems that the Soviet leader misunderstood the situation at a time when such misunderstanding could have had fatal consequences. He believed that the incipient quarrel between General Hoffmann and the diplomats about the resumption of hostilities would go in favour of the diplomats. He took no notice of Kühlmann's remark to the contrary, and believed himself to have scored a major victory at Brest Litovsk in forcing the Central Powers to accept his policy of 'neither war nor peace'. Trotsky's biographer generously comments on his achievement:[42]

He had given mankind the first great lesson in genuinely open diplomacy. But at the same time he allowed himself to be carried away by his optimism. He underrated his enemy and even refused to listen to his warning. Great artist that he was, he was so wrapped up in himself and in his ideal and so fascinated by the formidable appeal of his own work that he lightly overlooked its deficiencies.

The central committee was in session in Petrograd when the German and Austrian offensive on the eastern front opened on 17 February. The armies of the Central Powers moved swiftly and with ease, encountering no opposition. The Bolshevik committee was evenly divided between adherents of peace and of war. Trotsky, with his casting vote, would not commit himself, despite the fact that he had promised Lenin to support his peace policy if the Germans resumed their advance. By the evening of 18

February 1918 it had become apparent that the German armies were poised to move into the Ukraine and advance on the northern section of the front, toward the capital.

Trotsky proposed that the Soviets should get in touch with the Central Powers and inquire about their demands without requesting peace negotiations. Lenin was scathing about the proposal. He said that if there were to be a war, the Soviets should not have demobilized; that the Russian people would not understand the behaviour of their government. He added that Trotsky was 'joking with war', and it could lead to the breakdown of the revolution. Stalin thought that Trotsky's proposal could seriously be put forward only 'in literature'.[43] In the end, Trotsky, to everybody's astonishment, voted in favour of peace with Lenin's group. On the following day, 19 February 1918, the Soviet government made a formal offer of peace to the Germans.

For four days no answer came. The Germans had faced the same decision on war and peace as the Bolshevik central committee. On 10 February 1918, the day Trotsky interrupted the negotiations at Brest Litovsk, Kühlmann diagnosed the newly arisen situation.[44] He strongly advised against the continuation of the war on Russia. It would rule out the signing of the peace and bring about internal unrest in Germany. It had been decided, Kühlmann argued, to concentrate Germany's strength on the western front: in the east, there should only remain a border guard. The German Secretary of State again used the argument that had been coming up intermittently, since the early weeks of the revolution in Russia, in German diplomatic correspondence. It was the view that an attack by the Central Powers would rally the 'patriotic', or, as Kühlmann put it in this case, 'reactionary' forces to make another war effort, with the support of the western allies. In any case there was no guarantee, Kühlmann thought, that Germany could have real peace in the east at the moment. Berlin should therefore accept the *status quo* in the east and leave it at that: the mirror image of Trotsky's formula, 'neither war nor peace'. 'Who could throw us out by force, in eastern Europe', he wrote, 'from the positions we have acquired? In the immediate future, the Russians neither will nor can, and our enemies in the west have no way of getting here.'

Ludendorff wanted to introduce order into the fluid situation; he could not endure its open-ended quality. He insisted:[45]

if we act we strengthen our position in relation to the Entente, we reinforce the peace with the Ukraine, we achieve peace with Rumania, we strengthen our position in Lithuania (Litauen) and Kurland, we improve our military situation by taking possession of Dünaburg and parts of the Baltic provinces, we perhaps administer the knock-out blow to the Bolsheviks, thereby improving our internal conditions as well as our relations with the upper classes in Russia, we make available large forces in the east, free our whole military and moral power for the great blow against the west which His Majesty has now ordered.

At the Crown Council meeting on 13 February at Homburg, Kühlmann and Ludendorff faced each other across the conference table. Against the masterful inactivity advocated by the Secretary of State the war lords recommended swift action. Hindenburg feared Bolshevik advance into the Ukraine and the loss, for the Central Powers, of valuable supplies of grain. He thought that the struggle in the west would go on for a long time, and therefore 'we must defeat the Russians. Must overthrow the government'. The consultation went on, the argument often underlined by rising temper. Payer, the Vice-Chancellor, advised against an offensive in the east because it might set off strikes in the factories and questions in the Reichstag. The Kaiser snapped at Payer that in Germany there existed no 'republican circumstances'. The Bolsheviks were natural trouble-makers and they should be struck down dead; in that connection, the Kaiser mentioned the suggestion by Sir George Buchanan, the former Ambassador to St Petersburg, that England should ally herself with Germany to fight Lenin and his regime. The operation in the east was for the Kaiser simply a police measure, in aid of the Estonians – or, more precisely, the German landowners who lived in that province – who had come to ask him for help. He thought that such an action would encourage the people in St Petersburg to get rid of the Bolsheviks.

Ludendorff first suggested advance as far as Petrograd, but climbed down when he ran into stiff opposition from Hertling, the Chancellor. The Quartermaster General explained that he was not really concerned with the occupation of Estonia, but with pushing forward the front line at Dünaburg and taking the town. It would shorten the battlefront and release one German division for the west. Furthermore it would help the Ukrainians by drawing the Bolshevik forces away from the south. While Hertling and

Payer in the end agreed with Ludendorff's proposal, Kühlmann was unconvinced. Yet he remained in office until July, in frequent but ineffective conflict with the military.

The decision in Homburg on 13 February 1918 was in favour of a limited military action. The intention of the Kaiser and Ludendorff to advance as far as Petrograd and overthrow the Bolsheviks was abandoned, and so was Kühlmann's view on the advantages of letting Lenin's government 'stew in its own juice'.

Operation *Faustschlag* – the knock-out blow – was launched on 17 February and continued until the German troops reached the Narva–Pskov line. In 124 hours they advanced 150 miles in an area without roads, in the dead of Russian winter. They chased the shortening shadow of the old Russian army without coming up against the new Red Army, which was then in the making. The acceptance, by Lenin and Trotsky, of German peace terms on the following day was far too swift for the Germans. General Hoffmann used delaying tactics; the Bolshevik acceptance reached Berlin on 21 February. Two days later, Lenin had the German reply before him at the Smolny. It was presented in the form of an ultimatum and demanded new, harsh terms.

On 23 February 1918, the central committee met to consider the German ultimatum. The dilemma was still seen, by the majority of the members of the central committee, as a choice between war and peace, and it had lost none of its capacity to rouse and divide the committee. Lenin said at once that the policy of the 'revolutionary phrase' was over as far as he was concerned, and that if it were continued, he would resign his government and central committee posts. He insisted that the Soviets must buy time with territory. He got his way in the end. He asked the central committee whether the German conditions should be immediately accepted, and whether Russia should start getting ready for a revolutionary war.[46]

The choice, as Lenin formulated it, was not between peace and war, but between peace and the possibility of war, the preparation for it. The voting on the first proposition went in favour of immediate acceptance of peace, by seven to four votes, with four members of the central committee, including Trotsky, abstaining. The proposition that the Russians should start getting ready for war was passed unanimously. Lenin did not resign from the central committee, but Bukharin and three other supporters of revolutionary war did, and Trotsky gave up his post as Commissar for Foreign Affairs. Stalin sneered at Trotsky, and was made to apologize; he suggested that Bukharin and his friends had placed themselves outside the party, and after Lenin's and Trotsky's protests he was forced to withdraw the suggestion. The new pattern for political alignments in the central committee which became clearly recognizable a few years later began to emerge at that point of crisis.

It now remained for Lenin to convince the Petrograd Soviet and the central executive committee of the Congress of Soviets which were in session at the Tauride Palace. Lenin and the members of the central committee drove there immediately. Lenin took no notice of their hostile reception. He mounted the platform, regarded the delegates gloomily until the shouts died down, and then he told them:[47]

> Let us beware of becoming the slaves of our own phrases. In our day wars are won not by mere enthusiasm, but by technical superiority. Give me an army of 100,000 men, an army which will not tremble before the enemy, and I will not sign this peace. Can you raise an army? Can you give me anything but prattle and the drawing up of pasteboard figures?

After several hours' long, hard argument Lenin won the two bodies over to his point of view. The central executive committee in the end declared itself for signing the peace by 116 to 85 votes; there were 26 abstentions, and shouts of 'Traitor! Judas! You have betrayed your country! German spy!' as Lenin left the hall. It was early in the morning of 24 February, and he had just signed a telegram to the Central Powers accepting the peace terms.

On 1 March 1918 the two delegations again faced each other across the conference table at Brest Litovsk. Kühlmann was away in Bucharest, having turned to the problem of Rumanian peace; Trotsky had stayed behind in Petrograd. The atmosphere was sober, businesslike. Nobody was in the mood for verbal fireworks. No negotiations in fact took place. On 3 March, Sokolnikov, leader of the Russian delegation, signed the treaty. Its fourteen articles stripped Russia down to the territorial extent of Muscovy before the accession of Peter the Great and allowed the extension of Germany's influence into eastern Europe from the Arctic Ocean to the Black Sea. Poland and the Baltic provinces were taken away; so was the Ukraine: Russia lost almost one-third of its population. In addition, the Caucasian provinces of Kars, Ardahan and Batum, which were occupied by the Turks, passed under their control. The Russians had to undertake not to interfere in the internal affairs of those territories, to stop their propaganda offensive, and to demobilize their army. In his statement to the final session of the Brest Litovsk conference on the same day, Sokolnikov said:[48]

> It is a peace dictated at the point of the sword. It is a peace that revolutionary Russia is compelled to accept with its teeth clenched. It is a peace which, under the pretext of 'liberating' the Russian frontier areas, in fact turns them into German provinces. . . .

Lenin is reported to have said, when the delegation returned to Petrograd with the treaty, 'I don't want to read it, and I don't mean to fulfil it, except in so far as I am forced.' The price he was prepared to pay for peace and the continued existence of Soviet government was high. He still had some more persuading to do. The treaty had to be ratified by the seventh Party Congress. After three days of violent, passionate debate he succeeded in making the Congress accept the Brest Litovsk terms on 8 March 1918.

After the conclusion of peace with the Ukraine and with Russia, there remained the settlement to be made with Finland and with Rumania. Like the Ukraine, Finland had been a part of the Tsarist Empire: after the revolution in March 1917, the provisional government recognized the Diet in Helsinki as a substitute for the former Tsarist authority. The question of complete independence from Russia was then raised after the Bolshevik uprising in July, when, at a conference in Helsinki on 18 July 1917, the Social Democrats declared Finland an independent state and saw the *maktlagen* law through the Diet. The Petrograd government, however, did not recognize the law and dissolved the Diet. After the elections the Social Democrat minority in the new Diet obstructed its work: there was widespread popular unrest. This subsided when the agreement of 19 November between the middle-class and socialist parties accepted the socialist demands on the working day, on the formation of a new Senate, and on the Diet becoming the supreme governing body. But the truce was incomplete as well as brief. After the Diet voted, on 28 November 1917, for a middle-class Senate with Judge Svinhufvud, a well-known opponent of the Russians, at its head, the socialists again became very restless.

With the situation in Helsinki unsettled, a Finnish government delegation left, early in January 1918, on a tour of the European capitals, to seek diplomatic recognition. The King of Sweden gave his first: his action was approved of throughout Scandinavia, since it strengthened the peninsular system by placing another state between it and Russia, though there were politicians in Copenhagen who feared an increase in Swedish influence. On 6 January 1918 the Finnish delegation was received by the Chancellor in Berlin; on 11 January they arrived in Vienna. In December the Germans and the Austrians had agreed that a premature recognition of the Finnish republic was to be avoided by every means:[49] three weeks later, after the first round of negotiations in Brest Litovsk, they changed their minds.

By the end of January the first shots had been exchanged between the White and the Red Guards in Finland's civil war. The Russians supported the socialist Red Guard: the Whites were commanded by General Mannerheim, the former Tsarist officer who spoke Russian and Swedish, but no Finnish. The Reds had able political agitators; the Whites good professional officers. Mannerheim thought he could deal with the Reds himself; the politicians were of a different opinion. On 14 February 1918, the day after the momentous meeting of the Crown Council at Homburg at which Kühlmann's proposal for masterly inactivity was defeated by the military plan for an advance to the east,* the Finnish representative in Berlin, Professor Edvard Hjelt, asked the Germans for military assistance. A week later, the Supreme Command promised to send an expeditionary corps.

In the first days of March 1918 the question of the expedition was still being discussed in Berlin after it had left for Finland. There were strong political and financial objections against it, as well as an outcry in Sweden and Norway when the German troops landed, in transit, on the Aland Isles. Hindenburg asked the Kaiser not to cancel the expedition because it ran parallel to the operations in Estonia, Latvia and in the Ukraine. 'If we do not help the Finns the danger exists that they will be defeated', said Hindenburg, and added that it would mean 'the strengthening of Bolshevism and the possibility of another campaign against

* See above, p. 274.

Greater Russia [Grossrussland: i.e. the state in its 1914 extent] which would cost us more than the expedition.'[50] Germany could regard itself as safe only when the Russians understood that the non-Russian territories, formerly on the western fringes of the Tsarist Empire, could never again become a part of Greater Russia. There were other reasons for the insistence of the Supreme Command on the expedition. The extension of Bolshevism to the west had to be frustrated; the Bolshevik government had to be made to adhere to the clauses of the Brest Litovsk treaty; Germany needed new allies as well as sources of raw materials; there was the threat of English occupation of northern Russia: if there was no Finnish expedition, Finland would be driven 'into the arms of England'.

Before the final decision to go ahead with the expedition was taken on 12 March 1918, the peace between Germany and Finland had been concluded five days earlier, on 7 March. It was a separate peace: in Bucharest, where they were negotiating with the Rumanians, Kühlmann was almost as surprised by its conclusion as Czernin. Kühlmann, who had had differences with the Supreme Command about the Finnish expedition, told Czernin crossly that he wondered how they could conclude the peace 'behind our backs';[51] the Austrian Ambassador to Berlin, Prince Hohenlohe, was rebuked because he had reported, in an offhand manner, on the negotiations of a trade treaty between Finland and Germany.[52]

Two days before the conclusion of the Finnish treaty, a preliminary peace with Rumania had been signed in Bucharest on 5 March 1918. After the disaster inflicted on them by Field-Marshal Mackensen in the autumn of 1916, and after the collapse of the Russian front a year later, the Rumanians still had to be convinced that they had in fact been defeated. Czernin, when he arrived in Bucharest early in March, did most of the persuading. As Austrian Minister to Bucharest, he had known King Carol and the political scene well. Now, in March 1918, his audience with the King saved the dynasty.

The forces of Rumania's adversaries were closing in: the Rumanians had done little to make themselves popular with their neighbours. Though their troops had taken part in Kerensky's offensive in the summer of 1917, there had then been strong friction between the Petrograd Soviet and the Rumanian government, which made a point of persecuting the socialists. The life of Christo Rakovsky, the Rumanian socialist leader, was saved by the Russian soldiers and by his flight to Russia; his comrade, Marcus Wechsler, was shot dead by the Rumanian troops. After the fall of the provisional government in Petrograd, the Rumanians grabbed Bessarabia from Russia, their former ally; on 27 January 1918 the Soviet government broke off relations with Bucharest.

In a leader on 1 March 1918, the Vienna *Neue Freie Presse* pointed out that the King had brought his people into the war in the first place, and that 'he may have to pay for their misfortunes with his own person'. The day before, the King of the Bulgarians had toasted, at a banquet in Sofia, the prospect that 'all the children of our soil, after many centuries, will at last be reunited in one and only kingdom', meaning that the Rumanian Dobruja would soon become a part of Bulgaria. In the debates in the Budapest parliament it had become clear that Hungary would demand improvements, possibly far-reaching, of its strategic position on the eastern and southern slopes of the Carpathians in Transylvania, and protection of the key passes which the Rumanians had used when they invaded Transylvania, briefly, in the summer of 1916. There were the usual economic hopes: whereas the treaty with the Ukraine had been described as the 'bread peace', Rumania was to give the Central Powers an 'oil peace'.

The preliminary treaty of 5 March 1918 was signed in Bucharest against the background of the easy advance of the German and Austrian armies further into Russia: Kiev had fallen on 2 March. It went a short way toward a settlement. Rumania agreed to hand over the Dobruja, up to the Danube, to the Central Powers: to demobilize at once at least eight divisions and leave the still occupied Austrian territory, a corner of Bukovina, and to aid the Central Powers in transporting troops via Moldavia and Bessarabia to Odessa.

Czernin, when exploring the ways which might lead to a permanent peace with Rumania early in March, found that the Hungarians were the first obstacle he ran into. He was more interested in Rumanian supplies; the Hungarians, in Rumanian territory. As regards Rumania, therefore, Czernin remarked, 'a peace without annexations would be more difficult to bring about than with any other state'.[53] Demands as to the new Hungarian frontier were 'influenced by considerations not conducive to peace', and were to involve the cession of the Turnu-Severin and Sinaia provinces, and some valuable oil districts in Moldavia. The Budapest press was asking for much more than the politicians.

Before the Germans were able to make their own conditions, they had to abandon their original position that they would not treat with the King and government at all. They were also asking for a lot. They proposed that Rumania should give up most of its wealth – its oil, harbours, railways – to German companies for development, and that the whole country should come under Germany's financial control. It was to be for Berlin a small compensation for the territorial gains of Austria-Hungary. Czernin was caught between the German and the Hungarian demands.

In the course of the Brest Litovsk negotiations, the Bulgarians had been easy allies for the Germans and the Austrians to have. When Czernin visited their Prime Minister, Radoslavov, on 30 January 1918, he was told that, as far as Radoslavov was concerned, peace between Russia and Bulgaria already existed, only the signature was wanting.[54] As a reward for coming into the war on the side of the Central Powers the Bulgarians had been promised the Dobruja, a province in south-east Rumania. When the Rumanian army occupied Russian Bessarabia, the Bulgarians approved of the acquisition because they thought it would make giving up the Dobruja easy for the Rumanians. They were mistaken. In the course of the negotiations for the peace of Bucharest the Balkan problems emerged in all their complexity.

There existed, however, eloquent and influential advocates of the Rumanian cause in the Austrian Foreign Ministry. Their case made Czernin's position no easier. A few days before the opening of the negotiations in Bucharest, Count Pallavicini, the Ambassador to Constantinople, an Austrian diplomat who had spent most of his career in the Balkans, put down a few ideas for the benefit of his Foreign Minister.[55] Pallavicini argued that the conflict of interests between Russia and Austria-Hungary had made possible the well-known Balkan game of see-saw. The local politicians learned to benefit by it. But now it was over, anyway for the time being, because Russia had been knocked out.

The change was in the monarchy's favour, and Pallavicini's advice to Czernin was that Vienna should use the opportunity. The new situation, as the Ambassador pointed out, would become apparent in Bucharest in all its crude reality. Despite King Carol's cautious official policy, the Rumanians had looked forward to the break-up of Austria rather than to the dissolution of Russia. They were therefore used to casting their predatory glances in the direction of Transylvania rather than Bessarabia. Now or very soon, the Ambassador wrote, the shrewd Rumanian politicians would have to revise their attitudes. Any pickings would have to be done with Vienna's consent; Austria had survived, not Russia.

Pallavicini wrote that the promotion of such a mentality in Bucharest was to Austria's advantage. Rumanian politicians recognized that they had a community of interests with the Hungarians, surrounded by 'Slav sea'. Vienna had always regarded Rumania as a barrier on Russia's way to Constantinople. Now, with the disappearance of the Tsar's Empire, Pallavicini argued, Rumania's strategic importance had increased. It separated two 'Slav peasant republics': Bulgaria, which belonged to that category in fact if not in actual form, and the Ukraine. The possibility of their unification appalled Pallavicini. Rumania was the only wedge between some 'fifty million Slav socialists' who could influence their brethren inside the monarchy as well as cutting it off from the mouth of the Danube. It would therefore be a mistake to take away any territory from the Rumanians. Especially the Dobruja; that province was a matter of life and death to them; Bucharest could not breathe without the port of Constanza. Turkish interests were identical with those of Vienna, and there existed the danger that, if the Dobruja was to go to the Bulgarians, the Turks would immediately demand western Thrace, and there had been unmistakable signs of that in the press. An over-large Bulgaria, the Ambassador concluded, would come to dominate the Balkans, and take over the leadership of the South Slavs. The implication was clear: Austria had gone into the war to stop Serbia doing precisely that.

But if the Bulgarians were difficult about the Dobruja, the Turks were impossible about Thrace. Western Thrace was the only piece of territory that had actually changed hands during the war after a diplomatic agreement: the Turks had made that sacrifice in order to tempt the Bulgarians into the war.* Now they wanted it back. On 18 March 1918 Talaat Pasha told the Austrian Ambassador that Turkish representatives must not return from

* See above, p. 79.

Bucharest with empty hands; if they did, his government would fall. The best thing, the Ambassador thought, would be to make Bulgaria and Turkey hold the settlement over until the end of the war.[56]

This was done in the end, but not quite in the form Pallavicini recommended. Throughout March and April 1918 the disturbed balance of power in the Balkans continued to exercise the diplomats of the Central Powers. Rumania, the defeated enemy, had Bessarabia. Turkey and Bulgaria, the victors, felt that they had to pay a high price for Germany's friendship. The Turks' position was especially unenviable. They had lost half their territory in the Middle East to the Allies, and had given away western Thrace to Bulgaria. The Kaiser's current promise of 'the incorporation of the territories of the Caucasus lost in 1878'[57] helped only a little, but the threat of a government crisis, set off by the negotiations in Bucharest, remained, with the possibility of Turkey changing sides.

Half-way through April there came a glimmer of hope from Sofia when Radoslavov, the Bulgarian Premier, told the Austrian Minister that his government might be prepared to agree to holding over the Dobruja question until after the end of the war. His Minister of Finance, who had negotiated in Berlin, had been promised a considerable reduction of Bulgaria's war debt.[58] In any case the Austrian Minister to Sofia, Otto Czernin (a relative of the Foreign Minister, who had just resigned over Clemenceau's revelation of the Sixtus affair, and had been replaced by Count Burián) thought that the defection of Turkey would not hurt the Central Powers as much as the Bulgarians changing their minds, and he saw no way in which that could happen.[59] King Ferdinand, then riding a wave of popularity, would not agree to any major change in his country's political course.

The clash between the Bulgarians and the Turks went on until the end of April. The Turks insisted that they must get back the territory in Thrace; otherwise, they would not send their representatives to Bucharest. In the evening of 26 April 1918, the Turkish Ambassador to Vienna came to see Burián, the new Foreign Minister, and told him that, if Turkey did not get western Thrace back, the Dobruja would have to be partitioned, with its northern part remaining under the administration of the four Powers. The Turks would have to be promised, the Ambassador added, that that administration would not be lifted without their agreement.[60]

The idea of a condominium in the northern Dobruja was not new, but because the Turks themselves suggested it, it made the conclusion of the Bucharest peace possible. The treaty, signed on 8 May 1918, gave the Dobruja, up to the Chernavoda–Constanza line, to Bulgaria; the territory north of that line was to be run by the four allied Powers. Whereas Austria received only about 600 sq. kilometres of Rumanian frontier territory, Hungary's share amounted to 5,000 sq. kilometres. (A Vienna newspaper testily commented: 'Because of the divisions in Austria, because of the sins the Czechs commit against the population every day, Hungary has become the leading power in the monarchy.'[61]) The Rumanian forces were to be stripped down to the strength of the last peace budget. The Germans and the Austrians believed that the Rumanians would be able to defend themselves against the Soviets, and they were to stay out of Rumanian territory occupied by the Central Powers. There was to be a new Danube commission, excluding three of the signatories of the 1883 Paris treaty, i.e. the British, the French and the Italians: the Central Powers undertook to guarantee Rumania's access to the sea via Constanza. The economic agreements, vital to Vienna, were not revealed: the *Neue Freie Presse*[62] wrote that Germany

has the military leadership of the war, the command of battles and of occupation. It had secured influence in Rumania's oil industry before the war. Those elements of strength made themselves felt during the negotiations.

The peace with Rumania was the missing link in the chain of the eastern treaties concluded by the Central Powers early in 1918. The press in Berlin and Vienna greeted the Bucharest peace as the final seal on a policy of victory and peace.

The victory of 1917–18 in the east opened up fresh perspectives before the Central Powers. The Germans were now able to begin turning away from their policy of emulating the example set by the British Empire, a policy which had brought them into conflict with England in the first place. Their operations outside Europe had been marked by failure; they were losing their interest in the opportunities offered overseas. Continental expansion, on the other hand, held out high promise. There existed the hope that the victory in the east would help them to break the Allied economic blockade apart from releasing the troops for mounting a decisive offensive in the west.

Nevertheless, their successes were in several respects qualified. They adopted a forward policy in Finland and the Caucasus and advanced along the whole of the eastern front, far into the Ukraine and south Russia. They wanted to strip Russia of its outlying provinces, down to the barest bone of the purely Russian territories. But they stopped short of the country's nerve centres, Petrograd and Moscow, and negotiated with Lenin's government. They underestimated or completely disregarded the dynamic qualities of the Bolshevik appeal and gave Lenin the breathing space he so badly needed for consolidating his regime. Lenin knew that he had a reasonably good chance of defending successfully his government against its enemies at home. But military strength, combined with a clear-cut political objective, could have been fatal for the new Soviet state. Lenin was aware of that. It was the main reason why he went on negotiating at Brest Litovsk and why, in the end, he accepted extortionate, humiliating terms.

They were not adhered to by the German military, who came to regard Russia as an open country, where they could roam about at will. They advanced far beyond the limits set down at Brest, and further antagonized the Turks, who looked toward the Caucasus for compensation for the losses they had suffered in the Middle East. Indeed, all the peace negotiations had severely tested the cohesion of the four-Power alliance, and prepared the way for the military collapse in the Near East and in the Balkans in the summer of 1918.

The Brest negotiations strengthened the resolution, in both the belligerent camps, to carry on the war. In Berlin and in Vienna, they again held out the elusive hope of victory. In the western capitals, the victory of the Central Powers in the east demonstrated the relentless, far-ranging ambitions of their enemies. It caused panic in London and Paris, yet neither the French nor the English considered concluding peace from a position of weakness. They had another asset in the unexhausted, inexhaustible, strength of America. President Wilson had given up his desire for peace without victory.

Once again, Berlin staked everything on one card. This time it was to be the final, knock-out blow on the western front. Their offensive opened on the first day of the spring in 1918. Between November 1917 and May 1918, the Central Powers transferred, in all, eighty divisions from the eastern to the western and Italian battlefields. Of these, fifty-three divisions were German, and they all went to the west. They were expected to win the war.

But the ambiguity of Germany's eastern policy affected its position in the west. The policy of stripping Russia of its marginal territories and leaving a dynamic, revolutionary government in power, made heavy demands on the manpower of the Central states.

The Germans made smaller withdrawals from Italy as well, and left the Austrians to hold a bigger share of the front. But many of the Austrian troops released in the east and intended for Italy had to be used to combat the industrial and social unrest in Austria-Hungary early in 1918, which had been set off by the Bolshevik revolution and the subsequent pacifist agitation by the Soviets that accompanied the negotiations in Brest. When the German offensive in the west was launched on 31 March 1918 the armies of the Central Powers were still advancing on the eastern front. It was a walk-over, but it tied down almost a million German and Austrian troops.

8 Paris

When war came in August 1914 the alliance between France and Russia was over twenty years old. It had broken up Bismarck's diplomatic system and exposed the new German state to the danger of war on two fronts; it saved the French from isolation and made their desire for *revanche* for 1871 no longer an elusive goal; it confirmed Russia's position in Europe and, as a by-product, gave it the largest loans that had ever changed hands among friends.

A special relationship between the two countries developed while the alliance lasted. Poincaré, on his election to the Presidency in 1913, was awarded the Cross of St Andrew, a decoration reserved for members of the Tsar's family and for very special foreigners; in Paris, Izvolsky, the Russian Ambassador, was granted the privilege of addressing himself, in matters of urgency, to the President direct. In the war, a fortnight before the revolution, Pokrovsky, the Minister of Foreign Affairs, sent a note to Maurice Paléologue giving his government's final consent to the French choosing what their eastern frontier with Germany should be; Paris reciprocated on 11 March 1917 by giving the Russians a free hand in eastern Europe.

Before and after the revolution, financial links between the two countries set the tone of their relations. In 1913, investment in Russia amounted to 25 per cent of all foreign securities held in France; an estimate published by the Crédit Lyonnais on 1 July 1914 put the value of direct government bonds at 6,345m. francs and of the guaranteed railway bonds at 2,116m.[1] The small French investors, who subscribed most of the money, preferred fixed income securities, preferably guaranteed by a government. And the prestige of Russia in France was high. The Paris press, especially *Le Temps*, received from the Russian Embassy considerable subsidies for their good services. It did not seem to matter that French money went to a rich state in a poor country and that there was some imbalance between French financial and trading activities. (In 1913, Russia imported 57m. roubles' worth of goods from France; from Germany 652.2m.) No one in France took any notice of the warning, by the Russian revolutionaries in 1905, that loans made to the Tsarist autocracy would be repudiated.

Soon after the war with Japan in 1905, the Russian government became active again in Europe; the Bosnian and the Moroccan crisis pointed to the tensions underneath the surface of European diplomacy. In the new atmosphere Poincaré was able to say, without fear of contradiction, that his government would be guided in its policy of admitting foreign loans to the stock exchange by the principle of priority of national over financial interest.[2] The Russian military were thinking at that time about the improvement of their strategic railways: the big railway company bonds were issued in the years 1908–14. When Delcassé came to St Petersburg in 1913 as French Ambassador he brought with him a special brief. He was to make certain that construction of railways to the western frontier, as laid down by the two Chiefs-of-Staff, was speeded up. Nevertheless, in August 1914 the Russians had 13 lines with 23 tracks running up to their western frontier. Germany and Austria had twice the capacity, and it was better spaced: 32 lines with 46 tracks. French money had put Russia into a position to wage the war. The alliance had been buttressed by loans largely contributed by small savers. The French had held 80 per cent of Russian foreign debt before the war and 19 per cent of the war debt. They found it hard, in 1917 and after, to let the Russians forget it.

The idea of annulment of foreign debts had been originally put forward during the first Russian revolution in 1905; after the Bolshevik revolution *Pravda* restated the case without mincing its words:

The annulment of foreign debts deals the Entente Powers a blow which is scarcely less great than the victories on the western front of the Germans. The hour of punishment sounds for the Clemenceaus and the Poincarés. The small French bourgeois will forgive the thousands of victims on the field of battle, but he will never pardon his material ruin. The French government hopes to avert its fall by assuring the payment of the interest on the Russian debt.

In a debate in the Chamber of Deputies on 27 December 1917, Pichon, the Minister of Foreign Affairs, said that there could be no recognition of the Soviet regime so long as the Bolsheviks persisted in repudiating the financial obligations abroad of the former Russian governments. From then on, for six years, that grudge dominated French policy toward Russia. After the November 1918 armistice, Paris went on working for the over-throw of Bolshevism long after London and Washington had given up.

It was only in the first weeks of the revolutionary year of 1917 that the French thought they caught in the events in Russia a recognizable and flattering glimpse of their own revolution of 1789. The French press repeatedly referred to the 'grandiose spectacle' of the revolution which it regarded as inevitable and as a certain sign of the Russian determination to fight the war to a victorious end. Russian revolutionaries had always drawn heavily on what they regarded as the experiences of the French; early in 1917, Frenchmen also began to compare and forecast. Albert Thomas, the Socialist Minister who became the French government's representative in Petrograd, saw an analogy between the patriotic defence of France by the Convention in 1793 and the situation in Russia:[3]

> Our Convention knew how to fight the whole of Europe and organize democratic institutions at the same time. I cannot think you, the promoters of the first Russian revolution, incapable of correcting the vices of the *ancien régime*.

Like Michelet, the historian of the French revolution, Thomas saw the Russian events as an instrument of progress and he thought of them as 'the sunniest, most holidaylike, most bloodless'.

It was impossible to keep up such high optimism for long. When Thomas addressed the Petrograd Soviet on 21 May 1917 he told them that French Socialists also were, like the Russians, fighting capitalism and imperialism. He was duly applauded, but Rosenblum, for the executive of the Soviet, pointed out that the Russian revolution was directed against autocracy as well as against the war, and urged the French socialists to campaign for peace without annexations and indemnities based on the self-determination of peoples. Thomas later remarked that if the

Russians would insist on shedding their blood for a formula, then its interpretation might have to be changed.

Yet Albert Thomas got on with the revolutionaries better than any other French representative in Russia. A baker's son and a disciple of Jaurès, Thomas, so Kerensky thought, 'strikingly resembled a Russian intellectual who through his own effort has just escaped from a peasant background'. Maurice Paléologue, who was in effect superseded by Thomas in April, an aristocrat of Byzantine lineage, became useless as a source of information. The Tsar's court and its usual social functions disappeared; although the grand dinners and parties at the aristocratic houses in Petrograd still went on after the outbreak of the revolution, the hosts usually knew as little about the events in their own country as their diplomatic guests. Paléologue was uneasy in the new situation and glad when he was able to leave Russia. His successor, Joseph Noulens, the French Minister of War in 1914–15, who arrived in Petrograd in July, was a great believer in ambassadorial pomp and in the overriding value of disciplined action. When Noulens and his retinue passed through London on his way to Petrograd, Paul Cambon, the French Ambassador to the Court of St James, wondered what effect 'this display of Ambassadorial majesty will have upon the peasants of the workers' committee'.[4] Noulens's belief in discipline made him suspicious of the revolutionaries, and later led him to admire Mussolini. In any case, both Noulens and Albert Thomas were so committed to their task of keeping Russia in the war that they found it difficult to understand the desire of the revolutionaries to have done with it.

On 29 October 1917 problems of foreign policy were discussed, for the last time, in the parliament. The Menshevik, Fyodor Dan, charged the provisional government with their utter failure to understand the psychology of the masses. He said that the view that the revolution would facilitate the prosecution of the war was mistaken and that it was not the weakness and worn-out condition of the army that created the desire for peace, but the unsatisfied striving for peace that was playing havoc with the army.[5]

As the effectiveness of traditional diplomatic methods became less, the difficulties revolutionary Russia was having with its allies multiplied.* Ten days after the Bolshevik revolution, when Clemenceau became the French Premier, the chances of an under-

* See above, chapter 6, *passim*.

standing between the new rulers of Russia and the western Allies were low. In any case, Clemenceau had been no great partisan of the alliance between Russia and France: in 1906 he tartly remarked: 'After having furnished the Tsar with the financial resources which were destined to lead to his defeat abroad, it now remains for us to supply him with the financial resources destined to assure his victory over his own subjects.'[6] Clemenceau was committed to the energetic prosecution of the war on the western front. He was more single-minded in that regard than his predecessors, and the events in Russia were of interest to him only in so far as they had a direct and immediate bearing on the battlefields in France.

The Bolshevik victory did not clarify the situation in Russia for the western Allies. Quite the contrary; it was soon after the November revolution that Joseph Noulens informed the Quai d'Orsay:[7]

whether Trotsky or Chernov is in power tomorrow, whether or not Kerensky forms one of the coalition, the situation will be more or less the same. The terms of peace and of the agrarian solution will hardly be changed. The Germans will be free to develop all their intrigues against the Allies just as they please.

Such was the pessimistic view of the situation; the optimists went on hoping that Lenin's regime would gradually fade out, like the grin of the Cheshire cat.

The only well-established fact, in Paris as well as in London and Washington, was that Lenin had been allowed to cross Germany and that the Bolsheviks had been helped in various ways by Berlin. The London *Morning Post* commented that we had been betrayed by 'Russian Jews of German extraction' who were in the pay of Berlin; at the Foreign Office the writer of the weekly report on Russia believed that

Bolshevism is essentially a Russian disease; it is Tolstoyism distorted and carried to extreme limits. But in the present case it has been fastened on and poisoned by the Germans for their own purposes. It is not yet possible to say which of the Bolshevik leaders have taken German money; some undoubtedly have, while others are honest fanatics.[8]

It proved to be a misleading piece of information. The western Allies assumed that the Bolsheviks were under some obligation to the Germans, that there was a collusion between them which was bound to affect the political behaviour of the Bolshevik leaders. It did, but in an unexpected way. We have seen Trotsky at the time of the negotiations at Brest Litovsk going out of his way to disprove the charges against the Bolsheviks.

In any case it was the military situation of the Allies which dominated their attitudes to Lenin's regime. Looking back at the situation at the turn of the years 1917–18 the Chief of the Imperial Staff described it as

anything but encouraging. The armies of France and Great Britain were tired and discouraged, while the resources of manpower of both nations were nearing exhaustion. Italy was still reeling from the staggering reverse of Caporetto, and was a source of weakness rather than a support to the Entente. The armies of America were still in the making, and it was evident that long before they could intervene the Germans could mass on the western front the great numbers of troops set free by the collapse of Russia. At this period, and in the critical weeks that followed the bursting of the storm on 21 March 1918, it was above all things necessary to take a long view and to leave no stones unturned that could contribute to the eventual defeat of the German plans for the domination of the world.[9]

Lenin's decree of peace, Trotsky's revolutionary agitation in place of conventional diplomacy, the emergence of the Soviet regime from military defeat, set it aside from the warring European states. Many European socialists also found it difficult to come to terms with it. On 3 January 1918 Hervé, the French Socialist Party deputy, asked in *La Victoire*, when the question of sending another socialist delegation to Russia came up:[10]

Talk with Lenin? Talk with him after he has broken the Declaration of London with the Allies and has abandoned them in the midst of the war? What can we tell him that he does not know already? . . . with his visionary and fanatical pride as a possessor of the eternal truth, a French socialist delegation would merely increase his own exalted idea of himself and give him a kind of moral investiture that would allow him to put the screw yet tighter on our true friends in Russia. Lenin and his band are our declared enemies. . . . We have friends in Russia – the Ukrainians, the Cossacks, the Russian army, the Polish elements, the patriotic socialists, the Cadets and even the Russian monarchists – all those in short who want to restore order and close Russia to the Germans.

A few days later, another French socialist, Captain Sadoul, a member of the military mission in Russia pointed out:[11]

If we at last condescend to see in their programme that which is advantageous for the Entente, if we renounce every intention of meddling in their domestic struggles, of encouraging counter-revolutionary activities that are destined to be defeated, if we stop, in a word, favouring disorder and at the same time try to bring the Bolsheviks back to the bourgeois ideology, if we consent to revise our war aims, we can greatly profit by this government.

Though Hervé may have been too optimistic about the friends France had in Russia and Sadoul's remark about the conversion of the Bolsheviks to bourgeois ideology naïve, their attitudes pointed to the alternatives the Allies had before them in regard to the Bolsheviks and their new state.

An understanding with Lenin and his regime was one possibility open to the Allies. In a long and detailed telegram on 27 November 1917 Buchanan, the Ambassador to Petrograd, expressed the view that

the only safe course left to us is to give Russia back her word and to tell her people that, realizing how worn out they are by the war and the disorganisation inseparable from a great revolution, we leave it to them to decide whether they will purchase peace on Germany's terms or fight on with the Allies, ...[12]

Buchanan's view appealed to no one in Paris. The attitude of Clemenceau to the Bolshevik government was irreconcilable and he insisted that Russia must fulfil its obligations. His government described the German–Russian armistice of 15 December 1917 as a betrayal of the Allied cause, and Clemenceau said that if 'all the celestial powers asked him to give Russia back her word he would refuse'.[13] Buchanan, General Knox, the head of the British military mission to Russia, as well as Lloyd George shared the view, on the other hand, that the situation in Russia was such that rigid insistence on contractual obligations would only play into the hands of Germany. In London, on 10 December 1917, Balfour told the War Cabinet that Britain should 'avoid, as long as possible, an open breach with this crazy system'.[14] At a meeting in London on 21 December 1917 the War Cabinet decided: 'At Petrograd we should at once get into relations with the Bolsheviks through unofficial agents, each country as seems best to it.'[15] The

Americans had Raymond Robins of the American Red Cross mission, who called on Trotsky immediately after the Bolshevik seizure of power and asked the Commissar for Foreign Affairs bluntly whether it was worth while for his mission to stay on. After Trotsky's positive reply and the swift settlement of some outstanding problems, Robins changed his mind about his earlier judgement of Trotsky ('this curse of false spirit') and decided that it was possible to deal with the Soviets, in some matters, if not in all.[16] He thought that working with the Bolsheviks would give them self-confidence and help them resist German demands.

The French had Captain Jacques Sadoul, a socialist lawyer and a member of the military mission, who had known Trotsky as an exile in Paris. He kept on telling the government in Paris, from the time of the Bolshevik take-over of power, that Lenin and Trotsky were not German agents, that they were unlikely to be overthrown in the near future, and that if the Allies broke with them the Bolsheviks would be driven into the arms of Germany. Sadoul had sharp differences with Noulens; Albert Thomas, who had in the meanwhile returned to Paris, was his friend and ally. Sadoul besought him to appoint a young man with an open mind as the new Ambassador.

The Foreign Office in London sent Robert Bruce Lockhart as its unofficial representative with the Bolsheviks. A young and versatile Scot, Lockhart knew Russia well, having been attached to the Moscow Consulate General since 1912 and having acted as Consul since 1915. He had returned to London six weeks before the Bolshevik revolution; he was asked to attend a cabinet conference on Russia on 20 December 1917, which culminated in his meeting Lloyd George. The Prime Minister told Lockhart that his place obviously was in Petrograd and not in London; he left for the Russian capital on a British cruiser on 14 January 1918. His brief in Russia was simple, 'to keep unofficially in touch' with the Bolsheviks; there was no element of recognition of the Soviet government involved in the appointment. Noulens said of Lockhart's appointment: 'At once intelligent, energetic and clever, he was one of those whom the English Government employs, with rare felicity, for confidential missions, and whom it reserves, should the occasion arise, for disavowal.'[17] After his mission, which ended in August 1918 with his arrest by the Soviet government for complicity in a plot on Lenin's life, and then his exchange for Litvinov, his opposite number in London, Lockhart wrote: 'There is no one more quickly neglected than the man on the spot whose policy becomes discredited.'[18]

The policy of keeping in touch with the Bolshevik government brought the western Allies some small advantages. Certain consular matters were settled, and the necessary permissions were granted for Allied civilians to leave the country. In January 1918 the Bolshevik government allowed the establishment of a trading company, *Tovaro-Obmien*, which was to buy up merchandise in Russia that might otherwise have been useful to the Germans. But they were marginal agreements, the symptoms of a situation in which everybody tried to keep as many options open as possible.

Hopes of a more extensive co-operation between the Allies and the Bolsheviks rose higher in February 1918 than at any other time. The Soviet delegates were spinning out the negotiations at Brest Litovsk, or considering the possibility of a revolutionary war on Germany after the negotiations had been broken off. Some Bolsheviks – not Lenin – were still waiting for revolutions in the west to lift from the Soviet state the curse of military weakness. On the Allied side no obvious remedy had emerged for the failing strength of Russia.

The news of the German decision to advance on the eastern front reached Petrograd on 16 February 1918. Four days later Captain Sadoul, on his own initiative, offered Trotsky the support of the French military mission against the German advance. Trotsky was suspicious of the offer, and asked Sadoul for a confirmation from the Ambassador. Sadoul was fortunate. He did not know of the decision the French government had made shortly before his rash offer to Trotsky. It promised French military and financial assistance if the Bolsheviks resisted the Germans.[19] The central committee, as we have seen, decided otherwise.

The work of Sadoul, Lockhart and Robins, first in Petrograd and from the end of February in Moscow, remained ineffective. From time to time Trotsky held out the tantalizing promise of a revolutionary war on Germany. We know that Lenin opposed him and that Trotsky had to abandon that policy. A more modest aim, an intervention by the Allies with Soviet permission, a policy which Sadoul was the first Allied representative to advocate, also proved difficult to realize. Distrust of the Bolsheviks, of their motives and their intentions, was at the foundation of Allied diplomacy. It was not only a question of the Bolsheviks' German antecedents or their refusal to honour the obligations incurred by past governments. Buchanan was puzzled and hurt by Stalin's Sovnarkom (Commissariat of the Nationalities) appeal on 3 December 1917 which described the Great Powers as 'rapacious European plunderers', asked the peoples of Asia to overthrow 'these robbers and enslavers', and singled out British rule in India as the ideal target for revolution.

At the meeting of the cabinet on 21 November 1917, Balfour proposed that the British government should support Kaledin, a Cossack general who had declared himself an opponent of the Bolshevik regime. Kaledin and his troops were based on Novocherkassk, a town in the south of the Ukraine which was becoming a rallying point for anti-Bolshevik forces. Apart from Kaledin, General Alekseev was there, together with Boris Savinkov, the Vice-Minister of War in Kerensky's government; Rodzianko, the president of the Duma, and General Kornilov, who had unsuccessfully plotted against the provisional government, were reported to be on their way there. The cabinet made no decision on direct support of Kaledin; Colonel House's advice was that the Allies should ask the Rumanians to co-operate with the loyal forces. On the following day the Foreign Office sent a telegram to that effect to the British Minister at Jassy, the seat, since Rumania's defeat in 1916, of the government in the part of the country bordering on Russia.

The meeting in Paris of the Allied Prime Ministers on 1 December 1917, at which Colonel House was present, discussed the question of supporting pro-Allied groups on the Don and in Transcaucasia. South Russia then emerged as the most suitable area for a possible intervention. The Colonel's advice was ambiguous. He thought that there was no point in encouraging disturbances in Russia because the Allies neither had a definite programme nor any force to back it up with: he added, however, that if the pro-Allied groups were given no encouragement or money they would go to pieces.[20] On the following day the cabinet in London decided to give Kaledin all the financial assistance he needed. Neither the British Ambassador nor the head of the military mission were pleased about the decision. General Knox thought: 'To ask us to intrigue with Cossacks while we are here in the power of the Rebel Government is merely to get our throats cut to no purpose.'[21]

The first step the cabinet in London took toward intervention was the decision to give financial assistance to the opponents of the Bolsheviks and of the Central Powers. On 14 December the rule was laid down:[22]

Any sum of money required for the purpose of maintaining alive in South East Russia the resistance to the Central Powers, considered necessary by the War Office in consultation with the Foreign Office, should be furnished, the money to be paid in instalments so long as the recipients continue the struggle.

By then, two advances of £10m. had been made for use in South Russia as well as a smaller sum for use in the Caucasus. The financial arrangements had the highest security rating, and Britain's allies knew very little about them. In comparison with the cash sums that had been given to the Tsarist government during the war – £600m. from London alone plus £180m. from Paris – aid for the opponents of the Bolshevik regime was less generous.

It soon appeared that, in order to avoid duplication of effort, some division of responsibility among the Allies was necessary. In Paris, just as in London, South Russia was regarded as the most suitable for a military action in November and December 1917. Liaison officers were dispatched there, and General Tabouis of the French military mission became the 'Commissioner of the French Republic to the Government of the Ukrainian Republic'. On 23 December 1917 the French accepted the English plan for the division of responsibility between the two governments. The territory north of the Black Sea, Bessarabia, the Ukraine and the Crimea, became the responsibility of the French; to the east and south of the Black Sea, the British were to take care of the Caucasus, Armenia, Georgia, Kurdistan and the 'Cossack territories'. The French, with General Berthelot in charge of the Rumanian army, thought themselves to be in a good position to look after the operations in that area; the English had an interest in protecting the frontiers of India. The Anglo-French agreement was meant to give the Allied military some basic operational directive: one of the few they received in regard to Russia.

At the end of February 1918 the German advance threatened

Petrograd and dispersed the Allied missions. The American Ambassador, David Rowland Francis, thought it important that his country should go on being represented in Russia; he had done some exploration of a suitable alternative domicile for his mission. His choice was Vologda, a small provincial town some 350 miles east of Petrograd. The communications were good, with railway links to Archangel, Petrograd, Moscow and Siberia; telegraph to Archangel and wireless to Murmansk, with the English in control of the cable to London. It was, for the time being, out of the way of the German advance and unaffected by the revolution. The Americans arrived there on the last day of February. The British and French diplomats had also left Petrograd, and had struck out in the opposite direction, for Finland. Buchanan and his staff succeeded in leaving Russia, while Noulens and the French were intercepted by the Bolsheviks. He thought that his English colleagues abandoned him and never forgave them. The French were re-routed to Vologda, where they arrived some four weeks later: they were soon joined there by Francis Lindley, who had been the British Chargé d'Affairés in Petrograd and had succeeded in getting out of Russia via Finland at the end of February. Bruce Lockhart, who moved to Moscow with the Bolshevik government, thought that the Vologda diplomats frightened one another by wild anti-Bolshevik rumours and that the site of the new home of the heads of the three diplomatic missions was as if 'three foreign Ambassadors were trying to advise their governments on an English cabinet crisis from a village in the Hebrides'.[23]

When the heads of the American, English and French missions reassembled at Vologda, the value of the usual diplomatic channels was lower than ever. The two-way traffic between the missions abroad and the central office was exceptionally sluggish. The diplomats at Vologda had little reliable information to dispatch; London and Paris, in return, had few instructions to pass on concerning political matters. General Niessel, the head of the French military mission, had asked for political decision to precede military involvement in Russia.[24] In fact, the opposite happened. By postponing decisions, the politicians in Paris and London often left the soldiers to cope with the situation as best they could.

Of the Allied military missions in Russia, the French was the biggest and most important. It was commanded by General

Niessel, based on Petrograd; General Janin had led the French representation at the Stavka, the headquarters, until immediately after the Bolshevik seizure of power: he was later attached to the Czechoslovak Legion. General Tabouis, the head of the French mission at Kiev, became, we have seen, the representative to the Ukrainian government. He remained at his post until the Germans resumed their advance. French officers also stayed on at the front, mainly as technical and artillery experts, or were attached to Russian units in areas of special interest to the French. There were small French missions at Tiflis and Murmansk. General Berthelot, who later came under Niessel's command, was with the Rumanian army. Jassy and, for a short time, Kiev became the centres of French influence in south Russia.[25]

From the point of view of Paris and London, Russia was divided, for all practical purposes, into two distinct areas. The central Russian territory, including the two capitals, Petrograd and Moscow, and controlled by the Bolsheviks, was of little interest to the Allies. Though their representatives – Bruce Lockhart, General Lavigne, General Romei, Raymond Robins – stayed on in Moscow and kept in touch with the Bolsheviks, the ratification of the Brest Litovsk treaty further reduced the chances of an understanding with them. Lockhart and Sadoul, who did much for the cause of co-operation with the Soviets, fell out of favour with their own governments. Sadoul was later tried *in absentia* in France.

The rest of Russia was open to Allied military operations. We know that the French military had favoured the Ukraine, combined with the Rumanian base at Jassy, as the most suitable area for intervention. Their thinking resembled the policy of Berlin and Vienna, and the Central Empires were in a much stronger position in that area. The Allied plan was in the end frustrated by the German advance. Generals Berthelot and Niessel left Russia at the end of March 1918. After the loss of the Ukraine, the French and the British turned their attention to the north and the remote east of Russia. At Archangel and Murmansk in the north and at Vladivostok in the east, large stores of imported war material had accumulated. There were some 162,495 tons of war supplies, including large quantities of copper, aluminium and antimony, at Archangel; further north lay the newly constructed Murmansk port, together with a railway that ran due south until it joined the Petrograd–Vologda line. The railway was primitive, trains were arriving in Murmansk in the winter of 1917–18 at the rate of one a week, and the engineers looked forward without confidence to the effect of the spring thaw on the rails.

Toward the end of January 1918, the Soviet government dispatched an extraordinary commission to Archangel. It was to bring the local Soviet under Bolshevik control and arrange for the transfer of war materials. By late March, the stores at Archangel were being diminished at the rate of 3,000 tons a week. On 30 March, soon after Noulens arrived at Vologda and discussed the matter with Francis, the American Ambassador asked Robins in Moscow to find out what the plans of the Soviet government were in regard to the Archangel stores. The reply was that they were being moved to Moscow, the Urals and Siberia, and that the rumours of the Bolsheviks supplying Berlin with them were absurd. Though the reply was correct – war materials in Petrograd were being transferred, at the time, to similar destinations – it did not satisfy the Allied representatives. When the American Ambassador finally recommended intervention in Russia on 2 May 1918, the Soviet treatment of the question of the Archangel stores was reported to have played an important part in his decision.[26]

In Murmansk, on the other hand, the situation favoured the Allies. The harbour was controlled by Rear-Admiral Kemp's flagship, HMS *Glory*, and two Royal Navy cruisers: the French heavy cruiser, *Amiral Aube*, joined them on 19 March. Aleksei Yuriev, an anarchist worker, and Yury Vesselago, who had been an *aide* to the Russian admiral in command of the district, were in charge of the local Soviet. The news of the renewal of the German advance, together with the fears of a German and Finnish attack, favoured co-operation between the Allied and the Soviet authorities. On 1 March 1918 the Murmansk Soviet telegraphed Petrograd that the renewed German attack gave grounds for anxiety; in the evening of the same day Trotsky replied:[27]

Resistance is possible and obligatory. Abandon nothing to the enemy. Evacuate everything that has any value; if this is impossible, destroy it. You must accept any and all assistance from the Allied missions and use every means to withstand the advances of the plunderers.

(Professor George Kennan's close analysis of that incident shows that the reply was drafted in the hours when Trotsky was under the mistaken impression that the Soviet delegation at Brest Litovsk had not succeeded in its attempt to capitulate by accepting all the German conditions.[28])

On 6 March 1918 Admiral Kemp sent a detachment of marines from his flagship on the invitation of the Murmansk Soviet; in April, an Allied commander was put in charge of an armoured train and of the security of the Kandalaksha area in the southern part of the Murmansk peninsula. In March and April the co-operation between the Soviet and the Allies went further than either Lenin or Trotsky had envisaged, and it disturbed the Germans. On 14 May 1918 Lenin said about the Murmansk question that it had been a source of great friction.

The British and French have raised claims concerning Murmansk because they have invested tens of millions on the construction of the port in order to secure their military supply line in the imperialist war against Germany. They have such a wonderful respect for neutrality that they make free use of everything that is not nailed down. And the fact that they have an armored vessel and we have nothing with which to drive it away serves as sufficient grounds for seizures. Now there is an external wrapping, a juridical expression, called into being by the international situation of the Soviet Republic, which postulates that no armed force of a warring power may enter neutral territory without being disarmed. The English landed their armed forces at Murmansk, and we had no possibility of preventing this by armed force. In consequence we find ourselves faced with demands bearing a character close to that of an ultimatum: if you cannot protect your neutrality, then we will fight on your territory.[29]

Pressure by Berlin on the Soviet government, as well as German submarine activity in the Barents Sea, led to the hardening of attitudes both in Moscow and in Paris. The importance of Murmansk emerged for the whole policy of intervention. On 2 May 1918, the Supreme War Council at Abbeville decided that all the Czechoslovak forces – they consisted of Czechs and Slovaks who lived in Russia and of prisoners of war; they were technically under the command of Masaryk's National Council in Paris – that had not passed the Urals on their way to Vladivostok should be dispatched, as fast as possible, to Archangel and Murmansk. They would wait there for their departure for the western front and, while waiting, they could be 'profitably employed in defending

THE GENTLEMEN NEGOTIATORS

Archangel and Murmansk and in guarding and protecting the
Murmansk railway'.[30]

At the same time the British military authorities decided to send
a small expeditionary force to the two ports. Its task was to train
and equip the Czechs, raise a local Russian force of some 30,000
troops, prevent the occupation of Murmansk by either Germans
or Finns, and pin down the German army in Finland as long as
possible. There were long-term plans for the expeditionary force
as well. It was eventually to join with the pro-Allied forces in
Siberia, and, according to the reminiscences of its commanding
officer, Major-General Maynard, it was 'to assist in opening up
a new front against Germany'. But Maynard added:[31]

> The expeditionary force was to consist of a meagre 600 men, almost
> all of whom would be of a physical category so low as to render them
> unfit for duty in France; whilst 400 Royal Marines, a few Royal
> Engineers, a battalion of Siberian infantry, and some French artillery
> would come under my command on arrival.

Although no Czechs ever arrived at Archangel or Murmansk, the
British scheme went ahead. On 24 May 1918, USS *Olympia*, an
American cruiser under the command of Captain Brion B. Bierer,
steamed into Murmansk harbour, with General Poole, the
commander-in-chief of the Murmansk operation, on board. On
11 June, 150 American marines landed in the north.

The Moscow Commissars also started taking a more active
interest in the situation in the north late in May. On 24 May, a
special Bolshevik representative arrived in Murmansk, a day after
Chicherin's telegram which spelled out the policy of the Moscow
government:[32]

> No local Soviet organization should appeal for aid to one of the
> imperialist coalitions against the other. In case of an offensive by the
> Germans or their allies we shall protest and resist to the limit of our
> strength. We shall likewise protest against the presence of the Allies at
> Murmansk.

Early in June 1918, a special Soviet detachment was sent to
Murmansk to bring the province back under the control of the
central government.

The promise of an American man-of-war for Murmansk had
been made late in April 1918 in order to demonstrate Allied unity.
No such unity in fact existed. Neither Washington nor the

Foreign Office in London were at first aware of the full implications and extent of the task undertaken by the War Office. Their
acquaintance with the scheme was of a remote, general nature.
After Lord Reading, the British Ambassador, had discussed
Allied policy in Russia with Lansing on 11 May 1918, Lansing
wrote:[33]

> I further told him that intervention at Murmansk and Archangel
> would receive far more favourable consideration on our part than
> intervention in Siberia, for the reason that we could understand the
> military advantage of the former but had been unable, thus far, to find
> any advantage in sending troops into Siberia.

When the President sanctioned American military participation in
the Murmansk operation, 'provided General Foch approved the
diversion of troops and the necessary shipping for that purpose
from those now going to France . . .'[34], he believed that it would
be welcome to the Bolsheviks and confined to combating the
German-Finnish threat. He was unconcerned about the telling
reference in Balfour's memorandum of 28 May 1918, which was
passed on to him by Lord Reading on the following day. It stated
that ' . . . it is of vital importance to us to retain Murmansk, if we
desire any possibility at all of entering Russia'.[35]

There existed another possibility in the extreme east of Russia,
on the Pacific seaboard, where the problem of defending the stores
of war material came up as well. Vladivostok was used mainly for
supplies coming into Russia from America and Japan, and it could
be used as a point of entry for troops from the two countries. In
that way the three cardinal problems of the intervention arose.
First, there was the question of the American attitude to intervention in Russia; second, and closely connected with the first, was
the problem of Japan's participation in it; finally, there was the
problem of the control of the vast territory of Siberia, and of the
Trans-Siberian Railway in particular.

The United States had been in the war for just over a year. The
country was remote from the battlefields and the reality of war
had hardly impinged on it. At the time of the German offensive
in March, they had some 370,000 troops in France (instead of the
planned 450,000) and only some of them were engaged in active
combat. Though the monthly contingent arriving in France rose
sharply from 48,227 men in February 1918 to 83,811 in March and

244,345 in May,[36] neither the Americans nor their government realized the seriousness of the overall military situation after Russia had left the war.

There was therefore little bitterness in Washington over the behaviour of the Soviet government; the Americans were unable to feel the shock of Russia's defection with the same intensity as their French or British allies. That does not mean that American representatives in Russia got on noticeably better with the Bolsheviks than the British, the French or the Italians. In one regard the Americans even improved on their allies. Their head of publicity in Russia, Edgar Sissons, had procured forged documents purporting to prove that the Bolsheviks were German agents. They were published as a pamphlet entitled *The German-Bolshevik Conspiracy* by the Washington Committee on Public Information in May 1918.

Nevertheless, the American Ambassador to Russia had not advocated intervention before the beginning of May 1918, and President Wilson never quite agreed with either Britain or France on the meaning of that policy. Moreover, he suspected the Japanese of wanting to establish their political and economic positions on the mainland of Asia; the British, the President thought, were interested in new ways of extending their influence toward the Middle East and countering the German and Turkish advance into Russia from the south-west; the French wanted to salvage their investments by unseating the Bolsheviks.[37]

On 12 March 1918 the French Ambassador to Washington addressed a note to the State Department, bringing intervention yet again to the attention of the Americans, hinting that the Japanese would intervene anyway, with or without the consent of the Allies.[38] On 16 March Lansing replied to the note, stating firmly that Washington was unable to change its attitude toward the question of intervention.[39] On the same day in London an Allied diplomatic conference decided that President Wilson should be approached again; Balfour did so two days later through the Ambassador, Lord Reading.

The situation in Russia was, the Ambassador told the President, extremely dangerous. There were no Russian armed forces; the country was full of hostile agencies and it could fall an easy prey to the enemy. Only an intervention, launched from the north and Siberia, could bring about an improvement in the situation, and only the Japanese had men and shipping to spare. They would intervene as the Russians' friends and mandatory of the Allies. But for such a step American support was necessary.[40] Again, Wilson's reply to Reading was: 'I have not changed my mind.'

Officially Wilson did not change his mind until late in May 1918. Together with his Secretary of State, the President went on maintaining that 'it would be a great error for any of the Allied nations to send troops into Russian territory'.[41] Like Balfour, Wilson had misgivings about the effect on the Russians of a Japanese intervention. But while Wilson was opposed to the whole idea, Balfour had hoped, in the middle of March, to put it into practice with the Bolsheviks' consent. The weeks passed, and the Bolsheviks had still not asked the Allies to come to Russia; the insistence by Paris and Rome – they worried less about antagonizing the Russians – as well as by London played a part in wearing down Wilson's resistance.

Some time in April, the President became interested in the situation in Siberia and Manchuria: on 23 April 1918, Lansing instructed the Ambassador to Paris that the State Department would prefer it if two small detachments of Belgian and Italian troops in the Far East remained where they were: 'The position of the United States Government was predicated upon the possibility of intervention in Siberia ...'[42] Five days later, on 28 April, when Lansing received Viscount Ishii, the Japanese Ambassador, he found it most gratifying that

the Japanese Government agree fully with our point of view and that they do not see at present the military compensation for the danger of inviting the Russian factions to resist intervention and of throwing them into the arms of Germany.[43]

Later on in the conversation Lansing, 'assuming the necessity or advisability of intervention', asked the Ambassador what the attitude of his government would be. The answer was that

the presence at least of troops of the United States, Japan and China would go far to remove the suspicion of the Russians as to the purpose of territorial conquest which might be inferred if Japan acted alone.

In the following days there were several inconclusive exchanges between Washington and Tokio on the subject; on 8 May 1918 Wilson asked Lansing what Ataman Semenov, a young Cossack captain in command of a unit then east of Lake Baikal, was 'accomplishing and whether there is any legitimate way in which we can assist'.[44] The President was then moving toward a position that his Allies had maintained for some time. In fact, though not quite in theory. They were unable to agree among themselves at the critical point of the war, unable to deal with the problem of a defenceless Russia. No political decision in regard to Siberia was made by Washington and the Allies in May, and their policy remained what it had always been, a matter of military improvisation.

When President Wilson inquired whether Semenov could be in any way assisted, the French, the Japanese and the English had been doing that for about three months. Toward the end of January 1918 an officer sent by Semenov arrived in Peking and came to see the British Military Attaché there.[45] Semenov was based on Hailar and at Manchuria, where the Chinese Eastern joined the Siberian Railway. His force was some 750 men strong and he proposed to increase it to 3,000 troops by enlisting officers and Cossacks. He planned to begin with a local action in the Transbaikal region, occupying Kaminskaya, a village at the junction of the Amur and Siberian railways, and go on then to Chita and Verkhneudinsk; he expected some resistance from about 900 railway workers, organized into a Red Guard unit and based on Chita. His long-term, more ambitious plan was to lead his force westward, taking Irkutsk and Krasnoyarsk on the way, uniting with the Cossacks under Dutov's command and ultimately joining Kaledin. Semenov was apparently prepared to place himself under the command of Brusilov or Kolchak. The Military Attaché in Peking liked what Semenov's emissary told him of his commander's plans because they were military rather than political, and had a limited and definite objective.

Semenov wanted Allied aid, money as well as arms and ammunition: early in February the Japanese promised to supply the latter.[46] On 4 February 1918, Balfour telegraphed the Ambassadors to Paris, Rome and Washington to inform the respective governments:[47]

it seems clearly advantageous to encourage any purely Russian movement which shows signs of energy and success. As any support to be effective must be immediate, H.M. Government have therefore authorized H.M. Minister at Peking to give assurances to Semenov of financial support and they are endeavouring through their Military

Attachés at Peking and Tokio to secure supplies of arms and ammunition for him. You should express earnest hope of H.M. Government that Government to which you are accredited will participate in this action and expenses entailed thereby.

Though Balfour soon had doubts on the policy of supporting Semenov and resuscitated an earlier plan for a purely Japanese action, it was impossible to reverse the process once it had been set in motion. Semenov came to Harbin and told the British Consul that he was glad of the offer of money – £10,000 a month had been allowed – but that he would rather have guns. The Japanese Consul took over the matter, promising a delivery in the first instance of 8 mountain guns, 2 field guns, 20 machine guns, 1,000 rifles and a million rounds of ammunition.[48] At the same time the Admiralty instructed the Captain of HMS *Suffolk* to let the Ussuri Cossacks know that Britain would welcome an action by them in conjunction with Semenov.

Semenov needed guns more than money and in that way came to see a lot of the Japanese. In the middle of March the first supplies reached Manchuria – 36 machine guns, 4 field guns, 500 rifles, as well as 22 Japanese gunners to service them. The rifles and 6 machine guns went to the Ussuri Cossacks and the rest of the equipment to Semenov.[49]

When Captain Porter, the British Assistant Military Attaché, left Peking to inspect Semenov's unit early in April he found that it was composed of just over 1,000 troops, 600 of them Chinese, some of whom were ex-bandits. He was favourably impressed by Semenov and thought the unit, considering its improvised nature, quite serviceable. The difficulty was, Captain Porter thought, that Semenov's force

does not at present rest on any solid foundation either as being openly supported by Allies or by any form of Russian government which enjoys general confidence. It is a Cossack organization strongly anti-Bolshevik and possibly anti-Socialist and is regarded by many Russians with suspicion as a force of bandits and as an instrument of imposing a reactionary regime.

It therefore seemed desirable that Semenov's position should be 'clearly defined and openly recognized by Allies without delay'.[50] Captain Porter feared that Semenov's troops would make a bad impression on the many local Social Revolutionaries, and he believed that this could be minimized by a

public announcement that Allied support will be given to Semenov's force provided that its employment be limited to put down disorder and fight Germans and that it is not used for political purposes.

He was, however, instructed by London:

Such a declaration as you suggest will scarcely destroy the impression, which from your telegram appears to be well-founded, that Semenov's movement is fundamentally anti-Bolshevik if not counter-revolutionary.[51]

It soon became apparent that Semenov was a freebooter who accepted French, British and Japanese support and who sometimes flattered the highest bidder by carrying out a few of his wishes. The Japanese set the pace. They wanted, as President Wilson suspected, to establish themselves on the mainland in Asia, and they were interested in the iron and wolfram mines in Siberia which would help them diminish their dependence on America for steel. By the middle of May Semenov had received some 700,000 roubles from the Japanese.[52] While continuing their subsidies to Semenov, the British military authorities began to suspect the Japanese and the uses they made of Semenov and his troops. In the middle of March, Colonel Wedgewood had reported from his Siberian mission that the Japanese would not let British howitzers get through to Semenov from China; early in April Captain Porter noticed that the Japanese were popular with Semenov's officers and that a certain Captain Kuroki enjoyed the commander's confidence.

Early in April 1918 Semenov began planning an offensive: when the British asked him to postpone it, he refused. Later in the month his troops were advancing fast into Siberia, with the Japanese and French Military Attachés accompanying them. On 2 May 1918 the British Military Attaché in Peking telegraphed London that he presumed that

monthly allowance to Semenov should be continued in spite of his having taken offensive. Is it desirable that Assistant Military Attaché at Manchurian station should enter Siberia in connexion with Semenov's advance? He states that French and Japanese officers are doing so.[53]

On the same day Balfour informed the Ambassadors in Paris and Tokio of the news of Semenov's advance, and added that

as long as we are negotiating with Trotsky with a view to persuade him to invite Allied intervention we feel it important to give him no pretext for charging us with attempts to bring about counter-revolutionary movements. We have accordingly taken steps to restrain Semenov from making a further advance and have informed Trotsky that if he does so, it will be on his own responsibility.[54]

Semenov took the chance and pressed his attack until he was stopped by the Bolshevik troops late in May. In the meanwhile, in London, the Director of Military Intelligence wrote a minute on 4 May concerning the movements of the Assistant Attaché in Manchuria: 'I think Denny should *not* go, at any rate until the Bolsheviks had refused our definite proposals for the intervention.'[55]

In Moscow the Allied activities in the Far East did not remain unnoticed. The Soviet leaders had taken an interest in Colonel Wedgewood's mission to Siberia and Vladivostok in March, and the press recorded his statement that the British government would support a Constituent Assembly, should it materialize. On 31 March 1918 Lockhart sent another urgent, despairing telegram to London:[56]

You have before you two choices. One is to adopt my policy which promises you in a short time recommencement of war on this front with aid of Japanese and American troops, the other is immediate occupation of Siberia by Japanese for what object is not quite clear.

Lockhart was afraid, and he let London know of his fears, that General Knox was still responsible for the strategy of the General Staff in regard to Russia. Lockhart thought that Knox's complete misunderstanding of the situation in the country was one of the chief reasons for Britain's failure in Russia before and after the revolution: 'I should be more than sorry if at this critical hour a man of Knox's hasty and changeable judgement should be considered a more reliable authority than myself.'

Lockhart's view of the situation was based, at least in one important regard, on completely different information than that of London or Paris. French and Japanese intelligence, together with the British consular service (especially when it drew on anti-Bolshevik Russian sources) kept their governments well supplied with reports on the activities of the German and Austrian prisoners of war in Siberia and the uses that Vienna and Berlin tried to make of them. Captain Hicks, on the other hand, one of Lockhart's assistants who knew Russia and the language well, was convinced:[57]

The whole question of activities of German war prisoners has been hopelessly exaggerated. There is no danger of Siberian lines being seized by war prisoners. Some Austrian socialists who have renounced their own government have been armed with a view to being employed against Semenoff whose forces are composed mainly of Chinese and who is being financed and supported by the Japanese. These Austrians are few in number and there are no German officers among them. The latter are kept under strict guard and Bolshevik authorities in Siberia are quite willing to meet any Allied wishes with regard to this question.

Toward the end of April, Hicks travelled as far as the Manchurian frontier, visiting Omsk, Krasnoyarsk, Irkutsk and Chita on the way. With all his diligence, he was unable to find more than 1,200 armed prisoners of war along the line.[58]

In the meanwhile, early in April, tension mounted all along the Siberian line. In Vladivostok, owing to the murder of two Japanese subjects, 200 Japanese marines descended on the mainland and were reinforced by 50 British troops. The news of Semenov's advance east of Lake Baikal reached Moscow soon after. In London, reading a telegram on the Bolshevik treatment of the Russian Volunteer Fleet, the Director of Military Intelligence noted:[59]

This is another question which cries aloud for a definite break with the Bolshevists and a determined stand by us for all anti-Bolshevist elements like the sailors of the fleet who in other circs could be a definite asset to us.

Bruce Lockhart nevertheless went on working in Moscow for an agreement, by the Bolsheviks, to intervention. On 10 April 1918 he complained:[60]

... the whole eastern question raised again in a still more serious form by news of Semenov's activities. Chicherin stated that he had received news that Semenov well supplied with artillery and Japanese gunners was marching not against Soviet troops but against Vladivostok with evident intention of joining the Japanese.

Lockhart's position in Moscow was becoming untenable. He worked mainly with Trotsky there who perhaps raised the British agent's hopes on major issues by appearing reasonable on minor ones. Had Trotsky himself believed in the possibility of Allied intervention with Soviet consent, such a policy would have proved unrealistic. It would have run counter to the way in which Lenin dealt with the double problem of the immediate German threat and Russia's weakness, by buying time with territory, and by being seen to observe the Brest Litovsk conditions. It would have suited the circumstances as ill as Trotsky's earlier views on the feasibility of a revolutionary war.

In any case Balfour was alone among the Allied politicians in believing that Soviet consent was necessary for the intervention. The only country capable of carrying it out – Japan – had refused to act as a mandatory for the Allies unless American request and support were forthcoming, and insisted on retaining freedom of action whenever its national interest required it. Such had been Tokio's policy since the Brest Litovsk crisis at the end of February, and the local and international situation, frustrated Lockhart's endeavours in Moscow. By the end of April he himself started abandoning his lonely pursuit.

By then the first millions of roubles had been disbursed by the Allies in support of the Bolsheviks' adversaries, and the limited military actions in northern Russia and the Far East had taken place. While the Allied military in Russia expected some political lead from their governments, the politicians preferred the soldiers to deal with the situation. Though such unchannelled fluidity was to nobody's liking, its alternative – a firm, overall political ruling backed by insufficient military means – would perhaps have been even less desirable. In the circumstances, it seems to have occurred to no one to leave Russia well alone.

At that point the Czechoslovak Legion came into play. Its 39,000 troops, most of them prisoners of war, had been recruited by Professor Masaryk, the chairman of the National Council, the exile organization. It had fought well in the Kerensky offensive in the summer of 1917, its discipline marking it off from the Russian troops no longer prepared to fight. It became technically a part of the French army by Masaryk's arrangement; at the time of the Bolshevik revolution it was stationed in the south Ukraine. When they were not directly affected, the Czechoslovak troops took little interest in Russian domestic affairs. Masaryk's order of 9 November 1917 reminded them that 'the Czechoslovak army cannot be employed in Russian internal conflicts, but only against Russia's external enemies'.[61] Such a ruling could be observed as long as the western Allies had no other plans for the Czechoslovak unit.

Lenin and his government, who wanted to see the last of the Czechs as soon as might be, welcomed the decision to have them transferred to the western front. They made one condition: the Czechs were to travel not as 'fighting units but merely as a group of free citizens, carrying a certain amount of weapons for self-protection against the counter-revolutionaries'.[62] For some time the truce between the Czechs and the Soviets was observed, and there were no differences between them on the interpretation of the clause concerning a 'certain amount of weapons'.

On the way to Vladivostok in April 1918, some units of the Legion were compelled to give up their machine guns while others surrendered all their rifles before they were allowed to go on: many of them were simply held up. Then, on 21 April 1918, after the Allied decision to re-route the Czech units west of the Urals to Archangel, Chicherin asked that the trains should be stopped. The Czechs refused to obey the re-routing order. They did not want to be split up, and some of them suspected a German-Bolshevik trap. In the following weeks, tension between the local Soviets and the Czech Legion increased fast; there was the additional friction between the Czechs and the Hungarian and German prisoners of war who were proceeding on the same line in the opposite direction. A few officers among the Czechs were impatient of negotiating with the Bolsheviks and maintained that the Legion could, if necessary, shoot its way through to Vladivostok. This is what happened at the end of May 1918, after Trotsky's order, of 25 May 1918, instructing the Soviets along the Siberian railway line to disarm and detrain the Czech forces.

The Czech uprising against the Bolsheviks suited the Allied authorities well. The Allies had wanted to make use of the Legion in Russia before the rising in May. We have seen the way in which the Czech units would have fitted into the Allied plans for north Russia. The idea of utilizing the Czechs in Siberia had been discussed by the English and the French, at the diplomatic and military level, before the Czech uprising.[63] The uprising itself was not the same thing for the Czechs and for their Allies. Whereas in Paris and London the conflict between the Bolsheviks and the Czechs was expected to involve the Czechs in the policy of intervention and tie them down in Russia, for the Czechs themselves the uprising was the only way they could see of getting out of Russia.[64]

Masaryk had set off from Moscow for the United States on 7 March 1918, shortly before the conclusion of the Brest Litovsk peace. He left behind him in Russia a few loose ends. His view that the Allies were committed to transferring the Legion to the western front proved unfounded. The two representatives in Russia of the Czechoslovak National Council were not up to dealing with the complex problems of seeing the Legion from the Ukraine across Siberia, and in the end political control passed into the hands of the military commanders. It was a voluntary unit, with its morale dependent to some extent on what the troops thought of the uses that were being made of them, and at a low ebb during the February and March retreat from the Ukraine. The Czechoslovak Legion became the centrepiece in the Allied policy of intervention in Russia as well as in the struggle of Czechoslovak exiles for political recognition by the western Powers.

The easy initial successes, and the later calls for assistance, of the Czech troops affected the political situation in Russia as well as the thinking on intervention in the Allied capitals. In Russia, whether controlled by the Soviets or not, the diverse anti-Bolshevik forces were reactivated. The attempts to unify, to form government organs, even the plan of Boris Savinkov, the terrorist, writer of fiction, and former Vice-Minister of War, to get under his control an area to the north-east of the capital, where the Czechs and the Allied units from the north were presumably to meet – all that activity was set off by the events along the Siberian railway. In Paris, Edvard Beneš, the former teacher who became the Secretary of the Czechoslovak National Council, knew that French and British thinking on the employment of the Legion in Russia did not quite coincide with Masaryk's. On 1 April 1918, while Masaryk was still on his way to the United States, Beneš received a communication from the French Military Attaché in London. It was very pessimistic about the possibility of transporting the Czechoslovak troops to Europe. Beneš's own comment on that document was that it 'is also of historical interest. It inaugurates our politically important negotiations about the army, which I used for our political recognition in France and England'.[65]

The Czechoslovak rising gave the French and British military plans their backbone. At the beginning of May 1918 Captain Garstin, another of Lockhart's assistants, had evolved a grand plan for intervention, together with his friends among the Russian officers. One force was to come down south from Archangel while the other was to cross Siberia from Vladivostok; they were to meet in the Vologda area, the seat of the Allied Embassies, which would in the meanwhile be occupied by Russian anti-Bolshevik forces. By the time the plan reached General Staff level the Czech revolt had taken place and the planning then incorporated the Legion as one of the most important components of the operation.[66]

In spite of the developments on the Siberian Railway, Paris and London found it hard to move the American government from its position on Siberia. A Japanese intervention, it maintained, would push the Russians into the German arms. By using strong pressure, however, the British secured, early in June, the President's support for an operation in northern Russia. The Czechs were still expected at Archangel: most of the war material had been moved away by the Soviets. The size of the American force requested by London went on being discussed in June; the President finally gave in because he felt that he had refused too many requests by his friends. On 4 September 1918, 4,500 American troops, under British command, landed at Archangel.

Unable to make any headway in Washington in regard to Siberia, the western Allies resumed their consultations with Tokio on that subject. The Czechs were being 'miraculously' effective against the Bolsheviks, and Semenov was not doing at all badly: it was felt that the Japanese forces would add coherence to the Siberian campaign. On 3 June 1918 the French, British and Italian Foreign Secretaries, meeting in Paris, decided to inquire from the Japanese whether they would be prepared to observe Russia's territorial integrity in the course of the campaign, whether they would keep out of Russian internal politics and whether they would advance to the west as far as possible.[67] The intervention was again made conditional on American consent.

The last question of how far the Japanese would be prepared to advance dominated the subsequent exchanges. The Japanese Foreign Minister maintained that operations beyond eastern Siberia would meet with the most extreme difficulties. When the Foreign Minister's communication reached London early in July, Balfour was away in Paris, and Lord Cecil, the Under Secretary in the Foreign Office, received the Japanese Ambassador. He indicated to Baron Chinda that if the Japanese forces advanced as far as Chelyabinsk in the Ural mountains, Britain and France would regard that as the most valuable form of assistance, but no matter if they found themselves unable to do so. It was another way of saying that London and Paris would welcome Japanese intervention on any terms.

In the end, the Czech troops in Siberia played the key role in the securing of America's consent. A month after the beginning of their uprising against the Bolsheviks, the units of the Legion were strung out along the Siberian railway from Penza to the Pacific, with a concentration of troops, almost a third of the total force, at Vladivostok. East of Lake Baikal the continuity of the Czech command of the railway was threatened by strong Bolshevik forces, together with armed prisoners of war. The morale of the troops varied from one place to another, and political control of them was difficult. The French and the British on the one hand, and the Americans on the other, did not see the situation of the Legion in the same way. Whereas the optimism in Paris and London in regard to the Czechs was still being maintained, the Americans tended to be deeply concerned with their fate. The two attitudes nevertheless produced the same result.

Masaryk was received by President Wilson on 19 June 1918. They got on well together: Masaryk was neither a businessman nor a representative of one of the Great Powers. Like Wilson, he was an academic who had gone into politics; he had an American wife, and knew the United States well. Wilson was at the time looking for a way which would strengthen the anti-German forces in Russia, and demonstrate American interest in Russia, without antagonizing the Russians. He distrusted French and British schemes, and did not want to commit himself to a military adventure.[68] He found in the Czechoslovak Legion the justification for giving his consent to an action in Siberia. On 29 June 1918 the Czechs occupied Vladivostok; on 6 July, at a conference at the White House with his military chiefs, the President decided that small American and Japanese forces were to enter Siberia.[69]

In military terms the decision to intervene on the Baltic coast and in Siberia brought about little change. Of the two British operations, 'Elope' – a mission to arm and train the Czechs who were expected to come to Archangel – never got off the ground. Operation 'Syren', consisting of one infantry company, one machine gun company, and one field company (less two sections) sailed for Russia on 18 June and arrived at Murmansk five days later under General Maynard's command. They were joined, on 26 July, by a small French unit – 22 officers and 849 other ranks – of the French Colonial Infantry. Three days before the Washington decision on Siberia, on 3 July, the Supreme War Council had approved the proposal of the British government to send 14,000 rifles to Vladivostok for the Czechs. A month later, a British battalion arrived there, and was followed by 1,500 Japanese on 11 August, and by the first American contingent four days later. By the time the main force of American troops descended at Archangel on 4 September 1918, the point of crisis on the western front had passed.

Three months earlier, the Supreme War Council had discussed intervention in Russia at Versailles, against the background noise of the German guns at the front line. There had been a sense of urgency about every decision taken. In any case, military action had anticipated political decision; the politicians were even less able to make up their minds than to provide the necessary material resources. For that failure, Paris and London blamed President Wilson, while he, in turn, never gave up suspecting his western European Allies. In Paris, there existed a semi-proprietary attitude to Russia, and the French government went on being interested in intervention longer than any other Allied Power, long after the first Russian ex-colonel purchased his taxi-cab in Paris. The intervention went on exercising fascination on the military with time on their hands after the end of the war. A writer at the General Staff put it this way:[70]

At the beginning of 1919 we thus have a possibility of a united action from the east and south-east against Bolshevism, while Allied occupation of the Northern Ports, of the Black Sea ports and Bessarabia, together with their control of the Baltic, closes most of the channels by which the flood of infection can reach Western Europe. If the Poles can establish and maintain their independence, it only remains to close the gap between their southern frontier and the northern corner of Rumania to complete the '*Cordon Sanitaire*', which will set a limit to Bolshevik expansion, and, by confining it to its own devastated districts, bring about its ultimate collapse.

A confusion in the political thinking on intervention, and a touch of feebleness in its military execution, have been commented on by historians. It has emerged, from their writing, as a wholly ineffectual enterprise. To set against this opinion, we have the contemporary opinion of the Chief of the Imperial General Staff, Sir Henry Wilson. Early in 1919, Wilson thought that better results could have been achieved had the Americans not been so obstinate but that otherwise the policy of intervention was strategically sound. Indeed, Wilson argued, the flow of German divisions from east to west came to a standstill during the critical months of June, July and August, and Hindenburg, when he asked for ten divisions to be sent him from Russia during that period, was told that he could not have a single one.[71] In those three months, immediately after the Czech rising in Siberia and before the launching of the Allied offensive in the Balkans, the level of German strength on the eastern front remained steady at 35 infantry divisions, while the Austrians withdrew four of their 18 infantry divisions. The threat, more than the reality, of Allied intervention kept the Central Powers' forces on the eastern front. They also had to police the vast areas of Russia – from Narva in the north down to the middle reaches of the river Don and down to Taganrog and Odessa in the south, including the Crimea – which they acquired after the conclusion of peace.

9 London

Strategy on the Continent before the war, the military plans of Germany and France alike, were dominated by the idea of a brief and decisive campaign, of the knock-out blow. The highly developed railway network made swift transfer of large contingents of troops possible: shortage of raw materials, especially in the case of Germany, made such strategy necessary. British strategic thinking, on the other hand, ran along the traditional lines of the long-haul campaign, in which the weight of the alliance as well as of naval power would, in time, make itself felt. Despite the fact that its value decreased because it no longer held the monopoly in easy mobility, the habit of thinking in terms of naval power gave the British war leaders an advantage over their enemies on the Continent.

They fought the war for the security and extension of the Empire. In 1904 the Committee on Imperial Defence put forward the view that the Empire was 'pre-eminently a great Naval, Indian and Colonial Power'.[1] Among the Imperial possessions, India was the most highly valued, and the Indian reservoir of manpower was a factor of key strategic importance. Roughly a half of the regular army was stationed there before the war, and the Indian Army, commanded by British officers, amounted to about a quarter of a million men. During the war, 1,440,437 volunteers passed through its ranks; eight divisions saw active service in Palestine and five in Mesopotamia, in addition to twelve Dominion divisions, ten of which fought in France and two in Palestine. Imperial considerations were uppermost in the deliberations of British politicians in the war, and some of them – Lord Curzon, Lord Milner and General Smuts were the best-known among them – were ready to consider German gains in Europe in exchange for the consolidation and expansion of British interests overseas.[2]

Britain's allies, and France in particular, involved her in a Continental war. Of the sixty-six British divisions serving overseas, fifty-four fought in France and three in Italy. Only three were stationed in India, and six fought in other theatres of war – in Palestine, Mesopotamia and Salonika. Though the ports on the other side of the Channel were Britain's last-ditch defence, the British lost some of their customary freedom of action through the 'parochiality of the western front'. The concentration on that front, together with the demands it made on English resources, put relations between London and Paris under a strain.

Early in the war an English diplomat had complained that though Britain was making the biggest financial contribution to the war effort, it had not enough control over its conduct. Indeed, having allies was expensive. While Russia remained in the war, it had received £586m. in loans from London. France borrowed £434m. during the war, Italy £412m. Together with smaller loans, the total sum disbursed by the British amounted to £1,825m. More than half of it was raised in America: it was assumed in London that the loans would be repaid after the war.[3]

The British strategy in the war aimed at the defence of the Empire and its lines of communication and, at the same time, it was limited by the demands of the western front. The dual nature of the war was reflected in the way the English looked at it. The Germans had committed atrocities, it was reported in the London press, in Belgium, and the British public readily believed that the German atrocities in Africa were even more brutal. In the same way, German *Mitteleuropa* plans had their concomitant in *Mittelafrika* ambitions – an empire, that is, stretching from the Atlantic to the Indian Ocean. The press and a few politicians took in earnest the announcement of Emil Zimmermann, a leading German journalist: 'We are fighting for a Central African Empire.' A disciple of Lord Milner and a Secretary to the War Cabinet, Leo Amery, wrote in April 1917 that the object of British policy could be defined by the word 'security', meaning the

continuous creation of new sources of power in new worlds oversea to redress the balance of the Old World which is the really characteristic feature of British policy, and accounts for the fact that an essentially defensive policy has led to the acquisition of immense Empire.

Amery went on to say that German policy, 'that of sea power and colonial expansion at the expense of the British Empire', was, for the time being, defeated.

But if Germany can recover her colonies, or even add to them as she hopes, by the annexation of Portuguese colonies, or by the control of the Congo, she will be able to renew it with far greater hopes of success. She will take effective military measures to make her colonies secure against conquest, and she will establish in each of them bases for submarines and raiders. A base in Duala in the Cameroons, commanding the routes to South America and South Africa; a base in East Africa, whose radius covered the entrance to the Red Sea and threatened all communications between India and South Africa; one or more bases in the Pacific—once they are well organized the next war with the British Empire could be undertaken under far more favourable conditions.[4]

Amery attributed to the Germans a way of thinking that was not theirs. Their operations outside Europe had a hasty, improvised quality about them and we have noted, in chapter 3, their optimistic expeditions in return for the commitment of insignificant military means. This was so not only in regard to their colonial and Middle Eastern strategy: the same deficiency marked the execution of their policy of unrestricted submarine warfare. In a similar way and for similar reasons, the war leaders in Berlin underestimated the military and economic potential of America. They did, however, as we have seen in chapter 5, show themselves open to other temptations. Amery's suspicions were misplaced. The vast undeveloped spaces in eastern Europe and in Russia, the economic resources of Rumania and the Ukraine came to rivet the attention of the Germans during the war, after their victory in the east. There they grasped for power and influence rather than on the oceans and the colonial territories. They did not make a bid for world power in the English sense: their expansion was confined within continental limits.

The reasons why Britain fought Germany were not the same reasons why Germany went to war. The Continental Powers clashed over the control of the Continent: the compelling motives of the British war leaders lay outside Europe. Yet each of the two countries was the other's Enemy No. 1, and the obstinacy of Anglo-German rivalry was the driving force behind the war.

It may be that Germany's claim to a place in the sun, and the way it was made, put an edge on English hostility. It may be that the new horizons where the white man could carry his burden gave the conflict an ominous, visionary quality. It is certain that the longer reach of the arms, especially of the submarine and the aeroplane, made every German colony, in the eyes of England, a menace. The nature of the conflict was reflected in its settlement. After Napoleon's defeat all France's former colonies were returned to her. A century later every German colony was taken away, including Togoland, the smallest colony they had.[5]

On 5 August 1914, the day after the British ultimatum to Berlin, the Prime Minister gave his consent to the formation of a joint committee which would recommend to the cabinet the best means of dealing with the German colonies. Lord Hankey, then Secretary to the Council of War, wrote:[6]

The Admiralty earnestly desired this, for their capture was an essential factor in the protection of our maritime communications. There were, in addition, political reasons. German East Africa was a menace to the British Colonies which surrounded it and German South West Africa was regarded by the Union Government as a threat to South Africa. . . . In the Far East, until the intervention of Japan on August 23rd, Tsingtau with the cruisers based thereon was a menace to our trade and to our position in the Far East generally. Even the German island possessions in the Pacific—New Guinea, Rabaul and Samoa—were possible *foci* of intelligence, so long as the battle cruisers *Scharnhorst* and *Gneisenau* remained at large in the Pacific.

The 'Offensive Sub-Committee', as it became known, advised the cabinet on the campaigns which eventually brought the German colonial empire under Allied control.

Lord Lansdowne's treaty with Japan of 1902 paid dividends twelve years later. The Royal Navy was able to assert its mastery over the seas with the Japanese navy helping in the Pacific. The 'yellow peril' with which the Kaiser frightened the Germans became, in the columns of *The Times*, 'a chivalrous and honourable people upholding the principles of civilization in the Far East'. By the end of the year 1914, the last remnants of Germany's power had disappeared from the Pacific. The New Zealanders took Samoa at the end of August; the Australians occupied German New Guinea a fortnight later. In October, the Japanese occupied the Marshalls and the Carolines; early in November they captured Kiaochow after a seven weeks' siege. Soon the remaining islands north of the equator were taken and the five German cruisers in the Pacific destroyed.

Nevertheless, those operations revealed the extent to which the Japanese navy was the dominant force in the Pacific. To the Australians the 'yellow peril' was a more immediate threat than the Germans. While Lewis Harcourt remained at the Colonial Office, he exerted himself to protect the Australian Dominions and strengthen British influence in the Pacific. When he left in May 1915, Sir Ronald Munro Ferguson, Governor General of Australia, carried on the work under Bonar Law. Like Harcourt, Ferguson thought that by yielding their share in the New Hebrides to the French the British could firmly establish a third Power in the Pacific and thereby end 'our tête-à-tête with Japan'.[7] Another way was to offer Samoa to the Americans, but then the English did not see eye to eye with their cousins in regard to colonies.

The problem of balancing the need for Japanese help with the fear of growing Japanese influence put the relations between London and Tokio under a strain. The Japanese wanted a lot and Britain, because of Australian and New Zealand interests, had little to offer; the bonds of sympathy and common interest were wearing thin in the war. In 1916, it was feared in London that Japan might change sides; the Foreign Office expert on Japan allowed:[8]

> The quarrel between Japan & Germany is not a deep one, & owing to present conditions in Europe, Germany is Japan's least dangerous competitor in the Far East today. Calculating that the present war will not leave Germany on the best of terms with any of the Allies with whom Japan herself is immediately concerned, the Govt. of Tokio may see an opportunity for an Alliance there which does not present itself elsewhere.

The battle of Jutland, the outcome of which was not quite decisive, apparently convinced the Japanese that the war was at last beginning to run in favour of the Allies. And the Foreign Secretary reassured the Japanese Ambassador to the Court of St James that

> if Japan did not pursue expansion in Europe, America, or Africa, the Powers who did expand in these Continents ought to be favourable to the expansion of Japanese influence and interest in the Far East.[9]

The German possessions in the Far East were trivial in comparison with those in Africa, where the main colonial clash of the war took place. In South Africa, the uneasy peace between the Afrikaner and English communities was broken when an Afrikaner officer, Colonel Maritz, defected to the Germans. His flight precipitated an Afrikaner rebellion, which caused deep concern in London. The Union Premier, Louis Botha, however, turned down a British offer of troops and, by the end of November 1914, had succeeded in bringing the situation under control. The rebel leaders were driven into German South West Africa, a desert territory larger than Germany and guarded by some 3,400 officers and troops. In January 1915 South Africans invaded the German colony, and in July the Governor and his force surrendered. On 10 July 1915 *The Times* commented: 'So ends with a rare dramatic fitness the history of this first of German colonies.'

The conquest of West Africa was even swifter. The two hundred Germans in Togoland surrendered to British and French forces at the end of August 1914, after having blown up the Kamina wireless station, one of the most powerful transmitters in the world. By a provisional British-French agreement the British kept the capital Lomé and the control of the railways, while the French received a territory with twice the population of the British. Duala, the capital and the biggest port in the Cameroons, fell in the following month. There were differences between the Foreign and the Colonial Offices on the treatment of the occupied territory in west Africa; in the summer of 1916 Grey explained his view of the situation to the Secretary for the Colonies:[10]

The war has to be regarded as a whole & the fact that we hold all German S.W. Africa & are in process of getting German E. Africa & have all German colonies in the Pacific South of Equator puts us in a weak position for bargaining about Cameroons & Togoland.

Early in 1916, when all the German colonies in west Africa were occupied, Grey had his own way, and almost the whole of the Cameroon territory was handed over to the French. The Foreign Secretary was assured by the French Ambassador that 'the French Colonial Party were very excited'. The civil servants in the Colonial Office, however, felt let down by their colleagues in the Foreign Office.

The eastern part of the African continent had always been

strategically more important for London than the western, and there were no differences between the two departments on the subject of German East Africa. The British wanted to get the whole colony under their control, and they were at first reluctant to ask for Belgian assistance from the Congo, to the north-west. The Tanga operations in November 1914, conducted largely by units of the Indian army, were a complete failure and the German commander, General von Lettow-Vorbeck, proved a formidable adversary. The difficulties connected with the operations in East Africa forced the hand of the British government, and Belgian assistance was requested. In the course of the offensive which General Smuts commanded in the spring of 1916, he inquired of the Chief of the Imperial Staff:[11]

> Must I assume that each Allied Power administers the enemy territory occupied by its army and that three different systems of administration will thus arise? Or will the Allied Governments arrange for the temporary administration of all conquered territory by the British Government?

There was nothing Smuts could do about the Belgians who were entrenched in the north-western part of the German colony by the summer of 1916. No agreement could be reached between the two governments, and the matter had to be held over until the peace conference. In the military sense, the situation in German East Africa also remained unresolved until the following year. Though the numerically superior British and Belgian troops were in control of the greater part of the colony, they were unable to force a decision on Lettow-Vorbeck's compact army.

With that exception, Germany's influence in Africa and the Far East had vanished by the end of the second year of the war. Apart from giving the Cameroons away to the French the British were not in a mood for making concessions. They looked forward to annexations in Africa. In its vital eastern part, German East Africa was to complete the 'chain of British possessions from the Cape to Cairo'.[12]

In the reply to President Wilson's inquiry, in December 1916, as to the aims of the Powers at war, German colonies were not mentioned at all. The reply, the first major diplomatic act of the new cabinet under Lloyd George, had a disturbing effect on public opinion in the southern Dominions, and the Colonial Secretary thought it necessary to make a public statement, on 31 January 1917, that the German colonies would never be returned. In the following month, when Japanese naval co-operation was more than ever necessary under the threat of unrestricted submarine warfare, London undertook, by a secret agreement, to support its Far Eastern ally's claims in the Chinese province of Shantung and to the Pacific islands north of the equator. In return, the Japanese government promised to support British claims to German possessions south of the equator, as well as naval assistance.

Time was then running out for secret agreements: the assault on traditional diplomacy was about to begin. Ideas of international control, open diplomacy and self-determination of nations became the common coins of the radical currency. The slogan, 'No annexations or indemnities', hinted that neither President Wilson nor the revolutionaries in Russia accepted the view that wars should be fought for territory.

The victorious colonial Powers faced a dilemma. In terms of the simplifications of the First World War, colonies could be neither annexed nor left in the charge of 'the barbaric Hun'. The radical publicists in London – J.A.Hobson, H.G.Wells, H.N.Brailsford, Sydney Webb, E.D.Morel among them – offered a solution. It was the idea of an international 'trusteeship': some 'supernational' authority was to administer not only the German but all the other European colonies. In spite of strong Tory opposition, and the fact that *The Times* welcomed 'British East Africa' into the Empire on 5 December 1917, when von Lettow's force was pushed back into Portuguese territory (a piece of bright news at a rather gloomy stage of the war), the various radical pressures made their impact at the government level in London. Philip Kerr, Lloyd George's private secretary, put his private views to Smuts in these words:[13]

It is absolutely fatal to suggest that the German colonies must be retained because they are essential to British communications. The U.S.A. won't look at that for a moment, for this argument leads us at once to the proposition that every coaling station and port in the world must belong to us for the same reason. Personally I am against handing back the colonies, but I am of this opinion because I am sure it is contrary to the best interests both of the inhabitants and of the world that they should be given back to a nation inspired by Prussian ideals.

The Colonial Secretary, Lord Curzon, knew that the Russians and the Americans had 'a very strong feeling against what is called "annexations" ', but that they, and many others at the end of the year 1917, failed to

appreciate the difference between annexing territory as a result of victory merely to punish your opponent, and 'the policy I advocate which is the retention of the Colonies in the interests of good government and the peace of the world'.[14]

Lord Curzon saw internationalization of colonies as a 'nursery of international quarrel, and the prelude to greater disaster';[15] later he put his views on self-determination this way: 'I am inclined to value the argument of self-determination because I believe that most of the people would determine in our favour . . .'[16]

In the fifth of his Fourteen Points President Wilson stated:

A free, open-minded, and absolutely impartial adjustment of all colonial claims based upon a strict observance of the principle that in determining all such questions of sovereignty the interests of the populations concerned must have equal weight with the equitable claims of the Government whose title is to be determined.

The President's enigmatic statement had been anticipated by Lloyd George in the speech of 5 January 1918, in which he announced that exploitation of colonial territories was wrong and that the principle of self-determination would be applied to German colonies. We have no proof that his attitude to that principle was different from Lord Curzon's.

The Colonial argument, between the Foreign and the Colonial Offices on what to hold, and between the conservative and radical publicists on how to hold it, went on until the end of the war. But it was becoming less and less relevant. The war had shown up certain weaknesses in the Empire. It appeared that the Dominions had their own interests to look after; that the Royal Navy could not control all the oceans at the same time; that it was no easy matter to protect too many extended channels of communication. It also emerged that continental military strength could either result in a stalemate – in the west – or achieve a high degree of mobility – on the eastern front. And in the strategic situation created by Russia's defection from the war, 'the essential interconnection' between the attitudes to the western and eastern fronts lay at the centre of the British strategic problem. The 'Eastern Committee' was appointed by Lloyd George in March 1918 to deal with it. Lord Curzon, Balfour, General Smuts, E. S. Montagu, the Secretary of State for India, and Sir Henry Wilson, the Chief of the Imperial Staff, served on the Committee, which spent much of its time discussing the Middle Eastern problem.

We have noted, in the second chapter, the extent to which the adherence of Turkey to the Central Powers in November 1914 isolated Russia from the outside world. It was a major diplomatic defeat for London; Palmerston's axiom that 'Turkey is as good a guardian of the route to India as any Arab would be', the policy of supporting the Ottoman Empire, no longer obtained. Apart from the obvious military threat to the Suez Canal, it was feared in London that Egypt would be disturbed and that war with the only independent Moslem state would strain the loyalty of India's Moslems. London reacted swiftly to the new strategic situation brought about by the defection of Turkey. The Royal Navy bombarded the Dardanelles forts; reinforcements were sent to Egypt; an expedition was dispatched to secure the head of the Persian Gulf. In addition Cyprus, on lease since the Congress of Berlin in 1878, was annexed the day war with Turkey broke out and, in December 1914, Egypt was made a British protectorate.

All the military measures were initially more or less effective, with the exception of the shelling of the Straits fortifications. The Turks were angered rather than frightened by it, and the Germans found out what they needed about the weaknesses in the Turkish defences. But naval operations in that area looked attractive from London. After the Russian request for a diversionary action which would ease pressure by the Turks in the Caucasus, the Gallipoli campaign was launched.* Though the two operations at the extreme ends of the Ottoman Empire, in Gallipoli and in Mesopotamia, ended in disaster at the end of the year 1915, they had been observed with interest in Paris and Petrograd. The annexation of Egypt had had the same effect. (Like the Austrians in regard to Bosnia-Herzegovina six years earlier, the British cabinet thought that the position of Egypt would not be materially altered by its annexations. They were wrong, at least so far as the attitude of other countries to the annexation went.) On 4 March 1915 the Russians staked their claim to Constantinople, in the view of the

* See above, pp. 65 f.

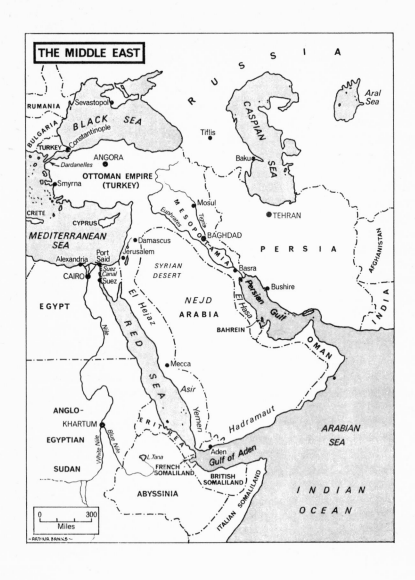

THE MIDDLE EAST

RUMANIA

BULGARIA

TURKEY

Sevastopol

BLACK SEA

Constantinople

R U S S I A

Tiflis

CASPIAN SEA

Baku

Aral Sea

Dardanelles

ANGORA

Smyrna

CRETE

CYPRUS

OTTOMAN EMPIRE
(TURKEY)

Mosul

Euphrates

MESOPOTAMIA

Tigris

BAGHDAD

TEHRAN

P E R S I A

AFGHANISTAN

MEDITERRANEAN
SEA

Alexandria

Port
Said

Damascus

Jerusalem

SYRIAN
DESERT

Basra

Persian Gulf

Bushire

I N D I A

CAIRO

Suez
Canal

Suez

NEJD

El Hejaz

ARABIA

El Hasa

BAHREIN

O M A N

E G Y P T

Nile

RED SEA

Mecca

Asir

Yemen

Hadramaut

ARABIAN
SEA

ANGLO-

KHARTUM

EGYPTIAN

SUDAN

White Nile

Blue Nile

ERITREA

L. Tana

FRENCH
SOMALILAND

Aden

Gulf of Aden

BRITISH
SOMALILAND

ITALIAN SOMALILAND

ABYSSINIA

I N D I A N

O C E A N

0   300

Miles

~ARTHUR BANKS~

British Foreign Secretary the 'biggest prize of the entire war'. The French, for their own part, put in their demand for Syria, including Palestine and extending to Damascus in the East.

Shortly after the outbreak of the war there was still no plan, in London, for the break-up of the Ottoman Empire; the habit of shoring it up had not yet been broken. Then the entry of Turkey into the war and the British military and political reactions to it, as well as the competition for the favours of Italy, led to the diplomatic undertakings, in the spring of 1915, in favour of Italy and Russia.* When Constantinople was promised to Russia, Sir Maurice de Bunsen's committee on Asiatic Turkey was established in April 1915. Its task was to clarify what the cabinet wanted: there had been no agreement among its members. Neither Asquith nor Grey wanted any more annexations; Winston Churchill thought that Mesopotamia, 'with or without Alexandretta', might be useful; Herbert Samuel was interested in the future of Palestine; Lord Kitchener's overriding interest was the land control of the route to India.[17]

The French were impatient to know what they would get in the Middle East. It was only after they had objected to the proposed British military action in Syria in the summer of 1915, and after the failure of the Gallipoli and Mesopotamian expeditions, that Sir Mark Sykes was appointed, in November 1915, to negotiate with the French. A young Member of Parliament whose second language was French, Sykes knew the Middle East well, and had written several accounts of his journeys there. A critic of middle-class democracy and its various aspects, such as industry, international finance and the profit motive, Sykes found his favourite ideals preserved intact in the Middle East. Under the name of 'Tory Democracy' there were among them the pastoral images of authority tempered by mercy, small intimate communities where everyone, lord or serf, knew his proper station. He had found no reason, before the war, to dissent from the traditional British policy of shoring up the Ottoman Empire. Its frontiers marked for him the limit to Russian ambition on the one side and to law and order on the other. In May 1913 he told the House of Commons: 'If we go back in history we find constant war in that part of the world which is the Ottoman Empire in Asia Minor.'[18] The Ottoman rule was for him the equivalent of British

* See above, chapters 1 & 2 *passim*.

administration elsewhere in the Middle East and run by men like Lord Cromer,

a big, solid, definite Englishman. That he spoke no Arabic and understood neither Arab nor fellah were probably the secrets of his success. A strong, dominant figure, dreaded by the inferior race whom he knew not and who knew not him.[19]

The Arabs were incapable of ruling themselves: the town Arabs presented to Sykes 'one of the most deplorable pictures one can see in the East', and he thought that it would be hard to find 'a more rapacious, greedy, ill-mannered set of brutes' than the bedouins. The Armenians were the lowest of the low: 'even Jews have their good points', Sykes recorded in one of his travel books, 'but Armenians have none.'[20]

Before the war Sir Mark Sykes had had too many opportunities to exercise his fluent pen: his conversion took a much shorter time. It may be traced to his disapproval of the Young Turks. They were corrupted by western influences and they, in turn, corrupted the state. Their joining the Central Powers gave the proof of their fall from grace.[21] The Arabs were now to take the lead in the return to the golden age of the Middle East. When he left London in June 1915, Sykes was entirely in sympathy with Lord Kitchener's pro-Arab policy. He was, however, left in charge of that part of Kitchener's plan which involved the securing of British influence in those Ottoman possessions strategically placed on the land route to India. He also had to pacify the French: M. Georges-Picot, the former Consul-General in Syria, was his opposite number in the negotiations.

The French historical memories in regard to Syria dated from the Crusades and the Frankish Kingdoms: France had always claimed to be the protector of Christians in the Ottoman Empire and especially in Syria. Napoleon's campaigns renewed that interest and the export of French civilization and capital in the second half of the nineteenth century confirmed it. In 1915 Paris pushed the British government hard to get its own way in that area. The principals – the Foreign Office and the French Ambassador to London – however soon dropped out of the picture, and Sykes and Picot were left on their own. They had their provisional agreement on the division of the spheres of influence ready in February 1916; in the following month, they travelled to Russia to confer with Sazonov, the Foreign Minister, and Grand Duke Nikolaevich in the Caucasus. They were ready to concur with the English and French proposals in exchange for an agreement to Russian claims in north-eastern Anatolia.

In Grey's letter to Paul Cambon, the French Ambassador to London, on 16 May 1916, and to the Russian Ambassador a week later, the points of agreement were set out.[22] The Russian sphere of interest was to include the Armenian and south Kurdish provinces beyond Trebizond in the west; France was to have Cilicia and Cappadocia with the provinces in the Armenian south as far as Aintab, and the Syrian littoral; England was assigned south Mesopotamia with Baghdad and the ports of Jaffa and Haifa. In the space left between the French and the British territories Arab sovereignty was to be exercised, and Palestine was to be placed under international administration, the details of which were to be settled later.

A Foreign Office memorandum after the war, commenting on the Sykes-Picot agreement, pointed out that 'Allied unity was at stake. That the Arrangement, in spite of grave and inevitable defects, carried the Allies over a difficult period cannot be denied.' In regard to the French claim to Syria it stated that it 'took no note of circumstances which had arisen in the Arab world in consequence of the war'.[23] Those circumstances were not due to the war alone. Soon after the Turks chose their side, pundits familiar with the Middle East began to consider the possibility of an Arab revolt against Ottoman rule. Lord Cromer mentioned it to Lord Crewe at the Turf Club; in Cairo, Ronald Storrs, Oriental Secretary to the British Agency in Egypt, and in the Sudan, Sir Reginald Wingate both had the same idea.[24] Lord Kitchener knew that the Arabs had no liking for the Young Turk regime and he had discussed the situation with a prominent Arab, Amir Abdullah, the son of the Sharif of Mecca. On 24 September 1914 Kitchener wrote to Ronald Storrs, asking him to send a messenger to Amir, to inquire about the attitude of the Arabs to a war between Britain and Turkey.

Several British officials in the Middle East thereafter kept in touch with the Arabs. In Khartum, Sir Reginald Wingate, the Governor-General of the Sudan, who had been responsible for intelligence about Arabia, was in contact with the Sharif of Mecca through a religious dignitary. Sir Henry McMahon, the High

Commissioner for Egypt, who had spent most of his working life in India, was, on his appointment to Cairo in 1914, 'slight, fair, very young for 52, quiet, friendly, agreeable, considerate and cautious'. Yet it was with his name that a major Anglo-Arab controversy was connected. It arose from his contacts with Mecca; McMahon was abruptly recalled and retired in 1916. Finally, there was Gilbert Clayton, who was appointed director of military intelligence in Cairo in 1914. He had served under Kitchener in the Nile expedition in 1898, was a friend of Wingate's and had a wide experience of Arab politics. His Arab bureau was responsible for guiding the Arab revolt throughout the war.

The correspondence with the Sharif had been opened by Kitchener on a note of high promise. In his second letter to Mecca, in November 1914, Kitchener wrote:[25]

Till now we have defended and befriended Islam in the person of the Turks. Henceforward it shall be that of the noble Arab. It may be that an Arab of true race will assume the Khalifate at Mecca or Medina, and so good may come by the help of God out of all the evil which is now occurring. It would be well if your Highness could convey to your followers and devotees who are found throughout the world in every country the good tidings of the freedom of the Arabs and the rising of the sun over Arabia.

Kitchener's gallant countermove to the German support of the Moslem Holy War was toned down in the subsequent exchanges. In October 1915 the Sharif complained to Sir Henry McMahon about the guarded language of his letters. In return, McMahon assured the Sharif that Britain would recognize the independence of the Arabs within the limits the Sharif had demanded. McMahon excluded the littoral lying to the west of the districts of Damascus, Homs, Hama and Aleppo, further areas where Britain had treaties with Arab chiefs, and hinted that Britain was not quite free to act because of France and its territorial interests.[26] The letter was dispatched three days after Grey made the opening move in the negotiations with the French, and a month before Sykes and Picot met for the first time. It differed from the subsequent agreement, and became a subject of controversy. The Sharif was never told of the extent to which London was prepared to meet French interests in Syria: nor was he aware of the promise made to the Russians of Constantinople. It may be that, had he known, he would have never joined the Allied side.

In India the Viceroy and his government at Simla were interested in making Mesopotamia a colony, and disapproved of supporting the Arabs against the Ottoman rule. The Indians, Moslems as well as non-Moslem nationalists, admired the Young Turks; the Viceroy was averse to the idea of stirring up trouble for the Caliph. India was therefore unco-operative about the Sharif revolt, which broke out in June 1916 (on the day Lord Kitchener went down on board HMS *Hampshire*) and which was supported, and to some extent directed, by the pro-Arab officials and soldiers in Cairo.

T.E.Lawrence became the best-known of them. His personality was more colourful than the personality of Sir Mark Sykes and so, often, was his thinking. Whereas Sykes appeared to seek some general rejuvenation through the Middle East, Lawrence pursued there a personal salvation. Like his friend and teacher, D.G. Hogarth, an archaeologist who became the head of the Arab bureau, Lawrence did not have to revise his views on the fate of the Ottoman Empire after the outbreak of the war.* Lawrence was convinced that the Ottoman Empire was both rotten and overextended, trying 'with diminished resources, to hold, on traditional terms, the whole Empire bequeathed to it'.[27] The Turks found no favour in Lawrence's eyes. All his actions in the war were directed toward the destruction of their Empire.

Lawrence had known the Middle East from archaeological expeditions before the war: being below the regulation height in 1914, he received a sedentary commission in Military Intelligence. When Turkey joined the Central Powers he went to Cairo. After two years at the Arab bureau and some three months after the outbreak of the Arab revolt, in October 1916, Ronald Storrs presented him to Sharif Abdullah, the second son of Husein, Grand Sharif of Mecca. He also obtained an introduction to Feisal, another of Husein's sons, whom Lawrence soon joined as an adviser. The Arabs taught Lawrence that 'no man could be their leader except he ate the ranks' food, wore their clothes, lived level with them, and yet appeared better in himself'.[28] He taught them what were the sensitive points of an initial civilization in the

* In an illuminating chapter on the formation of Lawrence's views, Elie Kedourie shows in his book *England and the Middle East*, pp. 90 ff. how Hogarth held two contradictory views of the Ottoman Empire. He suggested that it declined, on the one hand, because its attempt to reform on European lines was not pushed hard enough and, on the other hand, because the attempt was made at all.

desert, how to wreck trains, how to become 'an influence, . . . an idea, a thing invulnerable, intangible, without front or back, drifting about like gas, a vapour, blowing where we listed . . .' or, to put it briefly, how to 'tip and run'.

In May 1917 Lloyd George appointed General Allenby to the Egyptian command, telling him that he could have anything he wanted: new aeroplane squadrons were dispatched to Palestine. In return, the Prime Minister asked for Jerusalem as a Christmas present to the British people. In combination with Lawrence's Arab irregulars, Allenby's forces won memorable victories in the Middle East; Jerusalem, indeed, fell to the British in December 1917. The victories in the Middle East and in Africa brightened up a little a very bleak year.

Another, less noticed event lightened the load of obligations the cabinet in London carried. By opting out of the war, Russia gave up its claims to Constantinople. But just at the point when the situation in the Middle East looked like clearing up, another factor emerged on the scene. In a letter, of 2 November 1917, to Lord Rothschild, the banker who had founded a number of Jewish agricultural settlements in Palestine, Balfour wrote:[29]

His Majesty's Government view with favour the establishment in Palestine of a national home for the Jewish people, and will use their best endeavours to facilitate the achievement of this object, it being clearly understood that nothing shall be done which may prejudice the civil and religious rights of existing non-Jewish communities in Palestine, or the rights and political status enjoyed by Jews in any other country.

There was little public reaction to the promise made in Balfour's letter. *The Times* made no comment. A few questions were asked in the House of Commons the following week, but only to find out whether Paris was in agreement with the promise. Yet, in the words of a leading historian of the Middle East, the declaration by Balfour, 'measured by British interests alone, . . . was one of the greatest mistakes in our imperial history'.[30]

There were good reasons for making the declaration. As early as 1840, Palmerston had said:[31]

There exists at present, among the Jews dispersed over Europe, a strong notion that the time is approaching when their nation is to return to Palestine. . . . It is well known that the Jews of Europe possess great wealth, and it is manifest that any country in which a considerable number of them might choose to settle would derive great benefit from the riches they would bring into it.

The two ideas – that the Jews might return to their home in Palestine, and that they possessed great wealth and influence in Europe, not confined to any single European state – often occurred in British deliberations on the Palestine question in 1916–17, the two years before the Balfour declaration.

Palmerston had probably overestimated the desire of the Jews to return to Palestine. Zionism became an organized movement only toward the end of the century; at the outbreak of the war many influential Jews and their organizations opposed it. Vienna was its home. While the pogroms in the Tsarist Empire drove waves of Jewish emigration to the West, the growth of nationalism and political antisemitism in the Habsburg dominions gave rise to the Zionist movement. Its aim was to reverse the results of the diaspora and give the Jews their one national home; its founder, Theodor Herzl, a Viennese journalist, maintained that the Jewish problem would have to be raised to the international level before it could be solved. Though from its emergence the British government had taken an interest in the movement, its position in the years before the First World War was by no means a favourable one. Describing the situation at a Zionist congress, Chaim Weizmann said:[32]

After many years of striving the conviction was forced upon us that we stood before a blank wall, which it was impossible for us to surmount by ordinary political means.

That blank wall was the policy of protecting the Ottoman Empire.

After the outbreak of the war, responsibility for the conduct of the Zionist movement was divided between the old Berlin centre and the new headquarters based on Copenhagen. In Britain, Chaim Weizmann emerged as its leader. By origin a Russian Jew 'with the face and determination of Lenin', Weizmann had taught chemistry at Manchester University – in Balfour's constituency – before the war. He was busy on an Admiralty explosives contract in the first two years of the war when he came into contact with Lloyd George, then Minister of Munitions. 'Acetone converted me to Zionism', Lloyd George commented later. At the end of the year 1916 the demands made on Weizmann by his Admiralty work let up, and he began to give more of his time to politics. For Weizmann, the way to the Balfour Declaration led through some 2,000 interviews.[33] He convinced the people who were open to persuasion – Balfour and Mark Sykes were among them – that Zionist aims corresponded to British political and strategic interests.

When members of the War Cabinet met to consider the Zionist question on 4 October 1917 they had before them a formula which had been worked out by Milner and Amery, and which finally emerged, in a very similar form, as the Balfour Declaration. It stated that the government

views with favour the establishment in Palestine of a national home for the Jewish race and will use its best endeavours to facilitate the achievement of this object, it being clearly understood that nothing shall be done which may prejudice the civil and religious rights of existing non-Jewish communities in Palestine, or the rights and political status enjoyed in any other country by such Jews who are fully contented with their existing nationality.[34]

The formula aimed at satisfying the British Jews who held anti-Zionist views, without jeopardizing the pro-Arab policies which nourished the uprising against the Ottoman Empire. On 20 August 1917, General Clayton telegraphed Mark Sykes from Cairo:[35]

I am not sure that it is not as well to refrain from any public pronouncement just at present. It will not help matters if the Arabs . . . are given yet another bone of contention in the shape of Zionism in Palestine as against the interests of the Moslems resident there.

Edwin Montagu, the Secretary for India, who thought it difficult to find 'some convincing argument for not annexing all the territories in the world' into the British Empire,[36] found it impossible to agree with the Zionists. He thought that their plans threatened to undermine the position of the British Jews; his views were influential because he had direct access to the members of the War Cabinet. In a letter to Philip Kerr on 7 October 1917, Weizmann argued that the cabinet, and even Kerr himself, attached too much importance to the opinion of British Jewry:[37]

If it is a question of the Jews who have settled in Great Britain, well, the majority of such Jews are in favour of Zionism. If, on the other hand,

by British Jews one understands the minority of wealthy half-assimi-
lated Jews who have been in this country for the last three or four
generations, then of course it is true that these people are dead against
Zionism, but . . . Zionism is not meant for these people, who have cut
themselves adrift from Jewry; it is meant for those masses who have a
will to live a life of their own, and these masses have a right to claim
the recognition of Palestine as a Jewish National Home.

There existed no agreement, at the time, on the meaning of the
concept of 'National Home'. Mark Sykes, in his September 1917
memorandum, argued that it meant the 'recognition of the Jewish
inhabitants of Palestine as a national unit, federated with [?other]
national units in Palestine'.[38] In other words, he thought that the
Jews should not have their own state. At a conference Sykes had
had with the Zionists earlier in the year, Lord Rothschild said that
he was in full sympathy with 'the development of a Jewish state
under the British Crown'. Weizmann thought that a Jewish state
might eventually come into being, but added that 'States must be
built up slowly, gradually, systematically and patiently'.[39]

In the early autumn of 1917 pressure was growing on the War
Cabinet to take some positive action on behalf of the Zionists. The
Foreign Office believed that a German move was imminent, and
wanted to forestall Berlin; there was the precedent of the 'Two
Emperors' Manifesto' on Poland, published in November 1916.
Lord Curzon, by no means a supporter of the Zionist programme,
feared that 'delay may throw the Zionists into the hands of the
Germans'.[40] The pressure from newspapers came from two sides:
the British as well as the German. Early in September 1917 the
War Office monitoring service of the foreign press detected an
article in a Munich newspaper which showed interest in Zionism.
At the same time, Jewish newspapers in London were also under
the impression that Zionism was becoming a new and popular
theme in the German press. *The Times* commented that the
Germans wanted to prove that 'Palestine can only be regained for
Jewry under German auspices'.[41]

Such fears were unfounded. Since the beginning of the war, the
Germans had regarded the Zionist movement as part of their
policy of subversion directed against Tsarist Russia. 'The Committee for the Liberation of Jews in Russia' was established in
Berlin soon after the outbreak of war, and enjoyed the universal

support of German Jews, which cut across the Zionist and anti-Zionist divisions. It raised the hopes of the German government as to the potential of the third 'strongest movement against Tsarism'.[42] In Bucharest, some Jewish agents who were in touch with the German Consul promised to produce 'a rising in Bessarabia within ten days and later a general revolution against Russia'.[43]

The Germans succeeded in deepening the hostility between the Jews and Russian official circles during the war. In a conversation in March 1915 with Sazonov, the Foreign Minister, Sir George Buchanan was told that there was not the slightest doubt that a large number of the Russian Jews were in German pay and had acted as spies in the Polish campaign. Buchanan added:[44]

Nearly every Russian officer who returns from the front has stories to tell on the subject, and so far as I can form an opinion the case against the Jews is fully proved, though I cannot quote chapter and verse for it.

Berlin had made the Turks give away western Thrace for Bulgaria's entry into the war, and it could not press them to make any more sacrifices. The alliance with Turkey was more valuable for the German government than any assistance from the Jews could have been. It had no intention of making a promise to the Zionists of a new home for the Jews.

Apart from apprehension about the possibility of a German move, the War Cabinet believed that Zionist forces in Russia and in the United States could give the Allied cause valuable support. Sir Ronald Graham, the head of the Foreign Office Eastern Department, suggested that almost every Jew in Russia was a Zionist and a pro-German. If the Russian Jews could be convinced that the fulfilment of their ambitions depended on Allied support, an important section of the Russian people would swing behind the Allies.[45] Graham's memorandum, dated 24 October 1917, was meant to strengthen Balfour's hand in regard to the War Cabinet, where Curzon persisted in obstructing agreement. He argued that Palestine was a poor country without natural resources and with about half a million Arab inhabitants; that the Jews could perhaps be given equal religious and civil rights in Palestine, and arrangements for land purchase for the returning Jews could be made. But Curzon knew that such a policy was 'very widely removed from the romantic and idealistic aspirations of many of the Zionist leaders whose literature I have studied'.[46]

In spite of Curzon's opposition, the War Cabinet decided in favour of the declaration, on the lines of the Milner–Amery draft, on 31 October 1917. President Wilson, after some initial hesitations, had also agreed to it. Balfour argued his case on the basis of its merit as a propaganda move, directed at the Russian and American Jews. His views of the future development of Palestine had a certain tentative quality about them:[47]

As to the meaning of the words 'national home', to which the Zionists attach so much importance, he understood it to mean some form of British, American, or other protectorate, under which full facilities would be given to the Jews to work out their own salvation and to build up, by means of education, agriculture, and industry, a real centre of national culture and focus of national life. It did not necessarily involve the early establishment of an independent Jewish State, which was a matter for gradual development in accordance with the ordinary laws of political evolution.

On 2 November 1917 Balfour addressed his letter, containing the slightly altered Milner–Amery formula, to Lord Rothschild. It was made public a week later. The Bolshevik revolution had taken place in Russia two days before, finally freeing the British government from its undertaking to Petrograd in regard to Constantinople. Its place was now taken by the promise to the Jews of their national home. A political act without any binding or precise legal meaning, it indicated that the Ottoman state would be stripped of its eastern provinces, and threatened to clash with the recently aroused Arab nationalism. There existed sympathy in the cabinet for the aims of the Zionists, who succeeded in persuading the British that the realization of those aims would be in their best strategic interests. Like many other decisions in the concluding phase of the war, the decision to make and publish the Balfour Declaration was arrived at under the impression of Russia's failing strength.

It may be that the Middle Eastern 'side-shows', at any rate in 1917, made little difference to the overall strategic position of the Allies. Russia would have collapsed in any case, without the pressure from additional Turkish divisions. But the political significance of those operations was much greater. T.E.Lawrence's activities had introduced an element into the situation of making military trouble without taking much account of its political consequences. By giving both the Arabs and the Jews encouragement, the Allies made the final assault on the positions of the Ottoman Empire. Its dominions in Europe had all but vanished before the war; now it was time for the Turks to start shedding their possessions in Asia. For the time being, the war concealed the inconsistencies of the various commitments the Allies had undertaken in the Middle East.

Indications of the end of the Ottoman Empire did not counterbalance the departure of Russia from the war. At the turn of the year 1917–18, the mobilization of all available resources to meet the German onslaught occasioned the transformation of Allied policy toward the Habsburg monarchy. Though the Austrian and French Counts Revertera and Armand went on meeting well into the year 1918, the hopes of a separate peace between Austria-Hungary and the Allies, never very high, had disappeared soon after the Smuts–Mensdorff conversations in November 1917.

Among the Allies, Russia had been the Power most interested in the lands of the Habsburg Empire. The clash between Austria and Serbia, supported by Russia, in the Balkans, and between Austria and Russia alongside their common frontier in the north-east, had been the immediate cause of the war.* Soon after the outbreak of war Grand Duke Nikolai Nikolaevich, the Commander-in-Chief of the Russian army, issued a proclamation to the Slav peoples of the Habsburg Empire. It stated that the Tsar and his troops were fighting for the liberation of the Habsburg Slavs, and set off a witch-hunt by the Austro-Hungarian military

* Historians of the origins of the First World War have described, some of them in great detail, the Balkan rivalry between the two Powers. The enmity between them in the area where they came into direct contact has received less attention. Yet it seems to have been of great importance, especially in 1914. The loyalty to the Habsburg or Romanov Empires of the Ruthenes – now commonly described as the Ukrainians – was at stake. In 1913 and 1914 two trials of pro-Russian Ruthenes took place in Austria-Hungary. A few weeks before the Sarajevo assassination, Count Berchtold, the Austrian Foreign Minister, wrote a memorandum on the way the Ruthene problem affected the relations between the two countries; Count Tisza, the Hungarian Premier, had asked for a report on the same question. For the reasons set out above, the emergence of a Ukrainian nationality, separate from the Russian as well as the Polish, was supported by Vienna before and after the outbreak of the war. In that way, as we have seen, the Austrians and the Germans acquired, in the Ukrainian national movement, one of their most effective means of subverting Tsarist authority in the south-western margins of the Empire.

authorities which had an adverse effect on many Slav subjects of the monarchy.

There exists no evidence that the Tsarist government had made any decision on the future of the Habsburg monarchy. We know that late in November 1914, three Ministers who opposed the moderate policy of Sazonov in regard to eastern and central Europe filed in their minority report. The Ministers of the Interior, of Justice and of Education stated that if the war resulted only in the

unification of Poland, although under the sceptre of the Russian Sovereigns, without realizing our other historical tasks with a more direct bearing on the life of the Russian nation, such outcome, recalling the deplorable result of the Congress of Berlin, would arouse deep discontent and acute disappointment among the masses of the Russian people. . . . In regard to the order of importance for Russia of the war aims, we should remember

(1) to strengthen, as far as possible, the hard core of Russia [the authors used the description '*korenoi*', the adjective of 'root', and meant the purely Russian core of the state];

(2) to liberate, as far as possible, the other Slav nations from the domination of Germany and Austria-Hungary.[48]

The Grand Duke's proclamation to the Slav peoples of the Habsburg dominions was a propaganda move, without any political sanction. After Russia left the war, a similar situation arose, early in 1918, on the Italian front. Italy then began taking over Russia's role as the protector of the Habsburg Slavs, and the Italian front-line propaganda to the Austrian troops made references to the break-up of the Empire, and the liberation of the Slavs. In doing so it anticipated political decision by several months.

Over the centuries, the Habsburg dominion had acquired a certain territorial resilience. Its frontiers contracted here and pushed forward there; it constantly changed its shape, and no Habsburg ruler expected to look after exactly the same territory as his predecessor. The Habsburgs therefore never made common cause with any one people, and they required a flexible and strong civil service and army. They could have afforded to lose their Italian territories; the loss of their portion of Poland would have hurt, but would not have been fatal; even the South Slav territories could perhaps have been shed. The Habsburg power was based on the three capitals of Vienna, Budapest and Prague. Without the Austrian Germans, the Hungarians and the Czechs, the Empire could not have existed. The Czechs, with their economic strength and political grudges, were the odd men out in that arrangement.

Of the Habsburg Slavs, the Poles, divided as they were between Germany and Austria-Hungary on the one side of the battle-line and the Russians on the other, received the earliest recognition. In November 1916 the Two Emperors' Manifesto outlined the future of occupied Russian Poland; until the peace treaty with the Ukraine in March 1918 the Austrians and many Poles had hoped that Russian Poland would be linked with the Habsburg dynasty in some loose personal Union. In his 'peace without victory' speech in January 1917, President Wilson gave his blessing to the movement for Polish independence: a year later, in the Fourteen Points, he recognized the right of the Poles to a state of their own. The dilemma before the Poles themselves was whether to put their trust in the Allies or in the Central Powers. They resolved it by making no decision, and backing both sides: Roman Dmowski, Russia and the Allies; Józef Pilsudski, the Central Powers.

A month before the proclamation to the Slav peoples of the Habsburg state, the Grand Duke Nikolai Nikolaevich had addressed, on 16 August 1914, a manifesto to all the Poles. It was drafted by Sazonov: the promise of unity was followed by a steady stream of propaganda, a lot of it antisemitic. In the autumn of 1914, Austro-Hungarian troops on the Russian front found leaflets telling the Poles among them:[49]

> We turn to you as to our unfortunate brothers oppressed by the Germans. Why should you fight for the Austrians, who have delivered you as hostages to the Jews in Galicia? Why do you waste your blood for the Prussians, your contemptible oppressors and executioners of your children in Posen? The Germans and the Jews are your murderers and you humbly bow your head to them and are their slaves!

Until the outbreak of the revolution in Russia, the Allies regarded the Polish problem as one entirely within the sphere of competence of the government in Petrograd. The arrangement was continually being disturbed by the Poles in the west, especially by their organizations based on Paris and Lausanne. They were very active, talking to French deputies, writing articles in the French and Swiss newspapers, doing what they could to awaken public opinion. When Paléologue, the French Ambassador, mentioned the subject to Sazonov in April 1916, the result could not be described as a success:[50]

> Sazanov worked himself up into a great heat, as he sometimes does for a time, said that he had nothing to tell him as regards the intentions of the Russian Government, that the question was purely a Russian one, that he was afraid that the French were going to repeat their blunders under the second Empire, and that the Polish question, if unskilfully handled, was quite enough to wreck the Alliance. He also complained of the attitude of M. Berthelot at the Quai d'Orsay and of other Frenchmen in encouraging the Poles abroad.

When Sazonov calmed down, he explained to the French Ambassador that the divisions among the Poles themselves created additional difficulties, and that there was no point in talking about satisfying them unless one knew exactly whom one wanted to satisfy. The complete independence desired by the Poles in Paris and Lausanne did not appeal, according to Sazonov, to the moderate Poles. At another interview a few days later, the Foreign Minister asked Paléologue to tell his government to have nothing to do with the Poles. Sazonov said that he was prepared to discuss the subject privately: it was one which haunted him. He had lost the initiative as regards the Polish question. In 1915–16 Russian policy merely responded to the moves made by the Central Powers. Most of Poland was then under the occupation of Germany and Austria-Hungary, and Sazonov feared that the Germans would make some announcement, such as the declaration of the King of Saxony as King of Poland, which would cut the ground from under his feet.

Before the launching of the Brusilov offensive in the summer of 1916, Sazonov had a list drawn up of all the mistakes that the Russians had made during their first occupation of Galicia, and proposed that a Pole, Count Józef Potocki, be attached to General Brusilov's staff.[51] The manifesto to the Poles contemplated by Sazonov did not materialize before the offensive; after its conclusion – it had not been a great success – the German and Austrian negotiations on the future of Poland entered their last stage, and Sazonov's worst fears proved to be justified. On 5 November 1916 the Two Emperors' Manifesto was published. It promised the Poles an 'independent state with a hereditary monarchy and a constitutional form of government' though there was no 'more precise definition of the boundaries of the Polish Kingdom'. An army, built up with German and Austrian assistance, completed the undertakings the two Emperors were prepared to make to the Poles: they left it to the Governor General to sign the document.[52]

The proclamation marked a turning-point in the history of the Polish question. From then on Poland could not be restored to Russia or annexed by the Central Powers. Early in 1917, Roman Dmowski, the Polish journalist and former member of the Russian Duma who had worked unsuccessfully for a conciliation between the Russians and the Poles, became the head of the Polish National Committee in Paris; in June 1917, Poincaré authorized the establishment of a Polish army. As we have seen, President Wilson, following his 'peace without victory' speech, had called for complete independence of the Poles. The Russian revolutionaries were also free with their promises, but there was little they could do for the Poles. As in the previous two years, Polish statehood still lay within the gift of the Central Powers.

Nevertheless, the breakdown in Petrograd gave the Poles in the west a new lease of life. A week after the Bolshevik revolution and five days after the publication of the Balfour Declaration, on 15 November 1917, Count Sobanski, a representative of Roman Dmowski's Polish National Committee in Paris, sent a memorandum from his Committee to the Foreign Secretary. It reminded Balfour:[53]

> In spite of the successful military operations on the western front and in Asia Minor the cause of the Allies is threatened at present rather seriously
> (1) by the Italian defeat;
> (2) by the course of the events in Russia.
> These two failures show clearly the importance of the political offensive of Germany in her struggle against the Allies. The German success on the Italian front was due to a certain extent to the pacifist propaganda of the German agents in Italy and there are also the German political intrigues in Russia which brought about the disorganisation of her army and which drive her now towards peace.

The memorandum further stated that the weakness of the Allies in relation to the Central Powers lay above all in the fact that their struggle was confined to the military and economic spheres, leaving the political domain free for exploitation by their enemies.

The Allies 'up till now . . . have not attempted, except in Arabia, to attack the weak points of the enemy'.

While Germany was nationally homogeneous and therefore resilient to political assault, Austria-Hungary and Poland were wide open to it. The memorandum pointed out that the relations of the Germans to the Magyars on the one hand, and to the rest of the peoples of the Empire on the other, came under tremendous strain in the war.

In certain regions of the monarchy, i.e. Bohemia, there exists a state of fermentation which may turn out very easily into a revolution. If we bear in mind that in the Austro-Hungarian army, formed upon a territorial basis, regiments are to a great extent racially homogeneous, (which fact the authorities try to alternate in the time of war) we may easily imagine that revolutionary outburst among various nationalists of the Empire would find an inevitable echo in the army which might lead to its disorganisation.

The principal reason why that movement was kept in check was the belief that the Allies had no intention of breaking up the Habsburg Empire, and 'the political leaders of the oppressed nationalities find it impossible to start a determined struggle against the Austro-Hungarian Monarchy'. At the same time, after the disorganization of Russia by the revolution, the memorandum argued that the Polish problem became of the utmost importance:

After the war the only serious opponent to Germany in the East may be the Polish state if it is placed in conditions which will enable it to check the expansion of its Western neighbour. These conditions are:
(1) the overthrow of the German domination on the territory which separates Poland from the Baltic by the incorporation into Poland of all Polish territories which belong now to Germany, the mouth of the Vistula and the Niemen included;
(2) the overthrow of the German domination over the nationalities of Central Europe, which means the breaking up of the Austro-Hungarian Empire.

Dmowski's memorandum was followed by a spate of minutes in the Foreign Office. Since a separate peace had been attempted and remained unconcluded, the alternative policy was to support subversion of the established regime by revolutionary national agitation. The problem before the Allies was similar to that which had confronted the Germans in regard to Russia, before the revolution. Nevertheless, in the opinion of J.D.Gregory, who had served in Vienna and Bucharest before the war,

We may in fact have legitimate doubts as to how far all the peoples of the Dual Monarchy are thirsting for emancipation from the Habsburg yoke.

Gregory thought that, apart from Poland, if the Government were going to make any pronouncement at all on the subject of the Habsburg peoples, then

Bohemia with her 12,000,000 inhabitants must evidently receive individual attention, as her defection would be the most useful to us. But the question of Poland ought evidently to be kept distinct from that of the other nationalities and dealt with more solemnly and precisely, because it is clear that we are seriously threatened from that quarter, and that, if an Allied nationality policy elsewhere constitutes a political *offensive*, an Allied Polish policy is virtually a defensive policy, as events may so move that through lack of precaution we may find another and very inconvenient enemy in practice added to the rest.[54]

George Clerk, who later became the first Minister to the Czechoslovak Republic, wrote:

I would not quite accept all Mr Gregory's points, but I entirely agree with what I take to be his main contention, that the Allies should do all in their power to encourage the disruptive tendencies in the Austro-Hungarian Empire. I trust that the question will be seriously considered at the Paris conference.

Lord Hardinge, who had taken over from Sir Arthur Nicolson as the Permanent Under Secretary, ended the paper on a cautious note:

If we are to pursue a disruptive policy in Austria we may just as well advocate autonomy for Transylvania, Yugo-Slavia and Bohemia as well as the independence of Poland. But a declaration by all the Allies as to the independence of Poland would be most beneficial at present, as the situation there is not very favourable.

The line advocated by Hardinge was in fact taken at the Allied conference in Paris. The following text of a declaration was agreed to:[55]

The creation of a Poland, independent and indivisible, under such conditions as will ensure her free political and economic development, constitutes one of the conditions of a solid and just peace, and of the regime of right in Europe.

When it was communicated to Dmowski's National Committee in Paris, the Poles were very disappointed. There was no reference in the declaration to a 'united' Poland, and the words 'independent and indivisible' might apply to any Polish territory, however small; nor was there mention of free access to the sea. The Poles informed the Quai d'Orsay that they would prefer it if no declaration were published. An amended version of it was finally agreed on at the Allied conference at Versailles on 3 June 1918. The French supported those objections, and kept the slowly growing Polish unit – it amounted to barely 2,000 men in December 1917 – under their control. The financing of the Committee caused another difficulty. It had received money from various Polish organizations in Russia and America, but communications with Russia were cut, and the American Poles needed considerable funds for recruitment. It was suggested at the Paris conference that the Committee should be financed jointly by the Allies, at the rate of £12,000 a month.

The Allies, who had committed themselves to an offensive policy in regard to the Ottoman Empire in the same year, now took their first step in the same direction in central Europe. Russia, as we have seen, had taken up the weapon of national subversion of the Habsburg state early in the war, but Russia was no longer with the Allies. America had come into the war before Russia left it, but it had not the same direct interest in the territories of the Habsburg state. The United States became involved in the fate of the Dual Monarchy largely through its various ethnic groups and their organizations, which had kept up their contacts with the countries of their origin and had managed to preserve intact their national predilections. Britain and France, on the other hand, had nothing in common with the Habsburg state since the usual peacetime links of commerce and travel had snapped. Their territories marched nowhere together; their interests nowhere clashed. Since Britain had declared war on Austria-Hungary in 1914 as an afterthought, a week after the announcement of hostilities with Germany, no new reasons for animosity arose.

Alone among the Allied Powers, Italy had a direct interest in the territories of the Habsburg Empire. Earlier in the year, the Italian Prime Minister, Orlando, had obstructed the peace negotiations with Austria. At the end of the year, the fortunes of war

EUROPE IN THE SPRING 1918

the Entente Powers
the Central Powers
occupied by the Central Powers
neutral states
the battle fronts

• MOSCOW
(new capital from February 1918)

Note: Russia (including Finland and Ukraine) and Rumania concluded peace with the Central Powers early in 1918.

FINLAND

Helsingfors
(old capital)
Petrograd
Narva
Gulf of Finland

STOCKHOLM
Reval

Pskov

Riga
Libau

Memel

Königsberg
Kovno
Vilna

zig

Grodno
Minsk

Brest
Litovsk

Vistula

Warsaw

POLAND

Smolensk

R U S S I A

LINE AGREED BY TREATY SIGNED ON 3 MARCH 1918

ARMISTICE LINE OF 15 DECEMBER 1918

Kiev

Dnieper

U K R A I N E

Lemberg
(Lwow)

Dniester

Bratislava
(Pressburg)

Tisza

Budapest

Odessa

STRIA - HUNGARY
agreb
gram)

RUMANIA
BUCHAREST

B L A C K   S E A

BELGRADE

Danube

MONTE-
NEGRO

SERBIA

BULGARIA

SOFIA

Constantinople

ANGORA

ALBANIA

Salonika

GREECE

OTTOMAN EMPIRE
(TURKEY)

Brindisi

IONIAN
SEA

AEGEAN SEA

ATHENS

Smyrna

essina

RHODES

CYPRUS

SEA

CRETE

FINLAND

Gulf
of
thnia

had gone against the Italians. Late in October 1917, the Austrian and German offensive breached the Italian front in two places; Udine, the seat of the General Headquarters, was taken. At the turn of the year 1917–18, the military situation of the Allies, and especially of the Italians, opened up the way for the realization of the anti-Habsburg plans.

After three-and-a-half years' hostilities, national tensions in the Habsburg Empire were strained to breaking-point. The pre-war economic argument for its survival – a large market providing an economy of plenty – no longer held good. The Bolshevik revolutionary and pacifist agitations, as well as the doctrine of national self-determination which derived from its Russian and American sources, further weakened the hold of the dynasty on its peoples. Finally, to all the forces that made for the break-up of the Habsburg Empire, the sanction of the Allies was added.

In Rome and London, in Paris and Washington, expert advice given to the governments in the last year of the war – it had rarely been asked for, and never taken, before that – agreed on the one essential point. The Habsburg Empire had to die so that the Allies could win the war.

In London, there was to be found the most powerful indigenous lobby against the Habsburgs: Wickham Steed, the foreign editor of *The Times*, who worked for Lords Beaverbrook and Northcliffe in the Ministry of Information after its foundation in February 1918; R. W. Seton-Watson, employed in the Political Intelligence Department of the Foreign Office, a scholar who had travelled extensively in the Habsburg territories before the war; Lewis Namier, a naturalized Briton, by origin a Jew from a landed estate in Austrian Galicia, who had started working, early in the war, in Masterman's publicity office, a forerunner of the Ministry of Information. They all regarded Austria-Hungary as Britain's embittered enemy; Steed and Seton-Watson had strong, enthusiastic views on what the new, post-war Europe should look like. Namier had personal contacts with the Polish emigration; Steed and Seton-Watson specialized in the other exiles from the Habsburg Empire, especially the South Slavs and the Czechs.

By the end of 1917, the two historians, Seton-Watson and Namier, had established themselves among the politicians and diplomats. Seton-Watson's influence on the Workers' Educational Association was favourably commented on in the Foreign Office.

In a note for the Foreign Secretary drafted on 4 May 1915, Lord Eustace Percy pointed out that after the outbreak of the war there had existed 'some considerable danger of the development of anti-war feeling among working men', which was largely counteracted by the WEA.

In trying to explain the causes of the war, and justifying the war to its members, the W.E.A. not unnaturally came into close contact with Seton-Watson, and the W.E.A. 'groups' are largely feeding themselves on his works. The case of Belgium is easily grasped; the alliance with Russia is not; and Seton-Watson is about the only bridge which gets across the instinctive hostility to Russia felt by this class of Englishmen. He is therefore not only one of the few men who knows enough about south-eastern Europe to talk about it; he is also about the only man who can talk about it in a spirit friendly to Russia. The leaders of the W.E.A. have therefore been very dependent on his thought, and both they and the members at large have taken it for gospel.[56]

Lewis Namier, who in 1916 edited Austrian press summaries for the information of the government departments, inserted in one of his summaries in June 1916 the news, derived from Polish sources, that Dmowski had been negotiating with the Austrians in Switzerland. Namier had been authorized to do so by his chief, Charles Masterman, and had been attacked by the Russian Poles. The Foreign Secretary wrote to Sir George Buchanan in Petrograd, in case Namier had to travel to Russia in the future:[57]

Namier's information has been useful to us in many ways. . . . We naturally do not want to identify ourselves with anything hostile to Dmowski or take sides in these Polish squabbles at all, but as Namier wrote what he did write with the sanction of his immediate official superior it seems fair that he should be protected as far as possible from any consequences. . . .

Steed, Seton-Watson and Namier mediated between the anti-Habsburg exiles and the official quarters. In doing that they performed a necessary task. As late as 26 October 1917 Sir George Clerk wrote: 'A Mr Benes came to see me yesterday . . .'[58]

Steed's attitude to Austria-Hungary resembled in some ways that of Mark Sykes to the Ottoman Empire. Before the outbreak of the war he saw no reason why 'with moderate foresight on the part of the Dynasty, the Hapsburg Monarchy should not retain its rightful place in the European community'.[59] After the outbreak of the war, Steed and his friend, Seton-Watson, turned against the monarchy and worked, without sparing themselves, for its downfall. Their interest in it made them overestimate Austria-Hungary's importance. Steed in his memoirs wrote: 'From the outset, nay, even before the declaration of war, I was persuaded that Austria-Hungary would be the pivot of the struggle, . . .'[60] Namier never made that mistake. He did not lose sight of the order of priorities in the war, or of the fact that the hostility between Britain and Germany was its moving force. In that regard his advice was more consistent, and carried greater weight, than the views of either Steed or Seton-Watson.

Lewis Namier wrote his first book as a young man of twenty-seven; it was published in London in 1915 and introduced by H.A.L.Fisher, then Vice-Chancellor of the University of Sheffield. Its title was *Germany and Eastern Europe*. It presented Austria-Hungary as an appendage of Germany, as an instrument at the disposal of Berlin.

Austria-Hungary is Germany's Empire and comprises most of her non-German 'heritage'; it is therefore imperatively necessary for us to endeavour to break up its frame and organization. The Austro-Hungarian State gives Germany the power of disposing of the military resources of almost forty millions intensely hostile to the German nation.[61]

Such was the emphasis in Namier's argument, and it was one which was understood well in the Foreign Office.

Every time the diplomats addressed themselves to the problem of Austria-Hungary they had to decide whether that country was a check on the ambitions of Germany, or whether it was the instrument of those ambitions. In August 1916, when Sir Ralph Paget and Sir William Tyrrell wrote their memorandum on the territorial settlement in post-war Europe, they expressed the view that Austria-Hungary should disappear because it was a reservoir of military strength for Germany.[62] Throughout 1917, on the other hand, when the chances of a separate peace were thought to be high in London and Paris, the opposite view was taken by the diplomats. The Dual Monarchy was to become, as it had been on several occasions in the past, a counter-balance to Germany in central and eastern Europe. But as the chance of a separate peace diminished, that argument lost its force, until it was finally demolished by the Spa convention between Austria and Germany in May 1918. Austria then was on the way to becoming what the anti-Habsburg exiles and Namier had always declared it to be, a mere extension of Prussian power.

In Paris and Washington, politicians and diplomats were more directly exposed than in London to pressure from the exiles and their organizations. Paris was the home of Polish, South Slav and Czech national committees. Though the formation in Washington of such committees was never officially reported, the influence of the various ethnic groups and their organizations made itself felt there. When President Wilson brought the United States into the war he was open to the influence of the views propagated by the anti-Habsburg exiles. Long before the outbreak of the war and before he entered politics, he had noted that

the commanding difficulty of government throughout the whole course of Austro-Hungarian politics [had] been the variety of races embraced within the domain of the monarchy.[63]

He thought that

no lapse of time, no defeat of hopes, [was] sufficient to reconcile the Czechs of Bohemia to incorporation with Austria. Pride of race and the memories of a notable and distinguished history keep them always at odds with the Germans within their gates and with the government set over their heads. They desire at least the same degree of autonomy that has been granted to Hungary.[64]

And of Hungary Wilson thought that it 'has been a land of political liberties almost as long as England herself has been'.[65]

But it seemed that the peoples of central and eastern Europe met with Wilson's approval only so long as they stayed at home. Despite the links between Poland and America reaching far back into American history – Kościuszko was a military associate and personal friend of Washington; Count Pułaski, who was mortally wounded in the defence of Savannah, died on board the US brig *Wasp* – Wilson's views of the American Poles were not complimentary. In his *History of the American People*[66] Wilson had written:

. . . but now there came multitudes of men of lowest class from the south of Italy and men of the meaner sort out of Hungary and Poland, men out of the ranks where there was neither skill nor energy nor any initiative of quick intelligence; and they came in numbers which increased from year to year, as if the countries of the south of Europe were disburdening themselves of the more sordid and hapless elements of their population, . . .

Politics and the need for votes took away from Wilson the freedom of expression that had been his as an academic. Ten years later, during his presidential campaign in 1912, he wrote to a Polish-American leader:[67]

I yield to no one in my admiration of the Polish character. I have received the greatest stimulation from my reading of Polish history. If my terms were too sweeping they must be attributed to my clumsiness in expressing myself.

In the war, Wilson first interested himself in the Poles late in 1915, in connection with the problem of relief of starvation in eastern Europe. The President then appealed direct to the belligerent Powers to allow America to send relief. At the same time Ignacy Paderewski, the pianist, began to cultivate prominent Americans in the interest of Dmowski and the cause of Poland. He met and delighted Colonel House on 12 November 1915, and soon became 'colonel's pet'. House wrote many years later about the association with his Polish friend:[68]

It was solely through Paderewski that I became so deeply interested in the cause of Poland, and repeatedly passed upon the President Paderewski's views which I had made my own. That was the real influence that counted . . .

Some time in the summer of 1916, Paderewski was asked to dinner at the White House. He played Chopin's music after dinner; Poland was the sole subject of conversation. On 22 January 1917 Wilson said in his 'peace without victory' speech: 'Statesmen everywhere are agreed that there should be a united, independent and autonomous Poland.'[69]

Though, in the words of Lloyd George, 'nobody was bound by a speech', the other Slav peoples of the Habsburg Empire had, in terms of promises made to them, done much worse than the Poles. But, in the last six months of the war, in a situation of military crisis, promises were made which turned into hard political reality. The ground, as we have seen, had been prepared for them.

Late in the afternoon of 2 April 1918 the Director of Military Intelligence in London received a coded telegram from Steed, who was then at the Italian front, for Lord Northcliffe at the Ministry of Information. It read:[70]

Spent Sunday and yesterday morning with Lord Cavan who is ready to distribute all propaganda material available by patrols with rifle grenades, rockets and aeroplanes. It is distinctly understood that British troops will not engage in any direct conversations with enemy troops and that if eventually direct conversations with pro-Ally enemy troops become advisable they will be undertaken only under the supervision of competent Italian officers by Czech, Southern Slav and Polish soldiers now serving with Italian forces. Yesterday I made same arrangement pending arrival of new French Commander with principal Intelligence Officers of the French Forces. French officers eager to start propaganda as soon as possible and insist on necessity for high explosive methods. Enemy divisions opposite British Force contain large percentage of Transylvanian Rumanes and Carniola Slovenes. These would be susceptible to skilful propaganda. Opposite French troops is one purely Croat Division. We hope to seduce it. Most experienced Italian Intelligence Officers are confident that the Austro-Hungarian Army can be rapidly disintegrated if the Allies' appeals are sufficiently forceable [*passage garbled:*? forcible]. They strongly urge expediency of allowing Polish Czech-Slovak and Southern Slav National Committees to proclaim the independence of their respective territories on the understanding that Allied Governments would recognize such proclamations though they [? would not] pledge themselves to secure it. Possible then to assure Polish Czech Slovak, Southern Slav and Rumanes troops in the Austrian army that if they come over to the Allies they will be treated not as prisoners of war but as friends and allies and if they desire they will be allowed to fight on the Allied side for their own countries. In view of situation in France General Delmé-Radcliffe and French Intelligence Officers believe these methods highly desirable and that opinion is strongly shared by me. At this crisis of war Allies should apear [*sic*: ? spare] no efforts to break cohesion of enemy forces. Can you lay matter before the War Cabinet at once and secure prompt decision. I am convinced the French and Italian Governments would agree. At Congress of subject Austrian Hungarian races at Rome on April 8th proclamations could be made and immediately used on this front and in rear of Austrian Army as 'explosive' propaganda.

The reply from Northcliffe was sent through the Director of Military Intelligence on 4 April 1918:[71]

I am entirely in favour of an energetic propaganda at the Front.

I presume that the consent of the Italian Government and the French Government, especially the former, will be obtained to the particular statements contained in the propaganda.

As far as we are concerned, we should gladly recognise proclamations of independence made by subject nationalities in Austria-Hungary, though we could not pledge ourselves to securing it. Assurances to troops belonging to these nationalities that, in the event of their coming over to the Allies, they would be treated, not as prisoners-of-war, but as friends, and be allowed to fight on the Allied side, meet with our approval. If the French and Italian governments agree, you may carry out this policy at once.

As in the case of the intervention in Russia, soldiers were allowed to make decisions with implications reaching far beyond the military conduct of the war. A propaganda campaign was let loose on the Italian front which anticipated cabinet decision. Northcliffe's telegram of 4 April managed to be both enthusiastic and evasive. Eighteen days later, an agreement was signed in Rome on 22 April 1918 by Orlando and Štefánik, the Slovak astronomer and Vice-President of the Czechoslovak National Council, on the Czech army. (A similar agreement had been made in France on 16 December 1917.) Colonel Granville Baker, who saw Štefánik two days later, reported as follows:[72]

As Italy has recognized the Czechoslovak State by the signature of the above-mentioned convention, and it is hoped that the other Allied Powers will do likewise, it follows that their method of dealing with the Czecho-Slovak State in financial relations should be as between Governments, i.e. the Czechoslovak National Committee should manage its own finances and administer its own army and other State Departments (as it has already done in Russia) . . .

Colonel Baker added that recent intelligence reports from the Italian front showed an increase in the number of deserters from the Austro-Hungarian army, and that after a massive distribution of propaganda material within the last few days, strong enemy patrols were captured without any trouble. In the middle of May, Baker's high opinion of the effectiveness of anti-Habsburg propaganda on the Italian front was endorsed by General Delmé-Radcliffe, the head of the military mission in Italy. He argued that the internal situation in Austria, combined with the steps the

Czechs and the South Slavs were taking to secure their independence, would bring about the breakdown of the Habsburg army in the near future.

It is of the utmost importance that proper co-ordination of action with the Czecho-Slovak and Yugo-Slav elements in the Austrian army and in the interior of Austria should be discussed and agreed upon before serious operations begin. The Czechoslovak and Yugo-Slav National Committees are in touch with the political leaders in Bohemia and Croatia. The organisation for the political mobilization in the interior already exists and can be put into motion again for the purposes of deranging all movements and the economic life of the country and would thus constitute towards paralysing the action of the Austrian Army.[73]

If the Entente persisted in its equivocal tenderness toward the Habsburg Empire and failed to raise the confidence and patriotic spirit of the Czechs and South Slavs by making the appropriate public gestures, it might lose another great opportunity of inflicting a decisive blow on the Central Powers.

Three days later a draft was ready in the Foreign Office which recognized the National Council as the 'supreme organ of the Czecho-Slovak movement in the Allied countries', and the army as 'an organised unit operating in the Allied cause'. The Foreign Office opinion was that enough had been done for the Yugoslavs. Neither the independence of the Czechs and the Slovaks nor the position of their National Council as the government of the future state received mention. Lord Hardinge's view was that Britain had gone far enough; there was no point in adding to London's existing war obligations. It may be that the subtle distinctions that informed the minutes on that subject in the Foreign Office were obliterated in the propaganda on the Italian front. The thin end of the wedge was contained in the Foreign Secretary's note: 'The Czechs do not desire any promise or guarantee which they recognise to be useless. But we should take opportunities of speaking sympathetically of their national aspirations.'[74]

While the decision to intervene in Russia was being made in London and Paris, and after Austria-Hungary became more closely tied to Germany by the Spa convention of 8 May 1918, the Czech National Council achieved its objectives. Masaryk, we have noted in the preceding chapter, was received by President Wilson on 19 June; a month later, he put it thus to Lansing:[75]

You will understand our wish that the great American Republic would join the French Republic in recognising our National Council (in Paris) as the representative of the future Government of the Czecho-Slovak free State. I think that this recognition has become practically necessary: I dispose of three armies (Russia, France, and Italy), I am, as a wit said, the master of Siberia and half Russia, and yet I am in the United States as a private man.

A few days before, on 16 July 1918, Beneš, who was then in charge of the National Council in Paris, had received a telegram from Masaryk asking him to have the Czech provisional government proclaimed by the Czechoslovak army in France and Italy. Passing the message on to Wickham Steed, and asking him to find out whether Balfour would be prepared to recognize a government so constituted, Beneš returned, again and again, to the question of the Russian intervention:[76]

The position in Siberia gives us the right to do it. . . . I should like this to coincide with the Allied intervention in Siberia so that the proclamation of Czechoslovak independence may form part of the process of intervention in Siberia. . . . It is understood that our troops will remain in Siberia until the Allies are in a position to occupy the railway: eventually the greater part of them might remain in Siberia provisionally, in order to facilitate advance . . .

Though Beneš alleged that Masaryk's National Council was a 'delegation of the Provisional Government existing, albeit latently, at Prague', the demand that it should be recognized as the government went down badly in London. Sir William Tyrrell thought that it was fundamentally novel and likely to offend the Poles and the Yugoslavs; Lord Hardinge wrote: 'If we were convinced that the quasi-recognition of a Czech Govt in France would provoke a revolution in Bohemia it might be worth while to stretch a point in favour of Mr Benes' proposal'; Lewis Namier thought it wiser 'not in any way to forestall the verdict of the Czech revolution'. Namier, who regarded Masaryk as the finest intellect in Czech politics, believed that he 'would survive longest of all bourgeois politicians' because of his radicalism and outstanding moral character. But, Namier darkly hinted, the government in Prague would have to deal with problems on which there was no agreement among the Czechs.[77] In the end, on 9 August 1918, the British cabinet went further than any other Allied government in

making a promise to one of the Habsburg peoples, by recognizing
the Council as 'trustee for' the future Czechoslovak government.
The formula was invented by Wickham Steed. When Beneš asked
him what it meant he was told, 'Don't ask, my dear fellow. You
will never understand. "Trustee" is a mystical word. It is legal,
moral, metaphysical, anything you like, but it will do your
business for you.'[78]

In spite of all the promises and declarations of sympathy with
the Habsburg peoples, the Allies negotiated the armistice agreement, on 31 October 1918, with the Habsburg government. Beneš
protested and the Foreign Office apologized. On 4 November he
was for the first time invited to a conference of the heads of Allied
governments. The question was considered of using Prague
airfields for the bombardment of Berlin.[79]

While the Allies were trying to decide what they could do for
the Habsburg exiles, the military situation began to be resolved
in their favour. In 1917 the Central Powers had defeated Russia
and inflicted a severe blow on Italy. In 1918, they were themselves
in turn defeated by the western Powers. After the failure of
Ludendorff's fourth and final offensive against the French at
Rheims, Foch ordered a counter-attack on 18 July. It was successful, and in the weeks of August and September the French and
British troops beat the Germans back beyond their starting-point
in March 1918. But it was a long-neglected battlefield that precipitated a series of disasters which led to the defeat of the Central
Powers. Venizelos, the Greek Premier, had invited Allied troops
to Salonika in September 1915, when Bulgaria mobilized against
Serbia. The British offer of Cyprus did not tempt Greece into the
war, and Venizelos was forced to resign. After steady Allied
pressure King Constantine abdicated. Venizelos returned to
Athens on 26 June 1917; three days later Greece declared war on
the Central Powers. The Greek theatre of war remained a source
of irritation to the Allies until a year later, when Clemenceau
appointed General Franchet d'Esperey to the Greek command.
The offensive against Bulgaria, in which French, British, Greek
and Serb troops took part, was launched on 15 September 1918.
The Serbs overran Serbia and the Bulgarians were forced to conclude an armistice on 29 September. At the same time, General
Allenby rounded up the Turkish armies in Palestine and Syria.
The offensive in Bulgaria exposed Constantinople, and the Turks

sued for peace; the Austrians were forced to transfer troops from Italy to Bosnia. The Bulgarian surrender also convinced Ludendorff, who was hard pressed on the western front and without any forces to block the Bulgarian breach, that an armistice must be concluded. On 4 October 1918 the Germans asked President Wilson for an immediate armistice and peace based on his Fourteen Points.

It seems that Allied propaganda on the Italian front had some success: the approach of the forces under the command of General d'Esperey at the end of September and early in October was, however, more effective. The revolt against the Habsburg rule was set in motion during the last two weeks of October. In comparison with military success the operations of Northcliffe's department played a subordinate role. But they added another commitment to those accumulated by Britain during the war: they obliged the government to support self-determination of nations in general, and in particular the break-up of the Habsburg Empire. The government had no other policy to offer in place of that pursued on behalf of the Ministry of Information: there was in it no place for the subtlety and caution with which the diplomats moved. Within the concept of self-determination, the emphasis shifted from autonomy to complete independence; the question whether the competence of a national council was recognized in Allied countries alone mattered to a few people. Beneš, who was then in frequent touch with Prague, made political capital out of the promises by the Allies. Their effect was twofold. On the one hand they stiffened the resistance to the Habsburg rule and, on the other, greatly strengthened the position of Masaryk, Beneš and their National Council in regard to the local politicians in Prague.

The exiles and the forces they represented were, for their own part, used by the Allied governments to undermine the fighting strength of the Central Empires. They were a part of the great mobilization of forces that accompanied Russia's exit from the war. The Arabs in the Middle East, the Jews in Russia and America, the Slavs of the Habsburg Empire, as well as the anti-Bolshevik elements in Russia itself, were to fill the void left by Russia in the alliance.

When those policies were in the making the Allied governments first waited for the German offensive in the west, and then dealt with it. More than ever before, their attention was riveted on the western front. Elsewhere the military, or enthusiastic amateurs riding their particular hobby horses, were able to make decisions with far-reaching political implications. At the same time, expert advice to the governments was of uneven quality. The complications of encouraging both Arab and Jewish nationalism in the Middle East were ill understood. Sir Mark Sykes was enthusiastic for both causes. None of the experts on whose advice the Foreign Office drew pointed out that the national profile of the inhabitants in many parts of the Habsburg Empire was not as sharply defined as, say, that of the English and the French, and that, for better for worse, viable communities arose in central and eastern Europe out of the simple fact of people living in one place at the same time rather than because they belonged to one particular nation. Apart from one hint in a note by Lewis Namier, no one in the Foreign Office pointed out the social implications of the national upheaval in central and eastern Europe or the weakness of the middle classes who had the leadership of the national movement.

Political forces with a dynamic and will of their own were used to make up for a temporary military weakness. Thus their effect was greatly accelerated. Early in the war the Germans had tried to exploit national as well as social subversion in Russia. Their government had no sympathy with the aims of those movements. Now the Allied countries, with their extensive Empires, could only hope that the colonial peoples would decide in their favour.

On 4 October 1918 Berlin and Vienna addressed their notes to Washington after a period of intensive diplomatic activity. The pressure by Vienna on Berlin had been considerable. When the Emperor Karl visited Spa in May 1918, and bound the monarchy more closely to Germany, he asked that the two countries should take steps which would lead to the end of hostilities. The request was made at the wrong time; military advantage was still with Germany. The two Foreign Ministers, however, discussed the problem in August and September: early in September, the Secretary of State in the German Foreign Ministry, Admiral Paul von Hintze, visited Vienna in order to find out whether the two countries could agree on a common peace platform. Burián, the Austrian Foreign Minister, told the visitor that his country's economic situation was worse than hopeless, and that further conduct of the war was quite impossible. The Admiral, however, disagreed and told Burián that their two countries were in the same boat, and that they would sink or swim together. A few days after Hintze left Vienna, on 14 September 1918, Burián published his own appeal to the belligerent states, after pressure from the Emperor, whose patience was running out. Nobody took any notice.

At 7.30 in the evening of 25 September the Supreme Head-quarters of the Austrian armies at Baden received a telegram that Bulgaria was about to conclude a separate peace.[80] Two days later the Crown Council in Vienna discussed the political reform of the Empire, and decided to exert the strongest possible pressure on Berlin to conclude peace. On the following day Prince Hohenlohe, the Ambassador to Berlin, visited von Hintze, and told him that the situation was as bad as the Austrian authorities had painted it, but that they would do everything in their power to avert a catastrophe in the Balkans. Austria could last out, Hohenlohe thought, until December. But it would then take its last breath and die. On 29 September 1918, the Crown Council in Berlin decided, on Ludendorff's insistence, that the Central Powers should turn to President Wilson with a request for an armistice.

When the request was made German armies were everywhere entrenched on foreign soil. There was doubt whether they could hold their positions. There were no troops to spare to go and cope with an emergency in the south-east. The Americans, on the other hand, would have found little difficulty in putting an army of five million men into the field in 1919. For three weeks, the Germans and the Americans negotiated on their own, until the Germans accepted the Fourteen Points on 23 October 1918. Neither the French nor the Italians were prepared to go so far: the French had reservations about compensation from Germany; the Italians had to be told that the provisions of the treaty of London had nothing to do with Germany; the English objected to the point concerning the freedom of the seas. Lloyd George said, 'The English people will not look at it. On this point the nation is absolutely solid.'[81]

President Wilson, having defined their aims for the Allies, proceeded to advise the Germans on how to get the armistice from the commanders at the front. On 7 November 1918 the German delegation crossed the front line. They had only one asset

on their side: the Allied fear of Bolshevism. Colonel House told
Lloyd George and Clemenceau of the 'danger of bringing about
a state of Bolshevism in Germany if the terms of the Armistice
were made too stiff, and the consequent danger to England,
France, and Italy'.[82] German troops were to remain on the eastern
front as long as the Allies needed them there, and the Germans
were allowed to keep an additional 5,000 machine guns. It was
not much. It marked the beginning of a new period of European
history.

Notes

Chapter 1: Rome

Page   Note
 1   1 Antonio Salandra, *Italy and the Great War: From Neutrality to
          Intervention*, London, 1932, p. 18
 2   2 FO800/64: Sir Edward Grey's private papers; private letter
          from Sir Rennell Rodd, 7.vii.1914
 2   3 *Mezhdunarodnya Otnoshenie*, series III, volume 4, document 32
 3   4 FO800/54: Bertie to Tyrrell, 22.vii.1914
 3   5 Salandra, *La Neutralità Italiana (1914): Ricordi e Pensieri*,
          Milan, 1928, p. 68
 3   6 Alfred Franzis Pribram, *The Secret Treaties of Austria-Hungary
          1879–1914*, vol. 1: Texts of the Treaties and Agreements,
          Cambridge, Mass., 1920, pp. 249, 251
 4   7 ibid., pp. 68–73
 5   8 Salandra, *Italy and the Great War*, p. 55
 6   9 Luigi Albertini, *The Origins of the War of 1914*, vol. 2, Oxford,
          1953, pp. 229–30
 6   10 ibid., pp. 238–9

Page Note
6   11 Albertini, op. cit., vol. 3, London, 1957, p. 300
8   12 Salandra, op. cit., p. 26
8   13 ibid., p. 144
8   14 Sir James Rennell Rodd, *Social and Diplomatic Memories (Third Series) 1902–1919*, London, 1925, p. 224
8   15 Salandra, op. cit., p. 11
9   16 G. P. Gooch, *Recent Revelations of European Diplomacy*, 4th edition, revised and enlarged, London, 1940, p. 249
9   17 Benedetto Croce, *A History of Italy 1871–1915*, Oxford, 1929, pp. 225–7
9   18 *The Statesman's Yearbook 1914*, p. 1026: the figures include estimates for ordinary and extraordinary expenditure.
10   19 cf. W. W. Gottlieb, *Studies in Secret Diplomacy during the First World War*, London, 1957, pp. 142 ff.
10   20 *Annual Register*, 1914, p. 299
11   21 Michael Boro Petrovich, 'The Italo–Yugoslav Boundary Question, 1914–1915', chapter 4 of Alexander Dallin *et al.*, *Russian Diplomacy and Eastern Europe 1914–1917*, New York, 1963, pp. 164 f.
13   22 *Mezhdunarodnya Otnoshenie*, series III, vol. 6, part 2, document 86
13   23 Salandra, *L'Intervento (1915): Ricordi e Pensieri*, Milan, 1930, pp. 27 f.; Petrovich, art. cit., p. 169
14   24 cf. Z. A. B. Zeman, *The Break-up of the Habsburg Empire 1914–1918: A Study in National and Social Revolution*, London, 1961, pp. 33 f.
15   25 Petrovich, art. cit., p. 172
19   26 Milada Paulová, *Jugoslavenski Odbor*, Zagreb, 1925, p. 54
20   27 Salandra, *Italy and the Great War*, p. 151
22   28 Hugo Hantsch, *Leopold Graf Berchtold: Grandseigneur und Staatsmann*, Graz, 1963, p. 28
22   29 ibid., p. 48
22   30 ibid., pp. 664 f.
23   31 ibid., p. 62
23   32 ibid., p. 714
24   33 ibid., pp. 657–9
25   34 Salandra, op. cit., p. 92
26   35 *AA*: 985OH/H315941: a private letter of 21.xii.1914
27   36 cf. Gottlieb, op. cit., p. 139
27   37 Hantsch, op. cit., p. 687
28   38 *Mezhdunarodnya Otnoshenie*, series III, vol. 7, part 2, document 479

Page Note
28   39 Prince von Bülow, *Memoirs III: 1909–1919*, London, 1932, p. 216
29   40 FO800/64: private letter from Sir Rennell Rodd to Sir Edward Grey, 3.i.1915
30   41 *Tribuna*, 2.ii.1915
30   42 Giovanni Giolitti, *Memoirs of my Life*, London/Sydney, 1923, p. 391
30   43 ibid., p. 388
30   44 von Bülow, op. cit., p. 165
31   45 cf. C. Avarna di Gualtieri, Il Carteggio Avarna–Bollati, in *Rivista Storica Italiana*, year lxi, vols II, III, IV; year lxii, vols. I, III; especially Bollati to Avarna, 12.i.1915
32   46 Hantsch, op. cit., pp. 717–20
33   47 ibid., p. 721
33   48 ibid., pp. 733, 734
34   49 Klaus Epstein, *Matthias Erzberger and the Dilemma of German Democracy*, Princeton, N.J., 1959, pp. 120 f.
35   50 ibid., p. 125
35   51 Hantsch, op. cit., p. 735
36   52 Epstein, op. cit., pp. 127 f.
37   53 Salandra, op. cit., p. 346
37   54 Epstein, op. cit., p. 133
39   55 FO800/64: private letter from Sir Rennell Rodd to Sir Edward Grey, 7.xii.1914
39   56 FO800/64: Foreign Office telegram to Rodd, 18.ix.1914
40   57 Gottlieb, op. cit., pp. 319 f.
41   58 Salandra, op. cit., p. 267
41   59 For the terms, see ibid., pp. 268–70
41   60 Henry Wickham Steed, *Through Thirty Years 1892–1922*, vol. 2, London, 1924, p. 66
41   61 Serge Sazonov, *Fateful Years 1909–1916*, London, 1928, p. 264
42   62 Petrovich, art. cit., p. 182
42   63 Salandra, *L'Intervento*, pp. 167 f.; Petrovich, art. cit., p. 183
43   64 FO800/64
44   65 British White Paper, Misc. no. 7, 1920, Cmd 671
45   66 cf. Gottlieb, op. cit., p. 358
46   67 Salandra, *Italy and the Great War*, p. 309
46   68 G. M. Trevelyan, *Scenes from Italy's War*, London, 1919, p. 20
47   69 cf. Gottlieb, op. cit., p. 360
47   70 FO800/64: private letter from Sir Rennell Rodd to Sir Edward Grey, 12.v.1915
48   71 Epstein, op. cit., p. 137

Chapter 2: Constantinople

Page	Note	
49	1	*FO*800/29: Sir Edward Grey's private papers
50	2	W. S. Churchill, *The World Crisis 1911–1914*, London, 1923, pp. 480 f.
51	3	*FO*800/29
52	4	*FO*800/79: letter from Sir Louis Mallet to Sir William Tyrrell, 16.x.1914
53	5	*FO*800/79
55	6	Henry Morgenthau, *Secrets of the Bosphorus*, London, 1918, p. 27
56	7	Albertini, op. cit., vol. 3, pp. 612 f.
57	8	ibid., p. 614
57	9	*HH*: a telephone message, 7.viii.1914; Krieg, 1914, 4b
57	10	*HH*: T572, 20.x.1914, from Vienna to Pallavicini
57	11	*HH*: T541, 7.ix.1914, from Vienna to Pallavicini
58	12	*HH*: T486, 14.ix.1914, from the Foreign Minister to Pallavicini

59   13   *HH*: report no. $\dfrac{57\text{A–B}}{\text{P}}$, 22.ix.1914

60   14   *HH*: report no. $\dfrac{62\text{A–G}}{\text{P}}$, 22.x.1914, from Pallavicini

60   15   *HH*: T574, 27.x.1914, Vienna to Graf Tarnowski in Sofia

61   16   *HH*: report no. $\dfrac{63\text{B}}{\text{P}}$, 29.x.1914, from Pallavicini

61   17   Morgenthau, op. cit., p. 108

62   18   *HH*: report no. $\dfrac{68\text{A–H}}{\text{P}}$ by Pallavicini, 19.xi.1914

63   19   Gerard E. Silberstein, 'The Central Powers and the Second Turkish Alliance, 1915', in *Slavic Review*, American Quarterly of Soviet and East European Studies, vol. xxiv, no. 1, March, 1965, p. 79

63   20   *AA*: T1262, 7.xi.1914, Wangenheim to Berlin; cf. Silberstein, art. cit., p. 81

64   21   Full text of treaty in Silberstein, art. cit., p. 86

66   22   *FO*800/74: telegram to Sir George Buchanan in Petrograd, 19.i.1915

66   23   *FO*800/74: telegram from Sir George Buchanan, 25.i.1915

67   24   cf. E. Adamov (ed.), *Die Europäischen Mächte und die Türkei während des Weltkrieges: Konstantinopel und die Meerengen*, 1930, vol. 2, document 2, p. 9

69   25   M. Paulová, *Dějiny Maffie*, p. 153

Page	Note	
69	26	cf. Gottlieb, op. cit., pp. 333, 97
69	27	Adamov (ed.), op. cit., vol. 2, document 53, p. 130
70	28	Gottlieb, op. cit., p. 98
71	29	Maurice Paléologue, *An Ambassador's Memoirs*, vol. 1, London, 1923, p. 297
71	30	Gottlieb, op. cit., p. 100; Raymond Poincaré, *Au Service de la France*, vol. 6, Paris, 1930, p. 94
72	31	James M. Potts, 'The Loss of Bulgaria', chapter 5 of Dallin *et al.*, op. cit., p. 194
73	32	R. W. Seton-Watson, 'William II's Balkan Policy', *Slavonic and East European Review*, vol. 7, June 1928, p. 20
73	33	*Mezhdunarodnya Otnoshenie*, series III, vol. 1, document 291
73	34	A. Savinsky, *Recollections of a Russian Diplomat*, London, 1927, p. 213; quoted by Potts, art. cit., p. 200, n. 22
75	35	The full text of the treaty is in Albertini, op. cit., vol. 3, p. 616.
75	36	Potts, art. cit., pp. 206 f.
76	37	*FO800/57*: Lord Crewe to Sir Francis Bertie in Paris, 1.vii.1915
76	38	Potts, art. cit., p. 212
76	39	*FO800/42*: memorandum by Hugh O'Beirne, 31.x.1915
76	40	ibid.
77	41	Viscount Grey of Fallodon, *Twenty-five Years 1892–1916*, London, 1925, vol. 2, p. 198
77	42	*Mezhdunarodnya Otnoshenie*, series III, vol. 7, part 2, document 744; cf. Potts, art. cit., pp. 224 f.
79	43	*FO800/42*: memorandum by Hugh O'Beirne, 31.x.1915
79	44	cf. Potts, art. cit., p. 232
79	45	Alfred J. Rieber, 'Russian Diplomacy and Rumania', chapter 6 of Dallin *et al.*, op. cit., p. 264
80	46	Albertini, op. cit., vol. 3, p. 552
80	47	ibid., p. 574
81	48	Rieber, art. cit., p. 271

Chapter 3 : Berlin

Page	Note	
83	1	André Scherer & Jacques Grunewald (eds), *L'Allemagne et les Problèmes de la Paix*, vol. 1, Paris, 1962, no. 13: Bethmann Hollweg to Zimmermann, 19.xi.1914
84	2	*AA*: AS2769 in WK 2 secr. vol. 1
84	3	Scherer & Grunewald, op. cit., vol. 1, p. 26
84	4	ibid., p. 28

Page	Note	
85	5	ibid., document 33
85	6	ibid., document 14
85	7	ibid., document 20
86	8	ibid., document 21
86	9	ibid., p. 32
86	10	ibid., p. 33
87	11	ibid., document 114
87	12	ibid., document 117: memorandum by General Conrad, 21.vii.1915
87	13	ibid., p. 143
88	14	ibid., document 119
88	15	ibid., documents 27, 47
89	16	*Die deutschen Dokumente zum Kriegsausbruch*, II, no. 401, pp. 130 ff.; quoted in Fritz Fischer, *Griff nach der Weltmacht: Die Kriegszielpolitik des kaiserlichen Deutschland 1914–18*, Düsseldorf, 1962, p. 134
89	17	cf. Fischer, op. cit., p. 133
90	18	ibid., p. 137
90	19	ibid., p. 142
94	20	cf. Fischer, op. cit., p. 168
95	21	Z. A. B. Zeman (ed.), *Germany and the Revolution in Russia 1915–1918: Documents from the Archives of the German Foreign Ministry*, London, 1958, no. 1
96	22	ibid., p. 144. The quotation comes from a memorandum by Helphand for the Foreign Ministry, written early in March 1915. It can be assumed that he used the same arguments in it as in his earlier conversations with the diplomats. For a detailed description of Helphand's views and his relations with the diplomats, see Z. A. B. Zeman & W. B. Scharlau, *The Merchant of Revolution: the Life of Alexander Israel Helphand (Parvus) 1867–1924*, London, 1965
97	23	cf. Fischer, op. cit., p. 176; *AA*, WK 11, adh. vol. 2
98	24	Zeman (ed.), op. cit., no. 5
99	25	Zeman & Scharlau, op. cit., p. 164
101	26	*AA*: Brockdorff-Rantzau to the Chancellor: report of 30.xi.1915, in WK, 11c. secr.
102	27	Zeman & Scharlau, op. cit., pp. 185–6
102	28	Scherer & Grunewald (eds), op. cit., document 200
103	29	ibid., document 202
103	30	ibid., document 203
104	31	ibid., document 214
104	32	ibid., pp. 290 f.

Page	Note	
105	33	ibid., document 243
105	34	ibid., document 239
105	35	ibid., document 253
106	36	ibid., document 272
107	37	*AA*: Russland no. 74, secr., vol. 2
108	38	Scherer & Grunewald (eds), op. cit., vol. 1, document 281
108	39	ibid., document 305
108	40	ibid., document 305, p. 432
109	41	ibid., document 314
109	42	ibid., document 315
109	43	ibid., document 316
109	44	ibid., document 350
111	45	ibid., document 377
111	46	ibid., document 384
112	47	ibid., document 283
113	48	ibid., document 306
116	49	ibid., document 415
116	50	Karl E. Birnbaum, *Peace Moves and U-Boat Warfare: A Study of Imperial Germany's Policy towards the United States April 18, 1916—January 9, 1917*, Stockholm/Uppsala, 1958, p. 239
116	51	cf. ibid., p. 330
116	52	cf. Arthur S. Link, *Wilson*, vol. 5: *Campaigns for Progressivism and Peace 1916–1917*, Princeton, N.J., 1965, p. 210
118	53	Scherer & Grunewald (eds), op. cit., vol. 1, document 432
118	54	ibid., document 430
119	55	Birnbaum, op. cit., p. 257
119	56	Scherer & Grunewald, op. cit., vol. 1, document 441
119	57	Birnbaum, op. cit., p. 287
120	58	Scherer & Grunewald, op. cit., vol. 1, document 457

Chapter 4: Vienna

Page	Note	
121	1	C. E. Callwell, *Field-Marshal Sir Henry Wilson: His Life and Diaries*, London, 1927, vol. 2, p. 19
121	2	25.xii.1915: Fischer, op. cit., p. 396
123	3	*HH*: PA 524; quoted in Fischer, op. cit., p. 416
126	4	Fischer, op. cit., p. 403
127	5	Miklós Komjáthy (ed.), *Protokolle des Gemeinsamen Ministerrates der Österreichisch-Ungarischen Monarchie (1914–1918)*, Budapest, 1966, pp. 441–52

Page	Note	
	Page	*Note*

128   6   James Brown Scott (ed.), *President Wilson's Foreign Policy: Messages, Addresses, Papers*, New York, 1918, p. 249

129   7   FO371/3134: letter to Balfour from Maurice Hankey, 14.v.1918, and the enclosed memorandum

129   8   FO371/3133: memorandum by Sir Francis Hopwood, 17.iii.1917

131   9   Robert A. Kann, 'Josef Maria Baerenreithers und Graf Ottokar Czernins fragmentarische Darstellung der Sixtus Affaire', *Mitteilungen des österreichischen Staatsarchivs*, Band 16, Wien, 1963

136   10   cf. *Deutsch-Österreichische Nachrichten*, Berlin, 15.viii.1919

136   11   This and the following quotations on the policy of the War Cabinet are contained in a memorandum on separate peace feelers with Austria, drafted by Hankey in May 1918: FO371/3134

141   12   cf. Hankey's memorandum: FO371/3134

146   13   Matthias Erzberger, *Erlebnisse im Weltkrieg*, Stuttgart/Berlin, 1920, p. 116

147   14   Ottokar Czernin, *In the World War*, London, 1919, pp. 146–50

147   15   For an analysis of the July 1917 crisis in Berlin over the Reichstag peace resolution, see Epstein, op. cit., chapters VIII–IX

150   16   ibid., p. 225

150   17   Czernin, op. cit., p. 164

151   18   FO371/2864; cf. the minutes made on 22.viii.1917

153   19   FO371/2864: report of General Smuts's mission: David Lloyd George, *The Truth about the Peace Treaties*, London, 1938, vol. 2, p. 2462

153   20   ibid., p. 2463

153   21   ibid., p. 2464

154   22   ibid., loc. cit.

154   23   ibid., p. 2466

154   24   ibid., p. 2467

155   25   ibid., p. 2468

156   26   ibid., p. 2470

157   27   ibid., p. 2473

157   28   ibid., p. 2474

158   29   ibid., pp. 2474 f.

158   30   ibid., p. 2475

158   31   ibid., pp. 2476 f.

159   32   ibid., p. 2477

159   33   ibid., p. 2479

Chapter 5: Washington

Page   Note
162   1 *The Times Literary Supplement*, 4.i.1957
162   2 *Dictionary of American Biography*, vol. 20, s.v. 'Wilson'
164   3 Arthur S. Link, *Wilson the Diplomatist: A Look at his Major Foreign Policies*, Baltimore, Md., 1957, p. 5
164   4 In an essay entitled 'Democracy and Efficiency', *Atlantic Monthly*, March 1901
165   5 Link, op. cit., pp. 15–18
165   6 Link, *Wilson*, vol. 5, p. viii
165   7 Letter to C. W. Eliot, 17.ix.1913: Link, *Wilson the Diplomatist*, p. 24
166   8 R.S.Baker, *Woodrow Wilson: Life and Letters*, vol. 5: *Neutrality 1914–1915*, London, 1935, p. 20
166   9 Barbara W. Tuchman, *The Zimmermann Telegram*, New York, 1966, pp. 10 f.
167   10 J.D.Squires, *British Propaganda at Home and in the United States from 1914 to 1917*, Cambridge, Mass., 1935, p. 29
168   11 FO800/95: memorandum of 10.vi.1916
168   12 Squires, op. cit., pp. 34 f.
169   13 Harold D. Lasswell, *Propaganda Technique in the World War*, London, 1938, p. 187
169   14 Squires, op. cit., pp. 43 f.
169   15 Gabriel Hanotaux, *Histoire illustrée de la guerre de 1914*, ix, Paris, 1919, p. 56
170   16 Raymond B. Fosdick, 'America at War', *Foreign Affairs*, An American Quarterly Review, New York, vol. 10, no. 2, January 1932, p. 322; quoted in Squires, op. cit., p. 67
171   17 John Moody, *The Masters of Capital: A Chronicle of Wall Street*, New Haven, Conn., 1919, p. 171
172   18 ibid., p. 170
173   19 H. Montgomery Hyde, *Lord Reading: The Life of Rufus Isaacs, First Marquess of Reading*, London, 1967, p. 187
173   20 Charles Callan Tansill, *America Goes to War*, Boston, 1938, p. 54
174   21 Moody, op. cit., p. 156
174   22 Tansill, op. cit., p. 62
175   23 FO800/94
176   24 FO800/94: memorandum by Lord Eustace Percy, 16.vii.1915
177   25 FR 1915, supplement 794–798: Secretary of State to the Ambassador to Vienna, 12.viii.1915; quoted by Tansill, op. cit., p. 60

Page	Note	
177	26	FR 1915, supplement 804
178	27	FO800/95: Grey to Crewe, 16.xi.1916
178	28	Charles Seymour, 'American Neutrality: The Experience of 1914–1917', *Foreign Affairs*, vol. 14, no. 1, October 1935, p. 29
178	29	FO800/55: Sir Edward Grey to Sir Francis Bertie, 27.x.1914
179	30	*Annual Register*, 1915, p. 9
179	31	FO800/94: memorandum by Lord Robert Cecil, 19.vii.1915
179	32	FO800/94: Edward Grey's minute of 19.vii.1915, printed for the use of the Cabinet
180	33	FO800/95
180	34	FO800/95: Lord Eustace Percy's minute of 24.i.1916
181	35	Marion C. Siney, *The Allied Blockade of Germany 1914–1916*, Ann Arbor, Mich., 1957, pp. 252 f.
181	36	Seymour, art. cit., p. 36
182	37	Speech at Canton, Ohio, 16.x.1900
183	38	*The Intimate Papers of Colonel House*, vol. 2: *From Neutrality to War 1915–1917*, London, 1926, p. 167
183	39	*Philip Dru, Administrator: A Story of Tomorrow 1920–1935*, New York, 1919
184	40	House, *Intimate Papers*, vol. 2, p. 171
184	41	ibid., p. 176
184	42	ibid., loc. cit.
185	43	ibid., p. 181
185	44	*War Memoirs of David Lloyd George*, London, 1933, vol. 2, p. 687
185	45	House, *Intimate Papers*, vol. 2, p. 200
185	46	ibid., p. 201
186	47	Lloyd George, op. cit., vol. 2, p. 688
186	48	Grey, op. cit., vol. 2, p. 124
186	49	Link, *Wilson*, vol. 5, p. 209
187	50	Birnbaum, op. cit., p. 251
187	51	cf. Link, op. cit., vol. 5, p. 249
188	52	Scherer & Grunewald, op. cit., vol. 1, document 450
189	53	ibid., document 463, p. 669
189	54	ibid., loc. cit.
189	55	ibid., document 458
189	56	Link, op. cit., vol. 5, p. 257
190	57	ibid., p. 258
190	58	ibid., p. 260
191	59	ibid., p. 261
191	60	Scherer & Grunewald, op. cit., vol. 1, document 469

Page Note
191   61 Scott (ed.), op. cit., pp. 245 f.
192   62 ibid., pp. 248 f.
192   63 ibid., p. 249
193   64 ibid., p. 254
193   65 ibid., p. 255
193   66 ibid., p. 254
193   67 *The Times*, 23.i.1917
194   68 Scott (ed.), op. cit., p. 246
194   69 *The Edinburgh Review*, 1917, pp. 228 f.
195   70 Scherer & Grunewald, op. cit., vol. 1, document 472
196   71 ibid., document 474
196   72 ibid., document 475
196   73 Link, op. cit., vol. 5, pp. 277 f.
197   74 Scherer & Grunewald, op. cit., vol. 1, document 475. The
          telegram is printed in *Official German Documents*, II, 1047 f.
          and Professor Link uses that translation in vol. 5, pp. 278 f.
          of his biography of President Wilson. The earlier translation
          is done in a leisurely, literary style, and completely lacks the
          strong sense of urgency of the original. It contains a few
          mistakes, the most important being the omission of the
          word 'impossible' in the first sentence of the third paragraph
          (the official text reads: 'that our enemies had publicly
          announced their peace conditions').
198   75 Karl Helfferich, *Der Weltkrieg*, vol. 2: *Vom Kriegsausbruch bis
          zum uneingeschränkten U-Bootkrieg*, Berlin, 1919, p. 418
198   76 Admiral Georg Alexander von Müller, *Regierte der Kaiser?:
          Kriegstagebücher, Aufzeichnungen und Briefe 1914–1918*, Göttin-
          gen, 1959, p. 254: entry for 29.i.1917
199   77 Scherer & Grunewald, op. cit., vol. 1, document 476
199   78 ibid., documents 458, 463
200   79 cf. Link, op. cit., vol. 5, p. 290
201   80 For a detailed analysis of the President's thinking at the time,
          see Link, op. cit., pp. 298 f.
201   81 *Annual Register*, 1917, p. 312
201   82 FR 1917, supplement 1: Lansing's telegram to Page,
          8.ii.1917
202   83 FR 1917, supplement 1: Page to Lansing, 11.ii.1917
203   84 *Official German Documents*, II, 1337
203   85 Link, op. cit., vol. 5, pp. 345 f.
204   86 Tuchman, op. cit., pp. 184 f.
204   87 *Annual Register*, 1917, p. 9
205   88 Scott (ed.), op. cit., pp. 278 f.

Chapter 6: Petrograd

Page   *Note*
208   1 Alexis Goldenweiser, 'Paul Miliukov—Historian and States-
       man', *Russian Review*, vol. 16, no. 2, April 1957, p. 3
209   2 Major-General Sir Alfred Knox, K.C.B., C.M.G., *With the
       Russian Army 1914–1917*, 2 vols (continuously paged),
       London, 1921, vol. 2, p. 569
210   3 Robert Paul Browder & Alexander F. Kerensky (eds), *The
       Russian Provisional Government 1917*, Stanford, Cal., 1961,
       3 vols., vol. 2, pp. 920, 921
210   4 cf. Arno J. Mayer, *Wilson vs. Lenin: Political Origins of the New
       Diplomacy 1917–1918*, Cleveland/New York, 1964, 'His-
       torical and Political Framework' *passim* (there are no
       chapter numbers)
211   5 *Izvestia*, 31.iii.1917
212   6 id., 28.iii.1917
213   7 Browder & Kerensky (eds), op. cit., vol. 2, p. 909
216   8 Rex A. Wade, 'War, Peace and Foreign Policy during the
       Russian Provisional Government of 1917', University of
       Nebraska Ph.D thesis, 1963, pp. 108 ff.
218   9 Meriel Buchanan, *The Dissolution of an Empire*, London, 1932,
       pp. 196 f.
219   10 Paléologue, op. cit., vol. 3, p. 228
220   11 Lieutenant-General Nicholas N. Golovine, *The Russian Army
       in the World War*, New Haven, 1931, p. 254
221   12 Wade, op. cit., p. 193
222   13 Mary Agnes Hamilton, *Arthur Henderson: A Biography*, Lon-
       don, 1938, p. 132
223   14 *Izvestia*, 3.vi.1917
223   15 Wade, op. cit., p. 207
224   16 ibid., p. 212
225   17 cf. ibid., p. 180
226   18 Sir George Buchanan, *My Mission to Russia and Other Diplo-
       matic Memories*, 2 vols, London, 1923, vol. 2, p. 128
226   19 Foch, *Memoirs*, New York, 1931, p. 224
227   20 Wade, op. cit., p. 333
229   21 N. K. Krupskaya, *Reminiscences of Lenin*, Moscow, 1959, p. 335
229   22 ibid., p. 337
231   23 Fritz Platten, *Die Reise Lenins durch Deutschland im plombierten
       Wagen*, Berlin, 1924, p. 28
231   24 cf. Z.A.B.Zeman (ed.), *Germany and the Revolution in Russia*,
       no. 31

Page	Note	
231	25	ibid., no. 33
232	26	Platten, op. cit., p. 31
232	27	cf. J. Ley, 'A Memorable Day in April', *New Statesman*, 19.iv.1958
233	28	Zeman (ed.), op. cit., no. 37
233	29	ibid., no. 44
235	30	For an eyewitness account of Lenin's arrival in Petrograd, see N. N. Sukhanov, *The Russian Revolution 1917*, London, 1955, pp. 269 ff.
236	31	Platten, op. cit., pp. 7–13: 'Abschiedsbrief an die Schweizer Arbeiter'
238	32	Sukhanov, op. cit., p. 280
239	33	ibid., p. 287
239	34	Browder & Kerensky (eds), op. cit., vol. 3, no. 1039
239	35	*Rabochaya Gazeta*, 19.iv.1917
240	36	Browder & Kerensky (eds), op. cit., vol. 3, no. 1041

Chapter 7: Brest Litovsk

Page	Note	
244	1	For details of the estimated figures, see Golovin, op. cit., pp. 49, 90 f., 97
244	2	*Annual Register*, 1917, p. 21
245	3	Golovin, op. cit., pp. 249 f.; cf. Bernard Serrigny, *Réflexions sur l'art de la guerre*, Paris, 1921, p. 45
245	4	Golovin, op. cit., p. 251
247	5	cf. R. Gregor, 'Lenin's Foreign Policy 1917–1922', a Ph.D. thesis, London, 1966, p. 78
247	6	I. Deutscher, *The Prophet Armed, Trotsky: 1879–1921*, Oxford, 1954, p. 352
247	7	Sukhanov, op. cit., pp. 658 ff.
247	8	*Pravda*, 10.xi.1917
248	9	Zeman (ed.), op. cit., no. 73
249	10	cf. John W. Wheeler-Bennett, *Brest-Litovsk, the Forgotten Peace: March 1918*, London, 1938, p. 73
251	11	Sukhanov, op. cit., p. 225
252	12	Wheeler-Bennett, op. cit., p. 90
252	13	Jane Degras (ed.), *Soviet Documents on Foreign Policy*, vol. 1, Oxford, 1951, p. 18
253	14	ibid., p. 19

Page *Note*
255   15 Czernin, op. cit., p. 221
256   16 *Die Aufzeichnungen des Generalmajors Max Hoffmann*, Berlin, 1929, vol. 2, p. 200
256   17 Czernin, op. cit., p. 224
257   18 Bundesarchiv-Militärarchiv, Nachlass Haeften, quoted by Winfried Baumgart, *Deutsche Ostpolitik 1918: Von Brest-Litowsk bis zum Ende des Ersten Weltkrieges*, Vienna/Munich, 1966, p. 19
257   19 C.K.Cumming & Walter W. Pettit (eds), *Russian–American Relations, March 1917—March 1920: Documents and Papers*, New York, 1920, p. 64
257   20 Degras (ed.), op. cit., vol. 1, p. 25
257   21 ibid., p. 26
258   22 Deutscher, op. cit., p. 363, n. 1
260   23 J. P. Nettl, *Rosa Luxemburg*, London, 1966, vol. 2, p. 615
261   24 Julius Braunthal, *History of the International 1864–1914*, vol. 2, London, 1967, p. 102
262   25 ibid., p. 111
262   26 A. J. P. Taylor, *English History 1914–1945*, Oxford, 1965, pp. 96 f.
263   27 *Annual Register*, 1918, pp. 289 f.
266   28 Degras (ed.), op. cit., vol. 1, p. 35
266   29 *Protokoly CK RSDRP(b)*, Moscow, 1958, pp. 168 ff.
267   30 ibid., p. 173
267   31 cf. Deutscher, op. cit., pp. 371 f.
268   32 Zeman & Scharlau, op. cit., pp. 239–46
268   33 Deutscher, op. cit., pp. 375 f.
268   34 Zeman (ed.), op. cit., nos. 116, 117
269   35 John S. Reshetar, jun., *The Ukrainian Revolution 1917–1920: A Study in Nationalism*, Princeton, N.J., 1952, p. 107
269   36 Wheeler-Bennett, op. cit., p. 211
270   37 Theophil Hornykiewicz (ed.), *Ereignisse in der Ukraine 1914–1922*, Philadelphia, Pa., 1966–7, vol. 2, document 232
271   38 ibid., document 234
271   39 ibid., document 213
271   40 ibid., document 246
272   41 Baumgart, op. cit., p. 23
272   42 Deutscher, op. cit., p. 382
273   43 *Protokoly*, pp. 200 f.
273   44 In a telegram to the Chancellor; cf. Baumgart, op. cit., pp. 23 f.
273   45 Erich Ludendorff (ed.), *Urkunden der Obersten Heeresleitung über ihre Tätigkeit 1916/18*, Berlin, 1921, p. 472

Page Note
275 46 *Protokoly*, pp. 211 f.
276 47 Wheeler-Bennett, op. cit., pp. 260 f.
277 48 Degras (ed.), op. cit., vol. 1, p. 48
278 49 *HH*: T13246 from Hohenlohe in Berlin, 18.xii.1917
279 50 Baumgart, op. cit., p. 95
279 51 T4914 from Czernin in Bucharest, March 1918; PAX/151 in *HH*
279 52 *HH*: T4245 from Czernin, 14.iii.1918
280 53 Czernin, op. cit., p. 258
281 54 *HH*: Czernin's telegram from Sofia, no. 70
281 55 *HH*: report no. 18
283 56 *HH*: T169 from Pallavicini in Constantinople, 18.iii.1918
283 57 *HH*: report no. $\frac{29\text{A–E}}{\text{P}}$ from Pallavicini in Constantinople, 23.iii.1918
283 58 *HH*: report no. $\frac{\text{Z}37}{\text{A–B}}$ from Otto Czernin in Sofia, 19.iv.1918
283 59 *HH*: report no. $\frac{\text{Z}37}{\text{P–B}}$ from Otto Czernin in Sofia, 19.iv.1918
284 60 *HH*: T7140 from Burián at Vercioriva to Pallavicini in Constantinople, 27.iv.1918
284 61 *Neue Freie Presse*, 8.v.1918
284 62 ibid.

Chapter 8: Paris

Page Note
287 1 Olga Crisp, 'The Financial Aspect of the Franco-Russian Alliance, 1894–1914', London University Ph.D. thesis, 1954
288 2 ibid., p. 515
289 3 *Le Temps*, 26.v.1917; cf. A.C.E. Quainton, 'French Policy and the Russian Revolution 1917–1924', Oxford University B.Litt. thesis, 1958, p. 21
290 4 Paul Cambon, *Correspondance 1870–1914*, vol. 3: *1912–1924*, Paris, 1946, lettre à M. Fleuriau, 19.vi.1917
290 5 James Bunyan & H.H.Fisher (eds), *The Bolshevik Revolution 1917–1918: Documents and Materials*, Stanford, Cal., 1934, p. 44
291 6 *The Times*, 1.ii.1906
291 7 Joseph Noulens, *Mon Ambassade en Russie soviétique 1917–1919*, 2 vols, Paris, 1933, vol. 1, pp. 128 f.
291 8 Richard H. Ullman, *Intervention and the War (Anglo-Soviet*

Page	Note	
		Relations, 1917–1921: vol. 1), Princeton, N. J./London, 1961, p. 3
292	9	*WO*106/1470: a General Staff print of 28.ii.1919
292	10	cf. Quainton, op. cit., p. 80
293	11	Jacques Sadoul, *Notes sur la révolution bolchevique, octobre 1917—janvier 1919*, Paris, 1919, p. 184
293	12	Ullman, op. cit., p. 23
293	13	Lloyd George, *War Memoirs*, vol. 5, p. 2571
293	14	ibid., p. 2575
293	15	Ullman, op. cit., p. 58
294	16	George F. Kennan, *Russia Leaves the War* (*Soviet–American Relations*, vol. 1: 1917) (*Soviet–American Relations 1917–1920*, vol. 1), London, 1956, pp. 99 f.
294	17	Noulens, op. cit., vol. 2, p. 115; quoted by Ullman, op. cit., pp. 61 f.
295	18	Robert Bruce Lockhart, *Memoirs of a British Agent*, London, 1932, p. 347
295	19	Sadoul, op. cit., pp. 243 f.
296	20	*FR* 1918, Russia II, 583
297	21	Ullman, op. cit., pp. 47 f.
297	22	ibid., p. 52
298	23	Lockhart, op. cit., pp. 248 f.
298	24	Quainton, op. cit., p. 74
299	25	John Bradley, *Allied Intervention in Russia*, London, 1968, pp. 10 f.
300	26	George F. Kennan, *The Decision to Intervene* (*Soviet–American Relations 1917–1920*, vol. 2), London, 1958, pp. 247 f.
300	27	M.S.Kedrov, *Bez bolshevistskovo rukovodstva*, Leningrad, 1930, pp. 28 f.
301	28	Kennan, op. cit., p. 46
301	29	V. I. Lenin, *Sochinenya*, vol. 27, Moscow, 1950, p. 344; quoted by Kennan, op. cit., p. 259
302	30	Kennan, op. cit., p. 263
302	31	Major-General Sir C. Maynard, *The Murmansk Venture*, London, 1928, pp. 12 ff.
302	32	Kennan, op. cit., p. 273
303	33	*FR* 1918, Russia II, 160
303	34	ibid., p. 484
303	35	ibid., p. 476
304	36	cf. Ludendorff (ed.), op. cit., p. 364
304	37	cf. Kennan, op. cit., p. 82
304	38	*FR* 1918, Russia II, 75; cf. Kennan, op. cit., p. 89, n. 6

Page	Note	
Page	Note	
304	39	ibid., 80
305	40	Lloyd George, op. cit., vol. 6, pp. 3175–7
305	41	*New York Times*, 21.v.1918
305	42	FR 1918, Russia II, p. 135
305	43	ibid., p. 144
306	44	Kennan, op. cit., p. 356
306	45	WO106/1215: Military Attaché Peking to the Director of Military Intelligence, telegram of 28.i.1918; cf. Ullman, op. cit., pp. 98 f.
306	46	WO106/1215: Foreign Office telegram to Sir J. Jordan at Peking, 2.ii.1918
306	47	WO106/1215: telegram of 4.ii.1918
307	48	WO106/1215: telegram from Peking, 13.ii.1918
307	49	WO106/1215: telegram from Peking, 19.iii.1918
307	50	WO106/1215: telegram from Peking, 4.iv.1918
308	51	WO106/1215: Foreign Office telegram to Peking, 7.iv.1918
308	52	WO106/1215: telegram from Peking, 22.v.1918
308	53	WO106/1215: telegram from Peking, 2.v.1918
309	54	WO106/1215: Foreign Office telegram to Paris and Tokio, 2.v.1918
309	55	ibid.
309	56	WO106/1215: telegram from Lockhart in Moscow, 31.iii.1918
310	57	ibid.
310	58	WO106/1218: telegram from Lockhart in Moscow, 26.iv.1918; received in London on 3 May
310	59	WO106/1217: telegram from Tokio, 7.iv.1918
310	60	WO106/1215: telegram from Moscow, 10.iv.1918; received in London on 16 April
312	61	Zeman, *The Break-up of the Habsburg Empire*, p. 199
312	62	Edvard Beneš, *Svétova válka a naše revoluce (Dokumenty)*, vol. 3, Prague, 1935, p. 635
312	63	WO106/1218: a Note from General Spiers to the War Office, 25.v.1918
313	64	cf. Bradley, op. cit., p. 97
314	65	Beneš, op. cit., p. 636
314	66	cf. Ullman, op. cit., pp. 193 f.
314	67	ibid., p. 202
315	68	cf. Kennan, op. cit., p. 382
316	69	The President's decision is analysed in detail by Kennan, op. cit., pp. 381 ff. and Ullman, op. cit., pp. 213 ff.
316	70	WO106/1470: General Staff print, 28.ii.1919
317	71	ibid.

Chapter 9: London

Page Note
318 1 Lord Hankey, *The Supreme Command 1914–1918*, 2 vols, London, 1961, vol. 1, p. 46
318 2 W. R. Louis, *Great Britain and Germany's Lost Colonies 1914–1919*, Oxford, 1967, p. 2
319 3 A. J. P. Taylor, *English History 1914–1945*, p. 42
320 4 Louis, op. cit., pp. 3 f.
321 5 cf. ibid., p. 4
321 6 Hankey, op. cit., vol. i, p. 168
322 7 Louis, op. cit., p. 47
322 8 *FO371/2691*: minute by Alston of 30.iii.1916; quoted by Louis, op. cit., p. 48
322 9 Louis, op. cit., p. 49
323 10 ibid., p. 58
324 11 ibid., p. 65
324 12 ibid., p. 68
325 13 Smuts's Papers, 14.xii.1917; quoted by Louis, op. cit., p. 93
326 14 Louis, op. cit., pp. 93 f.
326 15 ibid., p. 94
326 16 ibid., p. 6
329 17 cf. Elizabeth Monroe, *Britain's Moment in the Middle East 1914–1956*, London, 1963, p. 29
329 18 Hansard, liii, 29 May 1913; cf. Elie Kedourie, *England and the Middle East: The Destruction of the Ottoman Empire 1914–1921*, London, 1956, p. 68
330 19 Shane Leslie, *Mark Sykes: His Life and Letters*, London, 1923, p. 191
330 20 Kedourie, op. cit., p. 69
330 21 ibid., pp. 78 f.
331 22 J. C. Hurewitz (ed.), *Diplomacy in the Near and Middle East: A Documentary Record*, vol. 2: *1914–1956*, Princeton, N.J., 1956, pp. 18–21
331 23 Leslie, op. cit., pp. 250–5
331 24 Monroe, op. cit., p. 26
332 25 ibid., p. 27
332 26 ibid., p. 32
333 27 *Seven Pillars of Wisdom*, London, 1935, p. 55; quoted by Kedourie, op. cit., p. 89
333 28 *Dictionary of National Biography* (1931–40), Oxford, 1949, p. 529

Page	Note	
334	29	Leonard Stein, *The Balfour Declaration*, London, 1961, frontispiece
334	30	Monroe, op. cit., p. 43
334	31	quoted by Stein, op. cit., p. 6
335	32	ibid., p. 59
336	33	ibid., p. 125
336	34	ibid., p. 521
336	35	ibid., p. 523
336	36	Louis, op. cit., p. x
336	37	Stein, op. cit., p. 518
337	38	ibid., p. 512
337	39	ibid., p. 523
337	40	ibid., p. 533
337	41	*The Times*, 13.ix.1917
338	42	Fischer, op. cit., p. 162
338	43	ibid., p. 163
338	44	FO800/74: letter from the Ambassador to the Foreign Secretary, 10.iii.1915
338	45	Stein, op. cit., p. 544
339	46	ibid., p. 546
339	47	David Lloyd George, *The Truth about the Peace Treaties*, vol. 2, p. 1137
341	48	cf. Titus Komarnicki, *Rebirth of the Polish Republic: A Study in the Diplomatic History of Europe, 1914–1920*, London, 1957, p. 39; *Russko-Polskiye Otnosheniya v period mirovoi voiny*, Moscow, 1926, p. 19
342	49	HH: report by the Foreign Ministry Liaison Officer at the A.O.K., Teschen, 7.xii.1914
343	50	FO800/74: letter from Lindley to Grey, 19.iv.1916
343	51	FO800/74: telegram from Sir George Buchanan, 17.vi.1916
344	52	cf. Werner Conze, *Polnische Nation und Deutsche Politik im ersten Weltkrieg*, Köln/Graz 1958, p. 226
344	53	FO371/3002; the English text is Sobanski's own.
346	54	FO371/3002: minutes on political offensive against Germany, 15.xi.1917; cf. Harry Hanak, 'The Government, the Foreign Office and Austria-Hungary, 1914–1918', *Slavonic and East European Review*, London, vol. 47, no. 108, January, 1969
346	55	FO371/3002: memorandum by George Clerk, 12.xii.1917
351	56	FO800/94
351	57	FO800/74: letter of 23.viii.1916
351	58	FO371/2864: memorandum for Lord Hardinge
351	59	Steed, *The Hapsburg Monarchy*, London, 1913, p. ix

Page Note
352   60   id., *Through Thirty Years*, vol. 2, p. 38
352   61   Lewis B. Namier, *Germany and Eastern Europe*, London, 1915,
              p. 118
352   62   Hanak, art. cit., p. 169
353   63   Woodrow Wilson, *The State, Elements of Historical and Practical
              Politics*, Boston, 1889; quoted by Victor S. Mamatey, *The
              United States and East Central Europe 1914–1918: A Study in
              Wilsonian Diplomacy and Propaganda*, Princeton, N.J., 1957,
              p. 58
353   64   Mamatey, op. cit., pp. 13 f.
353   65   ibid., p. 17
353   66   New York, 1902; quoted in Louis L. Gerson, *Woodrow Wilson
              and the Rebirth of Poland 1914–1920*, New Haven, Conn.,
              1953, p. 55
354   67   cf. Gerson, op. cit., pp. 56, 59
354   68   ibid., p. 70: letter to Orlowski, 15.i.1931
354   69   ibid., p. 71
355   70   FO371/3134
355   71   ibid.
356   72   FO371/3135: report of 30.iv.1918
357   73   FO371/3135: letter and enclosure to Lord Robert Cecil,
              19.v.1918
357   74   FO371/3135: Notes on possible effect on military situation,
              and steps Allies should take to extend that effect, 22.v.1918
357   75   FR 1918, Supplement I, vol. 1, 818
358   76   FO371/3135: message from Beneš to Steed, 16.vii.1918
358   77   FO371/3135: notes on Czech government, 22–24.vii.1918
359   78   Steed, op. cit., vol. 2, p. 232; cf. Hanak, art. cit., p. 194
359   79   Hanak, art. cit., p. 197
362   80   cf. Dr B. Krizman's contribution to the conference in Vienna
              in October 1968: *Die Tätigkeit der österreichisch-ungarischen
              Diplomatie in den letzten Monaten vor dem Zusammenbruch*
362   81   Taylor, op. cit., p. 111
363   82   House, op. cit., vol. 4, p. 121

Bibliography*

G. F. Abbott, *Greece and the Allies 1914–1922*, London, 1922

Ahmed Emin, *Turkey in the World War*, New Haven, Conn., 1930

Luigi Albertini, *The Origins of the War of 1914*, 3 vols, Oxford and New York, 1952, 1953, 1957

L. Aldrovandi Marescotti, *Guerra Diplomatica: Ricordi e frammenti di diario (1914–1919)*, Milan, 1936

J. Andrássy, *Diplomacy and the War*, London, 1921

Winfried Baumgart, *Deutsche Ostpolitik 1918: von Brest-Litowsk bis zum Ende des Ersten Weltkrieges*, Vienna/Munich, 1966

John W. Wheeler-Bennett, *Brest-Litovsk, the Forgotten Peace: March 1918*, London and New York, 1938

Norman Bentwich, *England in Palestine*, London, 1932

Lord Bertie of Thame, *The Diary 1914–1918*, 2 vols, London, 1924

Th. von Bethmann Hollweg, *Betrachtungen zum Weltkriege*, 2 vols, Berlin, 1919, 1921

Karl E. Birnbaum, *Peace Moves and U-Boat Warfare: A Study of Imperial Germany's Policy towards the United States April 18, 1916–January 9, 1917*, Stockholm/Uppsala, 1958

John Bradley, *Allied Intervention in Russia*, London and New York, 1968

Julius Braunthal, *History of the International 1864–1914*, 2 vols, John Clark trans, London and New York, 1966–7

Sir George Buchanan, *My Mission to Russia and Other Diplomatic Memoirs*, 2 vols, London, 1923

Prince von Bülow, *Memoirs*, vol. 3, *1909–1919*, London and New York, 1932

Count Stephan Burián, *Austria in Dissolution*, London, 1925

Paul Cambon, *Correspondance 1870–1924*, 3 vols, Paris, 1940–46

Winston S. Churchill, *The World Crisis*, 6 vols, London and New York, 1923–31

* Intended for the reader who does not happen to be a specialist. The more specialized works—books, articles, academic theses and archival references—are mentioned in the Notes.

Bibliography

Benedetto Croce, *A History of Italy 1871–1915*, Cecilia M. Ady trans, London and New York, 1929

Count Ottokar Czernin, *In the World War*, London, 1919

Alexander Dallin *et al., Russian Diplomacy and Eastern Europe 1914–1917*, New York, 1963

Isaac Deutscher, *The Prophet Armed. Trotsky: 1879–1921*, London and New York, 1954

    The Prophet Unarmed. Trotsky: 1921–1929, London and New York, 1959

    The Prophet Outcast. Trotsky: 1929–1940, London and New York, 1967

Klaus Epstein, *Matthias Erzberger and the Dilemma of German Democracy*, Princeton, N.J., 1959

Fritz Fischer, *Germany's Aims in the First World War*, London, 1967

David Lloyd George, War Memoirs, 6 vols, London, 1933–36

Louis L. Gerson, *Woodrow Wilson and the Rebirth of Poland 1914–1920*, New Haven, Conn., 1953

Giovanni Giolitti, *Memoirs of My Life*, London/Sydney, 1923

Nicholas N. Golovine, *The Russian Army in the World War*, New Haven, Conn., 1931

G. P. Gooch, *Recent Revelations of European Diplomacy*, 4th edition, London and New York, 1940

W. W. Gottlieb, *Studies in Secret Diplomacy during the First World War*, London and New York, 1957

Viscount Grey of Fallodon, *Twenty-five Years 1892–1916*, 2 vols, London, 1925

Paul Guinn, *British Strategy and Politics 1914 to 1918*, Oxford and New York, 1965

Lord Hankey, *The Supreme Command 1914–1918*, 2 vols, London and New York, 1961

Hugo Hantsch, *Leopold Graf Berchtold: Grandseigneur und Staatsmann*, 2 vols, Graz, 1963

Colonel House, *Intimate Papers*, 4 vols, London, 1926–28

Humphrey Johnson, *Vatican Diplomacy in the World War*, Oxford, 1933

Michael Károlyi, *Memoirs: Faith without Illusion,* London, 1956

Elie Kedourie, *England and the Middle East: The Destruction of the Ottoman Empire 1914–1921*, London, 1956

George F. Kennan, *Soviet–American Relations 1917–1920:* I *Russia Leaves the War*, London, 1956; II *The Decision to Intervene*, London and Princeton, N.J., 1958

Harold D. Lasswell, *Propaganda Technique in the World War*, New York, 1927

Bibliography

Arthur S. Link, *Wilson*, 5 vols, Princeton, N.J., 1947–65

R. H. Bruce Lockhart, *Memoirs of a British Agent*, London, 1932

W. R. Louis, *Great Britain and Germany's Lost Colonies 1914–1919*, Oxford and New York, 1967

Erich Ludendorff (ed.), *My War Memories*, 2 vols, London, 1919

Victor S. Mamatey, *The United States and East Central Europe 1914–1918: A Study in Wilsonian Diplomacy and Propaganda*, Princeton, N.J., 1957

Prince Maximilian of Baden, *The Memoirs*, London, 1928

Arno J. Mayer, *Wilson vs. Lenin: Political Origins of the New Diplomacy, 1917–1918*, Cleveland/New York, 1964

Henry Cord Meyer, *Mitteleuropa in German Thought and Action 1815–1945*, The Hague, 1955

Elizabeth Monroe, *Britain's Moment in the Middle East 1914–1956*, London and Baltimore, Md., 1963

Henry Morgenthau, *Secrets of the Bosphorus: Constantinople 1913–1916*, London, 1918

Albert Pingaud, *Histoire diplomatique de la France pendant la grande guerre*, 3 vols, Paris, 1938–40

Raymond Poincaré, *Au Service de la France*, 10 vols, Paris, 1926–33

Charles W. Porter, *The Career of Théophile Delcassé*, Philadelphia, Pa., 1936

Pierre Renouvin, *La Crise européenne et al grande guerre (1904–1918)*, Paris, 1934

Sir James Rennell Rodd, *Social and Diplomatic Memories (Third Series) 1902–1919*, London, 1925

Antonio Salandra, *Italy and the Great War: From Neutrality to Intervention*, London, 1932

A. Savinsky, *Recollections of a Russian Diplomat*, London, 1927

Serge Sazonov, *Fateful Years 1909–1916*, London, 1928

Marian C. Siney, *The Allied Blockade of Germany 1914–1916*, Ann Arbor, Mich., 1957

C. Jay Smith, Jr., *The Russian Struggle for Power, 1914–1917*, New York, 1956

J. D. Squires, *British Propaganda at Home and in the United States from 1914 to 1917*, Cambridge, Mass., 1935

Leonard Stein, *The Balfour Declaration*, London and New York, 1961

Charles Callan Tansill, *America Goes to War*, Boston, 1938

A. J. P. Taylor, *English History 1914–1945*, Oxford and New York, 1965

   The Struggle for Mastery in Europe 1848–1918, Oxford and New York, 1954

Bibliography

U. Trumpener, *Germany and the Ottoman Empire 1914–1918*, Princeton, N.J., 1968

B. W. Tuchman, *The Zimmermann Telegram*, New York, 1966

Richard H. Ullman, *Intervention and the War*, Princeton, N.J./London, 1961

R. D. Warth, *The Allies and the Russian Revolution: From the Fall of the Monarchy to the Peace of Brest-Litovsk*, Durham, N.C., 1954

Z. A. B. Zeman, *The Break-up of the Habsburg Empire 1914–1918: A Study in National and Social Revolution*, Oxford and New York, 1961

Z. A. B. Zeman & W. B. Scharlau, *The Merchant of Revolution: The Life of Alexander Israel Helphand (Parvus) 1867–1924*, Oxford and New York, 1965

Index

Aehrenthal, Count Alois Leopold Lexa, 21, 22
Africa, 41, 319–20, 321, 322, 323–4, 334
Albania, 11, 37, 42, 44
Albert, King of Belgium, 109
Alekseev, Michael V., General, 218, 296
Alexander I, Tsar of Russia, 194–5
Allenby, Edmund Henry Hynman, Field-Marshal, 334, 359
Allied Powers, and Italy, 11–13, 14, 19, 27, 53, 69, 139, 140, 143–4, 156; and nationalities question, 19, 155, 346–7, 357–9, 360; and Turkey, 21, 51, 57, 70, 71; and Bulgaria, 75–8; and Serbia, 79; on western front, 81, 108, 144, 360–1; on eastern front, 108, 112, 359; and blockade of Germany, 112, 123; and German peace moves, 116–17, 119–20; and Austria-Hungary, 131, 136, 140, 142–3, 153–4, 156, 160, 202, 340, 345–9, 360; and Russian revolution, 142, 209–10, 215, 219–20, 227–8, 248, 249, 252–3, 257, 291–303, 304–15, 338, 340; strategy of, 144; and President Wilson's peace proposals, 182, 185–6, 188, 191–2, 193, 202, 227, 362; in Middle East, 283, 331, 332; and Zionism, 338; see also Britain, France, Italy, Rumania, Russia, Serbia
Alsace-Lorraine, 123, 132, 158, 200, 262, 263
America, see United States of America
American League to Enforce Peace, 194
Amery, Leo, 319–20, 336
Andersen, Hans-Niels, 85–7, 88, 100, 130
D'Annunzio, Gabriele, 46
Arabia, 262, 331, 345
Arabs, 90, 330, 331–3, 336, 339–40, 360–1
Archangel, 82, 298, 299, 300, 301–2, 303, 312, 314, 316
Armand, Count Abel, 150, 159, 340
Armenia, Armenians, 61, 262, 297, 330, 331
Asia, 157, 165, 296, 304, 308, 340
Asia Minor, 44, 135, 216, 329

Asquith, Herbert Henry, 18, 20, 70, 121, 157, 166–8, 172, 184–5, 194, 329
Australia, 321–2
Austria-Hungary, pre-war relationship with Italy, 1–2, 4–5, 21; and war with Serbia, 3, 6–7; and Italian compensation question, 3, 5–6, 24; and the Adriatic, 4, 33, 37; Italians in, 4–5, 34, 37, 341; and the Balkans, 4, 5, 14, 58, 61, 123, 127; Slavs in, 4–5, 15, 19; Germans in, 5, 146, 342; and the Balkan wars, 5, 33, 156; on eastern front, 11, 25–6, 31, 77, 87, 92, 110, 121, 226, 243–4, 272, 280, 286; Serbs in, 14, 19; Croats in, 14, 19, 355; Slovenes in, 14, 19; and Bosnia-Herzegovina, 14, 53, 73, 156, 327; and Serbian subversion in, 14, 15–18, 133 n.; and Russia, 14–15, 68–9, 84, 87–8, 340–1, 347; and Poles, 20, 92, 123, 125–6, 127, 153, 270, 271–2, 341–2, 343–7, 351, 353, 354; negotiations with Italy, 23–5, 31–3, 35–8, 45, 48, 125; German pressure during Italian negotiations, 25, 31–2, 34–8; influence of Hungarians in, 33, 126; and Turkey, 53, 57–65, 125, 141, 282–4; opposition to Egyptian campaign, 38–9; opposition to Holy War, 61–2; Slavs in, 68–9, 146, 156, 282, 340–1, 350, 353, 354, 355, 357; and Bulgaria, 72–4, 75, 79, 140, 141, 156, 281, 282–4, 362; and Pless convention, 79; Rumania and, 80, 81, 123, 126, 156, 279–83; and possibility of separate peace with Russia, 84, 87–8; and the Ukrainians, 92–3, 269–71, 342; Lenin's arrest and departure from, 93–4; opposition to social revolution in, 94; and Czernin's pessimism, 112–13, 146; and peace initiatives, 115, 117–20, 123, 127–36, 150–1, 216, 340; difficulty of food supplies in, 123, 128, 270, 361–2; death of Franz Josef, 124; accession of Emperor Karl, 124; mistrust of Germany, 124–6; and Montenegro, 127; and Transylvania, 127, 156, 282, 346; Allied

389

Index

Austria-Hungary—*cont.*
consideration of separate peace with, 136-7, 138-45; and Russian revolution, 139, 147, 286; and papal peace-note, 148; on Italian front, 151, 160, 286, 350, 353; and Smuts–Mensdorff talks, 152-60, 340; and Bessarabia, 156, 282; relations with USA, 161, 205, 347, 350, 353; and trade with USA, 175, 177; President Wilson's view of, 201-2, 353; and the dismemberment of the Empire, 202, 262-3, 341-59, 360; Russian appeal to socialists in, 221, 257; at Brest-Litovsk, 250, 254-6, 258-9, 269-71; social unrest in, 259-60, 261, 266, 268, 286, 310; and Fourteen Points, 264; and peace of Bucharest, 279-84; Zionism in, 335; Czechs in, 342, 350, 353, 355, 357-9, 360; and Bohemia, 345, 346; and Yugoslavia, 346, 357; and armistice negotiations, 361-2; mentioned, 66, 170, 196, 248; *see also* Central Powers, Czernin, Count; Karl, Emperor

Baker, Colonel Granville, 356
Balfour, Arthur James, and Austro-Hungarian peace moves, 128-9, 130; and papal peace-note, 149; and Nabokov, 152, 227; and conference with Colonel House, 184-5; attitude to Constantinople, 185; and the Zimmermann Telegram, 203; attitude to the Russian revolution, 293, 296; and to Japanese intervention, 304, 305, 307, 311; and Semonov, 306-7; and the Middle East, 327; and the Jews, 334-6, 338-9; and the Polish problem, 344; and the Czechoslovak problem, 358; mentioned, 315
Balfour Declaration, 335-6, 339, 344
Balkans, effect of Triple Alliance on, 3-4, 5; Italy's view of, 5, 41; Russian interest in, 13, 68, 92, 340; Austria-Hungarian interest in, 6, 24, 64, 132, 340, 362; Italian interest in, 39; Central Powers expectation of Allied action in, 58; Turkish influence in, 59, 62; and Turkish treaty with Central Powers, 62, 64, 65; and Bulgarian-Turkish treaty, 74; Ukrainian activity in, 92, 93; set-back for Russian prestige in, 207; mentioned in Fourteen Points, 264; mentioned in peace of Bucharest, 281-5; Allied offensive in, 317; Austria-Hungarian and Russian rivalry in, 340 and n.; mentioned, 73, 156

Balkan wars, 5, 14, 35, 49, 54, 72, 78
Ballin, Alfred, 85-6, 88, 130, 171
Baltic provinces, 91-2, 276
Baltic Sea, 243, 267, 316, 345
Basok-Melenevski, Marian, 93, 94-5
Beaverbrook, William Maxwell Aitken, 168, 350
Belgium, investment in Italy, 27; German offensive in, 92; mentioned in German peace initiative, 109, 112, 126, 158, 200; considered in Austrian peace initiative, 123, 132; mentioned in Sixtus letter, 132; considered in Allied strategy, 137, 143, 149; mentioned in Papal peace-note, 148, 149; mentioned in Smuts–Mensdorff talks, 157, 158; Bryce report on, 167; socialists in Russia from, 217; mentioned in Lloyd George war aims, 262; in Fourteen Points, 264; action in East Africa, 324; mentioned, 24, 257
Belgrade, 25, 121, 133, 155
Benedict XV, 34, 117, 145, 147, 149, 191
Beneš, Edvard, 313-14, 351, 358-9, 360
Berchtold, Count Leopold, 6, 21-5, 31-3, 58, 64, 94, 126, 340 n.
Berne, 94, 129, 230, 232
Berthelot, General M., 297, 299
Bertie, Sir Francis, 2-3
Bessarabia, 81, 156, 280, 281, 282, 283, 297, 316, 338
Bethmann Hollweg, Theobald von, and Italian negotiations, 36; and the Turkish alliance, 63; attitude to coalitions, 63; relationship with Wilhelm II, 84, 109, 113, 114; and Zimmermann, 85, 115, 120; and separate peace with Russia, 85, 88, 108, 110-11; and Ballin–Anderson talks, 85; and discussion with Ferdinand of Bulgaria, 109-11; and Belgium, 109; France, 109, 126, 200; and Washington peace initiative, 110, 114, 119-20, 182, 187, 189, 198-201; and England, 110; opposition to submarine policy, 113, 115-18, 119-20, 187, 189, 199; and Austria, 113, 125-6; and German war aims, 126, 199-200; and Rumania, 126; and the Sixtus letter, 136; replaced by Michaelis, 147, 148
Bitsenko, Anastasia, 251, 256
Black Sea, 58, 59, 60, 66, 67-8, 82, 89, 90, 95, 104, 244, 276, 297, 316
Bosnia, *see* Bosnia Herzegovina
Bosnia Herzegovina, 14, 15-18, 42, 53, 73, 76, 80, 288, 327, 360
Brest Litovsk, 77, 250-9, 266-73, 276-7, 285, 286, 300, 311
Briand, A., 119, 134, 186

Index

Bulgaria, Austro-Hungarian attitude to, 24, 64, 72–4, 75; during Balkan wars, 54, 78; and Turkey, 54, 64, 74–5, 79, 82; neutrality of, 58, 72, 74–7; signs military convention, 64, 74–5; strategic position of, 72; and Russia, 72, 73, 75, 77; independence of, 73; and Serbia, 73, 75–6, 79, 156; France and, 73–4, 75–6, 77–8; activity of Central Powers in, 74, 76–7, 78–9; Allied negotiations with, 75–8, 79; and Rumania, 75, 76; territorial and military conventions signed, 78–9, 338; mobilization of, 100; offensives of, 110, 121, 243; British attitude to, 137, 141; mentioned in Smuts–Mensdorff talks, 156; Zimmermann's view of Allied intentions in, 196; represented at Brest Litovsk, 250, 254, 281; and the peace of Bucharest, 281, 282–4; and the Dobruja, 283–4; Allied offensive against, 359; surrender of, 360, 362; mentioned, 57, 60, 81, 109, 257

Bülow, Bernhard, Prince von, 21, 25–9, 30–1, 32, 33–4, 36–8, 43, 45, 85, 89, 115, 250

Burián, Count Stephan, 23, 32, 33, 35, 36, 38, 121, 123, 125–6, 283, 361–2

Bussche-Haddenhausen, von dem, 94, 112

Cadorna, Luigi, General, 141, 151
Cairo, 324, 332, 333, 336
Cambon, Jules, 134
Cambon, Paul, 290, 331
Canada, 171, 217
Carnegie, Andrew, 173–4
Carol, King of Rumania, 80, 81, 279, 280, 281, 282
Casement, Sir Roger, 91, 167
Catholic Centre Party (Germany), 146, 149
Cecil, Lord Robert, 180, 315
Central Powers, Italy's declaration of war on, 7; and negotiations with Italy, 21, 23, 30–2, 35, 36, 45, 53; and Turkish negotiations, 57, 60, 65; and Rumania, 64, 80, 112, 284; continental strategy of, 65, 284–5; and Bulgarian negotiations, 75–6, 77, 78, 281; occupation of Serbia by, 79; victory in the east, 82, 121; interest in separate peace with Russia, 87, 88, 100, 137, 225; and subversion in Russia, 85, 92; support for Ukrainians, 92, 269–71; and Czernin's pessimism, 112, 147; peace initiative of, 115, 119, 137, 150; and President Wilson's note on war aims, 119, 192; effect of Russian revolution on, 139; resources of, 144, 176, 181; mentioned in Smuts–Mensdorff talks, 158, 159, 160; and USA, 169, 181; effect of blockade on, 181; at Brest Litovsk, 255–6, 258, 263, 268, 269–72, 276; advance into Russia by, 273–4, 286, 317; and the peace of Bucharest, 280, 283, 284; on the western front, 286; defeat of, 359; Greek declaration of war on, 359; request for armistice by, 362; mentioned, 141, 207, 297, 327, 333; *see also* Austria-Hungary, Bulgaria, Germany, Turkey

Chernov, Viktor M., 213, 239–40, 291
Chicherin, Georgi V., 302, 310, 312
China, Chinese, 104, 305, 306, 307, 308, 310, 325
Chinda, Baron, 315, 322
Christian X, King of Denmark, 85–6, 87, 111, 131
Christiania, 128, 129, 130
Christiansen, Axel, 128, 129, 130
Churchill, Winston C., 49–51, 65, 72, 329
Clayton, Gilbert, General, 332, 336
Clemenceau, G., 131, 136, 150, 247, 283, 290–1, 293, 359, 363
Clerk, George, 346, 351
Committee for the Return of Russian Political Exiles, 230
Committee of Union and Progress, 49–50, 54
Congo, 320, 324
Conrad von Hötsendorf, Field-Marshal, 24, 87, 123, 127
Constantine, King of Greece, 359
Constantinople, Russia and, 41, 45, 110–11, 185, 207, 209, 213, 214, 327–9, 334; arrival of *Goeben* and *Breslau* in, 50; importance of, 89; socialists in, 94–6; Kühlmann and, 148–9; rationing in, 181; Lenin's attitude to, 236; British and, 329, 332; effect of Allied offensive in Bulgaria on, 359; mentioned, 143, 339
Copenhagen, 85–7, 88, 98, 99, 107, 130, 218, 229, 278, 335
Cossacks, 269, 292, 296, 297, 306, 307
Cracow, 93, 99
Crewe, Robert, Offley, Ashburton, 178, 180, 331
Crimea, 53, 297, 317
Croatia, Croats, 14, 19, 42, 355, 357
Cromer, Evelyn Baring, Lord, 330, 331
Curzon, George Nathaniel, 137, 318, 326, 327, 337, 338–9
Cyprus, 53, 327, 359
Czechoslovak Legion, 226, 301–2, 311–17, 356–8

Index

Index

Index

Moldavia, 127, 269, 280, 281
Montagu, Edwin S., 327, 336
Montenegro, 64, 127, 148, 200, 257, 264
Moravia, 22, 94
Morgan, J. Pierpoint, 173, 174
Moslems, 89–91, 93, 114, 327, 336
Murmansk, 82, 218, 298, 299, 300–3, 316
Mussolini, Benito, 46

Nabokov, Konstantin, 151–2, 226–7
Namier, Lewis, 350, 351, 352, 358, 361
Near East, 68, 84, 89, 285
New York, 172–3, 175, 198
Nicholas II, Tsar of Russia, and Constantinople and the Straits, 69, 70; and France, 70–1, 291; determination to continue the war, 109; Hollweg's view of, 110; abdication of, 208; arrest of, 218; and possibility of asylum in England, 218–19; mentioned, 214
Niessel, General, 227, 298–9
Nikolaevich, Grand Duke Nikolai, 66–7, 68–9, 331, 340–1, 342
Nivelle, General, 138, 219
Northcliffe, Alfred Charles William Harmsworth, 168, 350, 355–6, 360
Norway, 129–30, 177, 278
Noulens, Joseph, 290, 291, 294, 298, 300

O'Beirne, Hugh, 76–7
Odessa, 58, 60, 61, 280, 317
Oppenheim, Max von, 89–90
Orlando, Vittorio Emanuele, 347, 356
Ottoman Empire, see Turkey

Pacelli, Cardinal, 34, 148–9
Pacific Ocean, 105, 320–2, 325
Pact of London, see London, Pact of
Page, W. H., 176, 184, 201–2, 203
Paléogogue, Maurice, 70–1, 217, 219, 282, 287, 290, 342
Palestine, 262, 318, 319, 329, 331, 334–9, 359
Pallavicini, Count, 55, 56, 58, 59, 62, 63, 64, 281–2
'Parvus', see Helphand
Pašić, Nikolai, 14–15, 18, 19
Peking, 306–7, 308
Petrograd, 103, 107, 151–2, 207–4 passim, 244–5, 298, 299, 344; see also Russia
Piedmont, 38, 48
Pilsudski, Józef, 324
Pius XII, see Pacelli, Cardinal
Platten, Fritz, 230–3
Pless, 188, 198, 199
Pless convention, 79
Poincaré, R., 41, 69, 71, 132, 287, 288, 344

Pokrovsky, Mikhail N., 208, 254, 256, 287
Poland, Poles, Austria and, 92, 123, 125, 127; Germany and, 92, 100, 121, 123, 125, 200; Congress Kingdom of, 92, 100, 121, 123, 125, 256, 276; Brusilov's offensive in, 106, 343; and Two Emperors' Manifesto, 125, 200, 337, 342, 343–4; mentioned in papal peace-note, 148; Allied commitment to independence, 155, 262, 346–7; discussed at House–Grey conference, 185; in Brest-Litovsk negotiations, 256, 257, 270–2, 276; mentioned in Fourteen Points, 265, 342, 344; Russian attitude to, 341, 342–3, 344; and exiles in France, 342–3, 344; formation of Polish army, 344; and USA, 353–4; President Wilson and, 353–4; on Italian front, 355; mentioned, 20, 94, 104, 292, 316, 358
Polish National Committee, 344–5, 347, 351, 353
Portugal, 320, 325
Prague, 342, 359, 360
Pripet, 106, 243
Pszczyna, see Pless
Purdy, W. F., 261

Radek, Karl, 230, 234, 246, 249, 251, 268, 271
Rakovsky, Christo, 96, 280
Rasputin, 121
Reading, Rufus Daniel Isaacs, 173, 184, 303, 304–5
Revertera, Count, 150, 159, 340
Ribot, Alexandre, 134–5, 138, 144, 216
Robertson, William Robert, Field-Marshal, 140–1, 142, 144
Robins, Raymond, 227, 294, 295, 299, 300
Rodd, Sir Rennell, 2, 8, 25, 29, 38–40, 42, 47–8
Rodzianko, Michael, 209, 296
Romberg, Gisbert von, 94, 231
Rothschild, Lionel Waller, 334, 337, 338
Rumania, Rumanians, and France, 41, 81; and Austria, 58, 64, 80, 119, 123, 126, 127, 140, 143, 279–84; and Turkey, 64, 75; Allied negotiations with, 72, 76, 79–80, 81, 108, 112; and Bulgaria, 73, 75, 76, 78, 80, 280, 282–3; and the Dobruja, 76, 78, 280, 281, 282, 283–4; and treaty of Bucharest, 80; and Germany, 80, 97, 119, 126, 200, 257, 274, 279–84, 320; and Italy, 80; and Serbia, 80; entry into war, 80; and Transylvania, 80–1, 282; and Hungary, 80, 280–1, 282, 284; neutrality of, 80–1; and Russia, 81–2, 205, 207,

Index

Salandra, Antonio—*cont.*
  29, 31, 45, 48; as Premier, 9; and
  negotiations with Allies, 20, 28–9,
  36–7, 38–45; and Sonnino, 27, 48;
  and neutralists, 31, 37, 47–8; offer of
  resignation, 45–6, 48; mentioned, 33
Salonika, 79, 81, 141, 319, 359
Salvator, Archduke Leopold, 23
Samoa, 321, 322
Sanders, General Liman von, 55, 90
San Giuliano, 1, 3, 11, 13, 21, 39, 40
Sarajevo, 1, 2
Savinkov, Ataman, 296, 313
Savinski, Alexander A., 73, 74, 79
Sazonov, Sergei D., and Italian negotiations, 11, 12–13, 15, 18, 20, 41–3, 45,
  69; and Serbia, 11, 15, 18, 41–2, 45;
  and South Slavs, 15, 18, 20, 45; and
  Poles, 20, 342–3; and Constantinople,
  41, 45, 69–70; and the Straits, 41–2,
  69–70; and the Gallipoli expedition,
  70; and the Rumanian negotiations,
  81; succeeded by Stuermer, 81; determined opposition to Germany, 88,
  109; suspicion of Jews, 338; mentioned, 67, 103, 341
Scandinavia, 82, 98, 106, 128–31, 160,
  201, 220–2, 230, 268, 278
Semenov, Ataman, 305–9, 310, 314
Serbia, and the 1914 crisis, 3, 6; and
  Austria-Hungary, 3, 6–7, 14–18, 24,
  127, 143, 155–6, 282; and the Italian
  negotiations, 11–12, 13, 15, 41–2, 44,
  207; and Russia, 11–12, 14–15, 19,
  41–2, 45; and the Balkans, 11; and
  the Adriatic, 11, 14, 41–2, 44, 76, 207;
  gains after peace of Bucharest, 14;
  and death of Franz Ferdinand, 14; and
  South Slavs, 14, 15–18, 20, 42; and
  expansion, 14; and Bosnia-Herzegovina, 14, 15–18, 76, 156; territorial
  claims of, 15; vulnerability of, 15, 72,
  359; fighting in, 58, 79; and Bulgaria,
  73, 75–7, 79, 359; and the Pless convention, 78–9; occupied by Central
  Powers, 79; mentioned in Sixtus
  letter, 132–3; mentioned in papal
  peace-note, 148; mentioned in Smuts-
  Mensdorff talks, 155–6; in Fourteen
  Points, 264; mentioned, 64, 257
Seton-Watson, R. W., 350, 351, 352
Sevriuk, Alexander, 269, 270
Sharif revolt, 331–3
Siberia, 211, 218, 235, 269, 298, 300, 302,
  303, 305–6, 308–10, 312, 314–17, 358
Sixtus, Prince, 124, 131–5, 139, 140, 283
Slavs, in Austria, 5, 14, 15, 69, 84, 139,
  156, 341, 357; and Serbia, 14, 15–18,
  20, 42; and Italy, 18–20, 45, 341, 355;
  and Russia, 18, 45, 69, 156, 341;

and Allies, 119, 350, 354, 357, 360;
  influence of Russian revolution on,
  146; and Rumania, 282; in Paris, 353
Slovaks, 226, 301; *see also* Czechoslovaks
Slovenes, 14, 19, 355
Smuts, Jan, Field-Marshal, 152–9, 262,
  318, 324, 327, 340
Social Democrat Party (Finns), 277
Social Democrat Party (Germany),
  145–6
Social Democrat Party (Russia), 211,
  238–9
Social Democrats (Austria), 94
Social Democrats (Czech), 260
Social Revolutionary Party (Russia),
  226, 239, 241
Sofia, 61, 69, 72, 73, 111, 181, 280, 283
Sokonikov, Grigori Y., 251, 276
Sonnino, Sidney, as Premier, 7, 9, 27;
  and Salandra, 7, 28, 29; and Giolitti,
  9, 48; background and character,
  27–8; and von Bülow, 27–8; and
  negotiations, 27–8, 35–6, 38, 39–45,
  48; opposition to separate peace with
  Austria, 134–5, 138–9, 140; support
  given to Lloyd George by, 143–4; at
  St-Jean-de-Maurienne, 216; men-
  tioned, 134, 144
Souchon, Admiral, 58, 60
South Africa, 320, 321, 323
South African war, 172
South West Africa, 321, 323
Spa convention, 353, 357, 361
Spain, 97, 177
Stalin, Josef, 235, 273, 274, 296
Steed, Wickham, 350, 351–2, 355, 358–9
Stinnes, Hugo, 103, 104–5, 106–7
Stockholm, 88, 100, 102, 105–7, 145,
  188, 233–4, 248, 251
Stockholm conference, 221–4
Storrs, Ronald, 331, 333
Stuermer, Baron, 81, 106, 109
Stürgkh, 24, 31, 32
Suez Canal, 58–9, 61, 90, 91, 327
Supilo, Frano, 18, 19–20
Svinhufvud, Judge, 277–8
Sweden, 7, 91, 103, 108, 110, 233–4
Switzerland, 7, 26, 94, 98–9, 131, 150,
  230, 235, 238, 246, 343, 351
Syria, 54, 236, 262, 329, 330–1, 332, 359
Sykes, Sir Mark, 329–31, 332, 333, 336,
  337, 351

Talaat Bey, 49, 52, 54–5, 59, 62, 254,
  282–3
Tereshchenko, Mikhail, 213–14, 215,
  227–8
The Times, on German peace moves, 117;
  on Bolsheviks, 151–2; on Wilson's
  address to the Senate, 193–4; on the

400

Index